Guide of
Soul and Mind
The Story of Anderson University

Guide of
Soul and Mind
The Story of Anderson University

"Where Quality Learning
and Christian Service Come Alive"

by Barry L. Callen

Anderson University
and
Warner Press, Inc.
Anderson, Indiana

Arlo F. Newell, Editor in Chief
Dan Harman, Book Editor
Cover and interior design by David Liverett

TABLE OF CONTENTS

LIST OF TABLES

Foreword

We build our institutions, and then they build us. After seventy-five years of life, Anderson University shows evidence of being well-founded. She also has many who, like me, have been shaped by her dynamic life. Of course it is the people who become the stories and who are a part of the mentoring relationships. But from the life of the whole of this very good place comes something more, something I call the Anderson Experience.

For some, the Anderson Experience begins with annual visits to the campus during the great International Convention of the Church of God. For some, this is home as one matriculates for studies, nests in a crowded residence hall, tries one's wings of intellectual flight with freshman term papers, undertakes a service project all the way to a developing corner of the world, and learns chilling and affirming lessons from personal service. Such experiences lead some to careers in ministry, in business, in education, law, medicine, or social work.

For most, the Anderson Experience is wrapped almost unavoidably around a faith journey. That journey is not just the result of attendance in biweekly chapel or fulfillment of the religion requirement among courses of study. It is a way of growing, of considering all of life and all of learning from the perspective of Christ. Older and younger learners alike, pursuing an honest search for a meaningful life in this place, encounter at her center a faith in God. The mission of Anderson University finds fulfillment as the faith journey is pursued in all its dimensions. This holistic search is at the heart of what we mean by a Christian university at its best.

On the occasion of our diamond jubilee anniversary, it is the pleasure of Anderson University to offer this record of her life, the issues, persons, and events that have shaped her, and some glimpse of the ways in which she has shaped those whom she has served. Barry L. Callen is a dedicated and skilled reporter who has brought this collection to life in the pages to follow. His faithfulness and love for this dynamic, young place give evidence that he, too, has been touched by the Anderson Experience. We are grateful to him for this offering, a true labor of love.

President James L. Edwards, presidents emeritus John A. Morrison (statue),
Robert H. Reardon, and Robert A. Nicholson, June, 1992

xiii

In June, the graduates of the Class of 1992 were greeted in Commencement with these words:

"Kindle the Flame" is the University's theme for the year's celebrations. Through the years there have been those visionaries, those faithful stewards of this mission who have kept clear sight of the direction, the nature of the institution. Their efforts have been rewarded with remarkable success. Within Anderson University there is a wonderful light. It is a light that generations before us have fueled so that it might radiate knowledge, faith, and love to a hopeful world. It is a light that must never go out.

James L. Edwards
President, Anderson University

Introduction

The difference between an antiquarian and a historian is that the former collects antiques and bits of information that appear interesting while the latter engages in a much more serious task. The historian looks carefully at the past from the present and at the present through the enlightening perspectives of the past. History, then, is a never-ending dialogue between past and present, motivated by a concern about the quality of the future. This book does contain many antiques and interesting bits of information, but it is intended as a present attempt to recall the past for the sake of the future.

Truth sets free! This crucial assumption has been basic to the life of the Anderson campus since its beginning in 1917. Back then, and continuing to this day, the "truth" has been understood to include and be guided by Christian revelation. The freedom sought by the first students, mostly gospel workers employed in the local publishing company of the Church of God, was release from the lack of knowledge and skill development that was hindering the effectiveness of their diverse Christian ministries.

About a decade after the university's founding as Anderson Bible Training School, its curricular horizon widened. It came to include the liberal arts and a desired freeing of students from narrow cultural views and societal provincialisms that limit human development and relations. Doors to freedom now were opening more widely, even while the campus maintained the conviction that the person of Jesus Christ is the ultimate way to the life most free, most fulfilling, and most helpful to a needy world. Throughout its first seventy-five years, Anderson University has been a center for liberating people to be skilled and inspired learners, true and mature believers, and responsible servant leaders.

The annual campus publication, the *Echoes*, used as the orienting theme for its 1944 edition the message that "The Truth Shall Make You Free." That issue began with the stated assumption that people "are free as their minds are free and at liberty only as their spirits are unfettered." All of the material about the people and events that had comprised that difficult war year on campus was organized around the headings of five central freedoms, freedoms for which the nation was at war and for which the school itself was said to exist. They were the "freedom to worship, to pursue knowledge, to widen friendships, to express ourselves creatively, and to serve our fellow-man." All of these were focused around the prevailing perception found in the New Testament (John 8:32) and later featured in bronze at the front door of the newly united and automated university library dedicated on campus in 1989: "Then you will know the truth and the truth will make you free."

Do you remember when College Drive was Union Avenue and an interurban train line came right down the middle of what now is Third Street? Can you picture in your mind the East Side Jersey Dairy downtown at Tenth and Central or Gadberry's

Grocery and Lunch at College and Fifth, both favorite student hangouts? What about Higgins Cleaners, the Glad Tidings Chorus, or the "Tigers" who represented the campus in athletic competition before there were any "Ravens"? Do you know any of the women who once lived as single students alongside some aged saints in Sunset Hall, or any of the brave young men who at least survived in what they called the "Barnitory"? Did you ever hear of Toodles, the dog seen in chapel more often than many students and faculty members? Were you part of that late night parade to campus from the railroad station downtown just after accreditation finally was achieved in 1946?

Can you recall the marvelous play of Jumpin' Johnny Wilson, causing such crowds that some basketball games had to be moved to the "Wigwam"? Were you ever intimidated by a snap quiz in a class taught by Dean Olt—or maybe you are one of the hundreds who popped the marriage question at a special monument in Maplewood Cemetery? Are you an alumnus who was privileged to play in an NAIA baseball world series under coach Donald Brandon or one of thousands whose memories were fired again as you gazed at the beautiful homecoming luminaries? If you are, did or can, you either are an Anderson University old-timer or you have read ahead in this book!

Of course, institutional trivia such as the above can begin in mere curiosity and end only in passing nostalgia. So, while all of the above and much, much more is to be found in these pages, particular memories and delightful antiques of yesterday are hardly the more important things to be noted. What is central is an organized educational effort, stretching across most of the twentieth century, one which has had great impact on the lives of tens of thousands of students and thereby has managed to alter human lives and even human society.

Landrum R. Bolling once wrote that "the most important thing that can be said about a college is that it has a certain character, and that this character has helped, if it has, in shaping constructively the values, the purposes, as well as the skills of the students who pass through its doors" (Thornburg, viii). Anderson University surely has had a certain kind of character. The purpose in all that follows is to understand the several dimensions of that character and to review how those dimensions developed and have shaped the many people who have entered the educational doors in Anderson, Indiana.

President Robert H. Reardon began rather graphically his June 1977 annual report to the campus board of trustees. He tried to picture for board members the complexity of the life of the Anderson campus during the year then ending, saying with his characteristic touch of humor and wisdom:

> There are three things that are exceedingly difficult to do. The first is to climb over a barbed wire fence which leans toward you; the second is to kiss a girl who leans away from you; and the third thing is for the President of Anderson College [University] to write a summary, encompassing the kaleidoscopic activities of the school year.

If such were the case in 1977, the problem is even more difficult now that the time of the university's diamond jubilee celebration has come!

Necessarily, then, there is no attempt here to be comprehensive and exhaustive. Such is not possible. If it were possible, the resulting length of the book would make its reading prohibitive and the sheer mass of detail would overwhelm any sense of reader perspective on it all. So what does follow is selective and illustrative. I hope, nonetheless, that good balance has been achieved and proper perspective on the whole of things has managed to emerge. That at least has been my goal in writing.

The Anderson campus certainly has been about the business, to borrow Bolling's words, of "shaping the values, the purposes, as well as the skills of the students who pass through its doors." In this noble effort the assumed authority and guiding perspectives of the Bible have been a central treasure of Anderson University ever since its founding. The school's theme song, its beloved *alma mater* (see page 131), for decades has spoken of a "noble purpose." This purpose has been service centered and has reflected the institutional mission of being a "guide of soul and mind."

As with the biblical materials themselves, the university's history as told in these pages is hardly an impersonal and detached report of a long series of past events. Rather, it is an interpretative account, which takes for granted that there is meaning, purpose, and destiny embedded in it all. The life of Anderson University, of course, has been lived in the context of a maze of human activities and frailties. But it also has been infused with a distinctive mission. A divine dimension has always been part of this cherished enterprise of higher education. Vision, sacrifice, idealism, and a sense of God's call and guidance have joined to form a moving story rich in texture and enduring in meaning. Primarily it is because of these characteristics that rise above the ordinary that this history was worth writing and now is worth reading.

Combining the inevitable and enriching diversity of an academic community with the convictions and partnership of a committed religious community, the Church of God (Anderson, Indiana), Anderson University has produced a distinctive tradition well worth the careful recording. To record adequately the history of Anderson University, however, it was necessary to draw from the school's poets, prophets, storytellers, and the life-changing experiences of real persons, as well as from the contracts, catalogs, annuals, and numerous self-studies and other documents of many descriptions. Quite inadequate and boring would be any "history" presented only as a series of naked facts arranged chronologically like so many trapped beads on a very long string. The meaning really worth capturing and passing on is to be found in the rich tapestry of human hopes, memories, and transformations as they have revolved around and been enabled by the guiding mission of the university.

D. Elton Trueblood once said that "the poet goes beyond facts to meanings; he sees the world, not as something to be measured or even analyzed, but as something to which his whole being must respond. He catches a glimpse of what the world is like beneath its outer husks and what he sees makes him sing" (1936, 17). In this light it is fair to say that this present "history" seeks to be both descriptive and interpretative, both prose and poetry. It speaks both of the *what* and the *why* of happenings. There may even be a little singing and times of fun along the way!

3

This university history, then, is the telling of a wonderful story full of competent persons who were committed and compassionate, people who were part of events that have made a difference in this troubled world. Consequently, one will encounter in these pages more than a mechanical recounting of the happenings of past years. Also included are elements of the heart of the heritage, selected scenes along the way, plenty of photographs, a highlighting of some of the persons who have made the difference, and an attempt to evaluate a range of issues that have been pivotal. In addition to these pages, the reader also is directed to a companion volume, *Faith, Learning and Life: Views from the President's Office of Anderson University.* This supplemental source, published jointly by Anderson University and Warner Press in 1991, presents much of the wisdom of the school's heritage through the collected writings of its first three presidents.

Why so many pages devoted to the past of one school? The recovery of yesterday certainly is not intended to idolize blindly what has gone before. Careful assessment and selective reaffirmation always are necessary. Nevertheless, in the case of Anderson University, there is so much to be recovered and, even following critical review, so much worthy of reaffirmation that a lengthy telling of the story is justified. Here, then, is the presentation of a particular past that is full of perspective for the future. What has been in this school's past retains the ability to be a worthy "guide of soul and mind" for our todays and tomorrows.

All of us live in a stream of tradition that, whether we are aware of it or not, has shaped who we now are and what we now are doing. Too often that stream is unexamined. In his provocative book titled *The Vindication of Tradition,* Jaroslav Pelikan said that "tradition is the living faith of the dead; traditionalism is the dead faith of the living" (65). This present volume seeks the living faith of a particular past as one way of avoiding the dominance of dead faith among those who live on. The intent here is not a journey among fossils in an institutional museum; it is a pilgrimage into a tradition for the sake of tomorrow. We listen always for echoes from this past that are worthy seeds of a future still to come.

The phrase *truth sets free* helpfully identifies vital aspects of the university's history and mission. "Truth," particularly Christian truth, has been a strong institutional foundation from the beginning. "Sets" suggests an ongoing process of enabling, the path of questing, teaching and learning that sheds light on vital foundations and encourages the attitudes and skills necessary for students and faculty alike to live informed and inspired lives of service. "Free" refers to the mature, the released life of vocation widened by the liberal arts tradition, stimulated by an open and visionary church fellowship, and enriched by an interdisciplinary emphasis and international focus.

Truth and freedom require delicate balancing in a church-related university. Both, however, are essential elements of the special character of Anderson University and an appropriate balance between them is believed to hold great potential. Separated, each is its own kind of terrible tyrant. Joined, each brings richness and fulfillment to the other. So, in an important way, the history of the university is the story of a quest to understand and teach truth aright and to discover and use freedom wisely. You, the reader, now are invited to join this ongoing journey.

In the pages of this history there sometimes is information of significance that would burden unnecessarily a reading of the text. Such information appears in footnotes at the end of each chapter and in appendices at the end of the volume. Direct quotations appearing in the text that are not otherwise identified are drawn from the taped interviews listed in Appendix T. An extensive index is provided to serve the particular needs and interests of the reader

Appreciation is expressed to the many campus leaders, past and present, who have shared with me their memories and evaluations. While several persons read critically various portions of the first draft of this work as needed assistance to me as the writer, particular thanks goes to former campus presidents Robert H. Reardon and Robert A. Nicholson who each read the entire manuscript in draft form and offered a range of helpful suggestions. Research Assistant Deborah Hendricks also provided valuable assistance. Gratitude is expressed to Warner Press (earlier known as the Gospel Trumpet Company), which not only joined the university in enabling this publication, but in 1917 was parent for the university itself.

May that which has been in the past kindle a flame that will show the way to what should be. May the story of this exceptional educational institution continue its service as "guide of soul and mind!"

TABLE 1

Institutional Overview

Institutional Names:

    1917-1925 Anderson Bible Training School

    1925-1929 Anderson Bible School and Seminary

    1929-1964 Anderson College and Theological Seminary

    1964-1987 Anderson College

    1987-   Anderson University

Accreditations:

    1937   Indiana State Department of Education(secondary teacher education)

    1946   North Central Association of Colleges and Schools

    1963   National Council for the Accreditation of Teacher Education

            (secondary and elementary)

    1965   Association of Theological Schools

    1974   National League of Nursing (associate degree)

    1974   National Association of the Schools of Music

    1979   Council on Social Work Education

    1988   National Athletic Trainers Association

Chief Executive Officers:

    1917-1923 Joseph T. Wilson (principal)

    1923-1925 John A. Morrison (principal)

    1925-1958 John A. Morrison (president)

    1958-1983 Robert H. Reardon (president)

    1983-1990 Robert A. Nicholson (president)

    1990-   James L. Edwards (president)

Chief Academic Officers (College):

    1917-1925 (chief executive officers)

    1925-1958 George Russell Olt

    1958-1983 Robert A. Nicholson

    1983-1988 Barry L. Callen

    1988-   A. Patrick Allen

Chief Academic Officers (School of Theology):

    1950-1953 Earl L. Martin

    1953-1962 Adam W. Miller

    1962-1973 Gene W. Newberry

    1973-1974 Barry L. Callen (acting)

    1974-1983 Barry L. Callen

    1983-1988 Jerry C. Grubbs

    1988-1990 Barry L. Callen (acting)

    1990-   James Earl Massey

Recent Chairs of Board of Trustees:

    1981-1991 Ronald J. Fowler

    1991-   David L. Sebastian

1 Context and Caution
1636-1916

"These leaders were not really 'fighters of education'. Rather than being anti-educationalists, they were 'ultra-supernaturalists'."
(John A. Morrison)

Anderson University was born in difficult circumstances. By the time 1917 finally had arrived, the long tradition of higher education in the United States had developed widespread attitudes often critical of Christian faith. Partly in response to such negative attitudes, the Church of God movement was reluctant to sponsor what might become just another "hotbed of heresy," another institutionalized expression of human arrogance. Many of the earliest Church of God people had Methodist backgrounds and held the view common in American holiness circles that "book learning" tended to render one "less spiritual." It is not surprising, then, that the appearance of a church-related institution of higher education in Anderson, Indiana, had late, modest, and only cautionary beginnings.

Higher Learning in America

As early as 1619, when 10,000 acres of land were granted by the Virginia Company for America's first university, the goal was to combine classical learning and the Christian religion for the sake of cultivating "the humane person." Clearly this venture was in the tradition of England's seventeenth-century colleges at Oxford and Cambridge and of the Scottish universities. It sought to provide a general education that emphasized the art of clear thinking and effective communication and the principles that ought to direct all personal and public affairs. Unfortunately, by 1622 malaria and an Indian massacre ended this initial American thrust into higher education.

Soon, however, learning and religion joined forces. This time it was at the initiative of the Puritans. They established Harvard College in 1636, patterning it after Emmanuel College of Cambridge University in England. This new school became the first of a series of colonial institutions that lifted high the banner of Christ in the context of serious academic study. The central purpose of these new schools was represented by Harvard's famous statement of beginning:

> After God had carried us safe to New England, and we had builded our houses, provided necessaries for our livelihood, rear'd convenient places for God's worship, and settled the Civil Government: One of the next things we longed for, and looked after was to advance Learning, and perpetuate it to Posterity, dreading to leave an illiterate ministry to the churches, when our present Ministers shall lie in the Dust (*New England's First Fruits*, 1).

In general, collegiate education in America had found its parent and main sponsor in the Christian churches. Religion was unashamedly recognized as the keystone of the educational arch. The Christian faith in particular was the determining factor in educational theory and practice. This is exactly how most Americans wanted it and how it had been for centuries back in Europe before the birth of Harvard in the new world. The God of the Christian was recognized as the ground of truth and, therefore, the guiding light and ruling principle in the proper education of the young.

The nature of higher learning in America was more deeply concerned at first with forming character than with fostering pure academic research and theoretical comprehension. It placed great value on a carefully controlled residential pattern of life for students and oriented itself primarily around the training of a special elite for community leadership.

Early American higher education clearly was intended to educate gentlemen and professionals. At first the focus was on preparing ministers, but soon lawyers, doctors, and teachers were included. Hebrew, Greek, Latin, classical history, and literature were basic to the curriculum. The whole frame of reference for this curriculum was dominated by the assumptions and goals of the Christian faith.

During the nineteenth century Americans tended to group themselves by occupation, social class, religion, gender, locality, and ethnic background. Almost all of these groups found adequate reason to set up their own colleges, both to perpetuate their own subcultures and to give themselves an institutionalized legitimacy in the larger society. Hundreds of colleges owed their initial existence to the vision and energy of one person, often a gifted and enterprising Christian minister. The numerous Christian denominations in the United States, themselves significant subcultures, provided a strong impulse for college founding. They were motivated by the need for an educated ministry and by a missionary spirit that sought to establish new and vital centers of Christian education, living, and witness. They also tended to be motivated by concerns for strengthening denominational loyalty, competing with denominational rivals, and resisting the "secularistic" influences spreading rapidly throughout the culture.

Particularly after 1819, when the Supreme Court's decision in the Dartmouth College case essentially assured private institutions freedom from state interference, private liberal arts colleges multiplied. By 1860 more than five hundred new colleges had been founded, most of them under church sponsorship. Though many of these did not survive the Civil War years (particularly those in the South), and although often they were very weak institutions by modern standards, the American historians Samuel Eliot Morison and Henry Steele Commager have praised a strength they surely did have:

> For an integrated education, one that cultivates manliness and makes gentlemen as well as scholars, one that disciplines the social affections and trains young men to faith in God, consideration for his fellow men, and respect for learning, America has never had the equal of her hill-top colleges (1950, 514).

So it remained in the United States without significant change for several generations. Faith and learning went hand in hand. Together they were an essential part of the institutional backbone and moral fiber of a young nation.   Almost from the beginning, however, there were contrary forces. Changes of major proportions soon came along that caused many Christian people to distrust higher education and to fear that a cultivation of the mind might be dangerous to the life of faith and thus a direct threat to the health of the church.

The claims of the Christian faith may indeed have enjoyed great prestige and have influenced the basic nature of higher education in America from the beginning. But all of this came to face decades of significant change and turmoil.   Traditional religious piety began to be discredited and devalued in an ambitious and pragmatic young society. Theological and political assumptions, virtually unquestioned for centuries, came under attack—and much of the action inevitably came to focus on college campuses.

By the end of the eighteenth century the dominant beliefs and values of the early American colonial period already were being challenged directly.   Orthodox Christianity was beginning to struggle to hold its own against philosophies of the "Enlightenment," which were being adopted enthusiastically in some intellectual and

9

political circles. New approaches to truth and newly respected names filled the air, approaches like rationalism, deism, naturalism, and empiricism, and names like Descartes, Bacon, Hobbes, Locke, and Rousseau.[1] In America the bitter writings of Thomas Paine and the milder ones of Thomas Jefferson tended to encourage a style of religious unbelief typical of the European skeptics and political radicals of the time. From a Christian perspective, therefore, by the latter part of the eighteenth century there was a general decline in the American public's unquestioned commitment to traditional Christian faith and morals.

Timothy Dwight, who became the president of Yale in 1795, described increasing numbers of college students of the day:

> Youths ... with strong passions and feeble principles ... delighted in the prospect of unrestrained gratification ... and became enamored with the new doctrines.... Striplings scarcely fledged suddenly found that the world had been enveloped in general darkness through the long succession of preceding ages, and that the light of human wisdom had just begun to dawn upon the human race.

An antichurch play was staged at Dartmouth. When the dean of Princeton opened the chapel Bible to read, a pack of playing cards fell out. Someone had carved in the thick and supposedly sacred book a rectangular hole to accommodate the pack— and to embarrass and infuriate the school!

In the decades that followed there were times of dramatic spiritual awakenings on the nation's campuses that brought back some of the mutual supportiveness between learning and religion. But society-wide trends were pointed the other way. Interest in the natural sciences was rising. Pressure was increasing for higher education to be freed from the control of religious bodies. It now was being argued that the treasures of the human mind must be unfettered, loosed to reason boldly and act even in revolutionary ways on behalf of human happiness. The industrial progress of the nation was developing a need for persons with specialized training not available in the usual liberal arts curriculum that characterized most church-related colleges. So, for several reasons, there was significant call for fundamental change.

With the emergence of a more open society during the early decades of the nineteenth century, the inherited educational system began to be challenged. Historian Richard Hofstadter observed that "American society was too democratic to accept completely the idea of a gentleman's education, too practical ... to continue to accept complacently its classical content, too dynamic and competitive to accept indefinitely its static character" (Hofstadter and Hardy 22). Further, the attitudes and religious commitments of this more open society were being affected greatly by the society's mobility and increasingly rootless nature. By 1840 the westward movement had carried Americans in large numbers to the banks of the Mississippi River, and soon many hardy pioneers were rushing on to the Pacific Coast. When gold was discovered in 1848 near present-day Sacramento, California, the rush west became a flood. Whole lives, including traditional religious commitments, often were compromised. One overland diarist wrote in 1852: "He who starts across the continent is most sure to leave his religion on the east side of the Missouri River."[3]

Something very new was certain to come along in American higher education. That something would be more "secular" and pragmatic, more "scientific" and specifically related to the materialistic needs and desires of a changing society. No longer would higher education be designed to get as much as possible of the body of Christian truth into the heads and hearts of undergraduates because of the assumption that there is a more or less fixed body of truth worthy of conveyance to new generations. Rather, educators increasingly would view knowledge more as a process of critical inquiry freed from religious presuppositions and restrictions.

In 1862 the Congress of the United States passed and President Abraham Lincoln signed the Morrill Act, thereby endowing new colleges of agriculture and mechanical arts in many states. These land-grant colleges broke radically with the historic pattern of liberal education (the Ivy League classical ideal) by emphasizing the "practical" branches of knowledge so necessary for an expanding young nation.

They also separated their educational work from church control. Cornell University, founded in 1865, was the earliest example of a frankly secular university established to meet the needs of an emerging industrial society. Its charter stated clearly that "persons of every religious denomination or of no religious denomination shall be equally eligible to all offices and appointments." It was to be a new day. Money to finance a rapidly expanding academic community would come not from Christian bodies, which had been higher education's financial foundation in the past, but from the government and industrialists. The source of dollars and the nature of educational priorities, of course, tend to become closely related.

Another significant development, equally abhorred by most church-related educators of the day, was the importation of the German university model of higher education, something dramatized by the founding of Johns Hopkins University in 1876. Defenders of traditional church-related colleges spared little in denouncing this new direction for the American tradition of higher education. John Blanchard wrote in 1892: "German universities have done more to make the Bible contemptible than have all other causes since Luther rescued it from the convent of Erfort" (*Congregational News*).

Between 1815 and World War I more than ten thousand American students journeyed to Germany to secure their Ph.D. degrees from prestigious universities like Heidelberg, Leipzig, and Berlin. In those settings they learned a new model of education and absorbed viewpoints about the Christian faith often considered heretical at home. The new model gave priority to studies at the doctoral level, stressed faculty research, and degraded undergraduate education (the typical college years) to little more than preparation for postgraduate specialization. Heavy emphasis was placed on freedom for students to elect their own courses of study and for faculty members to teach subjects of their choice and to pursue sophisticated research as the centerpiece of their responsibilities.

Here was a far more scientific, technical and specialized notion of scholarship. The spirit of critical inquiry into any subject was fostered routinely. Nothing, including the Bible, was to be immune from the severest of "objective" investigation. No longer was there to be any established orthodoxy except belief in the scholar's right to pursue truth in a setting freed from nonacademic restraints on the process. Emphasis usually was placed on factual knowledge rather than on meaning and morals. The prime goal was the acquiring of relevant data and not the nurturing of persons. Such philosophic and curricular assumptions were a few of the key building blocks for what later would be a network of state-supported universities back in the United States, where most American youth eventually would be educated.

The methods of this German model of higher education soon were directed at the pages of the Bible. What resulted was a stress on the "human" side of sacred literature wherein, presumably, one could discover the cultural shaping and historical biases and frailties that comprised such revered writing. Professors became bold as they passed their independent judgments on what appeared to them to be the questionable validity of various parts of the Bible. The results? There were several.

German universities became famous worldwide for producing creative scholars in many fields of professional endeavor. Material prosperity came from some of the new knowledge gained from this approach. But this general approach to higher education, whether carried on in Germany or by its many American imitators, became infamous in the eyes of much of the Christian community.

Beyond the fact that challenges to accepted Christian doctrine were upsetting, these challenges became especially objectionable when such "enlightened" persons joined the faculties of church-related colleges. In some institutions the educational process soon deteriorated into bitter battles for control. In others the new trends were decried and every attempt was made to continue business as usual in isolation from such unwelcome developments elsewhere.

Reaction to the encroachment of this "modernism" was so severe in some quarters that many traditional and especially many church-related colleges found themselves alienated from the emerging culture around them. The historian of Wheaton College in Illinois, for instance, reported: "As the waves of 'modern thought' swept over America, Wheaton College gradually became an island of resistance in a turbulent sea of doubt" (Willard 68). Renewed concern for heartfelt religion swelled and joined with a disgust for this wave of seemingly arrogant unbelief, leading many orthodox Christians to a mistrust of the educational process itself. The reaction often was one of anger and shock and a pulling away from what came to be judged the increasingly corrupted scene of higher education in America.

Social and educational trends now were multiplying against the orthodox traditions of the church-related colleges in America. They even were suggesting that such colleges were relics of the past. By 1900 many persons had concluded that the small Christian college was living on borrowed time. William Rainey Harper, for instance, surveyed prospects for numerous denominational colleges scattered across the Midwest and judged that only twenty-five percent of them had a good chance for survival. The rest would either scale down their programs or die (1905, 349ff.). The trend away from a narrow, sectarian spirit in religion joined with the growing strength and vocational relevance and versatility of the state-supported institutions to spell difficulty if not doom for the small church college, which still championed traditional assumptions and now was desperate for operational dollars. Prospects were dim indeed.

A Reformation Movement Emerges

As the twentieth century was ready to dawn, then, evangelical Christian pulpits and holiness camp meetings commonly delivered tirades against formal learning, almost as if such learning were little more than a cunning wile of the devil designed to draw a person away from dependence on the grace of God. Seminaries were commonly condemned as "cemeteries." Many unlettered spokespersons for "the old-time religion" were given enthusiastic hearings on almost any subject they cared to address. They may not have been "educated," but they were said to be divinely inspired and not contaminated by the traps of "worldly" learning. Higher education had fallen under the dark cloud of being perceived as a haughty attempt to lean on one's own understanding.

Billy Sunday, probably the most flamboyant of urban Christian revivalists of the early twentieth century, boomed on this subject with a rugged rhetoric:

> Thousands of college graduates are going as fast as they can straight to hell. If I had a million dollars I'd give $999,999 to the church and $1 to education. When the word of God says one thing and scholarship says another, scholarship can go to hell.[4]

13

Often it is noted that such negative attitudes toward learning came partly from the social status of the persons involved. For instance, early nineteenth-century Methodism in the United States enlisted its greatest support among the lower classes, especially those living in frontier areas. Because of the rather primitive style of life, these people rarely had the time, money, or energy to devote to higher learning. As one historian concluded:

> What they could not obtain, many of them decried as inherently evil. Thus the Methodists of this period talked much of the dangers of "book learning"—especially about how it made ministers "less spiritual." They often confused being "less spiritual" with being less emotional than the average Methodist in one's approach to religion (Ringenberg 13).

Whatever explanation one chooses, by 1900 conservative Christianity in the United States had reacted dramatically. The resurgence of "holiness" teaching had brought with it a considerable isolation from "the world," including the world of "secular" learning. It had led to a devaluing of art, literature, science, and general culture. Christians by the thousands had virtually retired from the mainstream of society and instead had placed their faith squarely in the authority of their personal experiences with Christ.

While the "modernists" were undercutting the public's traditional confidence in the authority of the Bible, many conservative Christians had become rigid and reactionary, sometimes almost blindly defending their faith against all comers. Christian faith and the new world of learning were at odds. It was a troubled time for church-related higher education.

The Church of God reformation movement made its first modest appearance on the American scene in the late nineteenth century. By then church-related higher education in the United States already had known its days of glory and now was living through a controversial and chaotic period. The Christian community was at odds with itself, was sharply divided organizationally, and therefore was presenting a poor witness to an unbelieving world.

This new Christian movement was restorationist in nature and directly relevant to the central issues of the time. Emphasis was placed on holiness of life, biblical authority, and unity among God's true people. Here was a call for all Christians to return humbly to the normative beliefs and practices of the first-century church, a call that set these "saints" squarely against several major trends of the time. Here were bands of radical reformers offering a sharp critique of rampant denominationalism and all of its associated evils. The focus of their vision, as stated by the man to be the first president of a new school in Anderson, Indiana, was as follows:

> The church is the spiritual body of Christ.... The denominations are only religious organizations brought about by Christian people and are not in reality churches in the New Testament sense. The ideal was that, if all Christians could ... abide in Christ alone, that would be the road to oneness in the church (Morrison 1962, 165).

Feeling strongly that ecclesiastical organizations erode the leadership of the Holy Spirit in the church, these bold and visionary Christians began around 1880 to "come out" of all denominational entanglements. They sought to accept the apostolic faith as defined in the New Testament and to fulfill the gospel's mission in an open and free fellowship of sanctified and unified believers.

The pioneers of this new movement, therefore, were heavily experience-oriented (in common with many conservative Christians of the time) and also quite anti-institutional in general outlook. They were disgusted with denominational rivalries and were opposed to the tendency of denominations to found colleges as part of that competitive and divisive process. So the emphasis on spiritual experience and away from humanly devised church institutions, the commitment to highlight divine origin, control, and gifting as opposed to all human achievement, in addition to the general tenor of the times, led this young movement to considerable caution about the appropriateness of actually establishing "Church of God" institutions for the purpose of fostering the life of the mind.

In the earliest decades of the history of the Church of God movement it happened just about the way one would have expected. Founding standard colleges was not a high priority for Church of God people. To the contrary, formal learning and evangelistic believing tended to be seen more as competitors than as companions. Denominational colleges and seminaries, in fact, sometimes were identified as an obvious part of the very sectarian scene that God was said to be calling to an end. Obedience to divine dictates seemed to call for *coming out from* rather than *establishing* such humanly defined and dominated enterprises.

One "institution," however, did emerge almost immediately in the midst of this movement. Before the turn of the twentieth century the Gospel Trumpet Publishing Company had been organized formally as a necessary means of spreading the exciting news of this new reformation movement. It was an institution of expedience, something found to be necessary if God's work were to get done. But "higher" education was not a perceived necessity. It was, in fact, something many preachers cautioned against.

15

One day, almost four decades after this movement's beginning around 1880, a modest educational effort, a little Bible Training School, would develop in 1917 in the midst of the busy life of the Gospel Trumpet Company. It would be quite pragmatic in nature, like the trend in the nation's evolving public system of higher education. But the task to be served very practically would not be supplying the skills required by a growing and industrializing young nation. The task would be to provide support for gospel workers seeking to spread the saving, liberating, and unifying news of Christ.

That eventual development in 1917, however, was not without some tradition of a commitment to learning, even in an experientially oriented, anti-institutional church movement. Soon after his conversion experience in 1865, Daniel S. Warner, a prominent pioneer of the movement, attended Oberlin College in Ohio, enrolling for an English preparatory course. There he was exposed to persons of learning and refinement. The president of Oberlin at the time was Charles Finney, the nation's foremost preacher and writer of holiness. Later Warner attended Vermillion College where he studied Greek and New Testament.

In 1876, when Warner was a Winebrennerian minister, that body's West Ohio Eldership met in Findlay, Ohio, and expressed its belief "that in no other way can we so effectually build up the Church and retain the children of our brotherhood than by establishing an institution of learning to be owned and controlled by the Church" (Forney 566). Warner was one of three ministers appointed to plan a way to bring such a thing about (the resulting institution continues to this day as the University of Findlay).

But the presumed significance of such an educational institution was not high on Warner's personal agenda in the years that followed, even though he himself was a highly motivated reader, researcher, and writer. As a mature minister, later to be separated from the Winebrennerian fellowship, starting institutions of any kind (especially ones such as colleges intended in part to solidify denominational loyalty) would be seen as far from acceptable. He later would write in the *Gospel Trumpet*, of which he was founding editor, that the only credentials required for ministry were "to be filled with the Holy Spirit and have a reasonable knowledge of the English language." On another occasion he expressed his deep suspicion about much in higher education: "Colleges are necessary to fit men for the work of the devil and the business of the world. . . . They are but devil's playhouses" (1884, 2).

A major manuscript of Warner's was revised and completed by Herbert M. Riggle after Warner's death in 1895. It was an extensive critique of the "sects" and was based on a particular pattern of interpreting biblical prophecy. Especially criticized as a "mark of the Beast" was the denominational practice of instilling particular sectarian doctrines in the minds of their adherents. Warner and Riggle pictured "higher" education as one of several tools commonly employed to further human arrogance and solidify the disastrous disunity of God's church. How should it be instead? According to these early and prominent Church of God leaders:

> God's ministers received the everlasting gospel which they preach from the Lord. They receive it free. The anointing teaches them. They are "taught of God". . . . But all sects have their particular mark or doctrine with which they mark their subjects. They have erected preacher factories for the express purpose of marking their ministers with their particular mark (1903, 379-380).

Being formally trained, accordingly, was announced as merely the process of a person being boxed in a divisive human institution and tied by limited human thinking. It was understood to be a key section of the diseased backbone of the whole denominational system.

Probably it is most accurate to conclude that early pioneer leaders of the Church of God movement were not necessarily against education as such. But they certainly were against schools as they knew them. So much was this the case that the few leaders who had had the benefit of some formal education were known on occasion to hide that fact in order to retain status with their brothers and sisters in the movement.

No wonder, then, that some early Church of God preachers, once ordained to the Christian ministry, actually burned all of their books (except the Bible) as a witness to their singular reliance upon God and his Word. Such radical actions were a dramatic form of an earlier and related action of Warner. Sensing his call to the ministry and feeling that he must prepare to be a laborer in the Lord's harvest while it was yet day, he had cut short his studies at Oberlin College. He went home for a season and applied himself to prayer and Bible study, things he judged more directly necessary to ministerial preparation.

Certainly it was common for the pages of the *Gospel Trumpet* (new periodical of the Church of God movement) in those first decades after 1880 to carry very negative comments about education. Typically, however, the specific issue under attack was either the substituting of human learning for the grace of God, using schools for sectarian ends, or implying that the primary credentials for effective Christian ministry could be issued by a school. Warner, for instance, argued in 1883 that "as to men prescribing a course of study as a condition of preaching the Gospel, that is the vilest form of popery." Seminaries were branded as sectarian training grounds and hotbeds of heresy. Colleges typically were seen as institutionalized examples of human arrogance.

Despite all such negative references, it still is appropriate to assume that education was seen by key early leaders of the reformation movement as potentially good and helpful. After all, persons like Warner and Enoch E. Byrum, while writing strong antied-ucational articles, at the same time were building significant personal libraries and prov-ing themselves diligent students of the Bible and related subjects. But, in their view, little time was available to give attention to that academic potential.

More important issues were at hand. The gospel workers were hurrying around the country as a "flying ministry," rarely pausing long enough even to establish and sys-tematically nurture congregations and certainly not stopping to build things as costly and suspect as colleges.

Education Without Colleges

In the early 1890s at least the hint of a changed attitude about formalized educa-tion emerged within the young life of the Church of God reformation movement. A home for the children of itinerant preachers was organized in Grand Junction, Michigan, in relation to the publishing house then located there. Regular classes were conducted in music, taught by Andrew L. Byers, and penmanship, taught by Jeremiah Cole. Apparently Warner even envisioned something more, an "extensive educational project." Persons often had spoken and written to him about the possibility of a course in Bible study that would better equip them to labor in the Lord's vineyard. His heart had become stirred to make an effort in this direction. Even a simple curriculum was projected, with the possibility of three teachers. Suggested courses included Bible history and perhaps archaeology, the study of the New Testament, and lectures on prophecy, and experimen-tal and spiritual truth. Music and elocution were to be added later.

Then came a major turning point for this idea and for the young church move-ment itself. On the day of the first scheduled class in 1895, Warner fell ill. Within days he was dead. Soon Enoch Byrum replaced Warner as the new editor of the *Gospel Trumpet* and he was quick to make clear his own view and intent. He wrote:

> Some have asked if we have a theological school here. We answer, no. Neither do we expect to have. We have Bible readings and special faith meetings almost every evening which are wonderfully blessed of God by way of spiritual advancement and real soul food, and holiness is lifted up to the Bible standard (1895).

This hesitancy and even apparent defensiveness about the most modest of pro-jected educational ventures reflected a widespread attitude in the young church move-ment. Lawrence Brooks, for instance, started his ministry in Arkansas in 1915. Soon he felt the need for some systematic preparation for his life's calling. The advice he got

Daniel S. Warner (inset)
"Floating Bethel" docked near Moundsville, WV

from older ministers was what he later recalled as the common attitude still remaining in those days: "Why fool around in school while souls are going to hell?" So it was in the early years of the Church of God movement. Direct evangelism had clear preeminence over any systematic educational efforts.

This advice received by Brooks, however, came in the face of a growing discussion about the appropriateness of formal education for the work of ministry. This discussion, by 1912, included more than the status quo attitude of Brother Enoch Byrum and the negative opinion received by Brother Lawrence Brooks in Arkansas. While it is clear that the ranks of the young movement were filled with common people who had little or no school experience and little or no inclination in that direction, it also was true that many of that first generation of leaders were educated persons by the standards of the time.

Both Warner and Byrum had attended college. According to the sociologist Valorous Clear, the first person representing the movement to preach in Anderson, Indiana, was a physician-turned-preacher and, at one time, forty-one of one hundred volunteer workers were school teachers (1977, 20). Certainly the literary level of publications in the early years of this church movement suggests a highly literate leadership, if not readership.

On the other hand, most of these people came from a rural background and were not predisposed to use an educational approach to further general church work. Their attitudes often ranged from antagonism to apathy toward formal education. This situation, when combined with some trends of the times and certain theological emphases, encouraged the development of a deep and difficult cleavage between faith and learning, especially in the institutionalized settings of colleges and seminaries.

D. O. Teasley argued in the pages of the *Gospel Trumpet* in 1905 that spirituality must be central and the apprentice method must be basic to the training of gospel workers. He wrote:

> Having recently seen some sad effects of human effort to train men and women for the ministry, I feel led to set forth the New Testament method of training those whom God has called to his work. . . . All theological institutions and missionary training schools are run too much on the theoretical plan, which is detrimental to spirituality and tends to fill the head and empty the heart. . . . It is the special duty of pastors to encourage, and care for, and instruct young workers. . . . Workers are needed, but only those can be used who are able to convince the gainsayers, cast out devils, heal the sick, save souls, and perfect the saints (1).

H. A. Brooks, in the same publication in 1912, developed a somewhat different thesis. According to Brooks:

> To the ignorant and unlearned, the advantages of education are unknown. . . . Surely there is no evil in knowing how to do and say things well. Yet the unlearned maintain that it tends to pride and worldliness. That is not so; and indeed it is true that there are many more self-conceited people among the

uneducated than there are among the learned. . . . There is talent in the church of God lying dormant in the hearts and minds of men and women, through the lack of education (4-5).

Such differing perspectives represented more than a temporary tension, a dilemma that would fade quickly once the Church of God movement got itself better established. T. Franklin Miller was the executive officer of the movement's national Board of Christian Education for the period 1945-1966. He reported that even during those later years there still was this same cleavage among ministers in the Church of God. Some leaders were committed to evangelism and some to education, often with little appreciation shown for one another's views. It was an old and persistent problem. Sociologist Valorous Clear observed as recently as 1984:

That discussion, that dichotomy, that choice never has been eliminated. It juxtaposes the movement between the false extremes of trusting God or trusting humankind, and much of the Church of God institutional history and sociology consist of the ways in which we have dealt with that pseudo-issue (Massey, *Educating for Service*, 16).

Ways, however, were being found to deal with this issue because people needed assistance in their learning and growing. Initially it may have been education without colleges, but it surely was and would be education.

With the Church of God movement having an essentially negative and yet increasingly mixed attitude toward formal education in those first decades following 1880, there also was a growing band of enthusiastic gospel workers who were anxious to prepare for effectiveness in their Christian callings. They did not see a systematic program of training as necessarily either a compromise with sectarianism or a flaunting of human pride in the face of God's grace and gifts for ministry. As the need for increased preparation for service became more apparent, various kinds of educational experimentation emerged.

The Sunday school movement was popular among churches in the United States during the early years of the Church of God movement. It was a structured, lay oriented program often separated from the church bodies in whose buildings the classes met. Warner at first judged the Sunday school to be just another sectarian tool bringing more division to the body of Christ. Even so, he wrote in an 1885 *Gospel Trumpet* editorial that "where there are a sufficient number of saints to hold a service especially for the instruction of the children and youth, there is no reason why such a service should not be held."

   Classes of this kind became rather common, and some Church of God evangelists experimented further by conducting children's meetings alongside their revivals.
Special classes were held occasionally in the Gospel Trumpet Home (a large communal
living arrangement for workers at the publishing company). In fact, by 1892 there was a
Sunday school in the Trumpet Home. The editorship of E. E. Byrum, while showing no
enthusiasm for formal training schools, nonetheless did support Sunday school work. By
1903 George L. Cole was writing a weekly column in the *Gospel Trumpet* titled "The
Sunday School Work." Given a concern about employing "Babylon's" literature, and
having judged the International Sunday School materials to have "such a taint of sectism
and erroneous doctrinal views that it is not expedient to use them" (9), by 1910 the
Gospel Trumpet Company was publishing its own Sunday school quarterlies.   The
Sunday school avenue of education obviously had been accepted once it had been adapted to the concerns and perspectives of the Church of God people.
   Also of increasing prominence during the early years of the Church of God
movement was the growth and industrialization of cities. To these complex and problem-
ridden urban settings came pioneer ministers of the Church of God who were burdened
for the lost and the destitute. "Missionary homes" began to appear as teams of gospel
workers conducted revival services, distributed literature, and helped the needy. Probably
the first such home was started in 1895 in Chicago by Gorham Tufts. It operated as a res-
cue mission, an evangelistic center, and later, under the leadership of E. A. Reardon, a
place for a wide range of worship, service, and educational activities. Young people of
the church were attracted to this and similar "homes." They had idealism and energy for
service to others and they had needs of their own for growth and training. Doubtless,
these homes provided much needed leadership opportunities in their time.
   Robert H.Reardon, later to be president of Anderson University, recalled that in
1899 his father, E. A. Reardon, left West Liberty, Ohio, as a young school teacher of
twenty-three to live in the Chicago Missionary Home. The elder Reardon had been converted and felt called to Christian ministry during a three-week meeting in West Liberty
held by Barney Warren and a "flying band of reformation saints" (Reardon 1979, 6). At
that time, observed Robert Reardon, "we had the most elementary ways of training our
young ministers. My father simply caught hold of the coattail of an older, more experienced preacher and tried to learn how." In the young Church of God movement of the
time, he noted elsewhere, "it was expected that if he were truly called and filled with the
Spirit, signs would follow" *(Alumni News* 1959, 2).
   In 1909 F. W. Heinly was director of the missionary home in New York City.
He described the purposes of that and several other such homes:

This home offers an excellent place for the training and instruction of young workers whom God has called. No prescribed course of lessons is given, but . . . a number of established ministers and workers are always here, ready to give the young worker the benefit of their varied experiences in gospel work, expound the Scriptures, and present the best methods for the study of the Bible, how to win souls and conduct meetings in the most effectual way.

Adam W. Miller, much later to be dean of Anderson University School of Theology from 1953-1962, was once a participant in the "Study by Mail" program of the New York home. There significant courses of study had come to be developed by such noteworthy people as D. O. Teasley, G. P. Tasker, and A. D. Kahn. Robert H. Reardon was influenced deeply by life with his parents at the missionary home in Chicago. O. A. Burgess developed a correspondence course for ministers that was first offered through the Spokane, Washington Missionary Home in 1915. It was a rigorous, thirty-six week program in which students were expected to read one book per day, Sundays excepted. Young Albert F. Gray studied in this program and one day would be both president of a college which evolved from this "home" base (Warner Pacific College) and long-term trustee of another, the one that would evolve in Anderson, Indiana.

By 1910 these missionary homes had begun to decline in strength and effectiveness. Some eventually were sold as apartment buildings while others became strong and permanent congregations of the Church of God movement. But whatever the end of each, all in varying degrees had performed a critical educational function for the church. It had been typical in these settings that informal counseling and study sessions became regular classes for enthusiastic young gospel workers. Several of the homes developed for themselves the name "Bible school" or "missionary training school," including the Kansas City Bible School and the Spokane Bible School. One day there would be an "Anderson Bible Training School" growing out of the "home" for the workers of the movement's publishing company, which eventually located in Anderson, Indiana.

Some general softening of the harsh attitudes toward formal education had become evident. In a real sense the missionary homes were bridge "institutions" between what was slipping into the movement's past and what was about to come. They served for about a generation as the only existing "higher education system" in the Church of God. Possibly the best perspective on the attitudes of early Church of God leaders toward formal education during this whole process was provided by John Morrison, who became the first president of the school in Anderson. These early leaders were not really "fighters of education." Rather than being anti-educationalists, they were "ultra-supernaturalists." Concluded Morrison: "With the leaders assuming this positive attitude toward the divine and a passive or negative attitude toward the human as a means of evangelism, the rank and file of the ministry could easily leap to the conclusion that the divine was the only

means to the desired end of promoting the Kingdom."[5]

Over the years it was becoming increasingly apparent that the "flying ministry" days were coming to an end in the Church of God movement. Now there was the need for establishing more settled congregations with resident pastors. Converts needed stabilizing and nurturing. The deep bias against organization in church life, resulting from so many past perversions in Christian church history, was lessening in the face of the obvious need for some effective ministry structures. The publishing company itself had become formally organized, had finally settled permanently in Anderson, Indiana, in 1906 and was itself a significant training base. Some detail about these developments is crucial since it was in Anderson, Indiana, and out of the life of the Gospel Trumpet Company that Anderson University was soon to emerge.

Gas Boom and Gospel Trumpet

The earliest history of the city of Anderson is not well documented. Located in Madison County in east central Indiana, its early inhabitants were mound builders of unknown identity. Remaining yet today are nine earthworks located just east of town near White River in what now is Mounds State Park. These mysterious mounds likely were ceremonial and burial sites, with the largest, the Great Mound, about ten feet high and nearly one-fourth of a mile around.

Then came the Delaware Indians, led locally by Chief Anderson. In 1801 some Moravian missionaries established a Christian mission among the Delawares. But by 1818 the Delawares had signed a treaty with the government of the United States in which they relinquished claim to all land in Indiana and promised to move west of the Mississippi River by 1821.

So in 1827, with the Indians gone, Anderson became the county seat and in a few years was incorporated as Andersontown. Population growth came largely because of transportation, first featuring canal construction (stopped because the state of Indiana went bankrupt) and then the railroad, which reached Madison County in 1850. In 1892 local business leaders joined to build the Anderson belt railroad, which connected with each of the main lines passing through the area to make Anderson one of the better shipping points in the state. Anderson also was in the center of an extensive interurban electric rail transportation system covering much of the Midwest. One line coming from

(Top) New Home for the "Trumpet Family" in Anderson, Indiana
Soon would become the "Old Main" of the campus
(Bottom) Gospel Trumpet Company plant, Anderson, Indiana
Later the company became known as Warner Press

25

(Left) Rev. Eugene A. Reardon, with wife and sons (Robert on left)
(Right) Missionary Home and Chapel, Chicago, Illinois

Muncie and going on to Indianapolis ran through Anderson. When the new church school was established in 1917, this line went right past it and the church's adjoining campgrounds (down what today is Third Street through the middle of the campus).

Natural gas was discovered in Madison County in 1887 and soon Anderson was being called the "Queen City of the Gas Belt." The supply seemed inexhaustible. Out in the White River, on the edge of the downtown area near the Ninth Street bridge, "Old Vesuvius" flamed its light skyward. Being one of the largest-producing gas wells in the nation, it had been piped to the river's center and lighted so that it seemed to fascinated onlookers that fire rose perpetually, almost magically from the water. The railroad regularly brought tourists to see this roaring wonder of Indiana.

More seriously, a local board of trade was organized and began negotiating with various industries that wanted to relocate and take advantage of this wonderful, free energy resource. Soon operating in Anderson were the Fowler Nut and Bolt Works from Buffalo, New York, the Anderson Flint Bottle Company from Butler, Pennsylvania, and many others. The population grew, homes, churches and schools were built, and financial institutions were founded to serve what by the turn of the century was a booming, prosperous town.[6] Gas wells were in every township of Madison County, with one well in nearby Chesterfield producing nearly ten million cubic feet daily.

But the gas supply soon began to diminish. In 1902 there were 5,820 productive wells in the immediate area, 3,523 in 1906, and by 1917 only 1,830. A colorful and dramatic era of growth and development had begun quickly and almost as quickly was ending. That expansionist era had transformed a sleepy county-seat town into an active and ambitious industrial community of some 25,000 people. Anderson was located, according to the 1900 national census, just a few miles north of the population center of the country. So, early into the twentieth century, Anderson was looking for ways to fill the growing economic vacuum by attracting new business not heavily dependent on the diminishing supply of natural gas energy. A particular business was attracted and eventually was to prove one of the more important business, cultural, and educational developments in the city's entire history. To Anderson in 1906 came the small religious publishing company of the Church of God movement.

The first issue of this movement's influential periodical, the *Gospel Trumpet*, had come out in Rome City, Indiana in 1881, but soon the issues were being published on a press in the kitchen of the little home of its editor, Daniel S. Warner, then living in Indianapolis. This religious paper said that its object was "the glory of God in the salvation of men from all sin, and the union of all saints upon the Bible." In 1882 the little operation had moved to Cardington, Ohio, then on to Bucyrus, Ohio, the next year where it stabilized as a viable young business-ministry. A new masthead now had become more specific about its publishing mission: "Edited and published semi-monthly in the name of the Lord Jesus Christ. For the purity and unity of his body, the defense of all his truth, and the abomination of sect Babylon." The masthead was an advancement, but the home in Bucyrus was temporary. Problems forced this work to shift operations to Williamston, Michigan, in 1884, where it prospered, then on to Grand Junction, Michigan, in 1886 where there were better facilities and rail services for shipping. This latter move had required one freight-car for all machinery, office material, and household goods. It was here that Warner had envisioned the launching of a "school."

Still another move had come in 1898. Warner had died in 1895, but the publishing operation had survived, even prospered to the point of outgrowing what facilities and services the little Grand Junction community could supply. Some ninety persons then comprised "the Trumpet family," all volunteer workers who received subsistence, but not salaries. A substantial building, a former shoe factory, became available in a sheriff's sale in Moundsville, West Virginia, a town where coal could be bought for seventy cents a ton. So all of the people and equipment had been moved again by train. The July 7, 1898, issue of the *Gospel Trumpet* was the first to come from Moundsville.

That fall the publishing business was reorganized into a stock company governed by seven trustees. What had been essentially the dream of one man (Warner) and then a privately owned business now became a corporation held in trust for the Church of God movement, which was growing in large part through the outreach of this publishing ministry. Also that year were the beginnings of a wholesale and jobbing business with company products. Even though circulation of the *Gospel Trumpet* now had reached 35,000 copies, there was considerable debt and constant cash flow problems. By 1905 the Trumpet building in Moundsville, so adequate a few years before, had become very crowded and still had no electricity. City officials seemed less than helpful and company

27

leaders had interest in the possibility of relocating the operation west to Indiana where the church movement was growing and where the publishing operation would be more central to the population of the nation.

A company delegation visited central Indiana and was especially impressed by the possibilities in Anderson. The city's administration was favorable and a large brick building downtown at Ninth and Central was available for lease, could be adapted easily for company needs, and already had electricity to run the presses. Also a good tract of open land was located only a short distance away on the east side of the city, land that would make an excellent site for a new Trumpet home and campground.

The big decision was made and all arrangements negotiated successfully for a five-year lease on the downtown building and the purchase of about forty-four acres of land bordering on Union Avenue at the east edge of town. A vigorous young publishing company would come to Anderson in 1906 and begin a significant and long-term life in this city. With it would come the center of operations for the growing Church of God movement.

First, a large new Trumpet home for the many workers of the publishing ministry (about 160) would be constructed in the rural setting across the river east of the town (one day to be "Old Main" of Anderson University). Twenty carloads of lumber

Members, Gospel Trumpet Company, 1918. (Front, seated, left): F. G. Smith, N. H. Byrum, J. B. Peterman, R. L. Berry. (Middle): A. B. Palmer, J. W. Byers, J. C. Blaney, G. W. Bailey, E. E. Byrum, A. B. Stanberry, L. H. Morgan. (Back): W. D. McCraw, A. L. Byers, D. O. Teasley, J. T. Wilson, W. F. Chappell, A. T. Rowe, J. G. Anderson, E. A. Reardon, J. E. Campbell, W. E. Longbrake

were purchased from the closed World's Fair buildings in St. Louis, Missouri[7] and a sand and gravel pit was opened on the site to help supply materials for the 17,000 large blocks needed for the cement-block building to contain 114 rooms and full basement. Mostly volunteer workers began laboring round-the-clock through the spring and summer of 1906, with the first meal served in the completed structure on December 12, 1906. Robert Byrum supervised much of the construction work.

Within about a decade his gifted son Russell, who worked with him on this project, would be teaching in a new school that would be started in this very Trumpet Home. Meanwhile, plans were laid for new printing presses for the leased building downtown. They all finally would be supplied with abundant electric power and the good news they would print had immediate rail transportation to carry it in all directions.

Symbolic of the pioneering spirit and reliance on divine guidance foundational to these beginnings was a memorable action of Enoch and Noah Byrum. They were the company men who had visited the spacious site east of downtown Anderson before it even was known that these forty-four acres were available for purchase. Believing deeply that the Lord had led them to this good place on behalf of the company's future, they had knelt and dedicated this beautiful, rolling land to the Lord, and only then had they gone to town to inquire about its ownership! The *Gospel Trumpet* of September 27, 1906, highlighted that memorable moment this way:

> As the sun was nearing the horizon in the western sky, there in the evening of the day, we knelt and asked God to sanctify that place to his service and for his glory, to aid in sending the gospel to all nations.

On that sacred evening there was no way that these two men could have known that their prayer would be answered in part by the emergence on that very site of a church-related university that surely would "aid in sending the gospel to all nations." But that was still far in the future and well beyond their immediate intent or fondest imaginations. What they did know for sure was that God was involved in whatever was yet to be. From the viewpoint of the city of Anderson, the exciting prospects of this company's coming to town were described this way in the local newspaper:

> If the publishing Company can be located here it means an annual camp meeting attended by thousands. It means the permanent location in Anderson of many desirable families. It means the establishment of a great printing office which employs many skilled printers, pressmen and binders, but does not compete with offices already here (Phillips 1979, 103).

29

The decades to follow would bring fulfillment of all these hopes—and much more. Out of the life of this publishing company soon would emerge in Anderson a modest little school, one day to mature into the present Anderson University.

During the first years that the Church of God people were in Anderson, there was much construction of new facilities on that spacious tract of land east of town. The very large *H*-shaped, four-story Trumpet Home was completed in 1906 for use as a residence hall and dining facility for "Trumpet" workers. Later this structure would become the "Old Main" of the Anderson campus and serve as the center of campus life until it finally would be razed in 1968 to make way for the current Decker Hall. A new tabernacle also was built on the grounds, to be ready for use by the church's camp meeting of June 1908 (now the university's renovated Byrum Hall). An Old People's Home constructed in 1907 burned to the ground before being occupied, and was completed again in 1908 (later to be rented for a university residence hall under the names "Sunset Hall" and East Hall).

Then the decision was made to provide a permanent alternative to the leased building downtown by constructing a large structure opposite the new Trumpet home, one designed for the needs of the publishing work itself. The first issue of the *Gospel Trumpet* printed in the new structure on East Fifth Street was dated October 6, 1910. Eventually everything was moved from the building downtown. By the camp meeting of 1915 the company also had funded construction of a large new dining hall and dormitory for use by the camp meeting crowds (later to be used as a university gymnasium and dormitory). Soon a major new tabernacle would be made available for the general services of the church's annual camp meetings.

In the meantime, the publishing work had grown and with it the Trumpet family. Some new additions to this large "family" of Christian believers and volunteer workers included people who would play important roles in the early years of the new educational work that soon would begin. Bessie Hittle (Byrum) came as a proofreader in May, 1907. Otto F. Linn started work in June of that same year, arriving from Kansas to raise poultry for the Trumpet family. One day he would be a Greek scholar and earn the first Ph.D. to exist within the ranks of Church of God people. A few months later Joseph T. Wilson arrived from western Pennsylvania. A decade later he would be company president and founder of the coming educational work.

The Byrum brothers, Noah and Enoch, the principal leaders of the growing Gospel Trumpet publishing work around the turn of the century, had been drawn in 1906 to the rolling, high, wooded ground across the White River just east of the town of Anderson. It was land that appeared ideal for development of the work of a young church movement which then was growing more in the Midwest than elsewhere. The move to Indiana was a little like coming home since Daniel S. Warner had published some of the earliest issues of the *Gospel Trumpet* in nearby Indianapolis in the early 1880s. Even so, there appears to have been no organized effort to establish a congregation of the Church of God in Anderson prior to the arrival of the Trumpet company and workers in 1906. But when they did arrive, with the local gas boom fading rapidly, there came with them a whole new source of energy, now to come not from wells in the ground, but from the deep wells of the human spirit. That which would be taught, written, and published in Anderson would have significance worldwide.

1. A review of these intellectual tensions is found in R. F. Butts and L. A. Cremin, *A History of Education in American Culture*, 43-63, and in Howard Lowery, *The Mind's Adventure*, 20-33.

2. As quoted by C. Robert Pace, *Education and Evangelism*, 10.

3. As quoted by Winton Solberg in "The Sabbath on the Overland Trail to California," *Church History* (September, 1990), 341.

4. As quoted by Richard Hofstadter, *Anti-Intellectualism in American Life*, 122.

5. As in Barry Callen, editor, *Faith, Learning and Life*, 5.

6. A significant example was the Anderson Banking Company, which began business in January, 1890. Linfield Myers was an early investor and served as company president from 1930-1958. He became a key community leader and staunch friend of the Church of God college then located in the city. Later his book, *As I Recall: The Wilson-Morrison Years* (1973), told of the decades of challenge faced by the bank, college, and the whole community. To celebrate its one-hundredth birthday, the bank established at the local college (by then a "university") a significant scholarship program as a way to help the school and support young people from Madison County. The first recipient in 1989 would be Peter Soetenga, whose father was a local Church of God pastor (see *The Campaign Journal*, September, 1989).

7. The *Gospel Trumpet* of September 20, 1906, identified this St. Louis event as the "Louisiana Purchase Exposition," noting that Robert Byrum made trips to Chicago, St. Louis, and elsewhere to buy building materials. W. F. Shope planned the building and nearby farmers donated labor, wagons, and teams of horses.

31

2 A Bible Training School Begins

1917-1924

". . . though many have seemed to decrease in spirituality while increasing in knowledge, the reverse should be the case—better qualified men should be more spiritual men.**"**

(1920-21 Catalog, Anderson Bible Training School)

A Mr. Oldham raised alfalfa on his farm some miles from a little railroad whistle-stop called Horton, Missouri. His son, William H. Oldham, was a pioneer minister of the Church of God. William moved his family to Clinton, Iowa, in 1906 just as the Gospel Trumpet Company was moving to Anderson, Indiana. In 1911 William took his eight-year-old son Dale with him on one of his evangelistic tours, this one to be hosted back on the alfalfa farm near Horton. Since no church or school was available to house the services, the men built a "brush arbor" for protection from the sun. A guest preacher was Joseph T. Wilson. Dale Oldham fondly remembered later that Wilson, besides preaching, was a good shot with a .22 rifle.

The most important thing about this meeting was not that Wilson was a good shot or that one day the cattle got into a patch of wild onions and proceeded to produce unusable milk for days (Oldham 27). It was that one woman gave her life to Christ and that in the decades yet to come her sons, T. Franklin and Howard Miller, along with Dale Oldham, this J. T. Wilson and many thousands of other people, would all find common cause in a school not yet even founded. The school would be in Anderson, Indiana, and its launching in 1917 would be a little like that evangelistic campaign near Horton just a few years before. It would have to begin from nothing, be a venture of visionary faith, and have to face the results of patches of wild onions now and then. What would be most important in this school would be that people there would gain new insight, acquire new skills, even find new life in a place that both revered learning and honored Jesus Christ. From the school's first day J. T. Wilson would be in the lead. He was a determined man when he had an important idea. This school would be the most important idea he would ever have.

Something Better Than Nothing

Between 1912 and 1917 a series of little booklets for Church of God ministers appeared under the title *Our Ministerial Letter.* Here was a helpful and innovative communication link among leaders in the church who needed more than the news and inspiration typically found in the *Gospel Trumpet.* They needed vigorous and substantive dialogue and direction on topics central to their leadership responsibilities. Soon an even more organized and systematic effort would be launched to address this crucial need.

Attitudes about education for ministry clearly were changing in some quarters of the Church of God. This was reflected, for instance, in a 1912 article in the *Gospel Trumpet* by H. A. Brooks titled "Advantages and Value of Education" (4-5). Then came a sensitive, but vital concern. In the April, 1917, issue of *Our Ministerial Letter* a foreword was written by J. W. Phelps. Much as D. S. Warner had reported in 1895 when he was envisioning some systematic educational effort in Grand Junction, Michigan, Phelps reported:

> Young ministers and young men and women who are called to the ministry have been told again and again that they ought to prepare for their lifework. That the young people have realized the need of the best possible preparation is evidenced by the many earnest inquiries as to what they should study, what course of reading they should pursue. These questions are answered in this issue of *Our Ministerial Letter.*

Russell R. Byrum (1889-1980), then a pastor in Boston, authored the main entry in that issue, "The Preacher Among His Books."

In 1916 Adam W. Miller, a young convert from Baltimore, and several other aspiring ministers of the Church of God were attending a missionary convention at the Church of God Missionary Home in New York City. There they confronted the visiting Joseph T. Wilson, new general manager of the Gospel Trumpet Company now located in Anderson, Indiana. They had an important question: "When is someone going to provide young ministers with training for gospel work?" Wilson's answer brought them hope.

"The Gospel Trumpet Company is about to begin classes for workers, and we would be glad to have you come to Anderson and join us." These inquires and the thoughtful work and encouragement of Russell Byrum apparently had convinced Wilson that he must act and that a practical course of action surely was available for such an important cause. He was the kind of man who was willing to act on an important idea in spite of obstacles. A tall man possessed of a rugged pioneering spirit, only those with such a spirit tend to make difficult beginnings happen. While launching a school in Anderson would not be easy, it would happen just as he had promised.

An increasing number of competent leaders was needed for the expanding life of this vigorous, young church movement. Evangelistic teams needed singers with trained voices. The publishing company needed good writers, editors, and copy readers. There were young ministers like Adam W. Miller who wanted to learn about the Bible, the world, and their own ministerial calling. There also were persons writing to the *Gospel Trumpet* wanting to know if there were a Bible school where they could go to learn more about the message of the Church of God movement and how to preach and teach as ministers and gospel workers. Clearly it was time for something important to be born.

(Left) Joseph T. Wilson, founding school principal, with family, 1919
(Right) Russell R. Byrum

In the August, 1917, issue of *Our Ministerial Letter* there appeared Russell Byrum's "A Course of Study for Ministers." He wrote that "a minister who acts wisely may save an immortal soul for heaven, which is infinite gain; but by mistake, neglect, or wrong-dealing with souls he may be responsible for their being lost in hell forever, and to miss heaven is an infinite loss." He went further by stating that there are two kinds of qualifications for this heavy responsibility of ministry. The spiritual comes first and is God-given. The intellectual, however, comes also. It requires human effort and consists of knowledge relevant to ministry. This "information is obtained mostly from books," he argued, concluding with the observation that "we have no regular means of systematic training. It is not because we are opposed to preachers gaining knowledge, but the dangers and disadvantages that have sometimes attended training-schools have caused us to hesitate in adopting such means." Having laid the groundwork for justifying a course of study, he reviewed such a plan then being used by the Methodist Church and adapted it into a five-year study plan with an annotated bibliography of suggested readings for each year.

The year 1917 turned out to be pivotal. The General Ministerial Assembly of the Church of God organized formally in Anderson, Indiana, that year, beginning an eventful decade in which the Church of God "broke the organizational barrier" (Smith 1980, 205-225). That same year, after about four decades of the movement's life, the first enduring institution of higher education in the Church of God finally was established. That institution (a rather generous designation for its first years) would be located in Anderson, and Russell Byrum would be a prominent figure in the early phase of its life. He had taught an evening course in theology while functioning as the company's managing editor in Anderson prior to his return to Boston. J. T. Wilson, company president, had asked that Byrum take initiative in organizing the curriculum and selecting the first textbooks for the launching of a small school operation. This he gladly did.

Many changes were coming. Prior to 1917 the publishing company had functioned as a "family." Food, clothing, and shelter were provided to the volunteer workers who were sharing their own giftedness in the Lord's work. But by the time the company had moved to Anderson in 1906 this arrangement had grown cumbersome, almost unmanageable. So much was necessary to support the enlarged community that it was hard to concentrate on the central purpose of Christian publishing. There was housing, farming, food service, fire protection, a campground, an old people's home, a cemetery, livestock, and more.

So in 1917 the decision was made to view workers as employees and pay them cash wages so that many such necessities, especially housing, could become their own responsibilities. The range of company activities needed to be limited so that it could remain focused and viable. Even so, that same year, one significant new activity was added to the company's sponsored operations. Though potentially costly, it was seen as crucial. It was a school.

A reorganization of the Gospel Trumpet Company in June, 1917, had given it the power to publish religious and moral literature, conduct homes for the aged, and maintain schools. The time had come to act in the crucial area of educational need. Since many services to Trumpet Home members had been discontinued and some were moving to private residences, space in the big facility was becoming available for some new uses. Wilson was ready with a proposal. With visionary initiative, he prevailed on the members of the company to name a "managing committee" to plan for the launching of an educational effort. Comprised of J. T. Wilson, chair, H. A. Sherwood, secretary, J. E. Campbell, R. R. Byrum, and F. G. Smith, this committee of vigorous men went to work. They (primarily Byrum) arranged a course of study, selected textbooks, secured teachers, and advertised that a Bible training school was being opened in Anderson in October, 1917.

This little school would operate as an educational department of the company, with Wilson named as founding principal. It was to be financed, so the company hoped, apart from the general funds of the company. While any independent sources of support were uncertain at best, at least there would be an effort to begin in a way that would not jeopardize further the already ailing financial picture of the company. No tuition was to be charged students if they were company workers (three dollars per course for non-employees). Students, of course, would have to bear personal expenses. Rooms could be rented in the big Trumpet Home building for one or two dollars per week per person and, if boarding on the new cafeteria plan in the Home, the cost would be another three dollars per week. Since all of the members of the initial faculty except Henry C. Clausen (music instructor) were primarily employees of the Gospel Trumpet Company, giving only one or two hours per day to the new school effort, the school itself was responsible for little of their support. Even so, there still were operating expenses and somehow the church at large needed to be challenged to assist if this modest effort were to continue.

Almost immediately the growth of the school forced increased expense. As the school was about to open for its second year, for instance, the Training School's managing committee met on August 15, 1918, and made some hard but necessary decisions. "Allowances" now had to be set for three teachers not also employed in the publishing work. Hazel Soules (English) would receive $13.20 per week, Henry C. Clausen (music and voice) $20.00, and Bessie Byrum (history) $8.00. Since the number of classes to be offered had increased, two "recitation rooms" would be required instead of the one that was adequate the first year. So the sewing room in the Trumpet Home would have to be "fitted up to meet the emergency." By the end of the second year it was decided that there also would have to be a registration fee of $1.00 charged each student at the time of entry. Understandably, "Brother Wilson was requested to make an appeal through the Gospel Trumpet for finances." In the face of much church concern about the very existence of this small enterprise, the school was careful to state its working assumption about the relation of faith and learning. The first annual catalog (1917-1918) spoke clearly: "This training course is in no way compulsory or obligatory on the part of any, but is provided in order that those who need such training and desire to take advantage of the opportunity may do so."

Why might someone desire such training without violating the rich gifting provisions of true Christian faith? The answer was given: "No amount of training can take the place of real spirituality and no amount of human wisdom will lessen the need of divine wisdom. But our ignorance sometimes limits our usefulness and we could be more efficient workers in the Lord's vineyard were we only better informed. . . . Of course, if we educate a fool he will be a bigger fool. Educate a rascal and he will be a worse rascal. But educate a wise man and he will be wiser."

Why, then, was the school established? Clearly it was not a conscious effort to engage the major intellectual issues of the time by furthering in the public arena one particular ideological agenda. Clearly it was not thought of as a sectarian effort to establish and propagate a particular denomination as had been so common in preceding decades. Even the thought of such a thing would have been obnoxious to the sharp anti-denominational stance of the Church of God movement (although developing skills helpful to spreading the particular perspectives of this movement was a central motivation). Instead, the intent was to better prepare persons who were called to Christian service. The focus was on enhancing spread of the good news in Christ. So it seemed most appropriate to designate the new program of organized learning Anderson Bible *Training* School.

In addition to training, however, there was from the beginning an apologetic purpose, one that sounded almost denominational. That first catalog noted further that "there are many honest-hearted people who come to us from other religious bodies and are anxious to become better acquainted with the truth revealed in this last reformation." So here was to be a place where the distinctive perspectives of the Church of God movement would be available to any who were interested. The unmistakable intention was that the school would stay close to the church and prove itself relevant to the church's life. The school was born within the reformation movement, in part to serve the particular objectives of the movement.

The opening day for Anderson Bible Training School was Tuesday, October 2, 1917, in the Trumpet workers' home on East Fifth Street (to be the "Old Main" of the campus in later years). The notice in the October 18 *Gospel Trumpet* referred to the new effort rather reassuringly as the "Spiritual Workers Training School at Anderson." Most of the students could room in the Trumpet Home, a building of some 66,000 square feet. The large dining hall building on the neighboring campground doubled as an excellent gymnasium for indoor student exercise, and Park Place Church of God, located just three blocks away at Eighth and Union Avenue (College Drive), could seat about eleven hundred people in its brand new facility, thus helping to insure what was said to be the "greatest privilege" afforded all students, namely "opportunity for spiritual advancement."

That first term began with five teachers: Russell R. Byrum and his wife Bessie L. Byrum, Henry C. Clausen, Herbert A. Sherwood, and Joseph T. Wilson, with J. W.

Early Anderson Bible Training School faculty members (left):
Mabel Helms, Henry C. Clausen, Bertha Dye (?), Bessie L. Byrum,
John W. Phelps, Russell R. Byrum and John A. Morrison

Phelps also teaching later during the first year. This founding faculty was very much part-time (except for Clausen) and was not a very academically credentialed group; but it was a remarkable collection of gifted and dedicated people. Each brought something valuable to the assignment. For instance:

Bessie Hittle Byrum (1889-1971). Born in Greenville, Ohio, she came as a young Christian to the Gospel Trumpet Company in Anderson to work in the editorial department. She became the company's first editor of children's quarterlies and writer of the church school lesson commentaries and for many years pioneered in Sunday school work at the Park Place congregation. Having married Russell Byrum in 1916 and being a gifted teacher, she taught history, church history, and Christian education during her tenure of fourteen years with the new school. She received the school's honorary Doctor of Humane Letters degree in 1967 (see Appendix P).

Russell R. Byrum (1889-1980). Russell arrived in Anderson with his father Robert in 1906. Robert helped to direct the large project of constructing the Trumpet Home ("Old Main") and his son worked on the project as a carpenter. Russell became active in pastoral ministry and joined the Gospel Trumpet Company where his scholarly gifts soon elevated him to Managing Editor. While teaching Bible and theology at the new school, he continued his editorial work, became the first Executive Secretary of the Board of Church Extension and Home Missions, and published in 1925 his very influential book, *Christian Theology*. In an unfortunate set of circumstances that developed over suspicion about some of his belief and teaching (see chapter four), he chose to resign his teaching post in 1929, only two years after he had left the publishing company to be full time with the school and only one year after he had received an honorary Doctor of Divinity degree from the school (see Table 8). The balance of his long working life was spent building homes in Anderson as a respected construction contractor.

Henry C. Clausen (1880-1960). Mr. Clausen was the only full-time teacher on the original faculty. Born in Germany and reared in Nebraska, he attended business college, managed his own business, earned a two-year diploma from Moody Bible Institute in 1910, and finally was called by God to be a gospel singer and music evangelist. In 1917, while he was preaching and pastoring in North Dakota, he was asked to come and teach at the new school. He taught music on the Anderson campus for twenty-eight years, retiring in 1945, and was replaced by Robert A. Nicholson. He was founding director of the school's first mixed choir, the Glad Tidings Chorus.

John W. Phelps (1870-1947). In the Trumpet office building, just across the hall from J. T. Wilson's private office, was the office of J. W. Phelps. He had come to the Gospel Trumpet Company in 1911 and in 1917 was the Secretary of the Missionary Board of the Church of God. Phelps had a flair for public speaking, a subject he had taught in the public school setting in his earlier days in Kansas. Since effective communication surely was an essential for Christian preachers, he was pressed into part-time faculty service at the new school.

Herbert A. Sherwood (1877-1960). A native of Athens, Ohio,Pastor Sherwood served briefly as a Methodist minister before coming to Indiana to study at Taylor University. He encountered Church of God literature, was deeply convicted by it, visited nearby Anderson, and joined the Trumpet family as an assistant in the editorial offices. Soon after Park Place Church moved into its new building in November, 1917, J. T. Wilson, its pastor, resigned because of responsibilities in the publishing company, including heading the new school. So Sherwood became the congregation's first full-time pastor, serving from 1917 through 1919. Then he concentrated on teaching history and ministering to students on campus as though they were his own family (he had no children of his own). His wife Martha would carry on this grace of hospitality even after his death.

Joseph T. Wilson (1876-1954). A native of western Pennsylvania and from "fighting Irish stock," Wilson was an innovative and determined young man with, for the time, an unusual passion for education. He attended both Grove City College and the State Teachers College at Slippery Rock, Pennsylvania, then came to Anderson to work for the Gospel Trumpet Company and be part-time pastor of the Park Place congregation. He was founding principal of the new school in Anderson, left the company and school in 1923 to pastor, and received from the school the honorary Doctor of Divinity degree in 1929 (see Table 8). Soon he founded another, although short-lived school in Texas (closed in 1933). He continued as church leader for many years, even though after 1933 he was discouraged and faded from key national leadership.

The student body studying with this founding faculty consisted of some sixty persons who were workers at the company and part-time students. An eighth grade education was an admission standard hoped for generally, but not insisted upon initially. The first courses included Bible history and geography (R. R. Byrum), preparation and delivery of sermons (J. T. Wilson), ancient history (Bessie Byrum), vocal music (H. C. Clausen) and both beginners and advanced grammar (H. A. Sherwood), with J. W. Phelps of the Missionary Board soon to add public speaking. Each class was taught in daily "recitations" during afternoon hours to avoid conflict as much as possible with regular duties at the publishing company. Also scheduled on Friday evenings were practical lectures by prominent ministers—the teaching faculty plus F. G. Smith, D. O. Teasley, E. A. Reardon, E. E. Byrum, and J. Grant Anderson. The subjects ranged from "The Successful Revival" and "Altar Work" to "Woman's Place in the Church" and "Our Attitude Toward Brother Ministers."

There were three terms during the 1917-18 year covering the months of October through May and implementing the first half of the overall two-year program designed

TABLE 2

Selected Church-Related Colleges of Indiana

School	City	Year Founded	Founding Church Affiliation
DePauw University	Greencastle	1837	Methodist
Earlham College	Richmond	1847	Quaker
Franklin College	Franklin	1834	Baptist
Goshen College	Goshen	1894	Mennonite
Grace College	Winona Lake	1948	Grace Brethren
Hanover College	Hanover	1827	Presbyterian
Indiana Wesleyan University	Marion	1920	Wesleyan Methodist
Manchester College	North Manchester	1889	Church of the Brethren
Taylor University	Upland	1846	Methodist Episcopal
Wabash College	Crawfordsville	1832	Presbyterian

Most of these schools have published histories rich in information and perspectivethat shed comparative light on background, issues, and events significant in the history of Anderson University.

by Russell Byrum. He had studied the programs of many schools, envisioned a curriculum of considerable breadth, and chosen quality reading materials for the students, tending at first to use Methodist materials in theology and Baptist in ecclesiology. As the 1917-1918 catalog made clear, "no attempt at mere intellectual development is intended." What was intended was the preparation of persons to fulfill their divine callings through the life of the church. But exactly what kind of school it should be was not clear at all to some leaders in the church. Byrum recalled years later that he had intended it to be "a school of theology for the training of ministers." The name chosen, "Anderson Bible Training School," suggested something hard to be against.[1]

Excitement, challenge and caution were being expressed in the school and across the church. Now there was a place to go! Classes were held in the Trumpet Home, with dorm rooms on one of the floors above. Wilson continued to carry his regular responsibilities as general manager of the Gospel Trumpet Company. The school was modest, owned no property of its own, and gave no formal recognition for work completed. Its faculty and students spent much of their time working at the Gospel Trumpet Company. But it was a definite and welcome beginning. As Harold L. Phillips, historian of the publishing company, put it: "The need was great and Wilson had stepped in to meet that need by this audacious move to begin *something* in the way of systematic training" (1979, 156). Something, even something modest, surely would be better than nothing.[2]

This new school, it should be noted, came into being in more than the environment of the Church of God movement, the Gospel Trumpet Publishing Company, and the immediate Park Place community on the east side of Anderson, Indiana. It was surrounded by an already existing and rich tradition of church-related higher education in Indiana. See Table 2 for examples of such schools, all crucial in academic, athletic, and other ways to the future of the new school in Anderson.

Pieces Slowly Come Together

So the school had begun with an optimistic outlook despite the very fragile foundations. The city of Anderson, Indiana, seemed an excellent location. It was near the population center of the United States and was an industrial city then of about 35,000 people surrounded by rich agriculture. In 1916 the local Remy Electric Company had become a division of United Motors Corporation and later would become part of a major General Motors operation in Anderson. Beginning in April 1918, because of a state prohibition law, the city was said to be without saloons. Here is where the large publishing plant and centralized missionary administration of the Church of God now were located. Here also each June was the international assemblage of the church, including hundreds of ministers and inspiring services in the tabernacle (new in 1918), which would seat some six thousand people. Such church presence, such a wealth of gifted church leaders coming and going, such a congenial location—these appeared to be blessings that surely would enrich the life of a young school.

Finances, however, were an immediate and persistent problem. Wilson had announced to the church at large (*Gospel Trumpet* October 18, 1917, p. 10) that the intent was to make this new training cost students as little as possible. Thus no tuition was charged. Instead, reminding the church of how much it needed new pastors and evangelists, he said that the church should bear the expense of faculty and operations. He made clear that, although the publishing company was hosting the school's modest beginnings, regular funds for the publishing work should not have to be diverted to this new venture.

Even with this initial intent and appeal, however, the first year of the little school's operation did leave some unwelcome red ink on the books of the sponsoring publishing company. Some members of the company thought that a deficit operation, even in the name of such a good cause, could not be tolerated in light of the company's own and considerable financial problems. There had not been one dollar to begin with for this new educational venture, and certainly there was yet no clear evidence of wide-spread sentiment in the church that would encourage liberal donations for its ongoing support. Trying to be encouraging about the school as he made his June, 1919, annual report as president of the publishing company, Wilson announced with guarded optimism that "the Training School has closed its second year with a deficit of $594.83 as against $706.28 last year." That was progress! It also was pain.

Some ministers clearly opposed the whole undertaking and insisted that the intent to begin such a school should have been taken first to the General Ministerial Assembly for debate and approval or disapproval. That strategy had not been chosen by Wilson, a prudent choice according to Harold Phillips, historian of the publishing company. Rather than having acted hastily, Wilson "did what he was convinced had to be done if a school was to get going without more years of delay. He read correctly the opposition that would have instantly arisen in the Assembly, and he forged ahead carrying the dead weight of apathy and opposition. And the Company he headed bore the deficits year after year while the school got on its feet" (156-157).

War now was raging in Europe and many of the young men in Anderson left to take up arms "to make the world safe for democracy." Some were not able to return as students for the school's second year and enrollment dropped. During 1918 the Anderson Board of Health forced the school's closing for a time (along with all public schools) because of a terrible, worldwide influenza pandemic. Future prospects seemed gloomy. But there were those like J. T. Wilson and Russell Byrum who would not let the school die. Since it continued to exist into the second year of the planned two-year curriculum, the 1918 General Ministerial Assembly decided to give it considerable attention. What the school might become if it did survive excited some ministers and clearly worried others.

Of symbolic significance was the first action ever taken by the Bible Training School's managing committee that had been formed to guide the school for the publishing company. On that November day in 1917, with the first classes in operation only about one month, the school calendar for the coming summer was under review. J. T. Wilson, school principal, raised the question of the wisdom of continuing school operations through the time of the coming General Ministerial Assembly. "On motion of D. O. Teasley," the minutes read, "the committee voted to dispense with the school work during the week of the Assembly." Then by February, 1918, the committee found itself discussing another practical issue, the publishing of a proposed first school catalog; however, "it was decided that it would be the part of wisdom to defer its publication until after Anderson Camp Meeting in order to secure first the sanction of the ministry as a body regarding the further development and continuance of the Training School." The meetings and opinions of this national body of the church's leaders were not far from the minds of school leaders. It would remain that way for all the years to come.

An increasing number of ministers had come to appreciate the need for such a training school. Nonetheless, with only one or two exceptions, no pastors in the Church of God at that time held college degrees and there still were many negative attitudes about "liberal" colleges and "sterile" seminaries. Naturally concern arose that the new school might introduce into the life of the Church of God movement the titles and symbols of self-seeking and worldly sophistication and encourage reliance on credentials instead of the divine gifts of the Spirit. Some of the older pastors felt insecure with the prospect of a new generation of trained leaders. Ministers generally wanted a sense of ownership and control over the potentials and unknowns of this new school. So, as Wilson put it, "owing to the fact that certain ministers felt that they should have the privilege of voicing their sentiments, ... it was thought best to refer the matter to the general body of ministers" (*Gospel Trumpet*, July 4, 1918, 7).

After extensive consideration, the General Ministerial Assembly adopted the following in June, 1918, as appropriate and rather restrictive guidelines for any future operation of Anderson Bible Training School. These guidelines appear to have been intended as a general affirmation of the potential significance of the school to the church, if, that is, certain concerns were not violated. Said the Assembly:

1. We believe that such a school can be conducted to the glory of God and the welfare of the ministry and church itself if kept within certain bounds.

2. We believe that no effort should be made to create a sentiment to the effect that young ministers must attend this school in order to secure recognition.

3. It is our opinion that in many cases the education of ministers can best be obtained in those sections of the country where their ministerial work is to be done so that the practical can be more definitely combined with the theoretical. In other words, we do not believe that the Anderson Bible School should supersede or replace other training schools of the church.

4. Students should be left free to choose their own course of study from among such branches as the school provides.

5. No recommendation or diploma should be given any student. Satisfactory gradings in school constitutes no proof that an individual is called of God to preach the gospel. Hence every student must be left on his own responsibility so that he will not possess in this respect any authority proceeding from this school which will give him an advantage over those ministers who have not attended school. In the Church of God every minister must stand on his own merits and earn his place of responsibility whether educated or uneducated.

6. We believe that the training of ministers in this school should include more than their intellectual development along educational lines. The most prominent feature must be their personal development in spirituality, faith, and gifts of the Spirit of God.

Already this young school had gained the attention of the Church of God at large, something to be typical of the future. Over the years to come that attention would range from apathy or active opposition to generous support and intense pride. After only one year of operation there already was considerable caution mixed with obvious enthusiasm.

Restrictions or not, the school had been given the green light to proceed. Immediately the managing committee of the school advertised in the *Gospel Trumpet* for an additional teacher, a competent lady with some teaching experience preferred and "satisfactory evidence of Christian experience necessary" (July 25, 1918, 16). The result was the appointment of Hazel D. Soules. As she arrived for the fall classes of 1918 she would find a new program of "regular chapel exercises" in operation as one key way of addressing the "spiritual phase" of the school's mission. All campus members were expected to be present at these 6:20 a.m. (!) chapels.

In February, 1919, Principal J. T. Wilson wrote to John A. Morrison, then a young man only twenty-three years old and pastoring in Delta, Colorado. Wilson had wanted R. R. Byrum to assume more leadership in the school, but Byrum, partly in light of his own limited formal education, did not feel qualified, urged some alternative, and had suggested Morrison. While he did not know Morrison personally, Byrum had been impressed by material this younger minister had written for the *Gospel Trumpet.* Later Byrum admitted this about his recommendation of Morrison: "It was just a shot in the dark, but it worked."[3]

It may have been a shot in the dark so far as whether Morrison could function as an effective teacher/administrator in a new school. It had not been a blind guess, however, in regard to Morrison's perspectives and instincts. Those recent *Gospel Trumpet* articles of his had been revealing. They reflected a man committed both to the high calling of Christian ministry and to the needed discipline of careful preparation for that ministry.

John A. Morrison, with wife Eunice and children
(Left): Mona, Earl, Dorothy and Vivian (front)

In 1917 Morrison had called for people to seize their opportunities: "Too many young men and women are so absorbed in hoping for talents, rank, or money, that they fail to see them flow by, in a constant stream, in the form of present opportunities. A man can be master of his destiny if he will" (December 27, 1917, 8). He then had written in 1918: "The idea of depending altogether on the Spirit to qualify us is erroneous.... The diligent preacher avails himself of every possible means of self-improvement, and then earnestly beseeches God to fill his soul with a Pentecostal fire and zeal that will cause people to listen to him" (December 12, 19).

What probably attracted Byrum to Morrison as much as anything was the young minister's open and wholesome combining of commitment to divine gifting and to human learning. For instance, Morrison had said that "Paul was not great because he was a student of Gamaliel, neither because of his eloquence; but he was great because he lived close enough to God to keep fired with holy zeal; and his master intellect, coupled with pious humility and inspiration, enabled him to direct that zeal into such channels as empowered him to deliver terrific blows against the bulwarks of the devil" (*Gospel Trumpet* October 17, 1918, 2). Then, just as 1919 began, Morrison had written about the preacher as a student. He admitted that God does use ministers "unlearned in worldly knowledge" and noted that "many of the faithful brethren who stand in the front ranks of this grand and glorious reformation are men who entered the work under the most adverse circumstances, deprived of the opportunities many of us younger brethren are blessed with." Nonetheless,,"Blessed is that preacher who surrounds himself with good books and reads them." He even added that "the preacher who would be a good Shepherd must know his flock; and the study of human nature is a most engaging one" *(Gospel Trumpet* January 23, 1919, 22). Wilson's letter of invitation to the young John Morrison said in part:

> As you probably know, I have been not only president of the Gospel Trumpet Company, but also chairman of its School Committee and one of the teachers in the Bible Training School here. And now it seems advisable for Brother Teasley to go on a missionary tour during the next year. If he does I must take over his duties as general manager [of the Gospel Trumpet Company], which will make it necessary for me to turn over some of my duties to someone else.... Would you consider an opportunity to fill an important place in the Bible School? ... You may be able to accomplish much should you remain in the field, but if you by your work in the training school are able to help possibly several hundred ministers in preparing them-selves, you will thus accomplish much more than your individual work would accomplish. This work has a great future *(Alumni News* 1955, 2).

How right Wilson was, both in judging that this modest educational effort had a great future and that young Morrison could multiply his own ministry accomplishments by investing himself in that future. The letter received an affirmative response and on February 25, 1919, the School Committee set Morrison's "allowance as a teacher of homiletics" at eighteen dollars per week. The Morrison family, including John, wife Eunice, five-year-old Earl and five-week-old Mona, drove across country in their 1916 Model T Ford. John became a teacher and assistant principal of the training school beginning in June, 1919, and by July was elected secretary of the School Committee.

That same year Charles E. Wilson took the reins of Anderson's Remy Electric Company. Soon, through the efforts of local banker Linfield Myers, the paths of Morrison and Wilson would cross and a crucial partnership between education, industry, and the life of a city would be forged. But that still was in the future. Significant as such partnerships soon would be, they were far from anyone's mind in 1919.

For the first several months they were in Anderson, the Morrison family lived in one room in the north wing of the Trumpet Home, literally right out of their suitcases. John's educational background, like Byrum's, was modest. His natural gifts, also like Byrum's, were substantial. Later he reflected with some amusement on those first years of his in Anderson: "Since Bible schools usually are not prone to quibble over academic considerations, I taught an impressive range of subjects, almost as wide as it was thin" *(Alumni News* 1955, 2). The 1923-24 school catalog, for instance, listed John Morrison as assistant principal and teacher of homiletics, history of preaching, psychology, sociology, and pastoral theology. Beginning in December, 1921, he also was the School Committee's appointed representative to the Gospel Trumpet Company in relation to the business affairs of the school's life. Already his considerable gifts were bearing much fruit.

That's My *Alma Mater*!

Fond memories and warm, enduring relationships develop quickly in the life of a small college community. When persons, enriched by such intense and wonderful experiences, leave and become separated by distance and time, there naturally arises a strong desire to meet again and walk once more the campus halls and grounds. Rehearsing stories of how it used to be and renewing those precious relationships of the past are so encouraging and tend to deepen concern about how one might help the beloved school to carry on. Somehow the beloved *alma mater* must remain able to bring richness into the lives of new generations just as it had the ones now grown older.

The Anderson school highlighted its practical concerns in the 1919-20 catalog

ABTS students leaving campus for service at an Anderson orphanage, April, 1920

when only one class had had opportunity to complete the two-year program (see Table 3). Former students were recognized as "the school's most loyal supporters," especially because "the school had not been established long enough to prove its real worth to the church at large." The school's managers and teachers, through the pages of this catalog, encouraged former students to help the school in three specific ways. They could "favorably mention the school whenever the opportunity is afforded," assist in raising money for its needs and "help persuade those young people whom God has called to his work to attend the school." As a way of cautioning against misunderstanding in the church, it was stated plainly that "in the school much stress is placed upon the gifts of the Spirit" and, in representing the school, the suggestion was made to alumni that "you must not place too much emphasis on intellectual attainments."

In May, 1921, two classes of former students were now scattered around the nation and the world, a total of forty-five persons, mostly women, all having pursued the school's two-year ministerial course. With the annual Anderson Camp Meeting coming soon, thoughts began to focus on the possibility of a first alumni reunion. Maybe some network could even be established to link alumni as they pursued their various ministries. Keeping in close touch would be enjoyable and helpful both for former students and for the school itself.

On May 27 a meeting of seven local alumni was convened in the Anderson, Indiana, home of Elsie Bowser (class of 1919). Professor Russell Byrum and Principal J. T. Wilson had encouraged the idea of organizing some formal alumni activity. Amy Phillips (class of 1920) and Anna Koglin (class of 1919) were chosen at this meeting to be president and vice-president of a temporary alumni organization. Arrangements also were made for the first annual gathering of alumni during the big Anderson Camp Meeting soon to convene.

The reunion event was held in the reception room of the Gospel Trumpet Home on June 15, 1921. On that simple and yet emotional and historic occasion a constitution was adopted for an alumni association, the temporary officers were ratified, and Jessie Kleeberger (Martin) (class of 1919) was named secretary. An official motto was chosen: "Our Best for Christ." Most crucial, however, were not the formalities of a fledgling organization. It was the inevitable joys that were shared just because persons who had spent some months and years together in learning, worship, play, and service now were meeting again, remembering, updating, and enriching each other. People and service, two centers of the school's very purpose, were being celebrated! An ongoing alumni network had begun. Similar yearly gatherings were projected as alumni numbers would continue to grow.

The number of alumni totaled sixty-one by then, eighteen in the class of 1919, twenty-six in 1920 and seventeen in 1921. Included were people who soon would play

SCHOOL SCENES

Dining Room

Quartet

Students Room

Front Lawn

Quartet

G. T. Office

Waiters Senior Reception 1923

Reading Room

Center Stairway

Welcome

TABLE 3

First Graduating Class: 1919
Two-Year Diploma, Ministerial Course

Edith Bleiler	Richard Meyer
Mrs. Eskell Blore	Kate Morton
Fred. C. Blore	Aessa Mussery
Mrs. Elsie Bowser	Ada Pope
Louise Frederici	Rosa Schneider
Jacob Horne	Frank Shaw
Jessie Kleeberger	Mrs. Dorothy Timmons
Anna Koglin	Cora Weber
Carrie Larsen	Stella Weigel

major leadership roles in the school itself, such as Anna Koglin (class of 1919), Stella Weigel (class of 1919), and John H. Kane (class of 1921). Already examples of effectively ministering graduates stretched around the world, making increasingly clear that the school was worth all that was being put into it. Resources were modest indeed, but the available levels of commitment and vision seemed almost lavish.

The "Alumni Directory" appearing in the back of the 1922 *Echoes* (the first issue of the school annual) listed, for instance, W. J. Bailey (class of 1920) as missionary in British East Africa, Hjalmer Hansen (class of 1920) as pioneer church worker in Norway, Josephine McCrie (class of 1920) as superintendent of the Shelter in Cuttack, India, Richard Meyer (class of 1919) as church planter in Russia, Poland, Germany, and Switzerland, and J. Frank Shaw (class of 1919) leading the church in Trinidad. The 1923 Echoes proudly expanded this list, noting the Baileys and Ruth Fisher in Africa, Faith Stewart, Mona Moors, Burd Barwick, Josephine McCrie, and Mamie Wallace in India, Grace Alexander in Japan, and Frank Shaw in the West Indies. The Church of God movement certainly had a worldwide missionary vision. The Anderson campus, from its very beginning, reflected that significant internationalism. As stated in the 1923 *Echoes*: "Each student, as he leaves the school, takes a lighted torch with him, and we see this torch of truth shining bright as the morning star in our home land as well as in the foreign land" (33).

The building of alumni pride began to be nurtured in another way in 1921.

School scenes, 1923-24, as appeared in 1924-25 catalog

There appeared a new practice, one soon to become an annual tradition. The junior class each year would plan a reception for the seniors about to graduate. On May 30, 1921, just three days after that historic meeting in the Bowser home when the alumni organization was initiated, the class of 1922 staged a reception for the class of 1921. The event was held in the dining hall on the campground, with the Park Place Church orchestra bringing musical selections. According to the 1922 *Echoes*, "a prophecy of the senior class ten years hence was given in the form of an alumni meeting." There was the warmth of rich human relationships and the commissioning of seniors for their important tasks in the world.

That same 1922 *Echoes* carried a formal statement by Herman Ast on behalf of the junior class. The sentiments were strong and sincere:

> Some of us left the office or factory; some, the farm or business, all for Jesus' sake, in answer to the call of God, to train for service in His vineyard.

TABLE 4

Curriculum of Ministerial Course: 1923

First Year	Second Year	Third Year
Bible	Systematic Theology	Music
Music	Pastoral Theology	Missions
General Psychology	Sociology	Sunday School Methods, Organization, Pedagogy
Homiletics	Public Speaking	English
History of Preaching	Church History	
General History	English	New Testament Greek (elective)*
English		

*Anna E. Koglin, member of the first graduating class in 1919, was teaching the Greek, the first foreign language to be offered. She had a working knowledge of English, German, Swedish, Norwegian, Russian and Greek.

A few came from other schools, and several have been actively engaged in the work, but came to become more efficient soul winners. Thus we arrived from all parts of the country, from New York to California, and from Canada to Texas, from a variety of circumstances and with a wide difference in temperaments. We feared we might get homesick, but the A. B. T. S. is a wonderful place. It is truly a melting pot. We became acquainted almost immediately; such a spirit of fellowship existed; the faculty and second-year students did their best to make us feel at home. When we leave in June, we now fear we shall get homesick to come back (19).

A formal statement in the 1925-26 school catalog emphasized what wonderful and lasting friendships develop from time spent together in school. That statement, however, also made two appeals to alumni that highlighted the difficult life of a young school and key ways that its own graduates might be of assistance. First, since "during the School's short history it has had to withstand some honest opposition on the part of some who may not have been properly informed as to the true purpose of the Institution," every alumnus should live so as "to disabuse the minds of those who may have misgiv-

ings as to the important place the Seminary has in the life of the church."[4] Second, with finances being a constant problem, former students should remember the seminary in a financial way. "True, most of you are ministers and thus unable to make large donations to the School," the statement concluded, "but as evangelists and pastors you may exert a great influence in getting it represented in the regular church budget."

Among the first persons to complete the program in 1919 (see Table 3), the first of many thousands to come, were such remarkable people as these: Anna Koglin, later to be a long-term teacher of German and Greek for the school; J. Frank Shaw, who gave his life as a missionary in the West Indies and then among the Indians of the American Northwest; Louise Frederici, who became an assistant to the editor of the *Gospel Trumpet* in Germany; and Aessa Mussery, who soon would return for many years of effective Christian ministry in Lebanon and Syria. Decades later two sons of Aessa's son Adel, also a Christian pastor, would graduate from the Anderson campus, Fawzi in 1987 and Fouad in 1982. Fouad then returned to study in the School of Theology. Here is one committed family from the Middle East who has been represented actively on the Anderson campus both in its first and in its most recent years of existence!

End of the Beginning

In June, 1923, Joseph T. Wilson left his responsibilities at the Gospel Trumpet Company and that fall moved from Anderson altogether. There was considerable personal pain involved for him. The company had been facing financial problems, and complex circumstances now had led to this separation from the company and his resignation from the principalship of the school. Much, however, yet lay ahead for him in church leadership. He later would be chair of the General Ministerial Assembly (1929, 1932, 1937-39), first chair of the Board of Trustees of the Anderson school when it became independent of the company two years later, and president of a "university" he soon would found in Texas! He seemed a tireless, if not always a practical and fully appreciated pioneer.

On a September morning in 1923 the Wilson family car, a red Studebaker, stopped in front of the Training School on East Fifth Street. Teachers and students gathered around the car, sang, and said good-bye as the Wilsons left to pastor in Louisville, Kentucky. Wilson's years in Anderson had been eventful and stressful. He was a zealous man, had a passion for education, and sometimes was impatient with those who were opposed or just apathetic. On occasion, as John Morrison later put it, "this zeal also tended to beguile him into financial involvements which were impossible to dissolve" (*Alumni News* 1955, 2). But, whatever his weaknesses, Wilson was a worker, a daring pioneer, the founding principal of what one day would be a great institution of Christian higher education. He once was described by Morrison as "a man of maximum courage and minimum caution.... When he thought a thing needed to be done, he set about doing it, and thought about the consequences later" (1962, 142). His departure seemed like the end of an important beginning. John Morrison was left behind to carry on as principal. He now assumed the challenge of being the primary pioneering guide into a whole new era.

Wilson left behind a fragile young school that was to have a great future. Still no tuition was being charged students, and the school was not yet allowing the administration of any medicines to ill students, honoring rather the faith-healing stance strong in the church of the time. But the church's 1918 ban on the granting of any diplomas to graduates finally had been lifted by the General Ministerial Assembly in June, 1923. The Assembly recognized that in its six years the school had "proven itself to be a great asset to the work of the Lord." Realizing that "such diplomas would greatly benefit the graduates in seeking to enter other institutions of learning," the general church body had agreed that the school should grant "a suitable diploma, such diploma to be regarded in no sense as a license to preach or as conferring any ministerial authority whatsoever." E. A. Reardon, then pastor of the Park Place Church in Anderson, presented the resolution that lifted the diploma ban. There was only one dissenting vote, quite a shift from the action of 1918.[5]

These newly authorized diplomas now were being earned primarily inside the remodeled Trumpet Home, which contained everything from dorm rooms on the second and third floors (north wing for men and south for women), classrooms, chapel, cafeteria, and offices on the first floor, to laundry, boilers, baths, and a barber shop in the basement. The 1923-24 catalog presented the curriculum as (1) a "Sunday-School Course" leading to a two-year diploma for persons "who, though not called to the active ministry, feel a keen interest in religious work" and (2) a "Regular Course" designed for persons "who have a divine call to and wish to prepare for the regular ministry of the gospel." This regular ministerial course was now a three-year program that high school graduates often could complete in only two years (see Table 4). Also in operation was a home study course for preachers who were unable to do residence work at the school. As the catalog made clear: "It is not a correspondence course where the student submits papers each week to be graded by the instructor. It is an outlined course of systematic study." No doubt it essentially was the plan of work developed years earlier by Russell Byrum.

So Wilson drove away in 1923 and John Morrison was left in charge. Morrison reflected years later on "the low estate of education in our movement" that "one such as I would be invited to have a place in the one and only educational institution operated by the church" (1962, 126). He had never been to high school, although he had attended normal school for several terms to prepare for teaching in Missouri. But he was given a

55

place—and what a place it turned out to be! Linfield Myers, later to become a prominent business leader in Anderson and a good friend of the local school, said that it was Morrison's "earthy quality, together with liberal helpings of his equally earthy humor, that helped him achieve greatness." Myers concluded: "If the leadership role of the new college had gone to someone of lesser human endowments back in 1919, this whole story might have been completely different" (1973, 78).

But, fortunately, it did not go to someone else. The growing and gifted Morrison family was in Anderson to stay. Others also were coming, people who one day would stand tall in the growing life of the school. Among them was E. A. Reardon who came from Chicago in 1920 to assume the pastorate of the Park Place Church following H. A. Sherwood's resignation.

Reardon would be a great friend of the school and its people and he was the father of young Robert, born in the Faith Missionary Home in Chicago in 1919. Before the Reardon family moved to Anderson, J. T. Wilson had gone to Chicago and held baby Robert in his arms while offering a prayer of dedication. In a very few years Wilson would leave the new school and some decades later Robert would become its president.

In those very first years of the school's existence much credit goes to the Gospel Trumpet Company, which hosted the birthing of the school, with all the related church problems and financial deficits. It was an important new service ministry provided generously by the company for the needs of its own employees. It also was a crucial gift given in the service of the mission of the whole church.

Some of the established church leaders initially had found themselves with as many concerns as reasons to support the new educational project. But for many that had changed over time. By 1923, with the departure of Wilson, the end of the beginning seemed to have come for the school. The beginning, however, is all that it was. Much more was yet to come!

That much more on occasion would see other confrontations between the campus and elements in the church. But they would be honest differences, lovers' quarrels. They would be between parties who, by choice, would remain linked closely for the long term, and always would manage to be mutually supportive.

Many years later, when Robert Reardon was school president, he looked back reflectively on these beginning years. He saw the original ingrafting of the school into the life of the Church of God as "a remarkable feat" under the circumstances. His perspective was this:

> At perhaps the most critical moment in our movement's history, when we could easily have turned rigid and cultish, he (J. T. Wilson) ingrafted a small educational organism into the vitals of the Church of God reformation movement…. This college became the window open upon the world, a spawning

ground for fresh ideas and young leaders, a safeguard against the narrow parochial mind, and a home where theologians, biblical scholars, and practitioners of other disciplines could contribute to the upbuilding of the church and its young people.6

1. Taped interview, February 25, 1975.

2. Church historian John W. V. Smith judged that "in the first few years the school bore little resemblance to a college" (*The Quest for Holiness and Unity*, 1980, p. 245).

3. Taped interview, February 25, 1975.

4. It was common in those first years to refer to the school as the "Seminary" since ministerial education was its complete focus. See later chapters for information on the establishment on campus of a graduate-level seminary program.

5. See John A. Morrison's autobiography, *As the River Flows*, pp. 148-150, for an interesting account of how his resolution finally got to the Assembly floor.

3 Identity and Independence
1925-1928

"Therefore, be it resolved, that the Company approve the separation of the School from the Company and recommend to the General Ministerial Assembly that it take the necessary steps to organize the School on the same general principles on which the other general boards of the church are organized."

(June, 1925)

The Anderson Bible Training School was still very young and its new roots quite fragile. There was an identity yet to establish, credibility to build across the church, and a curriculum to refine, staff, expand, explain, and implement with integrity. Organizational independence from the Gospel Trumpet Company was soon to come, and increasing finances needed to be raised to insure the school's very survival. The early and mid-1920s surely were busy and pivotal years on the Anderson campus.

Image and Integrity

The attitude of the church constituency toward the school was still forming. Influencing that formation positively would be a significant challenge for the school in the years just ahead. The people of the Church of God movement at large comprised a body whose perspectives would have to be recognized, respected, and sometimes nurtured and altered at points. In that necessary and delicate process there would be much joy and occasionally some pain.

In 1922 John Morrison, then assistant principal, raised in the June 12 meeting of the school's managing committee "the matter of advertising the School in outside periodicals." The committee agreed to spend twenty dollars in this new way and asked Morrison to prepare a "motto" to be printed on school advertisements and letterheads. Then in August, 1923, he also was authorized "to put a sign board on the School lawn." It was time to project an image of the operation and spread word about the school more widely. There appeared on the title page of the 1923-24 catalog a fresh identification: "A Non-sectarian School for the Training of Ministers and Missionaries." Then on page two was this very clear statement of the school's important but clearly limited purpose: "The School does not attempt to give an extended theological course, but to give that practical instruction which will make the minister a more successful soul winner."

Very early the question arose about the proper relationship between the Anderson school and two other small educational efforts then associated with the Church of God, Kansas City Bible School and Pacific Bible Institute. Should each be considered national in scope or only regional? Should each seek church funding independently or be supported through some coordinated effort? On September 19, 1921, the school's managing committee in Anderson determined "that we should not be barred out of the territory west of the Mississippi River in soliciting School funds." The following year, having received inquiries about transfer possibilities to Anderson's program from students of these other schools in the church, the committee declined to set a firm policy until more information was available on the work being offered by them. Clearly the Anderson school wanted to establish a reputation of educational integrity and to be a national, not regional program, one free to serve and be supported by the whole church. This is what it was to become and always what it would seek to remain.

The Church of God movement also was trying to determine its own stance on these matters. As early as 1918, with Spokane Bible School, Kansas City Bible School, and Anderson Bible Training School then in existence, there already was some felt need to discuss the most appropriate relationship among the schools developing within the constituency of the Church of God. The General Ministerial Assembly of 1918

First school sign, on lawn of the Trumpet Home

addressed this need and appointed D. O. Teasley, J. W. Phelps, R. L. Berry, A. F. Gray and R. H. Owens to comprise a committee that would explore "the school question." As A. F. Gray recalled, this committee's subsequent discussion involved some significant disagreement. Wrote Gray:

> As the Spokane school was so far away it would be expected to draw students and support from its own territory. The Kansas City school was expected, so someone thought, to draw its students and support chiefly from Missouri, whereas the Anderson school would serve the church in general and be entitled to general support. Brother Berry opposed this conclusion vigorously. He declared that the Kansas City school benefited the whole church and if it was not entitled to general support neither was Anderson. He said that Missouri could support the Kansas City school by itself, if need be, but this would lessen its giving to other causes (1966, 91).

Finally the committee concluded that any work of a general nature was entitled to general support—and apparently all existing schools thought of themselves as "general" in nature and came to be recognized as such. The General Ministerial Assembly then proceeded to pass a resolution creating an "Education Fund" to be held by the Missionary Board of the Church of God and distributed "to the existing Bible training schools in proportion to the number of enrolled students" (*Gospel Trumpet* 1918, 4).

Here was the earliest attempt on record to muster general church support for institutions of higher education in the Church of God and to set some precedent for how the evolving schools should be interrelated and funded by the church.[1] As Brother Berry had argued for the national status of Kansas City Bible School (and thus no regional limitation on its student recruitment or fund-raising boundaries), so did the managing committee of Anderson Bible Training School in regard to its own prerogatives. It saw itself as serving the whole church and, in typical Church of God fashion, was opposed to the imposition of a humanly devised system of limitations. Some general coordination and certainly widespread support were seen as desirable by the schools and the church; however, centralized control of the several institutions was judged inappropriate. Anderson Bible Training School intended to be free of geographic boundaries to its service and student recruitment area. Its intent was to serve the whole church. Its hope increasingly was to seek and receive students and financial support from the whole church.

The goodwill and related support of the Church of God was essential for survival of the school. So was the church's willingness to assume some responsibility for the several ministries that had emerged in the life of the publishing Company but that were not central to the mission of publishing and that now the Company was having difficulty funding. Joseph T. Wilson offered a plan in 1920 to divest the company of some financial responsibility for what really were nonpublishing, general church ministries. The proposed first annual budget of the church totaled twenty-five thousand dollars and featured such company programs as the Old People's Home ($7,000), the Blind Work ($5,000), and the Camp Meeting ($4,300). "Conspicuously absent," noted company historian Harold Phillips, was the Training School. "It had been in the original askings but was dropped before the proposal was referred to the General Ministerial Assembly because," said Phillips, "of the expectation that it would meet too much opposition and/or apathy and might endanger the rest of the needs" (158).

Independence and Governance

One alternative for the future of the Training School was the possibility of its corporate independence from the publishing company. The desire of the company to streamline its diverse activities, its concern about often having to handle sensitive church relations matters involving the school, and the annual problem of more unwelcome red ink on the accounting books all encouraged thought about independent existence for the school. In June, 1920, for instance, the company pondered the costs of proposed modifications of the Trumpet Home facilities to better accommodate the growing number of students in the school and their various needs. The discussion turned to the larger question of "whether the school should continue under the charge of the Gospel Trumpet Company or whether the school should be managed separately, some suggesting that the church may not be willing to finance the school under the dictation of the company."

This matter was discussed during 1924-25 by the company's Board of Directors and the Training School Committee. The resulting joint recommendation was that the possibility of school independence be addressed at the company's annual meeting in June, 1925. So on the afternoon of June 11, after lengthy discussion, A. T. Rowe and Earl Martin placed on the company's table the following resolution:

> Whereas, the Training School has outgrown the meager organization provid
> ed for it in the Company's Bylaws; and
> Whereas, it represents one of the great general phases of the work of the
> church, for which reason it should be constituted a legal entity; and
> Whereas, with the present arrangement little doctrinal restriction is placed
> upon the school, the powers and duties of officers and teachers being
> scarcely defined at all; and
> Whereas, our Committee on Bylaws and our School Executive Committee
> have recommended that the matter of said change be submitted to the
> annual meeting;
> Therefore, be it resolved, that the Company approve the separation of the

School from the Company and recommend to the General Ministerial Assembly that it take the necessary steps to organize the School on the same general principles on which the other general boards of the church are organized.

This resolution was received with favor. Immediately an *ad hoc* committee was appointed to draft articles of association that might "govern the new Training School." Having consulted with the School Committee, the next day the special committee of J. Grant Anderson, A. L. Byers, W. D. McCraw, F. G. Smith, and B. E. Warren reported. E. A. Reardon then moved adoption of the proposed articles and their recommendation to the General Ministerial Assembly. No opposition was recorded to this historic move. It was done.

Just four days later the Assembly formally considered the matter and fully agreed. The name of the new corporation was to be "Anderson Bible School and Seminary" (see Table 1), and a separate board of trustees was elected by the Assembly.[2] It was to be a body of fifteen persons, elected for five-year terms by the Assembly, with all members to be "recognized members of the Church of God in good standing" and at least two-thirds of them always to be ordained ministers of the Church of God. The charter members of this new board are listed in Table 5. The board met for the first time and elected J. T. Wilson as chair and H. A. Sherwood as secretary. As officers of the "Seminary," the new board then proceeded to elect John A. Morrison as president, Russell R. Byrum as vice-president, and O. J. Flynt as treasurer.

Regarding arrangement for ownership of the Trumpet Home, now often being referred to as the "School building," company members felt that, since the school had not invested substantially in the structure, it should remain the property of the company. An agreement was reached for "a reasonable rental of the building for School use." The annual rental fee for the 1925-26 year was set at three thousand dollars. Very soon the school was anxious to have remodeling done to better suit its educational purposes. In the publishing company's minutes of June 18, 1926, for instance, particular school requests were discussed. But "it was the mind of the Board that just as few alterations as possible should be made and at just as little expense as possible." These few alterations, however, were significant.

In the early years three classrooms had been developed in the north wing and, along with the chapel and a modest library space, they met all essential academic purposes. In 1926, however, more space was needed urgently and the remodeling program was undertaken. It involved the dining room being moved to the basement and in the south wing the development of two additional classrooms, seven offices, a post office, and a reception room. By 1930 the growing library would be moved to the south wing of the second floor, two more classrooms added, and the decision made for the Gospel Trumpet Company to actually deed the building and the immediately surrounding grounds to the school. That process completed a genuine separation of the school from the publishing company, both legally and functionally.

Closely Tied, Well Led

As early as 1920 a crucial matter of school policy had been addressed by the publishing company on behalf of what then was still its training school. The question was foundational for defining the eventual range of the mission of the school. It was about the students who rightly belonged in the student body. Should the school serve exclusively those people who were called to Christian ministry in some form or should it also be open to those "who do not feel a call to gospel work"?

There was sentiment voiced by company members in favor of the more exclusive, restrictive view of the school's mission, limiting the curriculum to the immediate

TABLE 5

Charter Members, Board of Trustees: 1925

Berry, R. L.	Anderson, Indiana
Burgess, O. A.	Woodburn, Oregon
Byrum, R. R.	Anderson, Indiana
Dunn, S. P.	Chicago, Illinois
Gray, A. F.	Yakima, Washington
Guilford, L. W.	Los Angeles, California
Koglin, Anna E.	Anderson, Indiana
Martin, Earl	Everett, Massachusetts
Morrison, J. A.	Anderson, Indiana
Olt, Russell	Anderson, Indiana
Rowe, A. T.	Atlanta, Georgia
Sherwood, H. A.	Anderson, Indiana
Smith, F. G.	Anderson, Indiana
Wilson, J. T.	Dallas, Texas
Wright, Walker	Lougheed, Alberta, Canada

Note: A cumulative list of all members of the board
over the school's history is found in Appendix A.

63

Sitting room, southwest corner, first floor of the Trumpet Home (Old Main)

serving of those preparing to be Christian pastors, missionaries, educators, or musicians. Nonetheless, the company adopted the more inclusive view that envisioned the possibility of admitting and educating people in fields not related directly to traditional forms of Christian ministry. In principle, at least, this was a philosophical turning point. By the end of the 1920s the curricular vision would reach beyond "Bible school" goals to embrace also the "liberal arts." Such broader reaching, with its presumed motivations, implications, and greater costs, would receive substantial negative church reaction in the process of its introduction and first years of implementation. It, however, would prove to be the direction of a broadening future.

For the first years of operation independent of the publishing company, the curricular vision of the school remained rather singular. The 1925-26 catalog had on the front cover nothing except the new name of the school, Anderson Bible School and Seminary, and the phrase "Where Spirituality Predominates." Inside, reassuring to the ministers who were cautious about a formal training approach to the preparation of ministers, the catalog announced that the school "is preeminently religious." "The need of this age," it made quite clear, "is a Spirit-filled ministry, and at all hazards the Anderson

Bible School and Seminary intends to maintain a high spiritual standard." President Morrison, for instance, affirmed in his June, 1926, annual report to the newly formed board of trustees that "no person is offered a place on the teaching staff who is not saved and subsequently sanctified and fully committed to the reformation principles."

To what "classes of person" were the privileges of this special school said to extend? It was open to those called to Christian ministry, foreign mission service, Sunday school work, or leaders of sacred song. "Those persons not interested in any line of gospel work and desiring only a general secular education," the catalog made plain, "should seek their training elsewhere" (10). Persons, however, who hoped to serve the Lord better through avenues other than full-time ministry were welcome indeed.

This more inclusive approach to student admissions soon was used as a rationale for beginning the practice of charging student tuition for academic work pursued. The 1927-28 catalog affirmed again the school's continuing assumption and hope that the church would pay any tuition charges that might be necessary for ministerial students. "It is plainly unfair," argued the catalog, "that one who intends to devote his entire life to the ministry should be obliged to go in debt for his training" (14). But now there were dozens of students in the school whose intention was not full-time ministry. Some would become laypersons "and engage in secular work." Surely the church could not be expected to pay the tuition of such students, worthy as they may be. So the school said that, so as not to block nonministerial students from attending, it had devised a plan that allowed them to pay their own tuition. Now an annual tuition of $75 would be charged, ordained ministers would be exempt, and a modest financial aid program was started. For all students renting a dorm room, the fee averaged $2 per week—and each renter had to buy his or her own light bulb. Board costs in the school dining hall now were $4.25 per week.

Esther Elsaser (Weir) was a willing witness about the early focus of the school. She already had a degree from the Teachers College of Columbia University when she came to Anderson as a student in 1923. Her Church of God father in Boonville, New York, had insisted that she come to Anderson to get straightened out any theology that may have become crooked at Columbia. She had returned home after only two months because of her mother's illness, but was back in Anderson in 1924 as an English teacher. Given her youth and the possible awkwardness with students that it might create, President Morrison had told her to avoid social relations with male students. Nevertheless, Stella Weigel, the school social director who carefully monitored all such things, tried to interest Esther in various male students. Said Esther to Stella: "If anyone could be interesting to me, it would be Forrest Weir" (two years her junior). Stella went and told Forrest! Esther married him in 1928 and from 1930-1932 both were Anderson faculty members, Esther in English and Forrest in history (and debate coach).

In the *Gospel Trumpet* (March 26, 1925, 9) Esther evaluated her initial years of teaching as a single woman on campus. She knew of no student body, she wrote, that possessed "a greater degree of spirituality and earnestness in its work. In this wholesome atmosphere," she said, "one learns to 'find himself, know himself, and give himself' because he is inspired to live in such close communion with the Holy Spirit. Spirituality is the keynote, although scholarship is not slighted."

This spirituality was assumed to guide relationships on campus. Said the 1927-28 catalog under the category "government": "One entirely sanctified yields readily to reasonable and Christian discipline. Government at Anderson is a matter into which the administration, the faculty, and the student body enter with the mutual agreement to glorify the Master" (20-21). The use of tobacco in any form and "unbecoming" language were not tolerated. Chapel was to be attended regularly, but not "moving-picture shows, theaters, or other questionable places of amusement" (22). Student attire was to be "in conformity with the Bible standard of modesty and plainness" and "no student whose general conduct in the opinion of the management is such as to endanger the moral or spiritual welfare of other students will be allowed to remain in the Seminary" (22).

The strong church relatedness and spiritual emphasis also was to be seen in the choice of featured campus guests. From the very beginning of the school it had been management practice to bring significant persons to deliver special lectures to the student body. The 1924-25 catalog gathered these names (see Table 6) and stressed that their contributions had been "enthusiastically appreciated by the students and faculty." For the most part they had been prominent Church of God pastors and national leaders.[3]

A close relationship with the life and mission of the Church of God was the obvious intent of this young school. Even so, some tension between campus and church seemed inevitable. In the School Committee meeting back in February 25, 1919, for instance, there already had been discussion about "the misunderstandings that had arisen

(Left) Professor Forrest Weir   (Right) Professor Esther (Elsaser) Weir

in the minds of some over certain doctrinal points pertaining to the subject of sanctification which had been stated in a different way in the classroom than the ordinary method of teaching from the pulpit." While the Committee had judged that "no vital departures had been made in substance," it nonetheless called for "greater care to be used in the future in the employment of certain words or terms that might easily be misconstrued." Teaching in this school was to be carried on with a high degree of respect for and sensitivity to the believing tradition of the Church of God movement.

To assure the maintenance of such theological focus, while building a genuinely strong and respectable academic program, called for special leadership. When John Morrison became principal of the Anderson Bible Training School in 1923, as he later put it himself, "by no stretch of the imagination could I be thought of as capable of leading in the development of a worthy program of higher Christian education" (1962, 151). He was very capable of believing, however, that God was in this modest educational enterprise in Anderson and soon he became convinced that a particular young man over in Ohio was intended to be a key part of the divine plan for the school.

George Russell Olt (1895-1958) had grown up in a very ordinary community on the west side of Dayton, Ohio. John Turner, owner of a local novelty company and pastor of a Church of God congregation, gave young Olt both part-time work through high school and inspiration for Christian ministry. Soon the young man graduated from Lebanon National Normal University and joined that faculty. Then in 1917, when this school merged with Wilmington College, a nearby Quaker institution, Olt moved to that faculty both as student and teacher. He also continued in his leadership of a large and likewise merged extension education program operated for the benefit of public school teachers in southwestern Ohio. Wilmington's 1919-20 school annual identified Olt as "Professor of Education and Director of the Extension Work." By 1924-25, after earning a master's degree at the University of Cincinnati, he had become Wilmington's dean of the college, director of the Extension Department and professor of psychology.

Olt had emerged quickly as a vigorous young leader with an enormous capacity for competent work. During the period 1915-1927 John Edwin Jay was the president of Wilmington College. In his published memoirs he reflected glowingly on the service of Olt. "We could use him anywhere and everywhere, and did, almost. He was," said Jay, "willing to tackle a mountain if we handed it to him. We could not load him down, however much we loaded him up.... He was sergeant to all as well as general in command." That was quite a testimony of accomplishment for a man yet in his twenties who, all this time, also had been pastor of the Walnut Hills Church of God in Cincinnati. Jay concluded: "Dean Olt was one of the finest professional assets that Wilmington College will ever inscribe in its roll of honor" (1951, 232).

John Morrison became acquainted with Russell Olt and was impressed by his

TABLE 6

<u>**Special Campus Lecturers: 1917-1924**</u>

1917	E. A. Reardon	Pastor
1918	J. Grant Anderson	Author, Evangelist
1918	F. G. Smith	Editor
1919	J. C. Blaney	Pastor
1920	R. L. Berry	Writer
1920	H. M. Riggle	Author, Evangelist
1920	G. P. Tasker	Author, Missionary
1921	W. F. Chappel	Evangelist
1922	W. F. Chappel	Evangelist
1922	C. E. Brown	Pastor, Author
1922	J. Grant Anderson	Author, Evangelist
1923	A. T. Rowe	Pastor
1923	J. Grant Anderson	Author, Evangelist
1924	H. M. Riggle	Author, Evangelist
1924	John Paul, D. D	*University President
1924	F. G. Smith	Editor

*Taylor University, Upland, Indiana

effective combining of academic leadership and genuine churchmanship. Using his own unique, persuasive skills, Morrison determined to convince this exceptional young man to come to Anderson by "selling a dream." Olt already was well employed—and Anderson certainly had little money or institutional prestige to offer. The president of Wilmington College held a Ph. B. from Earlham College and an M. A. from Yale University, while the president in Anderson had never attended high school or college (only a "normal school").[4] But Morrison kept writing and visiting, pointing out that God had an important job to be done in Anderson and that Olt was the only one available to do it. Finally Olt agreed, probably in part because Morrison was prepared to give him full control of the faculty and curriculum and have unbounded trust in him as an academic leader.

This was one of the more important decisions ever to be made in the history of the Anderson campus, almost rivaling the coming to the campus of Morrison himself. "For thirty-three years," Morrison would write later in his own autobiography, "he and I labored together for a great cause in perfect accord. This in spite of the fact that we were different on practically every score" (1962, 152). In 1967, on the fiftieth anniversary of the school's existence, then President Robert H. Reardon would be able to look back and say: "The devotion to Anderson College by these two men, each with his own great gifts of mind and spirit, brought sterling leadership to the school during its most critical years. Together they gave more than seventy years to the College, and as long as Anderson College stands it will be a monument to them" (*Anderson College News* 1967, 4).

So when school opened in Anderson in October 1925, George Russell Olt was on hand as the new dean. He would commute on weekends for years to come in order to continue pastoring the Walnut Hills Church of God in Cincinnati. Here was a strong academic leader with a parallel strength in practical church life. This was a critical combination, which lay at the very heart of the mission of the Anderson campus. Dean Olt also was a real personality. He was both intimidating and fun-loving, staunch for discipline, standards, and excellence, and yet surprisingly given to practical jokes. Dale Oldham reported that, when he managed an early youth camp in Indiana, "the Dean" (as Olt usually was called) was one of the camp teachers. "I had more trouble with him than with all the kids put together," admitted Oldham. "He would put a sheet over his head at two o'clock in the morning, slip over to the girls' dormitory, and scare the daylights out of them with his ghosting" (1973, 133-134).

More was new on campus in the fall of 1925 than the dean, however. The school that year became legally independent of the Gospel Trumpet Company, had a new name, a growing curriculum, and its own board of trustees. It also faced the considerable task of articulating its broadening mission and, in the process, forging a workable relationship with its constituencies, especially the Church of God. In all the change and for all the tasks ahead, however, the school now had in the lead two exceptional young men, John Morrison and Russell Olt. As a leadership team, they would prove equal to every major task for decades to come, including maintenance of the essential, if sometimes volatile, relationship to the church.

By design there was to be an intimate and carefully monitored relationship between church and school. Such a closely tied relationship was made unmistakable in those original Articles of Association filed with the Indiana Secretary of State in June 1925. A central and official school objective was stated as follows:

> To conduct a Bible Training School, a Theological Seminary and any and all other courses, departments, schools or auxiliary schools deemed necessary, PROVIDED that any and all schools . . . shall be primarily religious and shall contribute to a general theological education.

Prominent also in those Articles was the establishment in Article XII, Section I, of a "Doctrinal Committee" accountable to the school's board of trustees and given sweeping responsibilities, including:

> This committee shall exercise a doctrinal censorship over the course of study to be pursued and taught, and the text-books to be used, and the verbal teaching in connection therewith, in the School. In the discharge of this duty, however, the committee shall in its rulings conform to the doctrinal standards of the Scriptures as taught and sustained by the ministry of the church [Church of God movement] and reflected in its accepted literature.

The work of this committee was backed up by the firm doctrinal standard that was characterized in entry XI of those Articles. Every teacher, like members of the board of trustees, would have to be recognized members in good standing of the Church of God. By accepting teaching responsibility in the school, all "shall be considered, by such an acceptance, as engaging to teach in accordance with and not contrary to the doctrinal standard of the Scriptures as taught and sustained by the ministers of the church and reflected in its accepted literature." Clearly, ministerial education was to be central, church-relatedness was to be taken very seriously, and a distinctive and faithful theologi-

(Left) President John A. Morrison   (Right) Dean George Russell Olt

cal focus was to be maintained by all teachers and in all instruction.

The first issue of the new alumni paper, the *Broadcaster*, sent out in April, 1929, highlighted the continuing development of this strong relatedness of the school to the church. The very first sentence of this first issue read as follows: "By means of this monthly publication The Anderson Seminary establishes a line of direct communication with all those who are interested in the educational phase of the church." Then the editorial written by President Morrison brought greetings, first "to the Preachers." The paper had been sent to all names appearing in the church yearbook, with this vigorous reassurance: "Anderson Seminary was created by the preachers; she is supported by the preachers; she is controlled by the preachers; their message is her message, and their success is her success." The president went on to describe the nature of this new paper in words reflecting much of his aspiration for the mission of the campus itself: "It hopes to be spicy without being frivolous; deep without being dry; religious without being sanctimonious; intellectual without being 'highbrowish'" (3).

Then the announcement was made that the annual commencement ceremony would be on Friday, June 14, that year, noting two key changes from the practice of the immediate past. Its location was being moved from Park Place Church to the old auditorium on the campground with its seating capacity of two thousand. This move was to accommodate the larger crowd expected since this date was the day immediately preceding the camp meeting itself, instead of the previous practice of scheduling the ceremony several days before. Said the *Broadcaster*, "Hundreds of camp meeting guests will now reach Anderson in time to get the inspiration of the Commencement" (4).[5] Ties with the church were being nurtured consciously.

In that year's commencement, E. A. Reardon, then pastor in Denver, Colorado, would be the guest speaker (see Appendix Q) and would be recognized with an honorary Doctor of Divinity degree (see Table 8). He was identified in the May, 1929, *Broadcaster* as "a devout and fearless preacher of righteousness" who also "is deeply in sympathy with youth and youth problems" (5). Three decades later his son Robert would assume the school's presidential reins and continue the tradition of seeking to combine constructively the twin aspirations of deep roots in the church's life and full intent for academic excellence in higher education.

By the 1927-28 year the young school had achieved a singular place as recognized representative of higher education in the church's national life. A coordinated national budget finally had been developed by the Church of God and the school was a significant participant. With the operations of the Gospel Trumpet Company paying their own way, the other ministries now were being supported as seen in Table 7.

A Developing Curriculum

The curriculum of the school in its first years was more than a listing of offered and required courses of study. It included a communal experience, a spiritual quest, and an attempt at the development of the human body, mind, and spirit. All learning and growing activity was designed deliberately for the cause of better serving God's purposes in this world. Six branches of study initially were projected, each with a modest sequence of courses spread over two years. These course areas were Bible, English, history, music, practical theology, and public speaking. The biblical emphasis, as intended, was evident across this curriculum. For instance, the first catalogs said that "in the teaching of history the constant aim of the instructor will be to call attention to those portions which throw light upon the Holy Scriptures." By 1927-28 the catalog prefaced its listing of history course offerings with this: "In the Department of History both the political and religious aspects of the subject are considered, with special emphasis on the religious" (52). That year the catalog listed a total of twelve faculty members (including the president and dean), with H. A. Sherwood teaching all history courses.

Facilities in which to implement this modest group of courses seemed adequate in 1917. The large Trumpet Home, while not designed originally for educational purposes, was spacious and adaptable for classroom, cafeteria, dorm, and chapel needs. All students were to gather in the chapel for worship at the very early hour of 6:20 A.M., six mornings each week. Students were reminded frequently "that while they are cultivating the intellect . . . this training must never be substituted for real spiritual power." Facilities other than the Trumpet Home also were available for the total student experience envisioned.

Students were told, for instance, that they "must give some attention to athletics and other forms of recreation if they would do their best work." The large campgrounds and lawns around the school building could accommodate various outdoor activities and the large dining hall on the campground was used as a gymnasium "where indoor games may be played and suitable exercise given." Pictured proudly in the 1917-18 catalog were two impressive new buildings, the large tabernacle on the campgrounds and Park Place Church at the nearby intersection of Eighth Street and Union Avenue. Note, of course, also was taken of the publishing plant itself located a short distance east of the school on Fifth Street.

This initial curriculum, however, soon took on the additional dimensions of the musical, literary, and dramatic. Of particular interest from the beginning was music. The Church of God shared in the rich musical heritage very evident in the American holiness movement and inspired much original music which celebrated and proclaimed the particular theological perspectives of the reformation movement. According to church historian Melvin Dieter, "Even a surface look at the history and music of the holiness revival quickly shows that the vigorous evangelistic theology of the movement quickly found fertile expression in song." The songs, he said, "resounded with the victorious note of freedom and power," of "Holy Ghost religion" (15, 17). The Church of God was part of that and soon had added many new lyrics and tunes of its own, focusing on Christian joy, biblical authority, God's church, and the unity that the church should express in the world.

Church of God music was a major vehicle for conveying and celebrating the heart of its reformation message. That message centered in Christian experience, full salvation, holiness, healing, hope, and unity among all true believers. Here was a happy, singing people. Just days before the first school classes convened in 1917, a group of persons assembled in the chapel of the Trumpet Home and organized a gospel band. Soon known as the Trumpet Home Band, the members practiced regularly and shared their musical enthusiasm and gospel witness in various settings. So, when the school first began, it was natural that music, especially vocal and choral, but eventually instrumental also, would be prominent in campus life.

Student Mona Moors wrote under the title "The Pleasure of Music" in the first school annual (Echoes 1922, 1). "One of the most important means of pleasure in this life," she wrote, "is music.... Music and Christianity go hand in hand." In the 1923 Echoes, under the title "Recreation," was the report that by then on campus there were "quartets for the vocalist, orchestras for the violinist and others who play stringed instruments, and a band for those playing the horns. The lovers of music will find real benefit and joy in spending a few minutes each day in this form of recreation" (33). The first full-time faculty member, Henry C. Clausen, was an instructor in music and the school's first recorded investment in faculty development involved the School Committee granting Clausen an allowance of ten dollars per week "to assist him in defraying expenses while attending school during the summer vacation, his purpose being to better prepare himself to teach music in the Training School" (June 26, 1918).

As would be expected from the cultural context and theological views of the church at the time, relatively little emphasis was placed on the visual and dramatic arts. As noted above, one printed rule of student conduct found in the first catalogs prohibited, in addition to the "use of tobacco in any form" and eight other unacceptable activities, attendance at "moving-picture shows, theaters, or other questionable places of amusement." In the 1921-22 Echoes, with student Mack M. Caldwell as editor in chief, student Emil Hollander editorialized on appropriate characteristics of social life for Christians, such as those comprising the school's student body. "When a chaperon of a party of students says, 'Let us pray,' no surprise or feeling of incongruity results. . . . This is worthy of note for many conceive of socials as times of recess from God's kingdom."

TABLE 7

General Church Budget: 1927-1928

Missionary Board	$132,000.00
Board of Sunday Schools and Religious Education	$ 1,000.00
Board of Church Extension and Home Missions	$ 35,000.00
Anderson Bible School and Seminary . . .	$ 31,000.00
Benevolences	$ 38,000.00
Total	$237,000.00

Nonetheless, even with suspicion of most prevailing forms of the visual and dramatic arts, the skills of group life and public expression were recognized as crucial for effective Christian ministry. Public speaking, of course, had been part of the very first set of courses offered in 1917-18. A Literary Society first was discussed in October, 1918, by the School Committee, but a negative decision about establishing such an organization was made at that time, partly because even the school's survival was very much in question. But in the fall of 1920 permission was granted to organize such a society during that school year, and in November of 1921 the School Committee decided that student membership in the Literary Society should be compulsory. Soon this organization was to be an important vehicle for several aspects of campus life and student learning.

In the 1922 *Echoes* Giles Jump described this Literacy Society as an organization of students and workers of the Gospel Trumpet Company. He reported that it met and had programs every two weeks "to familiarize the members with parliamentary procedure, to enable them to feel more at ease before the public, and thus to render better service in the kingdom of God." According to the 1923 *Echoes*, the Society provided the vehicle for a student to "participate in fiery debates in which he overthrows the views of his opponent and sways the opinions of the judges and audience."

In part, the intent was to help students learn parliamentary rules and how to conduct business meetings. At one meeting during that first year of 1921-22 there occurred what probably was the first "dramatic event" hosted on campus. R. L. Berry presented

Faculty, 1921-22, as appeared in 1922 *Echoes*

B. T. S.
FACULTY

J. T. WILSON, *Principal*

R. R. BYRUM	J. A. MORRISON
BESSIE BYRUM	MISS BERTHA DYE
H. A. SHERWOOD	H. C. CLAUSEN

MISS MABEL HELMS, *Class Advisor*

"The Snares of Satan," a vividly portrayed allegory of some of the temptations faced by young ministers. Soon members of Park Place Church and other citizens of the community began attending and enjoying various society programs. For the first years, then, dramatics on campus was limited to public readings, recitals of the public speaking class, and occasional programs of the Literary Society, all focused on supporting the church's mission in the world.

That mission was understood to include the caring for one's own body. People were recognized as physical, not only spiritual and mental beings. The very first catalog, 1917-1918, affirmed that "clerical workers and those who devote much time to study must give some attention to athletics and other forms of recreation if they would do their best work." By 1922, joining required membership in the Literary Society, "physical culture" became a mandatory part of every student's curriculum. Forty-five minutes each day were spent in such classes, mainly featuring calisthenics and group games such as basketball, volleyball, and relay races. The catalog said that "a minister to be at his best for God must have a sound body . . . . With the passing of asceticism, the world has grown away from the idea that a man must be pale in order to be pious." So, as Clara Combs put it in the 1922 *Echoes:* "The gymnasium work . . . has been a great factor in keeping up the physical strength of the boys and girls while they were busily engaged in their literary work and development in spirituality."

Selected students at first were employed to give the needed leadership in physical culture classes. In September, 1921, for instance, the School Committee authorized five dollars per week for student Mack Caldwell (B. Th., 1922) to function as "Instructor in Physical Culture for Boys." In 1924-25 recent graduate Steele Smith (B. Th., 1924) carried the title "Director of Gymnasium for Men" (much later he would become president of the church's publishing company). For about the first twelve years of the school's existence, then, the "gymnasium" program was seen as very important, with men and women meeting in separate periods under the leadership of upper division students or recent graduates who were employed part-time. Prior to 1930 there was no intercollegiate athletic competition. In fact, as the 1924 *Echoes* reported: "Since the gymnasium is for the students, and the students are here for gospel training, we have no outside match games with other schools" (58).

That gospel training did involve some planned dimensions beyond the course work, participation in the Literary Society, and the music and physical culture so evident in school life. The school itself was intended to be a real community, even an intimate and mutually supportive spiritual family. The "curriculum" necessarily included the whole process of life together. Value was placed on "residential" life. Just before the second year of the school's operation was to begin, the School Committee (J. T. Wilson, R. R. Byrum, J. E. Campbell, H. A. Sherwood, and F. G. Smith) met on August 15,

1918, and decided that, unless given permission to room elsewhere for very special reasons, all students would be expected to room in the Trumpet Home. Such a plan was very much in the tradition of the old Trumpet Family, except that now the family would be focusing more on learning and less on publishing activities.

This new focus on learning within a structured community would require special forms of group discipline. On September 19, 1922, the School Committee approved regular study periods each day. The time from 1:00 P. M. to the hour for Gym, and from 7:00 to 9:30 P. M. each day except Mondays, was to be regarded as study time when all students would remain in their rooms (the plan did not, of course, affect the Wednesday and Sunday evening worship services). Then in August, 1923, the committee determined that every student would be required to work for the school on Monday mornings from 7:30 to 11:30 A. M. If a student preferred to be employed outside the school at that time, he or she would be permitted to do so if fifty cents per week were paid to the school for the absent labor. After one school year's experience with this policy, the 1924 *Echoes* reflected positively on its results in student morale, commitment to the campus, and accomplishment of many practical needs in campus life.

As a rule, so it was reported, the students had worked cheerfully and were glad for this way that they could aid their beloved school. They had accomplished much building and grounds maintenance and other essential community tasks such as fruit canning and the making of tablecloths. The building had needed considerable attention, attention which the school could ill afford to hire done and which the Gospel Trumpet Company, still the owner, did not consider its responsibility. It was, after all, the home of the students and it had seemed appropriate, as well as financially advantageous, that those people comprising the community should take responsibility for the practical needs of the community. That 1924 *Echoes* went on to describe the result as a campus community of some two hundred people who were a happy family.

While the teachers were respected highly by students, faculty members did "not hold themselves above the students." There was mutual respect as well as much fun and shared responsibility, all resulting in a sense of real community. It should be noted, however, that real community is rarely without some presence of tension. For instance, in September, 1922, in the same meeting of the School Committee at which the discipline of regular student study hours was mandated, Principal Wilson reported that some students had called for the setting up of a Student Council, which "was to have a part in governing the affairs of the school." The committee's discussion was lengthy. The administrators finally agreed that "no such Council should be allowed at the present time."

This picture of the early life of the school would not be complete if the reach of the school were seen as restricted to this small Anderson community that was living,

77

learning, working, playing, and worshiping together in and around the big Trumpet Home that had been transformed into a very functional, multipurpose school building. Ministerial education by correspondence had been designed and implemented by Russell Byrum before there was the Anderson school in which he could teach. Then, within three months of the school's beginning in 1917, its managing committee acknowledged receiving a series of requests for a correspondence course and had proceeded to sanction the preparation of such a course, "making it parallel with the course at Anderson." In February, 1918, however, with the survival of the new Anderson school still in question, the committee had decided to delay putting the course into operation. Why? In part it was "the fear that a correspondence course at this early stage in the development of the Training School proper might induce prospective students to take the course at home rather than to go to the trouble and expense of coming to Anderson to take the school work, thus robbing themselves of the superior advantages of the Training School." This concern was not mere institutional protectionism. It also was influenced by a genuine valuing of the residential experience of intense, cooperative, and disciplined learning.

By September, 1920 that fear of launching the correspondence effort had been overcome, and Byrum was freed to complete the design of the course of study. In March of 1921 the course finally was approved, and five hundred copies of both elementary and advanced versions were printed. The commitment to this extension education effort, although slow in getting started, was genuine. So much was this the case that, when school independence came in 1925, the original Articles of Association would provide that "there always shall be a Bible Training Course afforded which may not be beyond such courses as can be pursued by persons not having more than a grammar school education." Educational elitism was not to be part of this school's character.

For those who were qualified and could come to the Anderson campus for their education, however, many advantages awaited. One was the presence of a dedicated faculty and a steadily growing collection of educational resource materials. Later, President John Morrison would recall the beginning of the campus library. It was in one room about twelve-by-fourteen feet located in the southwest wing on the first floor of the school building (Old Main). About five hundred volumes sat on the few shelves, "books as miscellaneous as the notions of the generous-hearted people who donated them." Only one table sat in the middle of the little room, lighted overhead "by a tungsten electric bulb dangled on a slender cord swinging from the ceiling" (*Alumni News* 1956, 2).

The School Committee quickly committed itself to securing a large and comprehensive library as soon as sufficient funds were available. In the meantime, students were reminded that the Gospel Trumpet Company had a comparatively good library for its employees and it now was available to students. In addition, the religious section of the public library about a mile away in downtown Anderson was said to be very good.

Still, the need for a much improved school library was obvious. In 1919 the first graduating class gave a modest cash gift to campus leaders for the purchase of books. Here was the beginning of much alumni generosity to be seen often in the decades to come.

In the earliest recorded decision about book acquisitions not limited by the notions of generous-hearted book donors, the School Committee in November, 1919, noted that it then had on hand thirty dollars for book purchases. It decided on *Clarke's Commentary* in six volumes, The *Sermon Bible* in twelve volumes, and John Miley's *Systematic Theology* in two volumes. These were to be placed for reference use by students in what still was referred to as the Trumpet Home Library. Then in the June, 1920, annual report to the Gospel Trumpet Company members by the company's president, ninety-six volumes were said to be shelved in the Training School library. The class of 1921 served a series of Sunday suppers and gave the proceeds, $125, to the school principal for purchase of a set of encyclopedias. According to the 1924-25 school catalog, the library by then had increased to about fifteen hundred books and the school was subscribing to "several current magazines." While this library beginning was modest, it was a beginning that would become a sturdy foundation for the future.

Another development deserves mention in order to complete an adequate overview of the early years. The young school meant much to those who were involved. One result was the desire on the part of some graduates to duplicate this educational effort elsewhere. In Augusta, Georgia, a small training operation was begun among black Christian workers, many of whom were active in the Church of God and needed a better educated ministry *(Gospel Trumpet* February 17, 1927, 8). Called the Southern Bible Institute, it was governed by the General Ministerial Assembly and sponsored and managed by Anderson Bible School and Seminary. Immediately after the Assembly in 1925 had elected the first trustees of the newly independent school in Anderson, it had turned to a resolution that noted the great need for a school in the South and affirmed the willingness of the Anderson school to establish it in cooperation with the entire church (June 17, 1925). The next day the newly formed board of trustees of Anderson Bible School and Seminary not only elected Morrison and Olt to be the president and dean in Anderson, but also graduate Mack Caldwell (B. Th., 1922) to be the dean in Augusta.

From almost the beginning it was clear that the likelihood of this Southern extension effort succeeding was limited. As early as December, 1925, A. T. Rowe of Atlanta told the Anderson trustees that he doubted the new effort could continue "unless radical steps were taken to insure better support." Even Dean Caldwell's sacrificial efforts could not make the difference. Only sixteen students took any classes during 1925-26. Unfortunately, because of lack of students and financial support, the effort in Georgia had to be suspended after only two years of operation despite enthusiasm for the importance of the work. Years later this work would be renewed in Mississippi and then

Texas (Bay Ridge Christian College). Fortunately, no such suspension of effort was forced on the vigorous young school in Anderson.

1. For detail on later developments, including brief histories of the schools other than Anderson, see Barry Callen, *Preparing For Service* (Warner Press, 1988).

2. In order to constitute this first governing board, the chair of the assembly appointed a committee of five to develop a slate of nominees, a pair of names for each position, to be presented the next day for election by the assembly. Committee members were B. E. Warren, J. T. Wilson, R. L. Berry, A. F. Gray and E. A. Reardon.

3. One distinguished guest during 1924-25 was the famous William Jennings Bryan. A special banquet was held in his honor, quite a venture for the young school to host. But host it did, inviting the faculty, representatives of the publishing company, other church agencies, leaders of Park Place church, and a few friends from the city.

4. Often Morrison told the story of the man he once met on a train. Learning that Morrison was a college president, he was persistent in wanting to know where Morrison had earned his doctorate. When it became no longer possible to evade the awkward question, he told the man straight out that he had never even attended high school. Recalled Morrison: "He was shocked and remarked that such a man would surely be either a genius or a donkey. Only he used the Bible name for that animal. I informed him that as to being a genius I had lived above suspicion, but as to the other there had often been a question" (Callen 1991, 9).

5. Many years later the school's board of trustees decided that the annual commencement would be separated from the camp meeting time, beginning in 1993, primarily for the convenience of graduates who had completed their work when the school year ended weeks earlier. In addition, the academic formalities and sometimes "secular" speakers featured in commencement addresses did not always prove a source of "inspiration" to camp meeting attenders.

4 Becoming a "Regular" College

1929-1934

"Anderson College and Theological Seminary opens her doors wide and welcomingly to the hosts of American youth who in humility of mind and in sincerity of purpose wish to enter upon the age-long quest for knowledge."

(President John A. Morrison, *Broadcaster*, July, 1931)

The number of Anderson alumni was increasing rapidly and the need for an expanded flow of information from the school to them was becoming obvious. The annual Anderson Camp Meeting of the Church of God had been and would continue to be a natural and convenient time for alumni gatherings. But clearly now there was need for effective communication between these wonderful gatherings of people able to be in Anderson each June.

By 1924, therefore, a decision was made that Bertha (Elsaser) Soderquist should function as editor of a mimeographed paper to be sent out from the campus every four months. The publication's name would be *Anderson Bible Training School Alumni Echoes* and the annual cost for each recipient was set at fifty cents. Then, with John H. Kane the president of the alumni association in 1928 (see Table 10), a new publication, the *Broadcaster*, was commissioned. The first issue of this more formalized vehicle to alumni was dated April, 1929. It was to be a monthly and would carry campus news, views, and occasional requests for alumni assistance of various kinds. Some of the more important news stories in those first years of the *Broadcaster's* publication were about an expanding curriculum.

Courses of Higher Grade

The year 1928 would be particularly memorable because it would be the culmination of a period of significant curricular expansion that had begun in 1925. Such expansion would have far-reaching implications and soon would stimulate a wide range of reactions both on campus and in the church. That culmination was reported in the July 22, 1928, issue of the *Young People's Friend,* a periodical published by the Gospel Trumpet Company. There appeared several feature articles and testimonies written by President Morrison, Dean Olt, and various "seminary" graduates. They all told of the benefits of the education now available on the Anderson campus. The Dean wrote about "a radical change" that had been brought about. It was, he said, the offering of "regular college work" and a reorganization of academic programs, which now would include a "College of Liberal Arts."

Introducing the liberal arts may have been a curricular dimension very new for the Anderson campus, but it hardly was new or unusual in the world of American, church-related higher education. In 1917, for instance, when the Anderson school was being started, nearby Taylor University (see Table 2) had been involved in teaching the liberal arts for many years. Taylor's catalog in 1917 admitted, very much as Anderson's had: "Alas! how many young people lose their spiritual life in a worldly college!" (17). It went on, however, to explain: "As Taylor University had trained so many young men for the ministry, some have thought that her work was devoted exclusively to the training of ministers and missionaries. This is not the case; while we have the Theological Department, we have the Academy and College, which offer the general culture necessary for any of the learned professions and which prepare for any honorable vocation" (18). Taylor's "college" courses in 1917 were said to have "as their chief aim the acquisition of a broad and liberal education" (39). Now a similar curricular vision was being introduced in Anderson.

This major curricular development in Anderson had begun in 1925 when, as President Morrison later was to put it, "there arose an urgent demand on the part of the church and students for courses of a higher grade" (Berry 27). Apparently more and often younger students were willing to invest as much as four years in preparation for their life's work in ministry. So, for students coming with a standard high school diploma, a four-year curriculum was designed to lead to a bachelor of theology degree. The 1925-26 catalog presented this program as "the first year of the Graduate Course," meaning one additional year built on the three-year "Regular Ministerial Course." Such "graduate" wording, however, suggested that potentially even more was in view. More would be built one day on what for now was limited to a fourth undergraduate year.

That extra year included fifteen "units" of work: New Testament Greek (3);

82

New Testament Introduction and Exegesis (3); logic (2); comparative religions (2); philosophy (1); sociology (1); Christian ethics (1); history of preaching (1); and an elective (1). The school gained its own charter from the State of Indiana in 1925. In recognition of this expanded ministerial program, identified in the 1925-26 catalog as "work of a seminary grade," it assumed the new institutional name Anderson Bible School and Seminary. An enthusiastic group of seventeen people, mostly recent graduates, returned in the fall of 1925 to expand their ministerial preparation with this B. Th. program. Among them were Walter Haldeman and Carl Kardatzke, graduates of the class of 1924 and both later to make significant contributions to their *alma mater* as distinguished faculty members.[1] Then, almost as soon as this first graduate degree program was in full operation, another kind of "graduate" degree appeared on Anderson's scene. This one was rather ironic in light of the recent and quite emotional opposition of many of the church's leaders to the school issuing any formal recognition to its graduates (a restriction lifted only in 1923). It was the new school practice of giving honorary doctoral degrees, beginning with the *Doctor of Divinity* (just years before sarcastically referred to on occasion as "dumb dogs" by prominent church leaders).

The first two of these honorary recognitions were awarded in June, 1927 to H. M. Riggle and F. G. Smith (see Table 8). Smith, editor in chief of the Gospel Trumpet Company since 1916, surely was a man committed to Christian ministry. He tended to rely on divine gifts rather than human credentials, and soon he would lead strong opposition to some of the school's new directions, fearing that they were elevating human credentials above divine gifts, possibly even threatening his own place of influence in the church. Nonetheless, in 1927 he accepted one of the first two honorary degrees ever given, a genuinely deserved, although a "human" honor. Writer of a guest article in the school's 1929 annual, the *Echoes*, he was identified quite formally as "F. G. Smith, D. D." In fact, the school's alumni association, noting the new practice of granting honorary degrees, revised its constitution in 1927 and voted to extend the now broadened membership to "graduates" H. M. Riggle and F. G. Smith.

Neither the new bachelor of theology program, while a real expansion of the curriculum, nor the new practice of giving honorary degrees was, however, the "radical change" to which Dean Olt had referred in 1928. That additional change would be the philosophic shift to the liberal arts. This shift would require considerable internal adjustments on campus and the weathering of some vigorous opposition that would come from many leaders in the Church of God. Why and how was this opposition set in motion? The story is rather complex, with perceptions varying as to meaning and motive. Clearly it was one of the more formative and stressful periods in the school's entire history.

President Morrison reported, looking back from the vantage point of 1931, that "in the Church of God the demand for secular higher education with a decidedly

TABLE 8

Honorary Degrees Awarded
1927-1936

1927	Herbert M. Riggle	1931	Alexander T. Rowe
1927	Frederick G. Smith	1931	Barney E. Warren
1928	Russell R. Byrum	1932	(None)
1929	Eugene A. Reardon	1933	G. Russell Olt*
1929	Joseph T. Wilson	1934	Sethard P. Dunn
1930	Charles E. Brown	1935	William E. Monk
1930	John A. Morrison	1936	(None)

*All honorary degrees in these first years were "Doctor of Divinity," except for the "Doctor of Laws" to Dean Olt. Degrees awarded in later years are found in Appendix P.

Christian interpretation of life had for many years been apparent" (Berry 28). Even so, the Bible Training School had not been quick to act. After all, to act on such a perceived demand would change some things for the school, would run some risks, and would carry quite a price in needed dollars for quality implementation.

Dean Olt was new to the Anderson scene in 1925. Certainly he was open to new thinking about curricular expansion and academic excellence, even including accreditation one day. His thinking and vision clearly were not limited to a Bible training school. Circumstances, particularly church relations, argued for caution. But Joseph T. Wilson, founding principal of the school who had left Anderson in 1923, had no reputation for heeding caution when he had what he judged an important idea. By 1924, with the Anderson school in competent new hands, Wilson was in Dallas, Texas, starting a new congregation and nurturing another new idea. It was a vision for a liberal arts school in the Church of God.

John Batdorf, a 1924 Anderson graduate, was now with Wilson as a ministerial assistant. He later recalled Wilson discussing contacts with President Morrison in Anderson about such a liberal arts broadening of the curriculum of that school. But prior to 1928 Anderson seemed not yet ready for such a bold move. So Wilson proceeded to do what came easily for him. He again became a venturing educational entrepreneur. In August, 1927, he was the active promoter of a dream that soon became the ill-fated but grandly conceived Warner Memorial University in Eastland, Texas. In its first year of operation (1929), one of the very few it would enjoy, primarily because of the Depression, the "university" was organized into a School of Music, a College of Science and Liberal Arts, and a Preparatory School.[2] This educational venture would not survive, while the one back in Anderson eventually would evolve into all and even more than Wilson's Texas dream had envisioned.

Time for Regular College Work

On June 15, 1928, President John Morrison recommended to Anderson's board of trustees that it approve the adding of "college courses" to the curriculum. He reported the following to the board members: "Brother Wilson tells me that the demand for a college [full liberal arts curriculum] in the southwest on the part of the church was so strong that, when he suggested that the Warner University project be dropped because of the fact that college work was being considered here, the ministry there refused to drop the project." Morrison said that such strong support for a broadened curriculum existed across the church, and if it were not provided by the church, the church's young increasingly were going to go elsewhere to have their legitimate educational needs met.

"Wherever I have been among the churches," he told the board, "parents and preachers and young people have been almost unanimous in the request that Anderson offer college work." He noted the awkwardness of considering such a change at the very time the Texas project was being launched, but he assured the board: "Since the change here would involve no financial drive and no change in budget affairs there need be no serious conflict."[3] In fact, the board not only agreed with Morrison's call for a broadened curriculum in Anderson, but it proceeded to elect Wilson as its own chair (see Appendix A).

One reason for the apparent lack of any immediate budget impact associated with the beginning of a liberal arts program was the assumption of a four-year process of its gradual introduction. Also, as Morrison told the board, "since fifty-five percent of our present curriculum is non-theological and most of this fifty-five percent is of such a grade and such a nature that it may properly be counted on college work, by adding one or two subjects we would be able to offer a strong freshman year's work next year." The main school building could accommodate expanded use and planners assumed that any added costs would be offset in part by the tuition from students drawn newly by the availability of the "regular" college work. Dean Olt had prepared the design of an eventual four-year program for board review. President Morrison noted that, during its period of implementation, the school's name and charter could be changed as appropriate and "other preparations made to meet the requirements of the standardizing agencies." The plan was a long-term one and full of major implications, including the intent and hope of the school's final accreditation by the appropriate state and regional bodies.

The board approved this expansion of the school's program and immediately the plan was submitted to the General Ministerial Assembly for final authorization (a move presumed wise and even necessary by the school since it was a significant change and involved potentially sensitive church relations issues). The Assembly, though cautious, was supportive. The formal resolution of approval noted that "the reformation has lost and is losing many of its most promising young people who imbibe unchristian and unscriptural philosophies of life while attending some of the institutions of higher learning of our country." Therefore, what was understood to be envisioned was a clear alternative, regular college work now to be offered in a distinctly Christian environment. Then, to speak to the concerns voiced by some ministers, the resolution concluded by stating a firm assumption meant to keep the new from ever overwhelming the old. "Be it further resolved," it read, "that the permanent policy shall be to keep the institution a servant of the church by always giving a large place to Bible and religious work and to preparation for the ministry, and especially shall it be the aim to keep the school preeminently spiritual and moral as it is at present."

Some ministers were fearful of this curricular expansion and questioned its appropriateness. But Morrison, with the considerable assistance of Dean Olt, had developed some strong convictions about the importance and even urgency of introducing the new liberal arts program. He knew that some ministers felt the church had no business sponsoring a "secular" education because, in their view, it would be a diversion from the evangelistic and missionary phases of the work. And yet he now was convinced that "if true religion and Christian morality are to be kept alive in America, the church . . . must promulgate her principles also by more indirect means." The state schools he saw as neutral or negative to religion, thus "our American civilization is headed in the direction of paganism."

So President Morerison's plea in 1931 would be: "Anderson College and Theological Seminary, as her name implies, is engaged in both theological and liberal arts education. She pleads for the patronage and prayers of devout people everywhere for both phases of her work." With the plea was a promise: "She promises to culture and inspire in the youth who come to her that faith in Christian virtues which make life meaningful, happy, and beautiful" (*Broadcaster* September, 1931, 1-2).

The freshman year's work in the new liberal arts curriculum at Anderson, then, was first offered in the fall of 1928, with an additional year of the program to be added each successive fall until the full four years was in operation in the fall of 1931. Broadening the curriculum in this way was quite an act of faith since the faculty had limited qualifications, there were virtually no facilities or equipment for science courses, the library was yet modest indeed (about 4,000 volumes), the total operational budget for

1926-27 was only thirty-two thousand dollars, and student tuition was not even charged until 1925. Once judged the right way to go, however, steps were taken to address these obvious deficiencies as rapidly as circumstances and resources would allow. An enlarged mission had been adopted and somehow a way had to be found.

Dean Olt increasingly stressed the importance of faculty members continuing their own education. During 1928-29 Professor Amy Lopez was granted leave to study at the University of Wisconsin. The following year Professor Anna Koglin enjoyed a similar arrangement at this same campus. B. F. Timmons, soon to receive his Ph. D. from Ohio State University, was appointed to teach ethics and sociology beginning in the fall of 1928. Morrison and Olt visited nearby Earlham College in Richmond, Indiana, to understand better what laboratory equipment was needed for teaching in the sciences. It then was reported by the president to the Anderson board of trustees in June, 1929: "We think that the expenditure of $1,000 to $1,500 for laboratory equipment will enable us to get by for one year."

Much more, of course, would be needed for this and many other things as the full program evolved. So an endowment campaign was conceived and launched in 1929 in an attempt to secure $500,000 from the Church of God and the city of Anderson (see chap. 5 for details). This was a first for the school. Aspirations were high and careful planning was done; however, for much the same reason that Warner Memorial University in Texas struggled for survival from its opening that same year, this campaign ran into the terrible timing of the crash of the nation's stock market and the mass unemployment that soon followed. So its success was limited at a time when the school's need was substantial and increasing.

Even though the Depression did limit the success of this campaign, financial hardship did not reverse the new philosophic direction of the school. In the fall of 1930 four full-time teachers were added, Otto Linn in Greek and education, Esther Weir in English, her husband Forrest Weir in history/public speech, and Paul Breitweiser in music (coming from the Warner Memorial University faculty in Texas). Otto Linn's service to the church went back to 1909 when he had been in charge of a Bible-study correspondence course in the New York City Missionary Home. Three of these new faculty members held a master's degree, and the fourth was nearing completion of his. Standards of academic excellence, judged in part by the holding of advanced academic degrees, obviously had become an issue of importance on campus. President Morrison told the board of trustees in June, 1930: "Just as fast as our financial strength will allow we are adding to our faculty persons who have educational credits which meet the requirements of the Indiana Department of Education."

The school amended its charter in 1929 so that it expressly allowed the conducting of a college of liberal arts. The 1928-29 catalog already had reflected both this organizational and philosophic change. The "Seminary," it said, was now organized into four schools. These schools, along with their programs and numbers of recent graduates, are seen in Table 9.

With a total student enrollment for the 1927-28 year of 213, the above academic program was implemented by a faculty of eleven people identified in the 1928-29 catalog, including the president and dean. The only earned graduate degrees held by this faculty were the M. A. of Dean Olt and the B. D. (Anderson, 1928) of Mabel Sanders, Professor of English. There was, nonetheless, considerable dedication and teaching competence among the faculty and, as all aspects of these programs became operational in the years immediately ahead, the size and professional qualifications of the faculty would increase accordingly.

By 1931 two science laboratories existed in Old Main. The chemistry lab in the basement of the southeast wing was serviced by water, gas, and electricity, and at least had tables, a few pieces of equipment, and an exhaust fan to help it not contaminate the whole school building. The biology lab was on the first floor and was equipped with simple and compound microscopes, glassware, and other minimal equipment. Above, on the second floor, was the library (Warner Hall) in the southeast wing, seating about one hundred. Music Hall, which filled the southwest wing, included vocal and piano studios and practice rooms

The school's revised charter specifically called for allowing the new college of liberal arts, "along with the theological work." That "along with" was important and conscious. Never was there any intent of lessening school emphasis on ministerial education. The change in school philosophy and curriculum was not a repudiation or outgrowing of the old. Rather, it was an embracing of a larger mission horizon.

President Morrison had anticipated such a broadened view the year before the liberal arts courses first were introduced. In his presidential message printed in the 1928 *Echoes* he posed the question, "What is an alumnus supposed to know?" At least three things, he answered. Knowing God, of course, was one. The others reflected a widening curricular vision taking hold of a young college president. One involved knowing "something of the vastness of truth." "To be unpossessed of an adequate appreciation of the vastness and complexity of truth," he insisted, "is to lay oneself a prey to extreme intellectual conceit." The other was that an Anderson graduate "should have learned that the human intellect, though marvelous, is finite, very finite.… So, in our quest for knowledge, we should content ourselves with a small portion, thoroughly obtained" (15).

Opal (Davis) Bengtson would be one of the members of the first liberal arts graduating class in 1932. In her student experience she was helped to grow along the lines of Morrison's vision of what an Anderson alumnus ought to be and know. One experience in which she was involved fixed in her memory a key aspect of that vision. It

TABLE 9

Academic Program: 1928-1929

Schools	Program Offerings	1927-28 Graduates
1. Bible School		
	Diploma, Religious Education, two years, 60 sem. hrs.	18
	Diploma, Ministerial Course, three years, 90 sem. hrs.	23
2. School of Music		
	Diploma, Teacher's Course, three years, 90 sem. hrs.	0
	Diploma, Vocal Music Course, three years, 94 sem. hrs.	0
	Diploma, Evangelistic Piano Playing, two years, 60 sem. hrs.	1
	(Mention made of a Bachelor of Music program, but not described)	
3. College of Liberal Arts		
	Bachelor of Arts, four years, 124 sem. hrs.	0
4. Theological Seminary		
	Bachelor of Theology, four years, 120 sem. hrs.	11
	Bachelor of Divinity, three years, 90 sem. hrs. (said to require the B. A. degree for entrance)	1

was a student-planned fun occasion that accidentally went sour. The students secretly had planned the event as a "Quaker" experience. The pianist sent hands all over the keyboard—lightly enough that no sound was produced. The soloist, rich in timely gestures, produced no accompanying sound. It surely was intended as hilarious, innocent fun. But there was a problem. Present that evening was the local high school teacher who was teaching biology part-time at the college. He was a Quaker. President Morrison, very aware of this man's presence, avoided any urge to laugh. Next day in chapel his embarrassment was made plain to the student body. Never make fun of anyone's religious beliefs! Gentleness, openness and tolerance, he stressed, are crucial marks of the educated woman or man.

OCTOBER

October 1—Physical training classes begin. We hear much of sore muscles.

October 2—We take our places in chapel according to classes, the Seniors getting front seats.

October 3—"Do you suppose it will *always* take four hours for one lesson?" and other groans from students beginning Greek.

October 4—The faculty royally entertains—first at a lively party in the dining-room, then at their several homes. A. T. Rowe stops at the A.C. & T.S. preliminary to his tour in behalf of the endowment, and speaks enthusiastically in chapel. We bid him Godspeed.

October 7—Brother Monk also stopping on his way to work on the field, prophesies victory.

October 8—The college department rejoice over new accessions by putting on a banquet.

October 9—The Dramatic Club advertises by a "fat lady—thin man" appearance that convulses the dining-room.

October 11—Open house. Extensive preparations before hand, and games in the dining-room afterward.

October 14—We are happy to be visited by Brother and Sister Neff on furlough from Egypt.

October 17—These are the days for class meetings, other organizations, and reorganizations.

October 24—The Endowment Drive is on full force in the city. We fast and pray at noon, and at night parade in a body to show Anderson that we are here and where from.

October 25—Two large gifts to the Endowment Fund are announced with rejoicing.

October 27—Two first appearances—the College Chorus in a song-service at Park Place Church, and the College Orchestra at Young People's meeting. Both are very pleasing.

October 28—Freshmen undergo the first intelligence test.

October 29—Elsie Egermeier in a chapel address reminds us that God also has faith in *us*.

October 30—Professor Hartselle reports on conditions as he found them in Syria.

October 31—We are glad to have John Neuhaus pay us a visit.

Student recollections of school activities, as appeared in 1930 *Echoes*, p.85

Park Place Church of God, Eighth and Union (College Drive), Anderson

Clash of Pastor and Professor

In 1925 it had seemed timely and mutually beneficial for the young training school to become an independent entity from its parent body, the Gospel Trumpet Publishing Company. Never, however, was there any thought of leaving home so far as the Church of God movement was concerned. John Morrison, in his role as school principal during the 1923-24 school year, had put this in the straightforward language for which he became so well known. "The Anderson Bible Training School," he said, "is the creature of the church. Aside from the church the School could not exist and need not exist. It is in the church that the School lives and moves and has its being. . . . The church has established the School to assist in perpetuating her doctrines" (*Echoes* 1924, 38).

Since the Church of God was not a creedal movement, with fixed and expected adherence to a carefully drawn set of doctrinal positions, at times there would be difficulty in measuring the school's faithfulness to the task of "perpetuating her doctrines." This delicate circumstance would provide for the campus over the coming years both room for constructive, original thought and uncomfortable vulnerability to church leaders who periodically would suspect the school of unacceptable waywardness. The lack of a formal statement of "denominational" beliefs always has been both an asset and a liability for the school in Anderson. In its formative years, the school did publish its own doctrinal commitments. The 1923-24 catalog announced that "the aim of the School is to 'earnestly contend for the faith which was once delivered unto the saints.' It teaches the orthodox or evangelical faith of Christianity with respect to all the fundamental truths of the Bible" (38). Then Principal Morrison reported in the 1924 *Echoes* that "the School, like our [the Church of God's] literature, is thoroughly committed to the reformation idea and is thoroughly imbued with the reformation spirit" (38).

Morrison proceeded to identify one key aspect of that "idea" and "spirit" by saying: "And by the very nature of things the Anderson Bible Training School stands related to the Church of God universal. It is not sectional or local in nature." He might have added, quite in keeping with the reformation ideal, that the school was not "denominational" in the restrictive, narrowing sense often associated with that word. Campus doors were open to new ideas, new relationships, fresh and honest thinking, but within the context of continuing loyalty to the reformation movement and the revealed biblical tradition. This combination of genuine openness and genuine loyalty would prove a crucial and sometimes fragile paradox.

Soon, despite how legally tied and how doctrinally committed the campus was to the Church of God movement, large storm clouds developed on the horizon of this relationship. The clouds were seeded by aspects of the reformation movement's own developmental dilemmas at the time, highlighted in part by an evolving clash between two strong men, F. G. Smith of the publishing company and R. R. Byrum, also of the publishing company, but increasingly with the school. It was a clash of educational philosophies involving honest disagreement among many school and church leaders about whether a broad range of academic studies was appropriate and affordable in a church-related school like Anderson. Beneath it all was this concern, as President Morrison put it in 1930: "When we developed the school into a college some of its friends were a bit fearful that the spiritual tone would be lessened and some of our ideals lost sight of. After two years of operating as a college I think we can say that the religious life of the School remains on the same high level."[4] Others were not so sure, or at least feared for the future.

In part the nature of that "high level" of religious life was Morrison's judgment, shared reassuringly with the board of trustees the year before, that, after having introduced the first year of college work, "so far as I have been able to ascertain, every individual student has at this time a positive testimony of full salvation." Nonetheless, the concern of some church leaders did seem reflected in what they feared was a shift in school philosophy and mission. The subtle shift appeared evident even in catalog course descriptions. For instance, the 1923-24 catalog had described the sociology course this way:

> Man stands associated with two worlds—heaven and earth—with God and man. Jesus said much about our relation to God; but he said no less about our relation to man. The Christian religion holds for the Fatherhood of God and the brotherhood of man, and he is unbalanced who disregards either. Sociology is the science of human society, and human society is the field in

which the preacher is called to labor. Hence the importance of such a subject to such a laborer. This course gives consideration to social origin and constitution, social laws, the family and state, crime, race, prejudices, labor troubles, public charities, etc. (17).

In the more liberal arts oriented 1930-31 catalog, however, the Christian language and emphasized ministerial relevance were missing from this course's description. Now it read:

An introductory course dealing with the general aspects of social life, including the study of human nature as its basis, the nature of society and the laws by which it operates, social institutions and the great social problems now demanding solution. This course is intended to give an introduction to theoretical and practical sociology, to unify and systematize the thinking, observation, and reading of the student (49-50).

Combining the academic and the spiritual, thought of as ideal, was implemented in various ways by different faculty members. As a student in the late 1920s and later a

Large wooden Campmeeting Tabernacle, scene of many college commencements

prominent pastor, Christian educator, and campus trustee, Esther Boyer (Bauer) recalled what many classrooms were like in her student days. Bessie Byrum was remembered as "an ideal teacher." Dean Olt "could scare you to death!" Then there was "dear Brother Sherwood." Sometimes students wouldn't have their lessons ready, so they would side-track this warm-hearted teacher by informing him that they "had a burden" on their hearts. Sherwood, said Esther, would "turn the whole class over to praying." Other faculty members were more rigorous, "all business" in the classroom, assuming that prayer belonged primarily in the chapel and private closet.

The student body of 1927-28 included persons from thirty-three states and six foreign lands, as well as more than thirty ordained ministers who had left their fields of labor "so that they might increase their efficiency." The president emphasized that gifted and prepared young people would be the hope of the church in the future. The dean insisted that the Anderson school had managed to rise above the two criticisms usually directed against seminaries, namely that they are spiritually dead, like cold, formal cemeteries, and that they are hotbeds of the often destructive conclusions of some forms of "higher criticism" of the Bible. Many alumni now were telling their stories of how obstacles to their attendance at Anderson had been overcome and how very much the education had meant to their lives and ministries. Good education and good Christian ministry could be quite compatible.

Even so, the school's new commitment to the broader goals of a liberal arts curriculum brought with it an unpredictable and, for some church people, a quite uncomfortable new potential. Should the relatively few dollars available for higher education in the church be diverted from ministerial education? Might the school increasingly influence church life in ways that could threaten traditional thinking and acting? Would the school become a force for change that could not be controlled by respected and divinely gifted leaders? Would not "worldly" concerns finally manage to prevail in the school? Out of such concerns was to emerge a period of troubling, almost disruptive and tragic turmoil for the campus.

F. G. Smith, editor in chief of the *Gospel Trumpet* from 1916 to 1930 and author of influential writings like the books *Revelation Explained* (1908) and *What the Bible Teaches* (1914), was a powerful person in the Church of God movement. He often warned of the dangers of human organization in the church and championed the "charismatic" process of the Holy Spirit alone placing servants of the church through the divine endowment of gifts. To many persons he had become the movement's spokesperson, its chief interpreter, the definer and protector of its distinctive treasures of truth. Nevertheless, some other persons were troubled by the influence he possessed and wished for more democratic procedures in the church's life, even wanting on occasion to entertain points of view other than those in the so-called standard literature of the movement, much of which Smith had written himself.

Smith saw dangerous trends in these "democratic" desires. He was particularly disturbed by his suspicion that Russell R. Byrum had begun using his Bible and theology classes in the school as places to test various points of view, including alternatives to Smith's own widely accepted interpretation of the Bible's apocalyptic literature. The school apparently was functioning already as a stimulator of new ideas, sometimes even new ways of understanding the Church of God movement itself! In 1927 Byrum left his editorial work at the publishing company to cross the street and finally become full time at the school, where he was more appreciated and very much needed.

Dean Olt now was standing by President Morrison's side and would do so for decades to come as an academic leader committed to excellence. "It was his dogged determination to bring strength and integrity to the educational program," recalled Robert H. Reardon, "that set the standard for a great deal of what has happened in higher education in the Church of God" (1979, 78). With Morrison and Olt, the school had a sterling pair of leaders with unusually complementary strengths. What was ahead would require all the strength that they had. The school was growing in stature, broadening its view—and heading toward a collision.

This planned addition of the liberal arts program had been authorized by the 1928 General Ministerial Assembly, but not without opposition, even though such a program was not unusual in church-related schools of this time and even much earlier.[5] What business, argued some, does the school have going beyond ministerial education? But the move had been made and had gained enough support to proceed. According to the now enlarged vision of this young school, its legitimate arena of academic inquiry and professional preparation would be, at least potentially, the whole spectrum of human knowledge and endeavor. The windows of learning were to be wide open. This college intended to be a college, a Christian one to be sure, but a regular college in the fullest sense of the word!

Back in 1919 F. G. Smith had published the book titled *The Last Reformation,* which emphasized that the Church of God movement was a fulfillment of biblical prophecy as understood by a particular interpretation of the biblical books of Daniel and Revelation. John Morrison and Russell Byrum disagreed with this scheme of prophetic interpretation and told Smith so. Thus a basic question had been posed openly. Did the movement's integrity rest in the good news of Christ and the fellowship of redeemed persons, or must there also be a common commitment to a particular understanding of biblical interpretation that saw the movement as specific prophetic fulfillment? Tension over this question grew in the church. Byrum continued to explore various options in his classes. He cautiously and gently raised questions about F. G. Smith's approach to interpreting prophetic literature and chose himself to rely primarily on the Gospels and

ANDERSONIAN

Vol. 49, No. 20   Anderson University's Campus Newspaper   April 30, 1992

Hartung expansion begins this fall

state-of-the-art science equipment in the Chemistry, Biol-
... and ... Psychology.

dedicated professionals.
The expansion will also
provide more classroom space
for the Bible and Religion department ... college.

THE Orange and Black

Vol. VII   Feb. 28, 1936   No. 17

CENTERING ON MINISTRY

Published by
The Center for Pastoral Studies
Anderson University - School of Theology
Anderson, Indiana

..., 1992   Volume 17, Number 2

An Introduction

The BROADCASTER

Official Organ Of Anderson Seminary

Anderson, Indiana, April, 1929

Vol. 1:   No. 1

DR. CARL KARDATZKE

I have just returned to the office from Maplewood
Cemetery where we laid Dr. Carl Kardatzke to rest. He
lies just beyond the north drive where the white birches

in the same place, with the same people,
work.
President Eisenhower's remark that a man
takes his work, and not himself, seriously.
rule Dr. Carl followed. Who can forget ...

---

fidelitas

Fidelitas, or *faithfulness*, as found on the campus seal

Alumni News

★ REPORT OF ANDERSON COLLEGE

December, 1949

Volume 32

SIGNATURES

Signatures

SPRING 1987   ANDERSON COLLEGE NAMES AND NEWS

ANDERSON COLLEGE NEWS

Vol. 59, No. 4   Anderson College / Anderson, Indiana 46011   January, 1977

Pre-Engineering Plan Adopted

Dr. Lawrence Shaffer.

Did you know the U.S. Postal
Service charges Anderson College 25 cents for each ANDER-
SON COLLEGE NEWS return-
ed to campus because of an
incorrect address?

Over the fiscal year this is
sizeable expense when many
hundreds of address changes
must be made each month.

In telling about address changes, you also can help update the
address lists by telling us if you
are receiving more than one copy
of ANDERSON COLLEGE
NEWS.

Too, if you prefer not to
receive THE NEWS, please tell
us and your name will be
removed from the mailing list.
Should you know of others who
See PAGE 3

You Can
Help Us
Conserve
Funds

Opportunities for pre-engineering studies have been established at Anderson College
through arrangements for an
affiliate relationship with the
Purdue University Schools of
Engineering.

It brings to 14 the number of
pre-professional and professional
studies offered at AC, according
to Dr. Robert A. Nicholson, vice
president for academic affairs
and dean.

Students may opt for the
pre-engineering curriculum beginning Feb. 2 with opening of
Semester II classes.

Dr. Nicholson said the new
affiliate relationship with the
state school at Lafayette makes
it possible for qualified Anderson
College students, taking a science and mathematics curriculum, to pursue an engineering
degree at Purdue University
after two years of AC studies.

Normally, it was emphasized,
the degree in engineering will
take four to four and a half years
of study, divided between the
two campuses.

Dr. Lawrence Shaffer, chairman of the physics department
and long-time recognized Oak
Ridge National Laboratories scientist has been named coordin-

ator for the pre-engineering
program.

According to the joint announcement by Dr. Nicholson
and Dr. John C. Hancock, dean of
Purdue's Schools of Engineering,
Dr. Shaffer will work cooperatively with Purdue's pre-engineering program coordinator,
Prof. Clyde Smith.

They will counsel students,
design and monitor curricular
development and manage administrative details of the affiliate
relationship.

"Anderson College has looked
forward for many years to a
pre-engineering program," Dean
Nicholson commented.

"I am pleased with this arrangement in which we anticipate sharing some of our best
students with Purdue a fine
sister institution with whom we
have had excellent association.
Now we can meet the many
requests we have had through
the years for pre-engineering
studies."

Dr. Larry Osnes, dean for
academic development, noted
course work prior to entering the
Purdue Schools of Engineering
will consist of approximately 44
class hours concentrated in mathematics and sciences-together
with 20 class hours elected by the
student.

Enumerating the benefits of
the new affiliate program, Dr.
Osnes emphasized it offers an
ideal situation for students desiring both a small, liberal arts
college experience and a professional preparation found at a
leading engineering university.

Dean Osnes said pre-engineering is added to the following
areas of pre-professional and
professional studies which have
See ...

Music-Art Campaign At $2.6 Million

"Phoenix Challenge" has
reached the $2,600,000 plateau as
activities continue to raise the
final $1 million dollars necessary
to start construction of AC's new
music and art complex by early
spring.

President Robert H. Reardon
has lauded efforts so far to
secure commitments as a "remark
ably successful" and said hopes
are good for breaking ground
soon.

He has been joined by Dr. Bill
Ellis (AB-52, MDiv-57, DD-76),
president of the National Alumni
Association, in inviting—and
encouraging—alumni in various
areas of interest to meet a
$300,000 challenge goal.

have pledged $29,649 while other
alumni and friends are commit-
ed to pledges of $22,400.

Members of Anderson College
Fellows and Sponsors have
pledged $60,840 and those in the
AC Business and Professional
Association have given $179,500.

Anderson College trustees
now are pledged to gifts of
$65,240 while those of the faculty
and staff have reached $77,822.

Friends of Anderson College in
the Madison County business
community have pledged $49,-
100.

The major gifts area has
reached $2,105,000, including the
initial challenge grant of $1
million dollars from Krannert
See BACK 3

Epistles as the foundation for understanding Christian unity. Byrum was not abrasive in style, not an intentional troublemaker. He was just an educator with both convictions and an open mind.

A showdown was coming and inevitably the school would be in the middle of it. It would be a clash that would involve an educational institution that, while loyal to the church, nonetheless was prepared to test, learn, and grow. The other party would be a group of strong church leaders. These leaders hesitated to support the "secular" aspects of higher education as a church priority or to encourage critical examination of even their most treasured biblical and theological assumptions. In part it would be a test of whether the church should be or could afford to be in the business of educating students for a wide range of life callings. A key question was the very purpose and legitimacy of the program of Christian, liberal arts higher education such as was being attempted in Anderson. The crisis would come to focus particularly in the Anderson Camp Meetings and adjacent General Ministerial Assemblies of 1929 and 1934

In 1929 there was a direct challenge to the orthodoxy of faculty member Russell Byrum on a range of issues. R. L. Berry, who had replaced Byrum as F. G. Smith's managing editor, brought the charges to the board of trustees of the school, thus initiating what Robert H. Reardon has called "one of the worst, most useless, painful—and shameful—episodes in our history" (1979, 53). A hearing, almost a heresy trial, was conducted over several days during the Anderson Camp Meeting that June. Although F. G. Smith was a chief witness against Byrum, Byrum's explanations and attitudes were generally acceptable to most of the trustees. He was exonerated of heresy by them, but increased caution was urged on him by the board in the exercise of his future teaching

Even though the college board pointed out the helpful distinction that Byrum had been functioning as a teacher, not an evangelist, and should be judged as such, nevertheless the trustees quickly drafted a statement of their own theological belief (uncharacteristic of the movement's noncreedal tradition). They then proposed that all faculty members of the school sign it as a concrete way of showing good faith, thus reassuring all concerned of their basic orthodoxy and loyalty to the Church of God movement and avoiding any further and unwarranted accusations. Byrum saw this as unwise, dangerously denominational, untypical of the school and the Church of God. He now also saw himself as a potential liability to the school. So, for the sake of the peace of the church and the good of the school as he then saw it, he resigned his key faculty position and became a builder of homes in Anderson for the rest of his long life. His departure was a serious loss to the school and the church. In a very different set of circumstances almost fifty years later, the General Assembly of the Church of God brought the now aged

Mastheads of various campus publications, beginning with *The Broadcaster* in 1929

Byrum to its session, gave him a plaque of appreciation, and stood and applauded in his honor.It had been so sad and such a long time.At Byrum's death in 1980 Robert Reardon, then campus president, lauded his contributions to the church and college. "It was Russell Byrum," he said, "who threw open the windows and doors of learning.... It was largely through the breadth and vision of this man that we were saved as a movement from theological rigidity and the same kind of closed-mindedness our movement had come into being to oppose" (*Vital Christianity* May 4, 1980, 5).

There also was loss other than Byrum resulting from that 1929 episode. Forrest and Esther Weir had returned to the campus in 1930 to teach history/public speech and English respectively. They each had rich Church of God backgrounds and memories of their own student days on the campus (Esther also having taught earlier).

By now the school had developed significantly from what it had been, especially with its "college" work and raised academic standards. The Weirs were creative and wholesome people, particularly able educators. Soon Charles E. Brown, the new editor of the Gospel Trumpet Company in 1930, recruited Forrest to write a regular column in the *Gospel Trumpet* that reflected on current events. The Weirs became involved deeply in campus life and avoided becoming possible targets of suspicion still being directed occasionally toward the school. But they were aware of what had happened to Russell Byrum and they knew of continuing conflict just beneath the surface, conflict that still had the school on one side and some church leaders, especially now pastor F. G. Smith, on the other.

Forrest and Esther felt some anxiety about what might yet happen and he was anxious to continue his own education. So when a scholarship to Yale University became available, they decided to leave in 1932. Forrest went on to earn a B. D. and Ph. D. at Yale, and then was to have a long and distinguished academic career. Unfortunately, partly because of the uncertainty of the ongoing church relations turmoil, they decided not to return to the place they always would love, Anderson. It was the school's loss.[6]

Final Showdown

It was a cold December evening in 1933. President Morrison and. E. A. Reardon, his pastor and close friend, walked out the old traction line to Jackson's Crossing (now Third Street and Route 32, east to the White River near the airport). Spirits were low. Student enrollment, school income, and faculty salaries all were down. College/church relations were strained and North Central accreditation "was only a distant gleam in Dean Olt's eye." They were coming back to the campus, quietly plodding over the frozen ground. Passing the old tabernacle, they saw the twinkling lights of Old

Clubs

The Music Club
Louise Hall

"Musical Muses" was organized by a group who realized that music is the expression of the soul. Its primary purpose is the study of master musicians and their works. Secondly, it is a medium of expression for its own members and a means of cultivating a greater appreciation for and a wider use of good music. The club includes the best musical talent of the school. Besides having its own club programs, it has furnished music for the other clubs of the school and has also made it possible for the whole student body to hear some noted musicians.

The Dramatic Club
Gladys Byard

The activities of the Dramatic Club have met with success throughout the year. Since the club was organized for the purpose of developing and using dramatic talent among our students, it has been a pleasure not only to the club but also to the visitors to observe the growth of abilities within the membership. Dickens' *Christmas Carol* was presented during the Christmas season to an appreciative audience. *The Butlers,* given at the local public school, was delightfully received. The club aims to present plays of classic worth as well as those of an entertaining type. The dramatic organization is a popular one in our midst.

The Literary Club
Edgar Williams

This organization is for the development of its members in literary activities. The programs include readings, dramatics, debates, parliamentary law, public speaking, and vocal and instrumental music. There are about forty members this year. Mrs. Mabel Sanders is faculty advisor and critic. The officers are President, Vice-President, Secretary and Chairman of the Program Committee, who are elected every six weeks, and the Treasurer and Sergeant-at-Arms, who are elected for the entire school year.

Description of some early school clubs, as appeared in the 1929 *Echoes*, p.88

Main gently piercing the winter darkness. They stopped. Pastor Reardon placed his reassuring hand on the burdened president's shoulder. "See those lights, J. A.? By the grace of God, we'll never let them go out!"[7] They never would, even though more difficulty lay just ahead.

Educational integrity had withstood a considerable challenge in 1929, but the skilled services of Russell Byrum and others had been lost in the process. Those people sympathetic with F. G. Smith's view still were frustrated, however, and were to become more so in 1930 when the Publication Board of the Church of God refused to reelect Smith to the editorship. That frustration would fester and soon be back for other confrontations—which again would focus on the school. One erupted over an action of Dean Olt.

This action nearly brought the house down. Dean Olt was interested in hypnosis as part of his study and teaching of psychology. One day Mary Husted, his secretary, complained of an abscessed tooth that needed immediate attention. Olt inquired of local dentist Dr. Rollie Bennett[8] if he would be part of an experiment—pulling the tooth under hypnosis, without the use of any anesthetic! Bennett was cooperative, the extraction was painless and, after Mary was awakened, all were delighted with what had happened. The dentist and dean went to the local newspaper to tell the tale and soon, not really expected or intended, the story was not only in the *Anderson Herald* (December 14, 1932), but also hit the Associated Press wires and Lowell Thomas noted it on his nightly radio broadcast. What happened next was put this way years later by Robert Reardon: "When the brethren [Church of God leaders] heard the news, storm signals went up all across the land. Letters denouncing devil worship and wizardry began to pour in, and in spite of an open meeting in the old chapel in which the Dean sought to allay fears, the angry clouds began to gather over the college" (1979, 63). Here was one of the occasions when bending without breaking became a necessary art in church relations.

There were people with no understanding of the psychological basis of hypnotism who were sure it was the work of the devil. That meant that Dean Olt had to be Satan's willing servant. What else might this man do or cause some hypnotized person to do if he weren't stopped now? Dale Oldham later told about "a conclave of ministers" called to Anderson "to sit in judgment on the Dean." Oldham, a school alumnus then pastoring and still in his twenties, chaired the session. He recalled the emotionally tense meeting this way: "Finally, however, as some of the better educated, more intelligent, and less inflammatory brethren began to make their presence felt, emotions began to subside. The Dean was rebuked and warned, but permitted to go on with his job" (Oldham, 134-135).

In his unpublished memoirs, *Little Journeys at Home and Abroad*, Dean Olt wrote his own version of this incident under the title "On Trial Before a Religious Mob"

(7-17). On December 28 the ministers of Ohio had met in Piqua, denounced Olt's action "as being inconsistent with the spirit of the New Testament and the Church of God" and called for corrective action. Olt reported that he wrote back to the Ohio ministers on January 3. He told them that he was amazed at their action since he had demonstrated hypnotism before ministers in the past and never had been questioned about its appropriateness. "I am convinced," he wrote to them, "that my brethren in this matter have acted upon preconceived ideas and uninvestigated prejudices." Having gone on to explain about respected research on the subject of hypnotism, even its possible use in the cause of Christ, and his dismay over the damage done to the school by such unwarranted public attacks, he nonetheless concluded: "Had ministers disturbed simply come to me they would have found me approachable and capable of yielding."

Olt, in his unpublished memoirs, elaborated on the "hearing" held in Anderson on this matter and the continuing calls for his resignation during that summer. He offered to resign, but Morrison would not agree. So on September 11, 1933, Olt wrote a long letter to all ministers of the Church of God, explaining his views on hypnotism and all that had happened, and offering a sincere apology for the problem the issue had caused in the church. The controversy began to fade away. In later years Olt would write his own book and say in the foreword: "I would approach religious phenomena with a reverent spirit and, at the same time, be brutally frank in exposing what I believed to be errors or misjudgments of religious phenomena" (1956).

The final showdown on the larger issues between the campus and opposing ministers came in the 1934 Anderson Camp Meeting and General Ministerial Assembly. President Morrison's ratification for a new term as college president was under consideration by the ministers. Between 1929 and 1934 opponents of both the idea of a church-sponsored liberal arts college and the continuing reports of liberal teachings at the college had joined in an organized attempt to force some changes. F. G. Smith, now pastoring in Akron, Ohio, was known to want the college controlled by "last reformation" teachings. He mistrusted John Morrison in this regard and used his own major influence in the "field" as a widely accepted spokesperson for the reformation movement to encourage opposition to Morrison's continued school leadership.

Beginning with a resolution passed and then circulated nationally by the Ohio Ministerial Assembly in 1933, various state assemblies adopted similar resolutions. They all assumed that the school was not "truly representative in doctrinal teaching and emphasis of the ideals firmly held by this reformation" and that "the progress of our school . . . is being sadly hindered in its spiritual development by the retention of other courses than theological courses." The call was for an end of the liberal arts college program, a return to a curriculum of "only such studies as are in keeping with a purely religious training school," and the placing of the school's administration "in the hands of

Early issues of the campus annual

men who are known to be wholly committed to this TRUTH, men who can and will pass it on, both in theological instruction and in burning reformational emphasis, to the body of students." Another influential Ohio pastor, C. E. Byers of Springfield, wrote: "The College (liberal arts program) is not the work of the Church. Let the Church train and prepare her youth to preach the gospel. It is not the Church's business to run an institution to prepare folks to go out into the world in a business way."[9]

Secular truth, the concern of colleges, is always being debated and changing, so the college's critics argued vigorously. But true Bible unity, based on divinely revealed truth and taught in the movement's standard literature, is the only center to which all

Christians can be brought. Secular "truths" and Bible truth, they concluded, should not mix in one institution, at least not in one expecting to be supported by the Church of God. Above all, this college in Anderson must not rule the pastors; it is the pastors of the church who must rule the college! There were many charges of the school's disloyalty to traditional teachings of the movement, with much of the focus on President Morrison and his term of office which was coming up for reconsideration. Morrison and the liberal arts program were facing a major challenge.

The college responded with mailings, carefully worded responses to accusations in its *Broadcaster* publication, and personal appearances by campus leaders in many church settings, explaining, defending, gently confronting. Morrison was sure of his ground and felt responsibility for the educational opportunities of thousands of the church's young people, present and future. Many letters of support flowed into Anderson. President Morrison did not question the motives of those ministerial colleagues who opposed his leadership, although he defended his complete loyalty to the Church of God movement and its highest ideals as he understood them. He spoke proudly of the constructive contributions the school's graduates were making to the church. Should the new college portion of the program be discontinued as requested?

Morrison wondered about the "twenty-five thousand young people among us.... Shall we send them away in their young years to the great state universities to have their faith ruined? Or, if we send them to the small denominational colleges, will they be taught the doctrines of the Church of God there?" (*Broadcaster* January, 1934, 3). Clearly not, he insisted.

In response to charges being made against some of the doctrinal teaching on campus, the faculty published in the March/April, 1934, issue of the *Broadcaster* (10) a statement of its beliefs. Signed by C. H. Hartselle, Carl Kardatzke, Alma Huston, George Montague, Harold Achor, J. A. Morrison, Earl Martin, Otto F. Linn, Russell Olt, Walter Haldeman, and Amy Lopez, it read:

> 1. We believe in and teach the doctrine of Christian unity as set forth in the New Testament.
> 2. We believe and teach that there is but one Church, the Church of God, that it was built by Christ Himself, and that the only door of entrance is through Christ by means of the experience of the new birth;
> 3. We believe and teach that the divisions of Christians into sectarian bodies is wrong and unscriptural, and, therefore, in love and humility we urge saved people to repudiate the walls of sectarianism and to abide only in the one true, spiritual Church, which is the body of Christ;
> 4. We believe and teach that Christ and his truth, divinely and authoritatively revealed, is the only basis of true Christian unity and the only center to which all Christians can possibly be brought, and that we should fellowship

all who believe on the Lord Jesus Christ and are saved by faith in him;

5. We believe and teach that this reform movement, which has as its grand ideal the unification of all true Christians, should not inculcate in its members a denominational consciousness or emphasize denominational legislative authority, and that it should guard against the spirit and practice of sectarianism;

6. We have urged and do urge our young people to go forth with enthusiasm and conviction to carry this great message to the ends of the earth.

If the faculty thought that publishing such reassuring statements would avert further confrontation, they were mistaken. There was too much disagreement and distrust.

Albert F. Gray, chair of the school's board of trustees, felt obligated to do whatever he could "to heal the breach." He wrote to C. E. Byers in Springfield, Ohio, a minister whom he judged "a leader in the agitation and a very good though excitable man." Gray was seeking middle ground by personally proposing to the "Ohio brethren" the possibility "of dividing the college into a thorough Bible Training School more fully under the control of the ministry and to form the other part into a secular school less responsible to the ministry, perhaps located elsewhere" (95). Gray was not sure that he favored this idea himself, but he thought it at least would trigger constructive conversations. He was wrong.

The idea was tried out on Dean Olt and "he turned it down flat." In a letter dated March 21, 1934, President Morrison told Gray that he and the entire teaching staff, with the possible exception of one, felt that "to separate the institution would mean the death of both of them." Ohio's response seemed no more positive. So the issue was joined and considerable political activity on all sides focused on the big June gathering in Anderson. Gray recalled that large numbers of alumni were encouraged by the school to be sure to attend and that the school also made arrangements "to ordain the graduating class of ministerial students so they might vote. This may not have been illegal," he said, "but was quite irregular" (95).[10]

When the showdown arrived in June, 1934, the college trustees reelected Morrison for another term as president despite the pressure to do otherwise and just end the whole matter. With a majority vote required for ratification of this election by the General Ministerial Assembly, Morrison subsequently was ratified by the very narrow margin of 243 to 231! A long meeting followed between trustees, faculty, and church leaders in an attempt to reconcile as many differences as possible for the sake of church unity. There was candid exchange, a reaffirmation by all of commitment to reformation perspectives on doctrine, and agreement by college officials to add a course in the school on distinctive doctrines of the Church of God.

From the vantage point of 1979, Robert H. Reardon, by then himself president of the Anderson campus for more than two decades, identified this Morrison ratification vote as one of those turning points that made a crucial difference. "At stake," he wrote, "was how the church was to address itself in the future—as a cult, calcified, turned in, windows closed; or as a people twice liberated from the rule of new and sterile creeds. I believe that no other single action by the Assembly has had more effect on the future of the Church of God movement" (73-74).

This judgment was substantiated by perspectives found in the 1953 doctoral dissertation of sociologist Valorous Clear.[11] For instance, concluded Clear, "the factor most responsible for the rapid rate and direction of change in the Church of God movement has been Anderson College and Theological Seminary." If true, that is precisely what some people in the church had hoped and others had feared.

The Church of God movement had engaged in a major internal debate and would survive. So would John Morrison as president, Russell Olt as dean, and the liberal arts program to which both were committed. In later years John Morrison and F. G. Smith were to be reconciled, finding joy together in their common commitment to Christ and his church whatever their continuing differences in viewpoint on some issues.

Morrison soon wrote to the school's alumni in the *Broadcaster* (May-July, 1934, 2) in order to put such an awkward period in church-school relations in proper perspective. There had been genuine disagreement on some matters. The president had urged all along that "this controversy can and must be carried on in a Christian spirit." He now was "unspeakably happy to report here that the finest Christian spirit characterized the entire procedure." When it was all over and he had watched the many ministers leaving that crucial 1934 meeting by car and train, he reported with gratitude: "I said in my heart deeper than I had ever said it before, 'surely these brethren are God's men.'"

---

1. Carl Kardatzke, professor of education, would be one of the most loved faculty members of all time. Walter Haldeman, professor of Christian education, one day would have the first and for a long time the only endowed faculty chair established in his honor (1959). This Christian Education chair has been held by Dr. Donald Courtney, Dr. Irene Smith Caldwell, Dr. Jerry C. Grubbs, and Dr. Kenneth F. Hall (retired in 1992).

2. For a brief history of this school, see Barry L. Callen, *Preparing for Service*, (Anderson, Indiana: Warner Press, 1988), pp. 103-109.

3. About eight months later the Anderson board, in launching a $500,000 endowment campaign, designed a plan to have a representative visit every congregation in the field "except the states bordering on Texas," an obvious good-faith attempt not to provide direct competition to

Warner Memorial University. What also seemed obvious by the early existence of such an ambitious campaign was that a broadened curriculum was to demand a stronger financial base.

4. President's annual report to the board of trustees, June 12, 1930, p. 1.

5. Such opposition was an understandable outgrowth of the brief history and special concerns of the Church of God movement. It was not, however, necessarily typical of other "holiness" fellowships of the time and the colleges they sponsored. Some Free Methodist colleges, for instance, were openly "liberal arts" very early in their existence. Asbury College in Kentucky was founded in 1890 by John Wesley Hughes, who said that the school's curriculum would be "to teach every fundamental doctrine of our holy Christianity in connection with the regular college curriculum, laying special emphasis on the Bible, clear Christian experience, on regeneration and sanctification, backed up with holy living." The strength of this religious purpose obviously was seen as fully compatible with a "regular" college curriculum, defined in Asbury's 1891-92 catalog as what school historian Joseph Thacker, Jr., called "a sound classical liberal arts emphasis for its day," leading to the Bachelor of Arts degree (1990, 19-20). Wilmington College in Ohio was the Quaker school founded in 1871 from which Russell Olt left the deanship in 1925 to come to Anderson. What he left behind was a well-established liberal arts curriculum which its president at the time, J. Edwin Jay, lauded this way in Wilmington's April, 1923, catalog: "Our college stands for the great and true ideals of American life as embodied in the class of Colleges known as the Liberal Arts Colleges. They are the real Colleges of America—the fundamental institutions of true education—benevolent in spirit, democratic in government, ennobling in aim and object. The Liberal Arts College is exactly the next stage of education which should come to young people after graduating from High School"(5). Clearly Dean Olt had brought with him to Anderson a strong commitment to such a perspective. Disciplined and broadening studies in a range of nonreligious subjects were seen as fully compatible with clear religious goals.

6. While at Yale, Forrest wrote a book titled *The Quest Begins*, which was published in Anderson. Dean Olt visited them at Yale and sought their return, but reluctantly they thought better of the idea. At present, Janet Brandon, daughter of Forrest's sister, is a longtime member of the Anderson campus community. A teacher in the public schools, she is the wife of Dr. Donald Brandon, physical education professor and baseball coach. The Weirs, despite the problems back in 1930-32, always would treasure fond memories of their years on the Anderson faculty. On February 14, 1949 Forrest would be a featured guest on campus to lecture in a "great issues" series. By then a significant ecumenical leader himself, his topic was "The Ecumenical Movement and the World Church."

7. As reported by Robert H. Reardon in Barry Callen, *Faith, Learning and Life*, pp. 3-4.

8. In 1972 Bennett Natatorium on campus was named for this generous community citizen and campus friend (see Appendix R).

9. Letter to A. T. Rowe of the Gospel Trumpet Company, quoted by Norman Beard, "Anderson College: Its Contribution to the Training of the Ministry of the Church of God" (Anderson School of Theology Masters Thesis, 1958), pp. 30-31.

10. In an interview in August 1991, I asked Robert H. Reardon to clarify the likely meaning of the suggestion that, at least in this case, the college may have used ministerial ordination for political purposes. He was ordained himself in 1941 by college officials. Said Reardon: "Warner's legacy of anti-credentialism was still prevalent. Ordination, like church membership, came from above and its validity was authenticated by those leaders who had won the mantle of authority—whether in informed geo-clusters, camp meetings, ministers' meetings, or at the college. If A. F. Gray, J. A. Morrison, Earl Martin, and R. R. Byrum agreed that a slate of graduates

should be ordained, they gathered them at the old Park Place Church and 'laid on hands.' Did Morrison use his office and influence to see that ministerial graduates were ordained? I think so. Did he work day and night to get friendly, ordained ministers to that critical Assembly in 1934? Yes. Did he resort to ordaining questionable or marginal candidates for voting purposes? I think not. Ordination by the college died out after World War II when the emergence of state organizations rightly claimed the authority."

11. "The Church of God: A Study in Social Adaptation." Ph. D. dissertation, University of Chicago, 1953.

5 Surviving with Dignity
1929-1940

"We heard John Morrison's passionate call for a wedding of education and religion. We struggled and grew under Dean Olt's insistence on academic excellence."
(President Robert H. Reardon)

Shadyside Park in Anderson was the site in 1934 of the first Homecoming planned by the alumni association. A large and enthusiastic crowd gathered to celebrate both the school's past and present. Brief speeches were given by a representative of every graduating class, from Stella Weigel (class of 1919) to Gabriel Dixon (class of 1933), and including Edgar Williams representing the class that had just graduated.

The school was surviving the nation's economic Depression, and the controversy with the church finally was about to run its course. Despite obstacles, now was the time for the campus to move ahead with chin high, and eyes fixed on the future. On the one hand, it did seem like an ongoing process of survival. On the other, whatever was to come, this school's existence was to be marked with a sense of dignity and appropriate times of remembering and celebration. The 1934 graduates reflected dignity and were leading the celebration.

Dreaming Big Dreams

The school was still young and its graduates relatively few. But already many of the alumni were serving in significant ways. The 1933 school annual, the *Echoes*, cautioned that the school had not yet been in existence long enough "for any of its graduates to have reached their prime." Even so, the annual noted with pride that in the field of religious education Lawrence Brooks (class of 1927) was secretary of a section of the

Cleveland, Ohio, Council of Religious Education, Mack Caldwell (class of 1922) was president of the Iowa State Board of Religious Education, and I. K. Dawson (class of 1928) was president of the Kansas State Board of Religious Education.

In the field of missions, Mona Moors (class of 1922) was superintendent of the Shelter in Cuttack, India, Nick Zazanis (class of 1922) was a church leader among Greek people and editor of the Greek language *Gospel Trumpet* then being published in Cairo, Egypt, Aessa Mussery (class of 1919) had returned to Lebanon and Syria to bring inspired church leadership to his native land, Mr. and Mrs. F. C. Blore (class of 1919) were missionaries in Belfast, Ireland, and Louise Frederici (class of 1919) was active in publishing work in Germany. In 1924 Canadian student H. C. Gardner had returned home burdened to begin a training school similar to the one in Anderson (eventually to become Gardner Bible College in Camrose, Alberta). American graduate Nellie Olson (class of 1924) had returned as a missionary to Jamaica with the same burden (eventually to become Jamaica School of Theology in Kingston). The school in Anderson may have been young, but its effectiveness already was significant and worldwide.

The pride of institutional accomplishment had only begun to mature. But mature it would. In spite of all the obvious obstacles, there were in the 1930s at least four major fronts on which institutional advancement was intentionally and aggressively addressed. Key leaders, especially President Morrison and Dean Olt, committed themselves to seeing that the school would do more than manage somehow to survive hard times. There also would be an ever-increasing dignity to that which survived and an ever-widening scope of the school's involvements and influence. Times may have been hard, but big dreams were being dreamed.

The four fronts of advancement to be addressed were the Church of God movement, the academic community of higher education at large, the cluster of private colleges in the Indiana area (see Table 2), and the city of Anderson itself. These were the primary constituencies to which the school wished to relate helpfully and by which it hoped to be recognized more appreciatively and formally. Such recognition would make several demands of a young institution. The school would have to find ways to prove itself appropriately spiritual, become worthy of recognition by the regional accrediting association, emerge as competitive in intercollegiate sporting and other events, and mature into a good and contributing citizen in its own local community. These would be central challenges during the years when the nation first struggled with near economic disaster and then plunged into the preoccupations of another world war. But, even though the Depression and World War II impacted heavily on the Anderson campus, these four overarching challenges were focused upon persistently and managed to get addressed with increasing success.

The 1930s certainly were difficult years for reaching high institutional aspirations. An enrollment as low as ninety-one students was experienced in 1932-33. Faculty salaries were most inadequate, and as the economy grew worse the faculty would volunteer out of sheer commitment to the school's survival to have them lowered even more. Sometimes salaries could not be paid at all. So, short of cash, a bartering system emerged which saw the trading of goods and services with no cash involved. Dollars and foodstuffs were collected for the students wherever they became available. An old college truck made trips to neighboring states to gather food from sympathetic farmers— once returning with five hundred quarts of sauerkraut from a single church! The one large concrete-block building, Old Main, was the only school facility as this decade opened. Dormitories, faculty apartments, classrooms, chapel, dining hall, carpenter shop, and laundry room were all housed under this one roof. Dollars and students were scarce, and many strategic friendships were yet to be developed. But there were generous friends and many heartwarming stories of personal sacrifice.

To reach high aspirations, some things just had to change. Three modest rooms still served as the total space for the library and student reading area. The State Department of Education in Indiana, to which the school already was looking for recognition of its teacher education program, clearly required more. So in the summer of 1930 considerable remodeling of the south wing of the second floor of Old Main was completed, resulting in "Warner Hall," the name of the new library now enjoying an area seventy-two-by-thirty-six feet. A perennial dormitory problem was solved at the same time. For years it had been somewhat awkward to handle the housing of both men and women in the same building. President Morrison said to the alumni in the July, 1930, *Broadcaster* that "we have remodeled and built partitions and changed halls and rooms until we are tired of it."

Incidents like the mouse and the man in the closet were both funny student pranks and a regular source of administrative annoyance. Daniel Schemmer was one of the three new students who came to Anderson from the Church of God congregation in Joliet, Illinois, in 1924. Graduate John H. Kane was the enthusiastic young pastor there. In 1925 seven freshmen came from that same congregation, Betty Clement (Schemmer) among them. Soon, with Dan, a playful sophomore living on the third floor of Old Main, and Betty, an attractive freshman, living just a floor below, a live mouse hanging on a string mysteriously found its way into the window of Betty's room. When the initial fright had worn off, Dan actually appeared at her door with the mouse. Men were strictly forbidden to be on the second floor. The girls screamed and matron Stella Weigel came running. Dan jumped into the closet in Betty's room as though Stella, trained to see all, might momentarily be blessedly blind. But she wasn't. He was caught and "campused" for a week. It was hard to keep the sexes separate in the same building.

So the school sought help from the Gospel Trumpet Company and got it in the form of the ability to lease the nearby Old People's Home for a women's dormitory. It had four spacious floors and a basement. The lease would relieve the company of a financial burden since there were very few aged church people continuing to live in the facility (all now clustered on the first floor). The school, obviously in deference to the few older rather than to the new and much younger residents, named the dormitory Sunset Hall. A few months later sixteen of the new student residents surprised the sixteen remaining aged residents at dinner with songs and individual flower bouquets. The *Broadcaster*'s report said that "tears of joy and gratitude flowed freely from the eyes of

(Left) Gifts of farm produce for campus use, from generous church families
(Right) George Edes, Horace Germany and Melvin Miller
unload contributions for the campus Harvest Festival, 1938

both the travel worn pilgrims nearing their journey's end and the younger pilgrims just starting out on life's highway" (December, 1930, 5). Here was a setting for student residential life with an enriching, intergenerational dimension traditionally absent in higher education.

The nurturing of church relationships was a must during these years when the expanding campus program was being criticized by many strong church voices across the land (see chapter four). President Morrison, noting that it seemed the age of big business, big factories, a general mass-production mentality, tried to make clear his own view of the distinct advantage of a smaller educational institution where the general spirit was akin to a family. He declared in the November, 1930, *Broadcaster* that "Anderson College and Theological Seminary has no ambitions in the direction of largeness. We are trying to be strong but not large." He hoped one day for a maximum student body of five to eight hundred, with all the necessary endowment and equipment to go with it, and he was confident that "we shall have them some day, by God's help" (2). That divine help, of course, would have to come in part through the active goodwill of the Church of God—and eventually it would.

When, in light of the new liberal arts curriculum, the institutional name Anderson College and Theological Seminary was chosen by the board of trustees in February, 1929, and approved by the church's national Assembly that June (see Table 1), the name Anderson University had been a consideration.[1] As President Morrison reflected on this possibility in the summer of 1929, he said: "A. U. would have been the short and handy name." But the school was not a university in the usual sense and, he had concluded, "an institution does not recommend itself to the educational public by calling itself what in reality it is not." Without doubt the school now did wish to recommend itself to that educational public. But the church also and necessarily was very much in view.

"Anderson College" would have been another "short and handy name." It had been dismissed as an option, however, because, Morrison continued, "we felt that we could not give up the name 'seminary' since we are to emphasize theological teaching no less than in former years" *(Broadcaster* July, 1929, 3). So the longer name had been selected to represent the new combination of curricular missions, with the church that summer given assurance that doctrinally the school still stood for the truths central to the reformation movement of the Church of God.[2] Accordingly, the school was structured into the church's national budget. In 1932, with John Morrison himself chairing the church's Associated Budgets committee, school alumni were encouraged through the *Broadcaster* to give to the church and school this united way. Wrote Morrison to them as a man of the church, "There is no such thing as financial success for any of the general phases of our work until the Associated Budget goes across" (May, 2). He and the school intended to be one with the general body, supporting it, and being supported by it.

On occasion such intentional oneness would require considerable understanding on both sides. That understanding would call for some special skills. President Morrison, for instance, was confronted by student Harold Boyer one day in 1935. Harold had a grievance he wanted addressed. Morrison listened, then leaned back in his chair, and gave some advice Boyer would never forget in his long pastoral and teaching career in the life of the church. "Harold, you haven't yet learned to bend without breaking!" But Morrison had learned, sometimes in relation to seemingly little things that were made into large and awkward issues in "the field" (the church at large) and sometimes in relation to significant issues where there was honest disagreement. Love, patience, and a sense of humor often were necessary. With such characteristics, fortunately, the president was richly endowed.

A Curricular Watershed

The year 1928 had been a watershed year for the school's curriculum. "Regular course work" was added formally to the school's offerings and the young institution, commonly referred to simply as "The Seminary," was divided into four schools, one of them being the "College of Liberal Arts" which now would offer the standard Bachelor of Arts degree (see Table 9 for a listing of all the schools and programs). According to the 1928-29 catalog, there was among the schools a "Theological Seminary" offering both the Bachelor of Theology degree (120 semester hours) and the Bachelor of Divinity degree (90 semester hours at the graduate level). This latter program was described as a "three-year course in graduate work. To enter upon this course the student must hold an accredited Bachelor of Arts degree or its equivalent." While many of the courses for this "graduate" program appear to have been the same as those required for the B. Th. program, with the faculty also the same, there obviously was at least a formal aspiration for offering genuine graduate work.

The idea of seminary work at the graduate level, however, was older even than the innovations appearing in the 1928 catalog. The 1925-26 catalog had stated that "students who have completed a standard high school course and who hold the Regular Diploma from this Seminary will be admitted to the first year of the Graduate Course.... Students completing the first year's work of the Graduate Course will be given the B. Th. degree." The next year it was said that "students holding an A. B. degree or its equivalent from a recognized college and completing forty-five units of work elected from the Seminary courses, with the approval of the Dean will be given the B. D. degree." Finally, then, in that 1928 catalog there had appeared the description of a full graduate program of ninety semester hours built on an accredited B. A. degree. It was to be spread across standard junior, middler, and senior years, and it called for the study of two years each of the Greek and Hebrew languages.

The first persons to receive this Bachelor of Divinity degree were Irvin Ferdinand Parker and Horace Hutchins Ward in 1927 and then Mabel Helms Sanders in 1928. None were awarded in 1929 or 1931, but Carl Kardatzke and Amy Lopez received B. D.s in 1930. During the decade of the 1930s there also were prominent recipients like Anna Koglin (1933), Walter Haldeman (1934), Earl Martin (1936), and Boyce Blackwelder (1938). In all, a total of twenty-two people completed this program. By 1940, however, the Theological Seminary division was offering only two four-year undergraduate programs, the Bachelor of Theology and the Bachelor of Religious Education. No longer was mention being made of the availability of any work at the graduate level.

This significant curricular change resulted from faculty discussions dating back to April, 1936. Then Professor Otto F. Linn, an outstanding scholar-teacher desirous of highlighting ministerial education, had proposed the following resolution, with its accompanying rationale:

> Whereas the ministry is one of the most difficult professions in the world today; and,
> Whereas an extended and progressive program of education is imperative in order to insure an equipment in knowledge and skill adequate for the effective discharge of ministerial duties; and,
> Whereas Anderson Theological Seminary has been established and is maintained by the Church of God for the purpose of equipping prospective

Christian workers in these two phases of ministerial education;
Be It Resolved:

1. That no B. Th. degree be conferred after June of 1937;

2. That students who have definitely decided upon the field of Christian service as a life work be allowed to enroll in the Theological Seminary throughout their four years of undergraduate work and take their B. A. degree from that school;

3. That our curriculum and schedule be so revised that ministerial students shall have the greatest possible opportunity for the development of skill, by dispensing with all Monday classes in the Bible School and Theological Seminary;

4. That this new plan be completed in time for publication in our annual catalogue for 1935-36, and that sections 2 and 3 of this resolution become operative upon the opening of school in September of 1935.

Action was taken to table this resolution and assign it to a committee for study. Finally, a recommendation from the faculty reached the board of trustees in June, 1937. Having been revised several times, it had come to call for several curricular adjustments in the B. Th. and B. A. degrees and an elimination of the graduate Bachelor of Divinity degree. The board concurred with the faculty's recommendation, including: "That the principle of guidance to be observed in registering ministerial students will be to recommend that those who contemplate graduate work register for the A. B. degree, whereas those who do not look forward to graduate work pursue the B. Th. course." That very summer young Gene Newberry (later to be the first faculty member and third dean of the future School of Theology) came to campus with a B. A. degree from Denison University in Ohio. Given his strong desire to prepare on the Anderson campus for Christian ministry, he was advised to pursue the B. Th. degree, which he received in June, 1938.

This early offering of a Bachelor of Divinity degree appears not to have been a genuinely graduate-level program for the most part, at least as it would be defined later. The aspiration was real enough, particularly on the part of Professor Linn, who was committed to focusing on quality ministerial education with no compromise of standards. He had dreamed of a true seminary program, not a B. D. largely in name only. But such a program would not be seen on the Anderson campus until 1950. In the meantime Dean Russell Olt was leading the campus in focusing its efforts and resources on building a strong and broadly based liberal arts program at the undergraduate level in preparation for regional accreditation.

That priority decision by the Dean contributed to Professor Linn's leaving the faculty in 1937 and the B. D. program being eliminated from the curriculum that same year. Albert F. Gray, chair of the board of trustees at the time and soon to be Linn's close colleague in a new Church of God college in the Northwest, put it this way: "Dr. Linn insisted that biblical work should have the place of prime importance in the college.

But Dean Olt won out and Dr. Linn resigned from the faculty" (96). Olt's judgment of priority prevailed, although it was intended by him as winning legitimacy for the liberal arts and real quality in all programs, ministerial education included.

The last B. D. granted was to Daniel F. Martin in 1939. From then until 1950 the only degree program the school offered in ministerial education was the Bachelor of Theology (B. Th.). That program was taken either as a four-year college degree or as a fifth year built on a completed college degree. In this latter case the fifth year was devoted specifically to theological and ministerial study and all was on the undergraduate level.[3] Those students who did intend to pursue graduate work in ministerial education needed to do that elsewhere, and many did. In a few years this circumstance would be used to argue for the reestablishment of a seminary program on campus, this time a standard graduate-level program separate from the undergraduate dean, curriculum, faculty, and even library.

The seminary eventually would come into being in its present form in 1950 and evolve its own library, to be named after G. M. Byrd, pioneer pastor (1869-1946), and his son Wendell (1910-1951). That naming would culminate another phase of the school's academic development, that of the library in the 1930s. Esther Sample was the daughter of G. E. Sample, pastor in Distant, Pennsylvania. As a student, 1933-37, she found her English major enriched by Professor Amy Lopez, "a brilliant teacher." Esther was a member of another Ladies Quartet, a prominent group that traveled four consecutive summers for the school and was said to have covered some 40,000 miles throughout every state east of the Rockies. Esther's bills were paid in part by her job as a desk attendant in the school's modest library on the second floor of Old Main. Professor Walter Haldeman had come to the faculty in 1933 as Professor of Religious Education and also was considered the librarian, but his direct and daily library involvement was limited. Esther usually met the users of the four thousand books available and provided reference service as she could.

One student user was Cecil Byrd, a student from 1932-37 with English and history majors. His brother Wendell had come in 1931 and together they were prominent on Anderson's basketball team. From a Church of God pastor's home in New Philadelphia, Ohio, Cecil began reading the *New York Times* in the library. The library may have been "bare bones," as Cecil later recalled it, but it was there "that I discovered I had a mind!" The teaching and scholarly excellence of Professor Otto Linn in particular added to Cecil's new academic growth. Cecil and Esther Sample would marry and carry from the campus the inspiration needed for a significant future. Cecil became an accomplished academic, professional librarian, the first curator of special collections and rare books at Indiana University, a worldwide leader in his field, and special speaker decades later when the new University Library was occupied and dedicated on the Anderson campus (1989). This couple tended to symbolize the developing life of the campus itself. From a modest background, one deeply rooted in the church's life, the school was maturing rapidly and had before it a truly outstanding future.

Campaign for Endowment

With the waters of church relations occasionally troubled but always valued and given significant attention, the school turned to the goal of gaining formal academic recognition. Dean Olt explained the situation in the May, 1929 *Broadcaster*. Many schools would not accept credit earned at Anderson. Often asked about this by prospective students, the dean admitted that "we therefore are placed in the embarrassing position of being unable to state that our work is recognized as being standard." He reported that faculty salaries were very low, more teachers were needed because the student body was growing, some classes had enrollments of 70 to 100 when 35 should have been the maximum for good education, and the library of less than 3,000 volumes was "miserably inadequate." The only solution was for the school to become endowed. He announced that "a careful study of the field leads us to believe that a half million can be raised." With such resources to draw upon, he assured church and alumni, the necessary steps could be taken to secure accreditation, thus giving dependable value to student credits, prestige to the church's college, and support to the mission of the church by bringing "men and women of every field to a knowledge of the truth."

In February 1929, with the new liberal arts program approved, launched, and the first B. A. class projected to graduate in 1932, the board of trustees decided that accreditation was needed by that special graduation time. Beginning a major endowment campaign was judged essential for achieving such a primary and expensive institutional goal. Here was the announced plan:

1. Secure pledges from faculty members, student body, alumni and former students, and other special friends of the School, to the sum of $100,000 payable in five years from October 1, 1929;

2. Secure the interest of the citizens of Anderson with the end in view of putting on a local campaign for the amount of $200,000, payable in three years from October 1, 1929, at about which date the campaign was to begin in Anderson;

3. Secure the services of a fund-raising concern approved by the Executive Committee;

4. Begin at once to create in the church sentiments in favor of such a campaign by advertising in the *Gospel Trumpet* and otherwise, with the understanding that the campaign was to be put on in the general church about October 1, 1929, for the amount of $200,000, payable in three years from that date;

5. General solicitations, except *Trumpet* advertisements, were to be withheld from Texas and the states bordering to avoid conflict with Warner Memorial University. Individuals or special groups of persons in this territory, however, could be solicited.

Soon President Morrison placed the campaign challenge before faculty and students in a chapel setting. The result? A total of $25,000 was pledged immediately from students, who "as a rule [are] not rich as the world counts riches," and from faculty, who "teach for love of their work and not for the love of the money they receive for their work" (*Broadcaster* April, 1929, 4). It was a good beginning!

The president saw the campaign as a vehicle for taking a yet infant school into a much larger and more mature future. One day a successful campaign would enable full accreditation. It was said to be "by far the greatest project the Church of God has ever undertaken" (*Broadcaster* May, 1929, 3). Morrison noted with particular pride how the city of Anderson was rallying behind the effort. The local *Anderson Herald* newspaper had reported to the public on April 5, 1929, that there had just been a meeting at the Grand Hotel at which a range of civic leaders "heartily endorsed a plan for the expansion of the Anderson Bible School and Seminary into an accredited college and pledged full cooperation."

A professional fund-raising firm, the Ketchum Company from Pittsburgh, Pennsylvania, was engaged by the school to run the city phase of the campaign. It had been its representative who had inspired that influential group in the Grand Hotel with how much a strong college could mean to the city's future. A special letterhead was printed, featuring the bold heading "Anderson College Endowment Fund" (note the omission of "and Theological Seminary," the part of the school name presumably less relevant or attractive to the public) and the crucial slogan: "Higher Education Is the Ignition of Community Prosperity." Local banker Linfield Meyers was named chair of a committee to confer with the school on just how the city could assist with this visionary effort.[4] He would write decades later, after having been a friend of the school all that time, that, unfortunately, "before the idea could become airborne, a crisis out in the worldly arena almost shot the project down" (1973, 81)—the stock market crashed on October 29, 1929!

But the campaign went forward anyway, especially in the church. School representatives toured the country, reminding pastors and people of their responsibility for the education of their own children. Anderson graduates of the future, church people were told, would fill the church pews with truth-conscious believers who would be leaders in all phases of community life, bringing strength and outreach influence with them. W. E. Monk gave full time to field solicitation. Despite the severe economic climate of the nation, President Morrison soon was able to inform the General Ministerial Assembly that $206,000 had been committed, enough to give hope that by 1932 the Indiana State Department of Education would extend its formal recognition to the school's teacher education program. As money came in it was designated as endowment and deposited with the national church's Board of Church Extension and Home Missions. That way the accumulating fund could be used to build churches, with future earnings helping to support school expansion and operations. Unfortunately, only about one quarter of the pledged funds ever were received.

Times seemed to become harder and harder. Anderson's sister school in Texas,

Warner Memorial University, only just established and also struggling against great economic odds, finally failed. The Anderson school did not fail, but, as seen from the vantage point of the school's fiftieth anniversary in 1967, in 1934 "here was a college that lacked prestige in athletics, had no accreditation, was constantly in the throes of poverty, could boast only a small number of students, had little standing in the academic world or in the community, and yet it had unbounded confidence in its mission, courage and endurance beyond imagining, and the sheer determination to succeed."[5] Failure would not be the fate of this school, regardless of all adverse circumstances.

In the middle of all difficulties there always were encouraging signs of success, growth, and hope. The year 1930, for instance, witnessed the graduation of significant people like Carl Kardatzke, Amy Lopez, Earl Martin, D. S. Warner Monroe, and Esther Boyer (Bauer). That long anticipated first liberal arts graduating class did come along in 1932, with bachelor of arts degrees granted to Opal Davis (Bengtson), John Lackey, Kenneth Ahrendt, Fred Schminke, and sixteen others. But there had been no achievement by then of accreditation by the Indiana Department of Education or any other body. There at least had been a formal inspection by the state agency in 1930-31, with a report of encouraging progress. That state accreditation finally would come in relation to the education of public school teachers, but not until 1937. In the meantime, the school would continue to survive all obstacles and do so with a maturing dignity.

Key faculty were added to the staff and a new chemistry laboratory, all at the same time that student enrollments and dollar donations declined and students had difficulty paying their bills. As 1931 opened, all school employees gathered in one room for a crucial meeting. They listened to the president review the severe financial problems being faced. Together, many with tears in their eyes, they reaffirmed their commitment to the cause and readily accepted salary reductions, from 25 percent of the highest salary to 10 percent from the janitor's modest wage. The call went out to church and alumni to send in produce from the farms to help feed the students.

Alumnus Dale Oldham (B. Th., 1923), then pastoring in Akron, Indiana, soon arrived on campus with a trailer hooked to his car. In it were 22 chickens, 40-dozen eggs, 150 pounds of flour, and quantities of butter, ham, lard, and potatoes. Here was the gratitude of an alumnus and the practical love of the church. The first "harvest festival" was held in the fall of 1932. Many "saints" drove to the campus with practical gifts that would help keep the school alive. Student Alfred Brown would never forget the day a discarded man's suit of clothes came in with a truckload of other things. He witnessed the beloved Professor Carl Kardatzke gladly accepting that gift as his own. He was a humble man and he really needed that suit.

Then in 1933, with the school openly proud of its strongest teaching staff ever, student charges were cut sharply to $247 per year, a reduction from the previous year of almost 40 percent! Now tuition would be $75 per year, with board and room together down to $3.50 a week. With $50 of employment also to be made available, that would bring the student's cash cost clear down to $197 for the year. The school successfully petitioned the Gospel Trumpet Company to reduce its rental charges to the school by the same percentage that the room rates had to be reduced for students. The president called this bold financial move of the school "a real step by faith." He told the board of trustees that there were many prospective students and that with a sharp reduction of student costs there was a good chance of doubling the enrollment. In fact, the enrollment did grow. The largest freshman class in history arrived in the fall 1933 and the financial operation for 1933-34 was not in the red. The school had bought its own truck and was hauling the coal it needed directly from the mines, saving hundreds of dollars. An estimated two thousand dollars worth of food was donated to the student cafeteria during that school year.

Already there were emerging traditions and signs of permanence. Some of the traditions were showcased in connection with the 1936 commencement. The smallest freshmen class had been in 1932, resulting in only seventeen graduates in 1936 (twelve of those completing degree programs). In the last chapel of 1935-36 the senior class presented a gift to the school, something already done for many years. Letters of achievement were awarded to a few seniors who had excelled in debate or intercollegiate athletics.

Then, as Dean Olt reported: "A colorful event of the day took place when the graduating class marched in dignified, stately procession carrying certain selected textbooks in funeral train. With fitting ceremony and an eloquent oration," the dean explained, "these books were consigned to the grave. The supposition lying behind such ceremony is that the four years spent in college have resulted in the transference of knowledge from the books into the head; hence the books are no longer needed, and should be given a respectable burial" (1936).

For a few years another tradition of graduating classes was to gather at Mounds Park in Anderson. Out among the natural surroundings made memorable by Indians of many generations past, those about to graduate would enjoy a sunrise breakfast and hold a private, senior class pow-wow. Then the seniors would return for the more standard graduation events on campus. President Morrison delivered the 1936 baccalaureate sermon in Park Place Church, the junior class held its traditional reception-banquet for the graduates, and Dr. W. G. Spencer, president of Franklin College, delivered the commencement address (see Appendix Q). Already being featured on official documents and at formal events was the campus seal. A flaming torch rose above an open Bible, all surrounded by the key Latin words *veritas, fidelitas,* and *utilitas.* They were chosen by the president and dean and translated into Latin by student Sidney Rogers (B. A., 1932).[6]

Clearly 1936-37 was "a banner year." It witnessed a major jump in student enrollment to 330, nearly a 100 student increase! The general economic condition of the country had improved and field representatives and alumni were credited by President Morrison with making the difference, particularly "our special solicitor" Elmer Kardatzke, who had traveled extensively in the church for six months. During the year a student work crew supervised by Harold Boyer, himself a student, renovated the old camp meeting auditorium into a fine new gymnasium (today's Byrum Hall—see detail below) and a men's dormitory was made available for about fifty single students by creating rooms above the old campground dining hall (soon, with some sarcasm, to be referred to often by students as the "Barnitory").

The following year the alumni association decided to ask for membership dues of one dollar a year, followed in 1938 by the "Greater Things Fellowship" campaign when all alumni were asked to share with the school. Real help had begun to come from the efforts of field secretary W. E. Monk, who was employed in the summer of 1939 in a plan worked out with the alumni association and the Board of Church Extension. New levels of revenue were needed urgently by the school and, as President Morrison told the school's board in June of 1939: "Many thousands of our church members are pastored by our alumni and we believe that these church members have both an obligation and a willingness to assist the institution that has trained the pastors who serve them." From May 1939, to May, 1940, a total of $7,735 of the alumni association's income of $10,692 came from a field tour Monk had made among the churches.

The *Alumni News* became the official alumni publication in 1938, with the two thousand copies of the first issue carrying the word that the school had real need and the alumni had a crucial role to play. That year the tradition was begun of the campus hosting a Harvest Festival and Homecoming Days just preceding Thanksgiving. Each year this event, one of the highlights of the year, featured a homecomer's dinner, a chapel service with dedication of gifts, and a basketball game and bonfire. An alumni goal of five thousand dollars was set to help relieve the school of debt. Plans were made for launching booster and state alumni organizations, with a goal of one hundred clubs by May, 1939.

Pride in the past was growing and high aspirations for the future were seen as achievable if alumni would band together. The specific aspirations were reported by the alumni association in the 1940 *Echoes*. They included an enrollment of five hundred students, accreditation by the North Central Association, removal of indebtedness, and establishment of a loan fund for ministerial students. These aspirations already were beginning to become reality. President Morrison was able to report in June, 1940, a significantly improved financial situation, and he gave much of the credit to alumni. That fall's Homecoming and Harvest Festival had raised about $1,000 and the field work of W. E. Monk had raised another $6,000. See Table 11 for a record of significant growth during the 1940s.

By January, 1941, the level of aspiration and related activity warranted the establishment of an alumni office in Old Main and the naming of I. K. Dawson as the first full-time executive secretary of the alumni association (see Table 10). Dawson's role included serving as a shock absorber between the school and alumni, raising funds, supervising the alumni publication, and encouraging an understanding of and support for Christian higher education. The intent was for him to visit every church pastored by a former student to suggest a plan for regular support in addition to that given through the Associated Budgets of the national church. Dawson brought outside perspective to the new role by his early contact with the publications and national convention of the American Alumni Association.

Expansion of the Extracurricular

The extensive development of extracurricular life on campus naturally accompanied the introduction of the "regular college work" and the expanded horizons that went with it. Young T. Franklin Miller, for instance, arrived on campus from Iowa in September of 1929 and "learned a lot, most of which was in extracurricular activities."[7] He played the saxophone, got involved in a new campus band, and participated in newly organized debate and track teams. It was a time of firsts for the school. Student life was increasingly active and diverse.

During the 1929-30 year discussion continued about some arrangement by which the student body could take a more active part in governing aspects of its own nonacademic life. In June, 1930, President Morrison told the board of trustees that "the students have proven worthy of the concessions which were granted cheerfully by the Faculty and Administration." There now was a formalized constitution for a Student Council. After one year's experience, this Council seemed to work well. At this time Professor Otto F. Linn was Dean of Men and his wife Dean of Women. H. A. Sherwood, identified as "student pastor," stated at the close of the 1930-31 school year that only three students "did not profess salvation," and one of those came to his office late in the year "and was reclaimed."[8]

One reason for such spiritual growth was the ethos of the campus community. Miller described it as "a loving, caring family, having a lot of fun." Meals in the cafeteria were served family style, usually six or eight to a table, each with assigned seating and a host and hostess. Eating together was a significant social and learning experience. Students were taught to be on time and, with the guidance of Amy Lopez, to employ the social graces of eating properly.[9] At Christmas break in 1929 some twelve students, including young Franklin Miller, were left on campus, unable to travel to be with their families. One of Franklin's most precious campus memories was being hosted by the Sherwoods with the other "stranded" students, cooking, eating, playing, laughing, being saved from homesickness in an open, loving home on the edge of campus. It was a place where people mattered and people grew. The gift of hospitality made such a difference!

As the 1930-31 school year ended President Morrison reported to the board of trustees that it had been "by far the most critical year in the history of the school." Yes, there had been many signs of welcome maturing in the school's life. But the modest maturing was in the face of almost overwhelming financial obstacles. Such obstacles, however, somehow seemed to strengthen resolve and stimulate willing sacrifices that kept the future viable. The president looked to the year ahead. Bessie Byrum, faculty member from the school's beginning, would be gone from the faculty for reasons of health and home duties. That seemed the ending of an era, with a new era symbolized by the returning to the faculty of two of the young school's own graduates, Anna Koglin from graduate work at the University of Wisconsin (she would complete an M. A. at Oberlin College in 1934), and Amy Lopez with a master's degree from Columbia University. Faculty salaries and student enrollment would be down in the fall and the financial deficit up, but the school was surviving. With Otto Linn on a year's leave of absence pursuing doctoral work in Chicago and with Anna Koglin, Paul Breitweiser, and three others teaching part time, the load would be carried by only seven full-time instructors, Russell Olt, H. C. Clausen, Earl L. Martin, Amy Lopez, Cecil Hartselle, and Forrest and Esther Weir. Somehow they would manage. They were a remarkable group of people!

Manage they did, with an enriched cultural dimension to campus life and an expanding volume of intercollegiate activity. A good example of significant extracurricular campus life was the chapter of Student Volunteers. This was a strong national movement on college campuses in behalf of Christian mission around the world. In February, 1930, the nineteenth annual conference of the Indiana State Student Volunteers was hosted on the Anderson campus, with delegates present from six other campuses. The keynote address was delivered by a missionary educator from India and broadcast from Park Place Church of God over local radio station WHBU. On the Anderson campus for several years, Student Volunteers was a prominent organization that assumed leadership of occasional chapel programs and produced missionary plays to raise funds for Christian mission projects. Local chapter presidents included Cecil Brown in 1934-35, Kenneth Crose in 1935-36, and Ray Keith in 1936-37. Some of the participating Anderson students also were elected to state offices over these years. This was one of the earliest and most significant of all student organizations, closely tied to the church dimension of institutional mission.

With emphasis on Christian mission always came a parallel emphasis on music. The Church of God movement was known for its vigorous evangelistic singing and its propensity to stimulate the writing of much new gospel music. This medium of spiritual expression and creativity, therefore, naturally had been in evidence in campus life from the beginning. In 1917 there was the faculty leadership of H. C. Clausen, soon to be joined by Cecil Hartselle and others. Additional dimensions of musical seriousness emerged. In the 1928 *Echoes* the music faculty announced that it was committed to the slogan, "Religion must motivate art, (and musical) art must idealize religious expression" (60). Professor Hartselle wrote in that same publication that "music has a definite function which is far greater than entertainment" and he called for "religious leaders [to] cease using music as a mere machine and [to] apply it more intelligently" (60). As early as 1930 the music club, the "Musical Muses," was honoring music as "the expression of the soul." Club members were studying master musicians and their works and were seeking to cultivate such musical appreciation in students generally.

At first the functions of a school choir were served by the second-year music class. But soon such an inclusive group, including some voices "not entirely satisfactory," proved inadequate (1930 *Echoes*, 63). So in 1928, under the supervision of Professor Clausen and accompanied by Paul Froehlich, a fifty-voice choir of gifted men and women was formed through an audition process. In its first year this "Glad Tidings Chorus" presented Christmas and Easter cantatas, a monthly song service at Park Place church, and a recital at the end of the year. The following year the Chorus broadcast local radio programs over WHBU and made a featured appearance at the annual meeting of the Church of God Ministerial Assembly of Indiana.

There were other musical groups, some with substantial church relations and student recruitment significance for the young school. Of particular note were two early quartets that ministered on weekends and then traveled the country in the summers, singing the gospel and representing the school from church to church in revivals and over radio stations. For the first years of the liberal arts program the Male Quartet was composed of Frank Towers (B. Th., 1932), first tenor, Earl Wells (B. Th., 1929; B. A., 1932), second tenor, Streeter Stuart (1931), baritone, and Oral Clemens (B. Th., 1934), bass.[10] The Ladies Quartet included Elsie Lackey (B. Th., 1928), first soprano, Esther (Laucamp) Johnson (B. Th., 1931), second soprano, Opal Davis (Bengtson) (B. A., 1932), first alto, and Eva-Clare Holbrook (Kardatzke) (B. A., 1934), second alto. By 1937-38 there was an A Cappella Choir led by Elizabeth Jackson, a Women's Glee Club, and a Men's Glee Club, the latter including young Robert Reardon, who became the college president some two decades later. As a student he was both the piano and organ accompanist for Miss Jackson's choir.

While the college received considerable benefit from the inspired service of these many gifted young musicians, it also gave them much. Opal Davis, for instance, member of the Ladies Quartet, had come to the campus from Missouri in 1927 to take the two-year Religious Education course. But after two years she elected to stay and pioneer with the school in the education and graduation of a first liberal arts class. Her problem was that she had not managed to graduate from high school before coming to Anderson. So she and others on campus in a similar circumstance participated in a plan of parallel studies, taking extra courses from a local high school teacher brought to campus especially to address their academic deficiencies. She worked at J. C. Penney's "uptown," traveled with the Quartet, and completed both high school and college in five years, being a member of that first B. A. class in 1932. A richness came into her life from contact with exceptional campus persons, including the president's "warmth and sense of humor," and the dean's "mixture of caring and dignity." There also was Bessie Byrum's "motherliness and yet brilliance in her teaching methods" and the leadership of debating coach and history teacher Forrest Weir, who started with the "now" in history and taught one "to think logically and critically" (Bengtson 1988, 11).

The richness also came from the personal touch in the midst of the economic hardships of the time. Opal married Paul Bengtson the same year as her college graduation in 1932. There was little money but much support from the campus community. The August wedding was in the flower garden of President and Mrs. Morrison's home. The president officiated, standing under a flowered archway, and Professor Paul Breitweiser played Mrs. Morrison's piano, which had been moved to the back porch within sound reach of the garden. Mrs. Morrison made many of the wedding arrangements personally. Given the times, this was real generosity and a personal touch never to be forgotten. Born to this new couple would be son Dale, who one day would be Dr. F. Dale Bengtson, faculty member, choir director, music department chair, and school dean on the Anderson campus.

The family atmosphere of the campus remained strong in these years of hardship. In May, 1932, the whole graduating class of that year shared the love and gracious hospitality of the campus at the annual Faculty-Senior Picnic in nearby Shadyside Park. There was group singing, vigorous games, humorous reflections, worship around a fire, and wonderful chicken and noodles, cole slaw and strawberries prepared as usual by Mrs. Morrison and faculty wives. The humorous reflections on such nostalgic occasions might well have included things like a disappearing class flag and electrically wired beds in Old Main.

A photo in the 1933 *Echoes* showed students proudly holding the 1936 flag. When the students of the class of 1936 were freshmen in 1932, some of them made this flag, suspended it between two wings of Old Main, and then had it mysteriously removed by upperclassmen. They got it back, put it on top of the flagpole in front of Old Main, and greased the pole on the way back down. Student Clair Shultz, school carpenter, made a special grease-avoiding ladder, got it down at night, helped hide it for the rest of the year, and got permission to present it back to the surprised freshmen class at the final chapel. That same *Echoes* has a picture of student Earl Dean standing on his head on top of Old Main—something for which he did not have permission or apparent good sense!

Then there were the beds. During the year 1936-37 Al Brown (B. A., 1941; B. Th., 1942) and Howard Miller (B. A., 1945; B. Th., 1946) roomed together in the attic of Old Main where student rooms had been enclosed among the open areas under the sloping roof. One night became very eventful as they slept, rather shocking in fact. They first tossed in mild discomfort, then bolted to their feet in fright and confusion. Shortly they discovered that there were electric wires hidden in the beds and shadowy figures outside the room regulating the current and enjoying the whole thing! Al remembered grabbing his ball bat and Howard his shotgun (!) and racing in the dark after Clifford Corns and Herb Neff. Fortunately they all wound up alive and still friends. They even found their chance to laugh at the revered Dean Olt who was reported on several occasions to have driven his car downtown, forgotten it, and taken the bus back to campus. Money always seemed in short supply; often laughs were not.

Various forms of dramatics soon joined music as a focus of student life. The Dramatics Club was organized by 1928 and then pictured for the first time in the 1929 *Echoes*. In December, 1928, the club presented on campus *A Christmas Carol* by Charles Dickens and later that school year staged *The Butler* at a public school. Years later Robert N. Smith, campus Director of Dramatics, drew the inference from these earliest productions that "the play choices done on campus were divided between the more religious and the 'safe' secular plays," a practice generally followed in the years to come (Smith 1987, 9). "Notably absent," observed Smith, "are plays which were known for their success in the professional theater. This would seem to indicate a reluctance on the campus to do anything that would connect it to the 'worldly' theater" (14). By the late 1920s there were courses in Elizabethan Drama and Shakespeare and curtains purchased to equip the Park Place Church sanctuary for dramatic productions .

In 1929-30 *The Three Bears* was produced by the French Club, presumably in French. While lower student enrollments and scarce resources helped to keep dramatic productions to a minimum until at least 1934-35, an "operetta" was staged by the Musical Muses in April, 1931, under the inspired direction of Professors Cecil Hartselle and Forrest Weir. Called by that month's *Broadcaster* "the most outstanding musical and dramatic event in the history of the school," student Ruth Coolidge played the lead in "Lelawala, the Maid of Niagara." In later years the music and drama departments would join annually to produce a major musical which had enjoyed great success in the public arena (see Table 19). The music, literary, dramatic and forensic clubs were centers of student activity by 1929. Forensics was new in 1928. By 1930 the school was a member of the Indiana State Debating League and had successful debating teams in intercollegiate competition, with superb coaching help from Professor F. C. Weir. Then student social clubs developed, not just as organized outlets for student energy but also as means of practical service to the growing life of the campus community. The first to organize was the Pep Club in 1934. "Pep" stood for Christian personality, education, and progress and was a women's club founded primarily to foster school spirit at basketball games. By 1936 there also was a men's club, the Boosters, organized to promote—boost—the college and its athletic functions.

Future campus president Robert H. Reardon (B.A., 1940) was involved as a student from this club's beginning. He and his friends David Houghton and Mitt Williams, Reardon later recalled, "got things organized, wrote a constitution calling for a high sense of honor and fidelity to Anderson College forever, called our buddies together, swore them in, and declared ourselves the Boosters, cream of the crop" (1991, 84). Soon another future president of the campus, Robert A. Nicholson, would come to Anderson as a student and also become a Booster. In 1939 the school's *alma mater* was written as a Booster Club project, with stanzas by Arthur Hoffman and Donald Smith. In that year's *Echoes* the Boosters said of their club: "Anything that promotes the good old A. C. T. S. we promote—for we're the boosters."

One other club appeared during this decade, Sachem, organized by Byron Westlake in 1937. "Sachem" was an Indian (Algonquin) word for "leader." For these students "God first, others second, self last" reflected their chosen philosophy of learning to lead by first learning to serve. This noble and humble attitude was not always obvious as they became the great competitors of the Boosters. Often these clubs sponsored dramatic productions, the first being "A Question of Clothes" by the Pep Club in 1936 and "Papa Behave" by the new Sachem Club the following year. Student involvement in the many activities of these clubs often provided their most lasting memories of college days.

Basketball had emerged as a major social attraction for the whole student body. With few student cars or dollars available to distract, a home game often was a rousing event drawing together much of the campus community. While President Morrison assured the board of trustees in June, 1937, that the school's stress continued to be on "physical education rather than intercollegiate athletics which, of course, is proper," he nonetheless reported to them with obvious pride the very next year that "in the field of intercollegiate activities considerable prestige and publicity have come to the college here in Indiana through the medium of intercollegiate basketball and intercollegiate debate."

In less than one decade the college obviously had done more than merely survive. It had begun to demand some respect. There now was considerable public awareness of the school, with the *Anderson Herald* newspaper of December 15, 1933, for instance, announcing to the public that the local college was hosting the basketball team from Concordia College, Fort Wayne, Indiana. Members of the Anderson team listed were Wendell Byrd, Cecil Byrd, Clair Shultz, Daniel Martin, David Gaulke, and Elmer Kardatzke. By 1934 there was a campus director of intercollegiate athletics and a basketball team known as the "Tigers," surely a fitting symbol for a tenacious young college determined to achieve, not only exist.[11]

The move beyond gymnasium as a curricular activity for all students to organized teams competing against teams from outside the campus community happened in the 1929-32 period. In 1929 the local YMCA's Darrist A. Denny was hired part time by the school as physical education instructor and with the intent of organizing competitive athletics. The 1930 *Echoes* refers to the existence of a baseball team,[12] men and women's basketball, tennis, and track teams. The Gospel Trumpet Company, by its action on March 20, 1930, in response to a college request, had made land immediately east of the plant available for a track to be developed. There was in this early period a series of part-time and student coaches for these sports, with only sporadic schedules and limited financial support. Basketball was the most popular and successful athletic venture as early as 1929, under the coaching of Mr. Denny, assisted by sophomore student Albert Donaldson. The men's team was competing with teams from churches and an industrial league in the city. The January, 1930, *Broadcaster* reported proudly to alumni that the men's team had beaten the "Gospel Trumpet Five" 32 to 29 "in one of the hottest contests that had been waged on the floor of the local gymnasium this season." Such competition was said to prove to "skeptics" that "properly supervised athletics will develop self-control, and thereby make our boys and girls better men and women in every walk of life" (3). Unfortunately, this report also said that the college girls' team had lost to the Trumpet girls 14 to 17.

By the opening of the 1932-33 season there was intercollegiate scheduling for the men's team and a regular faculty coach, George Montague. Anderson was beaten soundly, 49-16, at the Anderson YMCA by Indiana Central College of Indianapolis. But by December there was victory over the Indiana Law University of Indianapolis in the Gospel Trumpet gymnasium (the campground dining hall floor). Success finally had been tasted by team members Hubert Achor, Homer Beckett, Wendell and Cecil Byrd, Max and David Gaulke, Daniel Martin, Edward Miller, Earl Morrison, Clair Shultz, Herman Smith, and Virgil Tucker.

For years the school had used the Gospel Trumpet dining hall on the campground as a gymnasium. During 1934-35 several students and alumni began to agitate

Glad Tidings Chorus, with director Henry C. Clausen at right, as in the 1934 *Echoes*

for better gymnasium facilities and talked of somehow raising a mile of dimes, which was estimated to be about eight thousand dollars. That June the president admitted to the board of trustees that the need was very real. Current arrangements were no longer adequate for the expanding basketball program and, he added for emphasis, "many neighboring colleges refuse to come and play basketball with our boys because of poor gymnasium facilities." It was not only basketball. In 1935-36 Ray Edgar May had come as the first full-time physical education faculty member. He began building not only varsity athletics (basketball, track, and tennis), but a fine intramural program. The need for improved facilities indeed was growing acute.

`   The opportunity had evolved for the school to lease the old camp meeting auditorium and convert it into a reasonable gymnasium (much later to become the present Byrum Hall). So the achievement of this project became a focus of student expectation and administrative effort, and the theme of the 1935 alumni association meeting. Alumni pledges of $2,100 were received. The president successfully solicited local chain stores for contributions. In October, 1936, for instance, he wrote to the manager of Anderson's Sears store. He explained the gym project, saying that the new building would be used for basketball, physical education classes, chapel services, plays, and as a "community center." Already, he reported, he had received about $2,600 from city friends and businesses, naming S. S. Kresge, A & P Grocery, F. W. Woolworth, and others. He emphasized the positive economic impact of the student body on the local economy and reminded Mr. Shanahan that the school did not often approach the business community for money, in fact had not done so since the endowment campaign seven years earlier.

Adequate funds to proceed were secured. Apart from an architect, all work was done by students, mostly in the summer of 1936. Work proceeded under the supervision of student Harold Boyer, who was campus manager of buildings and grounds. He was paid thirty-five cents an hour, but in college credit more often than in cash. His work crew included Howard Miller,[13] Cecil Byrd, Milo Chapman, David Gaulke, and Louis Gough (all prominent in their various fields in later years). They tore down the old Gospel Trumpet Company's barn (no more livestock) and reused many of the materials.

(Top) Women's Quartet: (left) Elsie Patterson (Lackey),
Esther Johnson (Laucamp), Opal Davis (Bengston), Eva Clare Holbrook (Kardatzke)
(Bottom) Men's Quartet: (left) Frank Towers, Earl Wells,
Streeter Stuart, Sr., Oral Clemens

The sloping concrete floor of the old auditorium had to be replaced with a quality, level, hardwood floor suitable for basketball. Metal bedrails and springs from some dorm rooms in Old Main were used to reinforce concrete. These students learned construction techniques as they were needed. Student Clair Shultz, working for his brother Rolla, an earlier student in the school and now a local electrical contractor, climbed around the attic area to wire the new overhead lighting. A furnace and dressing rooms were added, along with a modest amount of seating for spectators. The final result was something about which all were justifiably proud. Cecil Byrd, outstanding basketball player of the time, surely appreciated the team being able to move over to this new facility.

In 1936-37 the new gym was ready for use and soon was claimed to be one of the finer physical education facilities in the state (despite its relatively poor lighting and limited seating for fans). It would, in fact, serve as the only physical education facility on campus until 1962 when the present Lewis Gymnasium would be constructed. Then in 1937-38 physical education was given academic departmental status, and the college became a member of the Indiana Inter-Collegiate Conference. The base had been laid for a diverse and proud future of athletic competition. Initially the success would come in basketball, with the city of Anderson being in the very heart of a general sporting enthusiasm popularly known as "Hoosier Hysteria." Archie Chadd had come to Anderson High School in 1933-34 and proceeded to lead those "Indians" to state championships in 1935 and 1937. Intense competition and a thirst for victory seemed to be in the air locally.

As early as the 1938-39 season, the college basketball team enjoyed a 15-5 record and generated a little hysteria of its own by qualifying to participate in a national tournament in Kansas City. There was considerable local newspaper coverage of Anderson's "Mr. Basketball," Jack Van Dyke. Jack, a graduate of Anderson High School, had been close to campus life as a boy. He often had watched the college's first basketball teams play in the dining hall gym with the low ceiling that frustrated many opponents.[14] As a freshman in 1937-38 he was point leader for much of season among all the state's colleges, finally finishing second only behind Jewell Young, an All-American at Purdue. Jack then won the state scoring crown as an Anderson sophomore, and as a junior was named to the All-Indiana first team. He and his teammates brought to campus life an unprecedented sporting excitement and the accompanying public attention.

President and Mrs. Morrison were avid fans, but they also were firm about strict rules of campus conduct. Van Dyke was suspended from school for a week more than once for some infraction, once because, despite warnings, he wore shorts without a shirt while playing tennis. Even so, in addition to the basketball success, he lettered four years in tennis and, as a senior in 1940-41, was named best all-around man on campus. He was joined by best all-round woman, Geraldine Hurst (Reardon).

129

Triumph Even in Trouble

These were troubled financial years, and yet rich ones in the lives of many students. Inspired people found ways to succeed in the face of significant obstacles. In 1932, for instance, a zealous, gifted, and young Boyce W. Blackwelder was accepted as a new student. He bought a suitcase for ninety-eight cents, packed what little he had, boarded a train headed for Anderson, Indiana, and for the first time left North Carolina to pursue a divine vision in his heart. Jobs were scarce, but Boyce was relentless in doing whatever he could to carry on, including wearing a sign over his shoulders to advertise meals at a local restaurant in exchange for his own noon meal and any leftover doughnuts (which he would take back to campus for hungry friends). By 1933 he was pastor of the Arrow Heights congregation on the west side of Anderson, walking and then riding a bicycle across the city to fulfill pastoral duties, all the while remaining a serious ministerial student (B. A. in 1936 and B. D. in 1938). His vision and discipline overcame every obstacle.[15]

People greatly admired Professor Hartselle, the music instructor who was blind and served on the faculty for thirty-nine years (1924-1963). He had developed the ability to move rapidly up and down the hallways and staircases of Old Main and to identify by name almost any student who approached his office, either by the sound of the footsteps or at least by the voice when the person requested to enter. "Toodles" joined the faculty in 1939. He was Hartselle's seeing-eye dog who, it was said, attended chapel more than some students. Hartselle was a gifted man who managed well despite a handicap

The experiences of Walter Tiesel (B. Th., 1938) and Margaret (Chambers) Tiesel (B. A., 1938) were typical and in their own way quite remarkable for the time and circumstances. They had married in 1932, after which Walter was called by God to Christian ministry. They found their way to the Anderson campus seeking ministry preparation. In their five years on campus the Tiesels lived in a little cottage on the campgrounds, in a modest apartment in the men's dormitory (the "barnitory" as this converted, drafty upstairs of the church dining hall was commonly called), and in an apartment in Old Main where a wonderful family atmosphere prevailed (some faculty families had moved in because they no longer could afford a private home). The Tiesels and three other student couples got permission to rent an extra room where they cooked together to save money. When a large truckload of gift potatoes arrived on campus, it seemed for a while as if every meal in the cafeteria was basically potatoes disguised in one way or another. But these couples had their little escape, a private cooking operation—which even included quality meat on occasion. Walter sold cookware while Margaret worked as a typist in various offices and was a clerk in a department store downtown.

Margaret became involved deeply in campus life, especially in music, dramatics, and as president of the Women's Organization being advised by Professor Amy Lopez.[16] Working for Dean Olt and various faculty members, Margaret observed times when these people were faced with very critical attitudes from some leaders in the

ALMA MATER

Second stanza by A. Hoffmann
Presented by the Booster Club, 1939

First stanza and arrangement
by Donald Smith

church. How patient and gracious they managed to be! Meanwhile, Walter was too busy with classes and employment to be very involved in campus life, but he certainly benefited greatly by the rich human resources available to support his ministerial education. There, of course, were exceptional classroom models like Earl Martin and John Morrison. There also was E. E. Byrum, for whom on occasion Walter gladly skipped a class so that he could drive the aging man to a home where Byrum could pray the prayer of faith for someone's healing. In addition, there was the bedridden songwriter, C. W. Naylor, who lived near the campus. Walter and other students visited him occasionally and came away inspired. People like Martin, Morrison, Byrum, and Naylor modeled how to achieve despite obstacles. It was becoming an institutional way of life.

In managing triumph in the midst of trouble, the family of President Morrison was a prime example. John Morrison's vision for the school and his dogged determination that somehow it would succeed were central reasons that it did survive—and with increasing dignity. The Morrison family had come in 1919 when the school was nothing but a fragile experiment. The Morrisons were a happy family, poor economically, but busy gardening, canning, sewing, and cooking, with the children using the campus opposite their home as a convenient playground.

Daughter Mona, for instance, only a few weeks old when the family first had come to town, went through the local public school system. She walked downtown to the high school and there experienced some negative attitudes toward Church of God people, often considered those "peculiar specimens" from across the river on the east side. This tended to spoil her high school experience, although she excelled as a student and pianist. Her brother "Jiggs" (Earl) was hurt in a similar way and her sister Dorothy recalled that in the eyes of her high school classmates "it was almost a disgrace to be in the Church of God." But each managed to prove his or her worth and things slowly changed. Sister Vivian Jean, five years younger than Mona, became the high school's prom queen in 1941 (although she had to promise her father that she would not dance at the big event!).

In 1938 Mona and Dorothy roomed together as college students on the third floor of Old Main, Mona a junior and Dorothy a freshman. Mona, still very active as a musician, got a D in a course from the intimidating Dean Olt, a real shock after all her A's in high school. Dorothy worked in the dining hall and was a cheerleader, helping Jack Van Dyke and the others on to victory. But the girls were never far from home and they knew about some of the problems. That close vote over their father's ratification for another term as president in 1934 was painful for the family. Dorothy, a young teenager at the time, could not understand why anyone would be so mean as to attack her dear dad, who was giving his whole life for the school.

(Top) "New" gymnasium (originally campmeeting tabernacle, later Byrum Hall)
(Bottom) Gospel Trumpet Company barn, just south of present School of Theology building

But financial sacrifice, local prejudice against the eastside church people, and an occasional crisis in national church relations were not all of the problems. John Morrison struggled periodically with significant bouts of illness. In the spring of 1929, with the liberal arts program just begun and the crucial endowment campaign about to be launched, he fell seriously ill for one month with erysipelas, nearly dying.

Then in the summer of 1938, when the school was coming out of the Depression and prospects for the future were brightening, Morrison was examined for tuberculosis, was found to have scar tissue from the now arrested disease, and was advised to take a year of rest away from the college to prevent the otherwise likely return of the disease. Son Earl ("Jiggs") was married by then and on his own, Mona and Dorothy were across the street in college, and Vivian was beginning high school. John's leaving the Anderson community for a year would be disruptive for the family and maybe the school, but it seemed necessary. So Jiggs and his wife Louise moved into the Morrison home at 327 College Drive, keeping Vivian with them, and the other girls lived in Old Main while John and wife Eunice went on half salary from the college (a net of $60 a month), borrowed money to buy a trailer, and set out for sunny Arizona to stay with Anderson friends living there.

It was a sad September day when they drove away (a little like that sad fall day in 1923 when the J. T. Wilsons had driven away). The first stop was the little Morrison cottage in the Missouri Ozarks where they decided to stay until Christmas when the children could come to visit. They lived in the trailer and worked hard to winterize the cottage in preparation for the excitement of the children's coming. John's spirit, if not his body, found healing in these quiet and beautiful surroundings. Of this time he was to write later in his autobiography:

> In late November and early December the nights crackled with cold. The branch that babbled under the bridge between the trailer and cabin was frozen into silence. Ice crept out from the edges of the river until it was frozen almost across. The woods were silent as a cemetery, and most birds had flown far away with only an occasional woodpecker and a skeleton crew of crows and jay birds to guard the citadel of the forest (1962, 196).

After the Christmas holidays spent with the children (who had brought along a small gift from nearly every person on campus!) and the rest of the winter spent in Phoenix in the home of Elver F. Adcock (B. Th., 1921), it was back to Anderson and reasonable health—until the spring of 1946. President Morrison and the college he led already had survived many things, and certainly had matured in the process.

As the dark clouds of World War II gathered, the Anderson campus was dreaming of and seeking to prepare for a great future. Robert Reardon began as a freshman in 1936 when the liberal arts curriculum was still young and the Depression was still taking its heavy toll. Judging by external things like buildings and dollars, Reardon said, "in many ways Anderson College was a pitiful place." Fortunately, there sometimes are more important criteria by which to judge. Reardon stated it this way as, in 1983, he himself was about to retire as president and did some historical reflecting for the benefit of that later board of trustees. Regarding the school in the 1930s, he said:

> Going to Anderson College generally was considered a disgrace locally. But, strange as it seems, those of us who came as students began a life-long love affair with the place. We heard John Morrison's passionate call for a wedding of education and religion. We struggled and grew under Dean Olt's insistence on academic excellence. We were enchanted with the world of literature and poetry opened to us by Amy Lopez and challenged by the unforgettably great teaching of Carl Kardatzke, Earl Martin, Otto Linn, and others.

It was the greatness in the people which made the real difference. Reardon concluded with these words:

> We saw in them the ideal of faith, learning and sacrificial service.... It was Whitehead's "habitual vision of greatness." When this is present, such things as architecture, endowment, and accreditation are meaningless.[17]

1. It would not be until 1987 that Anderson University finally would become the official name of the institution.

2. See: *Broadcaster*, Aug., 1929 and Jan., 1930.

3. Final Report, President's Study and Planning Commission (1955-57), A1.

4. By Sept. of that fall the fund drive committee in the city had contacted the Gospel Trumpet Company, asking for its commitment to the campaign. On Oct. 2 the company voted to give $200 per year for three years to the young school that it had brought into being just a few years earlier.

5. Quoted from the script of a historical slide presentation, 1967, written by then president Robert H. Reardon.

6. *Signatures*, Summer, 1990, p. 19.

7. "My Pilgrimage," presented to Park Place Church of God, Feb. 17, 1991. He was the first of two Miller sons to come, Howard arriving in 1936. Their mother had been converted back in 1911 on the Oldham farm in Missouri where J. T. Wilson, later founding principal of the school, had been guest preacher (see chap. 3).

8. President's report to the trustees, June 13, 1931, p. 3.

9. In the Spring of 1935 student Al Brown convinced President Morrison to hire him as the school bread baker beginning in the fall (he had never baked bread before). Al learned baking from a baker at home over the summer, then did it very well for two years, even becoming manager of the school dining hall. It was still in the basement of Old Main "where the cockroaches ran

rampant." During Al's years the cafeteria system replaced family style serving. Schedules had made it difficult for all students to be available at the same time and some took advantage of the family-style serving, getting more than their share of food.

10. The May, 1970, issue of *AC News* carried an extensive story about the men of this quartet, nearly 42 years after they had begun singing together. Pictured in Dale Oldham's *Giants Along My Path* (Anderson, Ind: Warner Press, 1973) is what he identified as "the first A. B. T. S. male quartet," consisting of Charles Smith, first tenor, Dale Oldham, second tenor, Homer Byers, baritone, and John Settlemyre, bass.

11. For a brief period in the earliest sports days, the campus teams were known as the "Moundbuilders," prominent imagery both in the history of the city of Anderson and, of course, back in Moundsville, W. V., from which the publishing company had come to Anderson. But "Tigers" soon seemed more graphic and vigorous, and then "Ravens" came along as the long-term name. This name, as Robert Reardon recalled, came from a contest won by the manager of the Penney's store in downtown Anderson.

12. This team defeated the "Armory" team in a practice game on April 23, with David Gaulke catching, Kenneth Ahrendt at second base, and Herbert Thompson at third.

13. Howard's brother T. Franklin had come as a student in 1929. Now Howard had his opportunity, starting with this summer job of construction on campus.

14. The ceiling reported to be only about twelve feet high, so that no real arch could be put on a shot except from quite close to the basket. The new gym (later Byrum Hall) possessed its own distinctive characteristics, which also had an effect on basketball play. Often, visiting teams would come out on the floor and ask when the lights were going to be turned on. What lights there were already were on!

15. See Barry L, Callen, *Listening to the Word of God*, especially pp. 1-12.

16. Miss Lopez was described by Mona Morrison Hoffman, one of President Morrison's daughters, as "absolutely a queen." She had a wonderful British accent, and when she read Shakespeare aloud it "would send chills up your spine." She was a pervasive and cultured presence on campus, teaching in the classroom, instructing in table manners in the cafeteria, and advising in various aspects of student life.

17. President Reardon's final report to the board of trustees, April 22, 1983.

6 Building Sturdy Foundations
1941-1947

"The administration is forward-looking."
(North Central Association,
visiting team report, 1946)

The major campus goals of the 1930s had been slowed in their accomplishment because of the Depression. Most were continued into the 1940s. Remaining as central aspirations were the building of good and mutually beneficial relationships with the larger Anderson community, the general academic community, and the Church of God across the nation. In 1938 President Morrison began pointing toward the school's silver anniversary to be celebrated in 1941-1942. That special occasion would be designated as a time for the school both to look back with gratitude and launch bold new initiatives for the future. It would be a time of building sturdy foundations on which could rest a greatly enlarged future.

Silver Anniversary Time

President John Morrison announced to the board of trustees in his June, 1938, annual report and to the Church of God through a major article in the *Gospel Trumpet* (May 14, 1938, 9, 14), that he intended to have several key goals reached by 1942. Student enrollment was one. From the annual student enrollment total of 355 that he had reported for 1937-38 (a school record to that date), he looked to a coming total of some

500. More young people now were in the church, college education was becoming more important in the society, and, said Morrison, such education should be pursued "in an atmosphere conducive to religious faith."

As the student numbers would increase, the need for increased residence hall space would increase also. In fact, the school already had been notified in 1938 by local authorities that the fourth floor of Old Main would have to be evacuated because no suitable fire escapes existed (twenty-five single men were being housed there).[1] Housing even more students, however, would have to be complemented with an increasing ability to serve them well. Therefore, Morrison continued, somehow the school's indebtedness of "several thousand dollars" should be eliminated and "alumni all over America [must] recognize that a large part of the responsibility for furthering their *alma mater* rests upon them." Meanwhile, the president assured the church, the intent was not to de-emphasize ministerial education. It rather was to stress it more than ever. This called for the projecting of a final goal, the raising of a ministerial loan fund to assist such students who, it was said, often "are rich in spiritual and intellectual endowment, but who are poor in this world's goods."

Such goals, insisted Morrison, were realistic, especially if the Depression would ease its terrible grip on the nation's economy. That grip indeed would be eased. Unfortunately for the school and millions of people worldwide, "prosperity" soon would come at an awful price. The world was about to go back to war. Shortly after the school had begun in 1917, many young men had been called from their studies, some to pay the ultimate price in their nation's service, never receiving the opportunity to complete an education. It was about to happen again. This time, when it finally would be over in 1945, many military veterans would flood onto the Anderson campus, often married, more mature, motivated, and with government assistance for their education. The campus would adjust as necessary and manage to serve with distinction.

With the president's goals in mind, the silver anniversary year of celebration approaching, and the horror of war in the air, the school's alumni association set an ambitious goal of raising an anniversary gift of twenty-five thousand dollars. That amount would eliminate all of the school's indebtedness, help meet its current operational needs, and provide for additional program expansion, all looking ahead toward the big goal of North Central accreditation sometime in the new decade. It surely was a time of real challenge and vigorous activity for a young alumni organization.

I. K. Dawson (B. Th., 1928, 1944), first executive secretary of the alumni association (see Table 10), had prepared a manual for presidents of state and district alumni associations because he knew that the executive committee of the national organization could work effectively only if such units were helped to be effective. By the spring of 1942 he noted that "at least eleven local units were organized and more or less active."

They were Anderson, Eastern States, Illinois, Indiana, Iowa, Kansas, Michigan, Minnesota, Mississippi, Ohio, and Kentucky. The association asked Amy Phillips to help prepare a comprehensive alumni directory to be published in the 1942 *Echoes,* the silver anniversary edition of the school's annual. It also decided to publish an attractive calendar calling the 1917-1942 years faithful and fruitful ones that had seen eight hundred graduates and a thousand former students, "pastors, evangelists, missionaries, teachers, executives, leaders all." The reported total of eight hundred graduates itself may have been a little "evangelistic" since the records of the registrar's office show that through 1946 only 735 degrees and diplomas were granted, including 422 bachelors degrees, 25 honorary degrees, 65 two-year certificates, 26 three-year diplomas, and 197 other certificates and diplomas. But evangelistic enthusiasm was then the mood in alumni circles! Aspiration and actuality apparently blended just a little on occasion.

A quarter of a century already had passed for the school. It now was time to remember, give thanks, and plan for much higher aspirations in the future. Most of those first twenty-five years had been difficult financially, some desperate. But the administration always had been determined, most members of the campus community had sacrificed as necessary, the church had remained supportive despite some vigorous disagreements, and the growing number of alumni had proved loyal and increasingly generous.

Persons had made the key difference from the beginning. By silver anniversary time the prominent persons in the national alumni program were W. Dale Oldham, Ohio pastor, Ida Byrd Rowe, editor of the Gospel Trumpet Company's *Young People's Friend,* John H. Kane, Michigan pastor whose alumni activity dated back to 1928, Amy Phillips, still active after having been elected the first alumni president in 1921, and I. K. Dawson, first full-time director of the alumni program beginning in 1941. A review of the presidents of the alumni association over those first twenty-five years reveals the names of these and other persons soon to become almost legendary in the history of the school and often in the Church of God at large (see Table 10).

More persons now were coming to the campus with no roots in the school's past but with potential for being significant to the school's future. One was young Robert A. Nicholson.[2] He came as a freshman in 1940 from a Church of God family in St. Paul Park, Minnesota, had no previous involvement in higher education. In his formative years, however, Nicholson's family had been pastored by two Anderson graduates, Max Gaulke (B. A., 1933) and Clair Shultz (B. A., 1936; B. Th., 1939). Later both were pleased to take credit for the decision that took young Robert to the Anderson campus.[3] Mrs. Nicholson visited her son's assigned room in the "Barnitory" over the old campground dining hall[4] and, understandably, was displeased with such makeshift quarters for her only child. But he would adapt, share a room with new friend, Maurice Berquist, for his final three years, excel with his natural academic ability, slowly emerge from his

TABLE 10

Leaders of Alumni Activities

Early Presidents of the Alumni Association

1921-22	Amy Phillips	1930-31	W. Dale Oldham
1922-23	Grace Phelps	1931-32	Lawrence Brooks
1923-24	Elver Adcock	1932-33	Walter Shriner
1924-25	John Ludwig	1933-34	Virgil Johnson
1925-26	Mack Caldwell	1934-35	Carl Kardatzke
1926-27	Elizabeth Jackson	1935-37	John Lackey
1927-28	Walter Haldeman	1937-41	George Edes
1928-29	John Kane	1941-44	W. Dale Oldham
1929-30	Carl Kardatzke	1944-48	George Blackwell

Alumni Executive Directors

1941-44	I. K. Dawson	1972-75	James Edwards
1944-60	John H. Kane	1975-77	David Edwards
1960-66	Joseph Espey	1978-80	(transitional)
1966-67	W. Shirell Fox (Acting)	1980-82	Trudi Hoffman Fulda
1967-69	Calvin Hanson	1982-84	(transitional)
1969-72	Helen Achor Shoemaker	*1984-	Michael Eastman

*In 1989 the alumni organizations of the college and seminary were merged into one body. Presidents of this unified associations have been James Martin (1987-90), Beth Stiers (1990-1992) and Lloyd Larson (1992 to present).

social awkwardness, and learn to accept his not being athletically gifted. His would be a great contribution to the school in the decades yet to come.

Nicholson's student experience reflected much about the level of maturity of the school at the time. He was voted into the Booster Club and found a warm, lifelong group of new friends like Milton Buettner and Arthur Eikamp, who all were learning to love this school. He helped staff the little Booster concession stand in the lobby of Old Main where the club sold "candy, Ping-Pong balls, and other necessities of life." A student deferment kept him in school when the war began, allowing him to go to the basketball games with nearly everyone else left on campus, work at the East Side Jersey Dairy, and be bored by the annual chapel talk of the local fire chief. Young Nicholson was very active musically, both on campus and in the city, drew great strength from the ministries

(Left) In 1947 Bessie Byrum, original faculty member, assisted President Morrison with the celebration of 30 years of school life
(Inset) President Morrison and I. K. Dawson celebrate the school's
Silver Anniversary in 1942

of nearby Park Place Church of God, and found his future wife in the student body (Dorothy Nelis from Dayton, Ohio). The school may have been young, but Nicholson's was a full, life-changing, and rather typical experience.

That life-changing experience was social, spiritual, and academic. The intensity and person-centered, often family-like nature of campus life brought to students like Nicholson substantial social growth.

Spiritually, the Student Volunteer Movement was still an influential force on campus. At a Religious Emphasis Week service during semester two of his freshman year, Robert Nicholson experienced a "true conversion" that stabilized his spiritual life and allowed him to focus on future vocation. The student speaker at that service was Geraldine Hurst (Reardon), a gifted young preacher who later would be campus first lady as wife of President Robert H. Reardon.

Academically, Nicholson managed to complete three majors, mathematics, history, and education. Each of these was essentially a major taught by one faculty person, with Joseph Wiley teaching the math, Frederick Schminke the history, and Carl Kardatzke[5] the education. Generally, Nicholson recalled, the quality of the classes was excellent. There was obvious weakness in all courses in a major being taught by one person. But at least these were outstanding persons. Soon regional accreditation would come, based in part on the quality of the instructional staff (see Table 12). When Nicholson, only months after his college graduation, found himself doing graduate work at New York University en route to his return as a faculty member, he was pleased to find that all of his work at Anderson was accepted in transfer, even though that undergraduate work was not accredited.[6] Accreditation, however, now was not far away.

Achieving Full Accreditation

Regional accreditation had been an aspiration of Dean Olt since the first day he had arrived on campus in 1925. The school back then had had a long way to go in meeting the necessary qualifications. Progress had been slowed by the severe resource limitations imposed by the Depression. Nonetheless, in 1935 President Morrison told the board of trustees that genuine progress finally was being made. He and Dean Olt, for instance, had just visited academic leaders at Indiana University and had received written assurance from them that Anderson students would receive full credit for work at Anderson if they transferred to and then performed satisfactorily at that state university. A series of other institutions already had said and even done precisely that. The reason usually was said to be recognition "of the high grade of academic work done by our professors."

The first formal breakthrough came in 1937. Mr. Arthur Campbell, superintendent of the Anderson public schools and friend of the college, was appointed by the governor to the State Department of Education. There he took initiative on behalf of the local college. In May there was an official campus inspection, and on June 4 the State

Cafeteria, lower level of Old Main, with student Robert Nicholson far right

(Top) Chapel session, northwest wing, main floor of Old Main, 1936. President Morrison speaking. Seated in front row (left) : Carl Kardatzke, Frederick Schminke, Dean Russell Olt, Otto F. Linn, Walter Haldeman
(Bottom) Chapel Session, 1950s, sanctuary of Park Place Church of God (Eighth and College) Faculty seated in choir loft as then typical

Department approved accreditation of the Anderson campus for the preparation of secondary teachers in public schools. Morrison told the college board that this recognition "will be a great boon to us in getting students and in keeping the respect of students once they are on the campus." The following year Arthur Campbell was granted an honorary Doctor of Laws degree by a truly grateful Anderson campus (see Appendix P).

So the decade of the 1930s had closed with limited state-level accreditation and

TABLE 11

Seven-Year Record of Financial Progress

	1943-44	1944-45	1945-46	1946-47	1947-48	1948-49	1949-50
Semester One Enrollment	508	536	479	800	857	831	825

INCOME (Percentages of total shown in parentheses)

	1943-44	1944-45	1945-46	1946-47	1947-48	1948-49	1949-50
Student Fees	80,466 (43.4)	98,392 (45.5)	96,220 (43.2)	183,978 (48.0)	225,525 (52.1)	232,381 (53.4)	251,171 (53.8)
Endowment	749 (0.4)	1,848 (0.9)	2,377 (0.10)	2,750 (0.71)	1,104 (0.25)	*1,193 (0.19)	3,752 (0.87)
Contributions Alumni	7,158 (3.93)	11,954 (5.53)	10,220 (4.59)	19,976 (5.21)	17,760 (4.10)	17,757 (4.08)	12,069 (2.58)
Other Contributions including World Service	27,656 (14.9)	42,685 (19.8)	55,639 (24.4)	54,204 (14.1)	57,483 (13.44)	54,033 (12.4)	54,319 (11.7)
Auxiliary Enterprises	63,881 (34.6)	52,915 (24.4)	56,218 (24.6)	105,822 (27.6)	109,098 (25.2)	111,147 (25.5)	133,171 (28.5)
Miscellaneous	5,144 (2.77)	8,200 (3.87)	7,104 (3.11)	16,187 (4.38)	21,233 (4.91)	20,966 (4.81)	11,901 (2.55)
TOTAL INCOME	185,054	215,994	227,778	382,917	432,203	435,091	466,383
TOTAL EXPENSES	159,758	185,639	223,843	319,585	405,949	449,712	476,388
SURPLUS or (DEFICIT)	25,296	30,355	3,935	63,332	26,254	(14,621)	(10,005)

the president's judgment expressed to the board in 1941 that "during the years since the close of the Depression we have made a steady advancement on all sides. True, that advancement has not been spectacular, but it has been deep-rooted and healthy." The biggest success was the systematic strengthening of the faculty, with 1939 showing fourteen full-time instructors, twelve holding either an earned master's or doctor's degree. A sturdy faculty foundation was being built.

The biggest challenge remaining, except for finances in general, was a significant upgrading of the library. As early as 1933 when Professor Walter Haldeman had joined the faculty and accepted the library responsibility on a part-time basis, the push had been on to build the meager book collection. Many used books were purchased to stretch modest budget dollars. When Warner Memorial University had closed in Texas in 1933, alumnus Elver Adcock, then with the Board of Church Extension and Home Missions of the Church of God, and Professor Carl Kardatzke drove a truck to Texas and came back to Anderson with about three thousand volumes. Growth would come in whatever ways possible.

There was a flurry of activity on the library front as the decade of the 1940s opened. A special campaign for new library holdings had been conducted in the city during 1939-40, involving representatives of groups like the Chamber of Commerce, the YMCA and the Council of Church Women. About five thousand dollars were raised. Along with this success came the announcement that the library soon would be moved up to the fourth floor of Old Main where there would be room for twenty-five thousand volumes and study space for 150 students. The necessary remodeling was done during the summer of 1940 at a cost of nine thousand dollars, including development of the new library space and renovation of the old library on the second floor into four new classrooms.

"When college opened in the fall of that year," reported the president proudly, "new and returning students were as amazed as they were happy to see what an inviting place had been made of an unsightly attic" (*Alumni News* April, 1956, 2). The shelves now carried some fourteen thousand volumes. In June of 1941 the school applied to the Indiana State Department of Education for the extension of its accreditation to the preparation of grade school teachers. The president assured the board that the main goal, full membership in the North Central Association of Secondary Schools and Colleges, now could be as little as two or three years away.

Systematic work toward this significant goal was underway. In the 1941-42 year alone the school developed a physics lab on the fourth floor of Old Main, bought the Enoch Byrum home, developing it into Kemp Hall for use by the music department, introduced a formalized retirement plan for faculty and staff employees through the Teachers Annuity and Insurance Association, and welcomed to campus Dr. John Dale Russell of the University of Chicago. Russell, a regular campus inspector for North Central, had been invited to come with two assistants to do a detailed study of the readiness of the campus for a full accreditation visit. He prepared a chart rating quantitatively the school's status in relation to the range of North Central's evaluation categories. The

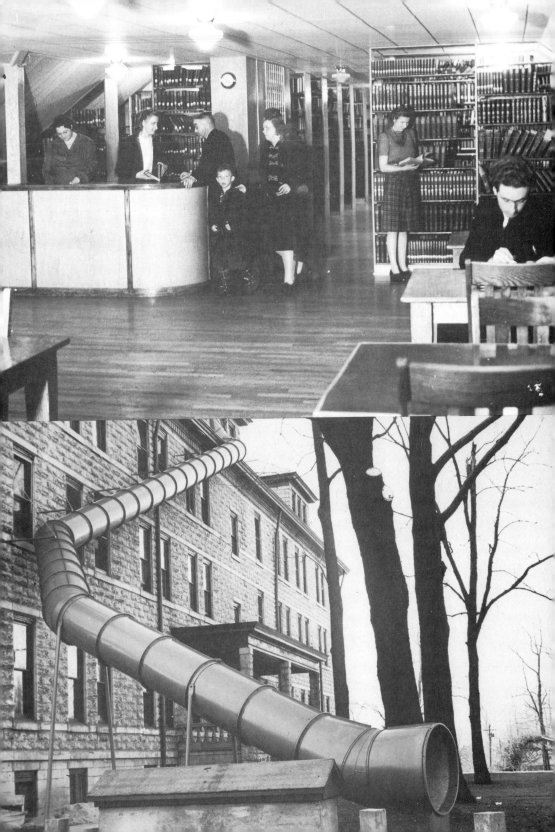

strength of the school, as noted in the subsequent Russell report, was the faculty's academic preparation, more than enjoyed by the faculties of many schools already accredited (see Table 12). The primary weaknesses cited were the expected ones, finances and library. School indebtedness was not great, but neither was gift income to support growing operating expenses (see Table 11).

President Morrison was encouraged about the prospects of better income, in part because of the recent work of the alumni association. In January, 1941, I. K. Dawson had joined the staff as the first executive secretary of the alumni association. As an experienced pastor, alumnus, trustee, and skilled promoter, the intent was for him to direct an accelerated effort to mobilize the growing body of alumni on behalf of the school. Action was to begin immediately with the school's silver anniversary year. By June, 1942, the president was expressing gratitude for the association's helpfulness financially, in student recruitment and in church relations. "The general morale throughout the church," he told the board, "is the best it has been in the history of the institution. This morale is partially due to the far-flung operations of the Alumni Office."

John H. Kane (B. Th., 1921, 1933) came to campus in September, 1944, to assume Dawson's responsibilities with the alumni association. At the end of Kane's first year he reported that giving to the Alumni Fund had risen from an annual total in 1939-40 of $3,789 to $16,264 in 1944-45 ($5,000 of which was designated for new library books). Kane was enthusiastic and aggressive in getting the accomplishments and needs of the school before alumni and the church in general. The circulation of the *Alumni News* publication, for instance, increased in Kane's first year from six thousand to ten thousand. Meanwhile, a similar thrust was being mounted in the city of Anderson. In 1944-45 a new Department of Public Relations was established on campus under the direction of E. J. Ronsheim, a local newspaperman. The public needed to be better informed about the maturing life of this special institution located on the east side of town. Ronsheim functioned very helpfully, retired in 1948, and was replaced by W. Shirell Fox (B. A., '50), still a student, a former G. I., and an experienced young newspaperman from nearby Alexandria, Indiana. From that time until his retirement in 1985, Fox would serve three presidents faithfully and be a key informational liaison between the campus and its publics. His outstanding service would be recognized at his retirement with the honorary Doctor of Laws degree (see Appendix P).

In the summer of 1942 the president also announced immediate action to further address the continuing library needs. The Russell report had recommended the employment of a full time and properly trained librarian and reclassification of all holdings from

(Top) Library, fourth floor of Old Main
(Bottom) Emergency fire escape from fourth floor of Old Main

TABLE 12

College Faculty, 1945

According to the catalog published in April, 1945, with announcements for 1945-46, the year North Central accreditation first was achieved, the following were the full-time faculty members. Each is listed with teaching field, highest earned degree, and in the order of catalog presentation.

Names	Teaching Fields		Highest Degrees
G. Russell Olt	Dean, Philosophy, Psychology		M. A.
Henry C. Clausen	Music, Vocal and Theory	M. Mus.	
Earl L. Martin	Bible, Applied Theology	M. A.	
Anna E. Koglin	Greek, German		M. A.
Cecil H. Hartselle	Music, Piano and Voice	M. Mus.	
Walter S. Haldeman	Religious Education		M.S. in Ed.
Carl H. Kardatzke	Education		Ph.D.
Vila Deubach	English		Ph.D.
Joseph W. Wiley	Mathematics, Physics	M. A.	
Frederick A. Schminke	History	D. l'univ.	
Paul Breitweiser	Music, Piano and Theory	M. Mus.	
Adam W. Miller	New Testament		M. A.
Charles E. Brown	Theology		(D. D.)
Clifton W. White	Physical Education		Ed. D.
Clarice M. Robinson	Business Education		Ed. D.
Lester W. Roubey	French, Speech		Ph. D.
Atwell M. Wallace	Biology, Chemistry		Ph. D.
Julia Eaton	English, Speech		Ph. D.
Nancy F. Osborne	Romance Languages	Ph. D.	
Virginia M. Bryant	English		Ph. D.
Ruthven H. Byrum	Art		B. A.
Alice L. Foudy	Piano		B. Mus.
Robert A. Nicholson	Choral Music and Theory	B. S.	

Total 23. Doctorates, 10. Masters, 9. Other, 4 (including C. E. Brown who was editor of the publishing company and only an occasional lecturer at the college).

The 1941 North Central Manual listed average percentages of faculty holding earned doctorates in various types of institutions then accredited by it. For privately controlled
liberal arts colleges, the percentage was 26.89, a level exceeded considerably by Anderson in 1945.

the Dewey Decimal to the Library of Congress system. By the following year Miss Glennie Norman, holder of a degree in library science, was supervising the library full-time. The following year she was replaced by Wilma E. Ponder who was to function as librarian for over a decade. In June 1946 the book holdings were reported to number only 13,899. The proposed reclassification to the Library of Congress system also would get done, but not until the 1980s.

All along, Dean Olt in particular had labored to bring the faculty and curriculum to new levels of maturity, always keeping a careful eye on the published accreditation standards of North Central.[7] Robert Reardon later summarized it this way: "Dean Olt, an academician, schooled in the German tradition, knew where he was headed, straight into the doors of North Central Association. . . . Early on he familiarized himself with their standards and all academic decisions were adjudicated thereby. . . . His teaching methods were based on fear and intimidation, yet there was such an air of moral and academic greatness about the man that we grudgingly endured it all."[8]

The academic program in 1945-46 included the 124-hour degrees bachelor of arts, bachelor of science, bachelor of theology, and combined arts-theology, as well as programs leading to a two-year certificate and a three-year diploma. The B. A. program reflected especially high academic standards, designed with attention given to North Central expectations. For graduation, either one major and two minors or two majors were required, with a series of related definitions and restrictions in place. If, for instance, a B. Th. graduate also wished to pursue the B. A., an additional thirty hours had to be taken subsequently, including a minimum of twenty-four more hours in residence. A range of course requirements were specified, including a foreign language. Premedical and preengineering tracks had been developed and publicized for interested students.

The Bachelor of Science curriculum offered fields of specialization in business education, teacher training, music, and religious education. The college was certified by the Indiana State Department of Education to prepare teachers for junior and senior high schools (see Table 1). Elementary education students still had to transfer elsewhere for their final two years. Ministerial education had two available tracks. One was the B. Th. program.

The other, reflecting a continuing commitment to emphasis on the liberal arts and a graduate dimension to an ideal ministerial preparation, was a five-year program involving the B. A. and then a B. Th. taken as a fifth or graduate year. This latter, combined track was "recommended to students of promise for the ministry of the Church of God" (1945-46 Catalog, 73).

The certificate and diploma programs were for older students who sometimes lacked a high school diploma and yet desired Christian service, often bi-vocational, and

(Left)   President Morrison and Dean Olt, 1946
(Bottom, right) Late night celebration
          at the Anderson train station

looked for "an opportunity to train for better service though they serve in a limited way" (74). All instruction was organized by "Divisions," namely, humanities, sciences, social sciences, Bible and religion, and music. Such structuring, while of descriptive use, had little or no functional meaning.

Student enrollment in 1944-45 reflected a growing student body comprised predominantly of women (many men were in the armed services) and men with ministerial deferments. Clearly the school was national in scope, with students coming particularly from states where the Church of God constituency was largest. Indiana led with 210, then came Ohio with 62, Michigan 45, Pennsylvania 27, Kansas 25, Oklahoma 23, and so on.

Table 12 identifies the teaching faculty in place as the potential of accreditation increased. In large part the academic preparation and teaching commitment of these people, combined with respected and visionary executive leadership, soon would qualify the school for full accreditation. The large majority of the faculty were people associated with the Church of God and, as the president told the board of trustees in June, 1944: "Owned, operated and supported as we are by the Church of God, we think that it is only consistent that the bulk of the teaching staff be made up of Church of God men and

150

women." Noting, however, that he and the dean now were reluctant to appoint new faculty members without the earned doctorate because of accreditation standards,[9] the president admitted that finding qualified Church of God people had become difficult, especially in the sciences.

The quest for regional accreditation had been long and hard, but finally it was about to succeed. Following a campus visit by North Central inspectors Dr. H. C. Coffman, president of George Williams College in Chicago, and Dr. Theodore P. Stephens, president of Aurora College in Aurora, Illinois, the time came in March 1946 for the Association's meeting in Chicago. President Morrison and Dean Olt journeyed north by train. Morrison wrote in his personal journal while riding on the train, Sunday afternoon, March 24: "Dean and I appear before the Board of Review tomorrow afternoon. *Will We Make It?* I Don't know. We at least have a chance." They met that board, then had to wait two days in Chicago for the fateful decision.

The decision was affirmative! Wrote Morrison in his journal: "What a relief. Now after all these years of struggle we are fully accredited. Dean and I came at once up to the room to phone the news to the College. Supposed to have a full headline in the *Herald.*"

And indeed, there it was in the *Anderson Herald,* March 28, 1946. A very bold headline on page one read: "ANDERSON COLLEGE IN TOP RANK." Along with photos of Morrison and Olt was a feature story leading with the subtitle, "Institution Takes Place Among Academic Leaders in Country." Obviously the city of Anderson was genuinely proud. Twenty-nine years earlier when the school had first opened, the local newspaper had taken no note at all. Back then the school was seen as having no public consequence. Now it did.

The scene soon to follow was unforgettable, one of those truly magic moments in the school's whole history. Morrison and Olt boarded the train home at 9:20 P. M. on Wednesday and, half asleep, arrived at the Anderson station at 2:00 A. M. the next morning. Here is what Morrison's personal journal entry of March 29 said about what happened next. "Dean and I got off and what did we see? Five or six hundred students and teachers with the college band—all jubilant over the fact that Anderson College had been fully accredited. We formed a long and noisy procession up Eighth Street and College Drive to the Main Building and hundreds of them crowded into the lobby to hear a short talk by the Dean and me. We went to bed at 4:00 A. M. I did not sleep until 6:00. We got up at 8:00. We met at chapel at 9:30 and I spoke for 30 minutes on the meaning of our new accomplishment.... No school today. Dr. Martin had announced a full holiday."

Seniors like Howard Miller had been in that joyous night parade. They were so excited that their degrees would be accredited! A freshman like Lucille Strawn, later to be school registrar (1974-1989), would never forget the excitement of that late-night march. Glenn Falls, a former G. I. now on campus, a man who one day would be a long-term and influential business faculty member (1952-1987),[10] marched in the parade and shared the joy. Shirell Fox, who soon would begin work as a long-term director of publicity for the school, had just come to campus that semester as a recent G. I. For years to come he would have relatives who teasingly would announce that his arrival finally had made the accreditation possible! Neighboring Taylor University in Upland, Indiana, received its regional accreditation by North Central only in 1947.[11] That school was much older than the one in Anderson. In fact it had a fully developed program by the time of Anderson's beginning in 1917. But Anderson had managed to mature rapidly to the point of accreditation despite all the limitations. That maturity now was a good foundation for much more yet to come.

What President Morrison said in that historic morning chapel revolved around gratitude for the past, excitement about the present, and firm resolve about accomplishing the very much that yet lay ahead. The North Central report, while recommending accreditation, nonetheless had cited the school's considerable facility needs as the campus was growing in numbers of students. It also had noted the range and quality of academic offerings. So the president spoke directly and optimistically about such future challenges. Morrison's intent was to build, in the years just ahead, student residence halls, a library, a science building and a physical education plant. There even would be, he said, the launching of a "School of Theology" to operate fully at the graduate level. The largeness of this vision was more evidence of something the North Central examiners had applauded in their accreditation report: "The administration," they had said so rightly, "is forward looking." In fact, somewhat earlier, President Morrison had offered to resign his office, thinking that his own educational background, so lacking in academic degrees, would hinder the final achievement of accreditation. The expressed North Central opinion, however, was that this unusual man was a key asset of the school, one it could not afford to lose. So his resignation offer was dismissed as a generous gesture and a very bad idea.

On June 14, 1946, President Morrison explained to the college board of trustees that the war had caused North Central to discourage schools from making application for accreditation. But that had changed beginning in July, 1945, and the backlog that had developed accounted for the unusual number of twenty-six schools that had applied during 1945-46. Anderson had moved immediately, bringing an academic leader from Miami University in Ohio to survey carefully the status of the campus in relation to North Central's many standards. This survey updated the Russell report of three years earlier. Dr. Russell, who knew the campus well from his earlier visit, now was

Student James Macholtz in early chemistry lab in Old Main

152

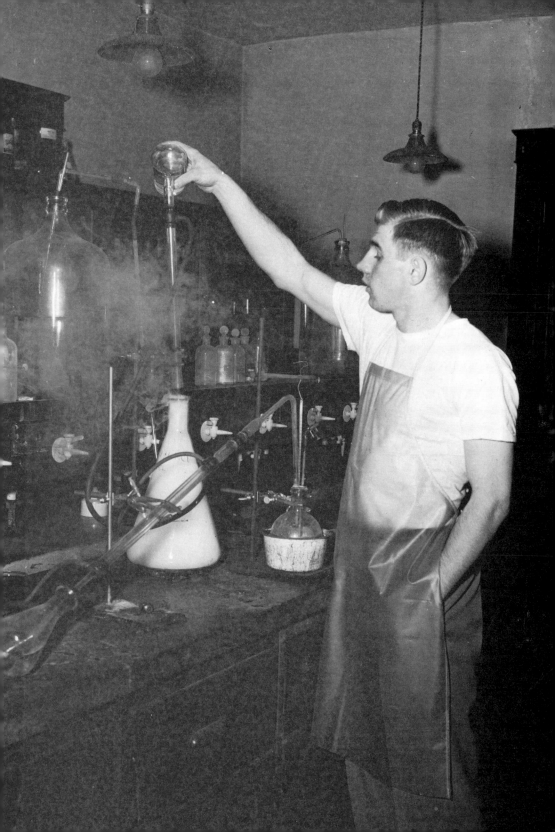

Executive Secretary of North Central. Of the twenty-six applicants that year, only seven institutions were admitted to membership—and, of course, Anderson had been one. North Central records indicate that an "advisory committee" was named by the Association to continue monitoring beyond accreditation various concerns about the development of the Anderson campus. This committee's reports were accepted by North Central in 1947 and 1949, when it was disbanded with no further action. Another formal North Central visit would not be scheduled until a full accreditation review would come a decade after the last advisory committee report.

The president certainly had visionary plans, but the strain of it all made an unwelcome and untimely appearance in his quite fragile body. Arthritis brought him great discomfort and at times considerable loss of mobility. The months ahead were filled with periods of intense suffering and resulting depression. It became necessary for Earl Martin to function as acting president from June, 1946, until April, 1947. Morrison appeared in chapel on April 23, 1947, to attend a brief ceremony marking his official return. Greeted with hearty applause, he also managed, with crutches, to be on the commencement platform to introduce the speaker, D. Elton Trueblood. By July of 1947, Robert H. Reardon had arrived from his pastorate in Pennsylvania to bring welcome help as a presidential assistant. A dark year in the president's life was ending, with many challenges just ahead and fresh administrative help now at his side.

We Need Our Own Seminary

The long-range North Central accreditation goal had finally been achieved. Administrative attention and institutional resources had been focused for years on broadening and strengthening the programs, personnel, policies, and supportive resources required to satisfy the requirements of such an important institutional recognition. Eventual success had been a real accomplishment, thought by some to have come at too high a price. Two central concerns of Professor Otto F. Linn and of some influential church leaders in the 1930s had been voiced occasionally. In the press for accreditation, feared some, serious church relatedness might be compromised and a primary focus on ministerial education likely would be sacrificed. Thanks in large part to the strong and balanced church and academic commitments of the Morrison-Olt leadership team, however, the first of these concerns was avoided largely and the second, always resisted, at least in principle, now would be addressed directly by the emerging dream of establishing on campus a true graduate School of Theology. The coming 1950-51 Bulletin of

(Top) President Morrison appears in chapel in his wheelchair, February, 1947.
Dean Olt and Robert Nicholson, future dean and president, seated to right
(Bottom) Earl L. Martin as Acting President during Morrison's illness

the School of Theology, its first, would attribute the seminary's eventual founding to "repeated and insistent requests of the ministers on the field." The real burden for a graduate seminary, however, had rested primarily on the hearts of men like Earl Martin, T. Franklin Miller, Adam Miller, John Morrison, Gene Newberry, Russell Olt, Harold Phillips, and Robert Reardon. That burden had not been mere personal preference, but rather a strong conviction which had been strengthened by a series of rather dramatic and sometimes painful circumstances.

A worldwide sense of relief had followed the end of World War II in 1945. Hope was reborn and for millions of people, whose existence had been completely disrupted, it was time to get on with life. In the United States the G. I. Bill was passed and large numbers of soldiers, sailors, and airmen exchanged their military uniforms and weapons for school books and college campuses. The mood was expansive and aggressive. On the Anderson campus the achieving of accreditation by the North Central Association in 1946 had been the realization of a long-standing dream, an outside validation of quality about to be enjoyed by many new and often older students. The foundation finally had been laid and larger things soon would be built on it.

But dissident voices were being heard in the Church of God. They began speaking loudly enough that there was considerable disruption of the church's life, both at local and national levels, particularly in the 1945-1948 period. The central concerns centered in the fear of some ministers that the perspectives of the Church of God movement's pioneers were being "liberalized" and the Anderson-based church agencies, the "headquarters people," were growing so powerful and even arrogant that they were beginning to strangle the church like an "ecclesiastical octopus." While this criticism was not directed primarily at the Anderson campus,[12] a constant irritation to many pastors was the practice the campus then maintained of ordaining its own ministerial graduates when they received their degrees. Thus these graduates went out to pastor with both academic and church credentials, not needing to stand the judgment of older and often less educated ministerial colleagues.[13]

The chief voice of concern was L. Earl Slacum, a 1926 graduate of the Anderson campus. Eventually the main charges were rejected for the most part by the General Ministerial Assembly and the opposition leaders were neutralized, although not satisfied in many cases.

Much pain and many broken relationships resulted in this awkward process. Among the leaders of the Anderson agencies, however, the result tended to be a welding together of persons whose work had been under vigorous attack. They became a strong and united community as never before. Many of them had experienced personally the advantages of higher education and tended to judge that some of the church's recent problems came out of simple ignorance and lack of exposure to and appropriate appreciation for alternative viewpoints and ways of operating. A natural conclusion was that finding a way to develop a better educated ministry was crucial to the church's future. Several of these national leaders already had gone somewhere to seminary themselves, and they were very sympathetic to the idea of a new seminary being started in Anderson.

President John A. Morrison, limited in his own formal education, initially had little direct awareness of the nature and potential of graduate theological education (despite the earlier B. D. program on campus). But in 1942 Robert Reardon, a 1940 Anderson College graduate and now a graduate student at Oberlin Graduate School of Theology in Ohio and pastor of a small congregation near that campus, invited Morrison to preach a week's revival for him. A room was arranged on the Oberlin campus, and during those days young Reardon and President Morrison talked much, attended a few classes together taught by prominent professors, and had a good exchange with Oberlin president Ernest Hatch Wilkins about matters of common concern. Morrison appeared to be impressed, stimulated, and certainly held his own very effectively in lively exchange with his fellow president. He now had walked the same campus that Charles Finney and Church of God pioneer Daniel S. Warner had walked many years before. It was a good place, an exciting model of effective ministerial education.

This probably was the time that Morrison began to reflect seriously on whether such a seminary program should be in Anderson's future. He was impressed by Robert Reardon, whom he had known as a boy and college student and whose minister father was a dear friend. He probably also noted privately the possibility of this vibrant graduate student, organist, and pastor one day having some important leadership role to play back on the Anderson campus.[14] Further, both Oberlin and Butler University's School of Religion in nearby Indianapolis were seminaries organized in a way that easily could become Anderson's model, that is, not an independent seminary, but a seminary in a single campus structure, jointly governed by one president and board of trustees in coordination with an undergraduate college.

By June, 1947, just before Robert Reardon arrived back on campus to give Morrison some valuable administrative assistance, a campus committee comprised of Adam Miller (chair), Russell Olt, Dale Oldham, C. Lowery Quinn, and John Kane reported to the board of trustees on evolving plans for the possible establishing of graduate ministerial study in Anderson.[15] This report noted considerable interest in this possibility being expressed by potential students, and it stated why such a graduate school was thought to be needed. In part the report read as follows:

> Since the Church has not been able to offer its ministerial students anything beyond the five years of training now set up at Anderson College and Theological Seminary, many of our very fine students have gone to such seminaries as Oberlin Graduate School of Theology, Butler University

School of Religion, Duke University Divinity School, Princeton Theological Seminary, Berkeley Divinity School, Divinity School of the University of Chicago, Chicago Theological Seminary, Hartford Theological Seminary, Yale Divinity School, and others.

Why was such attendance at these fine schools seen as a significant problem requiring substantial and expensive attention? The report continued:

We are well aware of the wide variety of religious philosophies and theological emphases to which students are subjected in doing graduate work in these institutions. We are deeply concerned that our young men and young women of ability get their advanced training in the wholesome religious and theological atmosphere which will surround them in the type of graduate school which can be set up on the campus of Anderson College and Theological Seminary, and where the training will be especially designed to fit them for the pastoral, evangelistic, religious education, and other fields of activity in the Church of God.

This "denominational" thinking, somewhat uncharacteristic of the ideals of the Church of God movement, was nonetheless very real and seemed justifiable in light of the circumstances that were being experienced in those years. Some of the most capable and promising young ministers now were choosing to go to seminary. Since the Church of God had none, they had been going elsewhere. The earliest probably was Forrest Weir, who left the Anderson faculty in 1932 to attend seminary at Yale Divinity School, completing both the B. D. and then the Ph. D. in Yale's graduate school. His significant career then had found avenues for fulfillment largely outside the Church of God.

Oberlin College and Graduate School of Theology in Ohio was a main center of this seminary attendance by Church of God students. Anna Koglin, member of Anderson's first graduating class in 1919, received an Oberlin M. A. in 1934. Earl Martin's son, Daniel, began his seminary work there in 1937. Robert Reardon, wanting to study organ at Oberlin's Conservatory, spent the summer of 1938 living with the Martins and enjoying a wonderful educational experience. Gene Newberry, having finished the B. Th. in Anderson in 1938, traveled for the college the next two summers in an effort to generate more student applications for admission. He stopped by Oberlin that first summer, visited Reardon, and learned all he could about that seminary. By 1941 Newberry had completed a B. D. at Oberlin, as did Reardon himself in 1943.

Soon there were many other Church of God persons attending Oberlin, including Irene Smith Caldwell, James Earl Massey, Louis Meyer, Hollis Pistole and John W. V. Smith, all persons later to teach full time or part time in the coming new seminary in

Departure of early choir tour, director Robert Nicholson at right

Anderson. Generally, these and others, who sometimes had only pastoral ministry in mind, enjoyed good seminary experiences in these settings. Gene Newberry, soon to be a theology professor in the Anderson seminary and later its dean, recalled with deep appreciation the teaching methods and general approach to systematic theology of his Oberlin teacher, Walter Marshall Horton. Robert Reardon also expressed his debt to Horton, with whom he had worked closely (*Andersonian* Feb. 24, 1948). Boyce Blackwelder, later to be New Testament professor in Anderson, often expressed high regard for Toyozo Nakarai, his teacher at Butler University's School of Religion in Indianapolis.[16] Other persons key to the future of the coming Anderson seminary earned graduate degrees at Butler, including Adam W. Miller, T. Franklin Miller, and Harold L. Phillips. Dale Oldham, then pastor of Park Place Church in Anderson, had completed his ministerial education at United Seminary in Dayton, Ohio. He later wrote about United: "I owe a deep debt of gratitude to the professors who put up with me in my greener years.... I was a stranger and they took me in" (202).

In institutions like Yale, United, Oberlin, and Butler, Church of God persons were exposed to viewpoints which at times brought aspects of their own church tradition into question. They wrote theses, often for the first time analyzing critically various aspects of the heritage of the Church of God. One master's thesis, written at Oberlin by Robert Reardon,[17] was critiqued publicly and vigorously by Earl Slacum in a publication called "Watchmen on the Wall." Often these Church of God seminarians received attractive offers to pastor fine churches in "denominational" settings. A few elected not to remain identified with the Church of God.

Such a loss of potential leadership was compounded by another church concern. The Anderson campus was beginning to graduate increasing numbers of persons, and it anticipated even larger enrollments coming. Many of these gifted young people soon would take their places in the lives of local Church of God congregations. If they were to be retained as loyal laypersons, they would tend to expect pastors whose professional preparation they could respect—and that was coming to be seen as ministers educated at the seminary level. Further, there was some talk around the country of the possible founding of new schools in the life of the Church of God, schools focusing on ministerial education. Whether or not that was a serious possibility, especially involving graduate-level education, Anderson traditionally had been recognized as the primary place for the education of Church of God ministers. Now that the need for seminary education was being recognized more widely, the continuing welfare of the Anderson campus seemed to rest in part on its being the institution to take the called-for initiative.

But there were other concerns as well. There was at issue on the Anderson campus a clear question of educational philosophy. Dean Russell Olt had high aspirations for the young college in Anderson. He admired the educational model of the University of Chicago and was committed to the highest of accreditation standards. While the B. Th. program would continue until after his death in 1958, Olt aspired to the greater educational potential available in a true seminary program that built professional education on a strong liberal arts base.

The Anderson College administration believed a quality graduate program of

(Left) Professor Carl H. Kardatzke   (Right) Professor Amy K. Lopez

TABLE 13

Meet Your Professors: 1947-48

A series of articles appeared in the first issues of the student newspaper, the Andersonian, giving much helpful information to students about prominent faculty members. Examples follow, with the issue dates in which the faculty members were featured.

Anna Koglin	5/6/47	Leona Nelson	12/9/47
Cecil Hartselle	5/20/47	Paul Breitweiser	2/3/48
Walter Haldeman	6/3/47	Candace Stone	2/10/48
Robert Nicholson	10/7/47	Robert Reardon	2/24/48
Nancy Osborne	10/21/47	Zylpha Hurlbut	3/9/48
Mary Lou Barr	10/28/47	John Buehler	3/16/48
Florence Orr	11/4/47	Ruthven Byrum	9/7/48
Val Clear	11/11/47	Amy Lopez	11/16/48
James Sibert	11/18/47	Marie Strong	11/23/48
Vila Deubach	11/25/47	Cleda Anderson	11/30/48

ministerial education to be crucial to the church's future. From the beginning of the planning for a new seminary, the assumption had been made that the basic degree to be offered would be the standard, three-year bachelor of divinity degree and that the school would function at the graduate level in every respect. Standards of the Association of Theological Schools[18] were very much in view and its accreditation of a new seminary was expected to be sought as soon as possible. In the meantime, the hope was to change the institution's status from North Central's classification II to III so that the offering of the new graduate work could be considered regionally accredited as well.[19]

With this educational philosophy and accreditation assumption very much in mind, Robert Reardon said, in summary, that "the overriding concern was for a responsible, well-educated ministry and the School of Theology seemed the appropriate way for us to go." In fact, the *Alumni News* of February, 1949, went so far as to reprint an editorial by Charles Koller, president of Northern Baptist Theological Seminary in Chicago, titled, "As Goes the Seminary So Goes the Denomination."[20] Even so, being sensitive to central emphases of the Church of God movement, the following was made clear:

Let it not be said that we are making the mistake of thinking that education is

The "Barnatory," early gymnasium, then a residence hall

the only requirement for ministerial qualification. In the Church of God we believe in a God-called ministry, and in spiritual qualifications as being basic to all forms of service in the church. But we are aware also that preparation can be the means of placing the best possible instrument in the hands of God to be used for his glory and the upbuilding of the church (Phillips *Alumni News*, June,1950,3).

So, serious discussion and planning began. Gene Newberry had gone to Baltimore as pastor in 1944. By 1945, with World War II ending, the G. I.'s rushing to the campuses, and the dream growing in Anderson for its own seminary, Dean Olt encouraged Newberry to push ahead with his graduate work in anticipation of teaching. Earl Martin traveled from the campus to Baltimore and explained to the church there that the College was asking their pastor to attend Duke University and then return to Anderson for a significant teaching ministry. Newberry spent the 1945 year at Duke, taught in Anderson in 1946, returned to Duke in 1947-48, and finally came back to Anderson to teach theology and help with final plans for the launching of a new seminary. A graduate school focusing on preparation for pastoral ministry would need faculty members with church experience and quality academic credentials. Newberry had prepared well to be its first full-time faculty member and later its dean.

Frontiers of Student Life

While all of this church activity and planning for a new seminary was going on, life among the undergraduate students was proceeding even more vigorously than before. A good source for understanding many dimensions of that life is the *Student's Handbook* which was published by the Student Council in 1945-46 as an informational and policy

Kemp Music Hall (former E. E. Byrum home)

guidance document for the 1946-47 student body.

Paul Whalen, a senior, chaired the Council that year and sophomore Kenneth Hall was editor of the publication. It began with greetings from the president, which included this message to the student body: "Every teacher and employee of the College is your friend.... The whole physical equipment is here at your disposal. You are invited to respect it, use it, and benefit by it. Attendance at college is a privilege and not a right. May this be a year of happy and helpful Christian associations" (7).

Such greetings were meant to make clear both that the campus was a special place with rich learning resources and that there were definite student conduct expectations. The use of liquor or tobacco in any form was prohibited. There were various rules about student dormitory hours and access, both of which were controlled carefully. Programs sponsored by any individual or student group, it was said, had to be cleared well in advance by the dean or president. A list of "approved chaperons" for social gatherings or out-of-city trips was posted on the bulletin board. Student couples "keeping steady company" could obtain permission to use the faculty reception room in Old Main for their officially sanctioned dates. From Monday until Friday no meetings were to extend beyond 7:30 P. M.. However, head counselors could grant special social privileges to the following, "providing their disciplinary records are excellent": seniors, students over twenty-five, and engaged couples. Dress was to be such "as not to attract attention" (37).

Students were allowed as many absences from a class as that class yielded hours of credit. A two percent demerit in grades was given for each unexcused absence, administered by the registrar's office after the instructor had submitted the final grade. Chapel convened three times a week. Attendance also was required there, with seats assigned and careful records kept. Only eight absences per semester were allowed. Any more resulted in "one point demerit in each grade" for each unexcused absence. A wide variety of religious, cultural, and community-building events happened in chapel. In 1948-49, for instance, included among the outstanding speakers were E. Stanley Jones, D. Elton Trueblood, and Henry Schricker, governor of the State of Indiana.

During 1946-47, with President Morrison on a medical leave of absence and Earl Martin functioning as acting president, a new school publication was launched, a weekly student newspaper called *The Andersonian.* Martin informed the board of trustees at the end of the school year that "it is serving a useful purpose" and then reassured the members that, while the work was being done by students, the newspaper was "under the direct control of the administration and the student-faculty publications committee." Students Kenneth Hall[21] and Melvin Goerz were editor in chief and business manager respectively. In order to gain the school's permission to begin, they had sold 435 annual subscriptions at two dollars per year and met other requirements to convince the administration of their constructive intent and financial responsibility. Hall had had considerable editorial experience in high school and was prepared to do quality work, well beyond the level of the *Orange and Black*, a modest student paper of some years earlier.

The first issue of the *Andersonian* was dated February 18, 1947, and carried the following in its lead editorial: "The administration of Anderson College has made an honest effort to grant democracy to the *Andersonian* within the bounds set by the Board of Trustees and the Church of God at large. We of the staff shall not be toadying to the administration for the mere sake of toadying, nor shall we, on the other hand, encourage or launch mutinous attacks on established college policies." Considerable local business advertising was carried, such as Gadberry Grocery and Lunch at East Fifth and College Drive, a place just across from Old Main where students often met while buying gro-

(Top) Student Lawrence Reynolds (military veteran),
with wife and son at their campus trailer, 1946
(Bottom) College Haven trailer community on campus

164

ceries or eating a light lunch. In its first years of publication this paper had ample news to share. There was much writing about the busy life of campus social clubs and the many activities of drama, music, debate, and athletics.

From 1942 to 1948 Dr. Julia Eaton functioned as the first faculty member ever to head formally the campus drama program. Although the war years affected the volume of many activities, several dramatic productions were staged each year, and some maturing of the class offerings was evident in drama, speech, and English literature. Robert Smith, current director of drama, began as a student in 1948-49, making his first acting appearance in "Our Hearts Were Young and Gay," which the college staged at the Anderson High School auditorium. The decade of the 1940s also saw Arlo Newell (future editor in chief of Warner Press) as an officer of the Drama Club in 1946-47, the chartering on campus of Alpha Psi Omega (national honorary theater fraternity) in 1948, and the coming to campus in 1950 of a key drama leader of the future, Malcolm G. Gressman.

Meanwhile, the college choir was maturing rapidly under the skilled and energetic direction of a young music professor, Robert Nicholson. The April 15, 1947, *Andersonian* carried a front page story about the choir leaving on a spring tour to churches in Ohio (Middletown, Cincinnati, Hamilton, Columbus, Canton, Akron, and Lima). This was the first formal tour of its kind, the beginning of many reaching to the present time. The choir's tour program that first year opened with "To Thee We Sing" by Schvedov, and concluded with the "Hallelujah Chorus" by Handel and "Benediction" by Lutkin.

Only three weeks before the choir left on this tour, for the first time in the college's history there had been a large-scale intercollegiate debate tournament (more than three teams) hosted on campus. The national topic for intercollegiate debate that year was used: "Resolved that labor should be given a direct share in the management of industry." Dr. Julia Eaton was Anderson's debate coach. Her teams, arguing both the affirmative and negative, faced teams from colleges and universities across Indiana.

A "Meet Your Professor" series had begun with the first appearance of the *Andersonian*, each article sharing with students considerable personal and professional information about a given faculty member (see Table 13). While these were appearing in successive issues, there were two campus topics of particular prominence appearing frequently in the student newspaper. They were the urgent need for improved student hous-

(Top) Men's basketball team, 1941-42
(Bottom, left) Cheering crowd at a basketball game in the old gym
   (called the "Roundhouse," later Byrum Hall)
(Bottom, right) "Jumpin" Johnny Wilson

ing and the expanding program of intercollegiate athletics.

Adequate Housing, Winning Teams

Student enrollment during the war years shifted considerably. Local employment opportunities multiplied. Student numbers grew and, because of the war, came to consist mainly of women and ministerial students. The campus administration found itself working with draft boards all over the country to verify the status of ministerial students, some of whom were conscientious objectors opposed personally to the taking of human life. Occasionally these boards were not well informed about or sympathetic with the religious programs and student religious claims of a school like Anderson College. A college attorney had to be retained to deal with the many draft and deferment claims and appeals.

(Top) Morrison Hall under construction
(Left) President Morrison speaking
at dedication of the residence hall named in his honor

The graduating class of 1943 was larger than usual, forty-six, with seventeen receiving the bachelor of theology degree, twelve the bachelor of arts, nine the bachelor of science, one the bachelor of science in religious education, four the three-year diploma, and three the two-year diploma. Of these graduates 85 percent were either ministers or ministers' wives, with twelve persons being ordained at Park Place Church in conjunction with their graduation ceremony. The graduating class of 1945 would number fifty-nine, largest in the school's history, with forty-two of them ministerial students. But the war would end soon and the student body would undergo even more substantial change. With this change would come urgent student housing problems.

In June, 1941, President Morrison had reminded the board of trustees of what was painfully obvious. Living facilities for men on campus were inadequate. Many mothers of students, other than just Robert Nicholson's the previous year, were displeased with the conditions above the old dining hall, nicknamed the Barnitory. Morrison admitted that discipline out there was a problem, partly because during the winter it was almost impossible to heat adequately those leaky, makeshift rooms. These rooms had paper-thin walls, which students, like Roscoe Snowden, had put their fists through. But now a solution had arisen. The former Old People's Home, used previously for a women's dorm—"Sunset Hall"—was being leased from the Gospel Trumpet Company. There were yet three "inmates," aged saints to be cared for by the company. With some interior remodeling, this large block facility, a small scale of Old Main down the street, could house eighty men and now would be known as East Hall.

The following year the E. E. Byrum property (site of the present University Library) was purchased with the generous help of T. J. Kemp of Ocala, Florida. It quickly was remodeled into Kemp Hall and became the home of the growing music program. Here was a visionary move. Morrison had been concerned for some years that this property, about three acres immediately joining the campus to the north, not just to be divided into lots and sold to the public at Brother Byrum's death. The campus had a future, and soon it surely would need that land for something. Some decades earlier Byrum was thought to have been rather cool to the idea of a college. Now, said Morrison, "he is eager for the college to be able to purchase it from him." The college did. Then, according to President Morrison, with the main building, the gymnasium, the "new" men's dorm, and a music hall, "although they are not what we would build were we building now, they should take care of our needs for some time to come." With the rapid growth of the student body just ahead, however, the status of student housing would re-emerge quickly as again far from satisfactory.

As the Old People's Home, briefly a women's dorm, had been transferred to the greater need of the men in 1941, now in 1945, with the student body predominantly women, it was changed back to the use of women (supplementing the third floor of Old

Main yet housing women). Men were living in the Barnitory (now remodeled), the YMCA downtown, and in several undesirable old residences close to campus. But men, often with young families, began arriving on campus in large numbers by 1946. In the 1947-48 year more than three hundred former G. I.s were on campus, with Helen Holton now serving as Director of Veterans Affairs in addition to being President Morrison's secretary. Student Glenn Falls recalled the large number of veterans on campus. They were "scared to death, having been away from schooling for several years." At the same time, the younger non-veterans were scared that they couldn't compete with these older, obviously very motivated students." The *Alumni News* of June, 1946, listed 192 former students who had served in the armed forces during World War II and fourteen reported killed or missing in action.

The college accepted a government offer to help install some used trailers for housing veterans and their families. Soon twenty-four trailers were in use, a number that shortly would more than double when private trailers joined this new housing community called College Haven, parked with the publishing company's consent in a grove near the gymnasium. One trailer was occupied by Lawrence Reynolds (B. A., 1948), who had grown up a Baptist in Anderson and had met several Church of God young people attending Anderson High School with him before he went off in 1942 to serve thirty-nine months in the Air Force. Once home, he entered Anderson College "as a steppingstone only" since the school was convenient and in spite of local prejudice against those "different" people over in the Park Place area. He began semester two, 1945-46, moving his bride and young son into College Haven. Elected the first "mayor" of this trailer community, Reynolds helped make arrangements with the school to use a self-imposed residential tax for laundry machines, which were placed in the nearby gymnasium building. These former G. I.'s engaged in much horseplay, helping one another unwind from war experiences. Many also modeled exemplary Christian lives, one reason why Reynolds "saw the church" and, during his twenty-eight months on campus, committed to ministry through the Church of God movement.

But the trailers only began to speak to the housing problem. According to the *Andersonian* (October 21, 1947), in the fall semester of 1947 only 373 of the 664 students coming from outside Anderson found housing available on campus or in campus-owned property. Said Morrison to the board of trustees in June, 1946: "When can we have the new men's dorm is the question that is on everybody's lips. How I wish I could answer that question!" While the answer was being found, numerous wives in College Haven were becoming pregnant and Reynolds, having one of the few cars, drove many to the hospital for their deliveries.

Professor Carl Kardatzke, the faculty's family life specialist, studied all this and its effect on the ability of the students to concentrate on academic life. He reported that a major factor in the rapid population growth in College Haven was the interurban train that passed (down today's Third Street) at 5:00 o'clock each morning, its horn blowing away. The awakened students and their wives, he concluded, couldn't get back to sleep and often spent the time before breakfast in intimate activities quite unrelated to academics!

A three hundred thousand dollar drive was launched for the needed college advancement. The national church was asked to become responsible for the first one hundred thousand dollars, with a second one hundred thousand dollars to be raised locally. The new accredited status and now bulging student enrollment of the school just had to be protected and served.

A new residence hall, to be located west of Old Main across College Drive and large enough to house 140 men, was under construction by the summer of 1947 as an early phase of the expansion program. With federal aid, a new classroom annex, a war surplus building called "Government Hall" also was being constructed just east of Kemp Hall in the area of the current School of Theology building.

Soon, however, came the crisis of no money in hand to proceed on the residence hall, now a big, unfinished shell just sitting there awkwardly for all to see. By the time of his report to the board of trustees in June, 1949, fortunately President Morrison was able to announce that the campaign for one hundred thousand dollars in the city of Anderson finally had been successful.

It had been planned and directed by local businessmen Linfield Myers, president of the Anderson Banking Company, T. C. Werbe, president of Lynch Corporation, Frank Zoll, general secretary of the YMCA, and Everett Hartung of Broadway Sales Company. The wonderful new residence hall, neighboring the president's home on College Drive, was dedicated in 1949 and named Morrison Hall after the beloved president himself.

There was some surprise, however, and even anger among a group of male students, including Gustav Jeeninga, when the board of trustees announced its decision not only about the new hall's name, seen by all as fully appropriate, but that this fine residence facility would be occupied by women and not men! Earlier, the president had given a stirring chapel address during which he had invited the student body, many of whom were in dire financial circumstances themselves, to pledge toward the struggling project. As Robert Reardon wrote in the 1949 *Echoes*, "a great sea of hands went up all over the chapel. It was a great spiritual experience to see the sacrifice and devotion of these students.... There was hardly a dry eye in the house...." More than four thousand dollars had been pledged. But for some students like Jeeninga, a young Dutchman still learning English and on campus after having been a Nazi prisoner during the war, part of the giving motive had been that the severe housing problems of the men soon would be solved. The gender switch by the board was never explained to the satisfaction of many male students, despite a series of rather heated meetings on the subject and a presidential explanation, even apology in chapel. Soon another new residence hall would be built and it would be for men.

While the student housing needs were being handled as well and as rapidly as resources allowed, the intercollegiate athletic program of the campus was expanding rapidly. Most prominent among the sports was basketball, which dated back to the beginning of the 1930s (see Table 27) and had reached a zenith in the 1938-39 season with a 15-5 record and a genuine star in Jack Van Dyke. Gas rationing during the war had reduced the 1942-43 season to only seven games and had forced a complete cancellation of the next season. After the war Lieutenant Quentin Withrow (B. Th., 1947) was the first of the former students to return to campus as a war veteran.. He soon became the new center on the basketball team, only to lose that spot the next year to a young, black all-star graduate of Anderson High School, Jumpin' Johnny Wilson. Some real glory days for basketball lay just ahead and all of Van Dyke's records were about to fall. Robert Reardon said that President Morrison's formula for institutional success was, in part, "to show the sports world we were winners."[22] It was about to happen in basketball.

During 1945-46 the Gospel Trumpet Company granted the school a forty-year lease on about ten acres of land lying to the east of the publishing plant, just beyond East Hall (Old People's Home). The plan was for the school to develop a new track and baseball diamond, in fact a whole athletic complex.[23] Joining the physical education and athletic staff to assist with expanding coaching needs was Frank "Pop" Hedden, former coach at Butler University who was used to running a "big time" program. A new football team was authorized (see Table 27), in part because President Morrison judged that a lack of emphasis on athletics "lost us a good many Church of God students who in their high school career had taken great interest in athletics."[24]

The new football team first took to the field in the fall of 1947. Coached by Pop Hedden, the team soon enjoyed its initial victory. The *Andersonian*'s October 21 issue reported that the "Ravens unleashed all of their potential power last Saturday afternoon when they trounced the McKendree College aggregation 38-0." Starting at fullback for the Ravens was James Macholtz (B. A., 1951) from St. Joseph, Michigan. For decades to come he would be a campus leader in athletics, physical education, and general academic life.

Despite that excellent McKendree game, Morrison summarized the first season this way: "The showing was not so good so far as games won.... We believe with the experience of this past year we shall be able to have a much better. . . program in football next year (board report 1948). That next year brought a winning season, and a local lawyer, Henry "Hiney" Schrenker, came to assist with the football coaching. He had played at Notre Dame University and would share his knowledge as a very colorful part-time coach for many years. With some of those years not very successful on the score-board, Schrenker helped to hold the program together. He was loved by players, even though some of his language and personal habits were hardly the norm for a conservative, church-related college.

Basketball was the real news. In 1947-48 the college had won the Hoosier Conference championship in basketball, track, and golf. But basketball had demanded most of the public attention. The 1946-47 season saw sixteen wins and nine losses, while 1947-48 was an even better eighteen and five (no home losses). This team had become one of the best in the whole region, with some home games having to be moved downtown to Anderson High School's large Wigwam gymnasium to accommodate the swelling crowds. John (Jumpin' Johnny) Wilson, a state high school star recruited by Pop Hedden, was bringing national recognition to the college, leading the team with 515 points in 1946-47 and 565 the next year when the "Heddenmen" were ranked third among small colleges in the nation in team offense. This local and highly skilled black man was accepted readily and loved on the campus in a time when racial prejudice was strong in the city.[25] After leaving the college, he toured with the Harlem Globe Trotters, 1949-1954.

Back in 1938 R. Edgar May, then director of physical education on campus, had admitted to the church in the *Gospel Trumpet* (May 14, 14) that much criticism leveled against intercollegiate athletics may be merited. It is "so liable to corruption." It, however, also can be valuable, he said, if conducted properly. "I am happy to say that Anderson College is not so rabid to win that we are willing to sacrifice a single principle for the attainment of that object." There had been no conscious reversal of this institutional stance by 1947. Even so, in the spring of 1947 letters went out from President Morrison's office to the colleges of the Hoosier College Conference, which Anderson College had joined as a charter member just one year earlier. They announced Anderson's intent to withdraw from conference membership. Scheduling was said to be one key reason. Basketball was enjoying some real success against a few rather large institutions outside the conference and schedules were being finalized for a new football team. Independent status would give more freedom and flexibility.

But more was involved. The president reviewed the whole situation with the Executive Committee of the board of trustees in September, 1951. Then the issue, he said, was "the problem of whether or not certain persons who play on athletic teams were to have some of their expenses taken care of, and if so in what manner." He recalled the coming of Coach Hedden in 1946, his successful efforts to recruit some quality athletes, and the winning records that followed.

Soon an Anderson College Athletic Association had formed, with its relatively few members, some alumni and a few Anderson citizens, all seeking "to raise money to pay the tuition of approximately half a dozen athletes on the theory that it was impossible to get these men to Anderson College ... unless we did something for them." They did raise and use for this purpose about two thousand dollars. The resulting success on court and field was so great that the "Conference raised grave questions as to whether we were abiding by the regulations" (no athletic scholarships). So, "fearing that we might be dropped from the HCC" and feeling "that we wanted a freer hand in playing bigger schools outside the conference," Anderson had decided to withdraw.

Reactions around the state to the withdrawal were not enthusiastic. Some of the colleges felt that Anderson was overextending itself, altering institutional priorities in favor of athletics, really wanting to gain students, dollars, and public acclaim by going "big time." Vernon Schwalm, president of Manchester College and respected educator in the eyes of the North Central accrediting body, was one who was displeased.[26] Robert Reardon and Dean Olt represented Anderson at North Central's annual meeting in Chicago in the fall of 1947. Schwalm suggested to them that the North Central Association probably would be displeased with Anderson's decision and might even rescind its accreditation decision of the previous year! Reardon recalled that "Dean Olt looked pale. When we returned home, my first assignment [from the president] was to visit each Hoosier Conference school and beg for reinstatement...."[27] Athletics had become a real frontier of student life. But it would not be permitted to jeopardize the centrality of the academic program.

The college was welcomed back into the conference, with the understanding that the Athletic Association be disbanded so that any continuing, special assistance to athletes at least would be limited and informal. Dean Olt explained this compromise to leading Association members Harold Achor, Everett Hartung, Earl ("Jiggs") Morrison, the president's son, and Kenneth Ahrendt. They understood and agreed to cooperate. By 1951 a crisis again arose because several athletes with outstanding bills had assumed that someone would be covering them. A committee was set up to discuss the possibility of the school beginning to budget for grants-in-aid for this purpose. The tension around these kinds of issues, of course, would not go away for any of the schools in the conference. How does a school keep education first and yet not be embarrassed in the public arena of athletics and in a society that loves winners? An adequate answer never has come easily.

1. Soon the library would be moved to this upper floor and a steep, shaft-like fire escape installed. During a fire prevention week, Professor Haldeman explained library safety rules and students practiced emergency leaving of the library by way of this long, tubular escape. Occasionally it was used by students in quite unauthorized ways. A piece of waxed paper and a little push at the top would provide quite a ride down!

2. Not long after his graduation in 1944, Robert Nicholson would join the faculty in music, remain on the faculty longer than anyone else (forty-five years), and be the college dean from 1958-1983 and the school's president from 1983-1990.

3. Gaulke had encouraged young Robert toward Anderson. Then Shultz arrived as pastor just as the decision was to be made. The Nicholsons were unsure, having heard of problems on campus like smoking, card playing, and dancing by some students, despite rules against them. Shultz told the Nicholsons that there are problems anywhere and there was a good spiritual side to the school also. They should send Bob. They did and it would turn out to be a historic decision for him and the school.

4. Dr. Val Clear, while a student, addressed President Morrison in a chapel setting concerning the needs of the men then living in this facility. He used the pejorative "Barnitory" for the first time on this public occasion. Recalled Clear, Morrison's "eyes sparkled with ire."

5. Carl Kardatzke was admired by Nicholson and many other students of the time as an outstanding model of a Christian educator and active churchman. Recalled Nicholson, "He was out in the church every weekend, speaking and selling his wares (Christian education and family life materials). He was the campus marriage, family and sex expert. He was a Christian man in the full-orbed sense, a great model."

6. When Robert Nicholson graduated in 1944, he had gone to Dean Olt and said, "This is a marvelous place. Someday I would like to come back here and teach." He listed for the dean possible fields like history and Christian education. The following fall Olt wrote to Nicholson, then a new associate pastor in Hickory, North Carolina. Professor Clausen, the first full-time faculty member in the school's history, would be retiring in music that year after 28 years of faithful service. Would Nicholson get into a master's program immediately and return to teach music that next fall? He did, beginning a record-setting tenure of 45 on the faculty, to include 25 as college dean and 7 as school president.

7. Dean Olt's own copy of the 1941 revision of North Central's *Manual of Accrediting* still exists in the school's archives. It contains a complex chart of all standards, grouped by eleven aspects of school life, with a clearly marked percentile ranking of Anderson's then current accomplishment for each.

8. Robert Reardon, *This is the Way It Was*, 75. Dean Olt's private record book of student names, attendance, and grades for the psychology class he taught semester two, 1930-31, still survives. It is revealing. Of the thirty-two students enrolled, fourteen received either a D or F as the final grade. The dean never was shy about setting and holding standards.

9. In fact, in 1940 a set of faculty standards was presented to the board of trustees for information and affirmation. It set the goal of every faculty member under the age of sixty holding a doctorate by 1945. Professional growth and formal academic credentials were high institutional priorities as accreditation was anticipated. Those holding the doctorate also were to meet specific standards of continuing professional growth and productivity.

10. Falls remains to the present a half-time member of the campus development staff.

11. Taylor's president and dean, also in Chicago at the North Central meeting the year after Anderson's accreditation, did much as Morrison and Olt had done when the joyous news of the initial accreditation of that school was heard. They called home to Upland, Indiana, also setting off a campus celebration. See *Taylor University: The First 125 Years* by William Ringenberg (Wm. Eerdmans, 1973), 145.

12. This criticism, however, certainly did not exclude Anderson College. For instance, the 1947 General Ministerial Assembly had appointed a special committee to pursue complaints about the teaching of two faculty members (Walter Haldeman concerning the issue of conversion and J. D. Black, a Methodist, concerning atheism and evolution). That committee referred its concerns to the Doctrinal Committee of the school's board of trustees, which interviewed both teachers in detail and then decided that neither was "teaching matters contrary to what we as a group teach generally" (March 25, 1947).

13. See footnote ten, chapter four.

14. On October 3, 1946, E. A. Reardon died. After the funeral in Anderson, his son Robert, then a seminary graduate and pastor in Pennsylvania, shared his grief with the Morrisons, dear family friends. The president proposed on that occasion the idea that Robert become his assistant. Morrison then was struggling with his own health and felt the increasing weight of the administrative burdens. Soon the decision was made and in July, 1947, the Reardons were back in Anderson, living in the old family home at 914 Walnut Street, ready to do whatever would be of help to the president. As Wilson had invited Morrison in 1919 and then Morrison had invited Olt in 1925, now the coming of Reardon would prove significant indeed for the future of the school.

15. President Morrison had sought the board's permission the previous year to launch this study. He saw the goal as *reestablishing* a graduate school "upon a more reputable and creditable basis" since "some years ago, because of inadequate staff, library, and other facilities, the graduate school was temporarily discontinued."

16. See Barry Callen, editor, *Listening to the Word of God* (Warner Press, 1990), 4.

17. "The Doctrine of the Church and the Christian Life in the Church of God Reformation Movement," S. T. M. Thesis, Oberlin School of Theology, 1943.

18. Known earlier as the American Association of Theological Schools.

19. Earl Martin, the new seminary's first dean, reported to the board of trustees on June 16, 1950: "By changing the classification . . . from Group II to Group III (in which, by the way, standards are more difficult to meet) it will be possible to give graduate work in the present framework of our offerings with full accreditation of North Central to the graduate program." Even though his report to the board in June, 1951, gave some assurance of such accreditation, it would not be reality for another 24 years. President Reardon's annual report to the board of trustees in June, 1975, announced the formalization of such regional accreditation for the seminary. It has been in place ever since, coordinate with the ATS accreditation that would be gained initially in 1965.

20. This Anderson publication made clear, however, that "if we were writing it, we would use the word 'church' where Dr. Koller had used the word 'denomination.'"

21. This gifted young man also would become involved in editorial work across the street from the school at the Gospel Trumpet Company, remain there for many years in editorial capacities, and finally return to the school in 1978 as Professor of Christian Education and then chair of the Department of Bible and Religion, retiring in 1992.

22. From his final president's report to the board of trustees, April 22, 1983.

23. On March 29, 1946, the *Anderson Bulletin* carried the story of the extensive plans for this new complex. Much of it never did come about. Years later the company called the lease on this land for its own needs (there had been no building or permanent stands erected). The later athletic complex would be developed on another site on the north side of the campus. The originally projected athletic complex, it was said, would be "a complete, modern athletic and physical education plant" which would "afford the Park Place institution facilities comparable to those possessed by larger schools in Indiana." This headline newspaper story was reproduced as a full page in the 1946 *Echoes*.

24. President Morrison's annual report to the board of trustees, June, 1948.

25. At the college, Wilson became a friend of Truman Harris, a young white man soon to be a Church of God pastor in the South. When Wilson was touring with the Globe Trotters later, they played before a white crowd one night in Birmingham, Alabama. Wilson was leaving the floor when he heard, "Hey Jumpin' Johnny!" Down the steps ran a white man, who caught up to and embraced John right in front of that Southern white crowd of about 6,000 people. His wife joined him and did the same. They were the Truman Harrises. John never would forget that wonderful moment. To him it was a spontaneous symbol of some very special, some very human and racially inclusive things that characterized his beloved *alma mater*. After a successful career as a college coach, Wilson later would retire to Anderson and become an assistant basketball coach on his home campus (1990).

26. Vernon Franklin Schwalm was Manchester's dean, 1918-1927, and later its president, 1941-1946. See Timothy K. Jones, *A Century of Faith, Learning and Service: Manchester College, 1889-1989* (Manchester College, 1989), 111-112.

27. Final president's annual report to the board of trustees, April 22, 1983.

7

Citizen of City, Church and World
1930-1950

"I have had three consuming passions . . . (1) the fight for peace . . . ,(2) the fight for the working man . . . , and (3) the fight to abolish racial discrimination."

(Dean George Russell Olt)

Aggressive and very costly expansion projects, such as those envisioned by President Morrison immediately after accreditation in 1946, would require many new institutional friends and substantial financial resources.

But another kind of expansion was in process. Moral obligations inherent in the Christian faith itself also were requiring that the maturing school be increasingly active and demonstrate responsible involvement "in the world." Crucial issues could not be ignored in good conscience. New constituencies were being cultivated. They were raising new questions as well as providing new opportunities.

The mission of the college inevitably called it into significant and sometimes uncomfortable roles as a Christian presence and good citizen in the larger world. Building bridges and proving relevant were essential tasks for institutional growth. Having a prophetic voice on occasion was crucial for institutional integrity. Included as primary constituencies to be served were the students, of course, but also the church, the local, and even the world communities.

This campus did not intend to be a closed-door enterprise. Nor did it intend to educate students who would be narrow in their thinking and selfish in the investment of their lives.

178

On the Air with the Church

By 1950 the campus would formalize at the graduate level a program central to its mission from the very beginning, ministerial education. Preparing leadership for the church always was and would be a crucial focus for the campus. But another way of relating to and serving the church also had been prominent in campus life from its beginning. That way was music. After the end of World War II some significant developments in music emerged both in the church and on campus.

Radio broadcasts by Church of God pastors had begun to multiply in the 1940s, with Warren Roark having been on the air in Canton, Ohio, as early as 1936. Typically, music was featured alongside preaching. By 1946 forty-five such local or regional broadcasts were led by Church of God pastors, a growing phenomenon that encouraged exploration of the launching of a national radio program. Church historian John W. V. Smith credits Anderson College student Richard Meischke (later known as J. Richard Lee) with originally conceiving the idea in 1946 (1980, 338). An active student and employee at a local Anderson radio station, Meischke initiated the first conversations with W. Dale Oldham and the Board of Church Extension and Home Missions, which already had been discussing the possibility.

Called "Christian Brotherhood Hour," the resulting new broadcast ministry went on the air in January, 1947, with the preacher being college alumnus Oldham, then pastor of Park Place Church in Anderson, Indiana, Meischke (B. A., 1946) as program director and announcer, and the Board of Church Extension and Home Missions as sponsoring agency. In later years campus faculty members James Earl Massey and then Gilbert W. Stafford would serve as speakers for CBH, either concurrent with or immediately after their important assignments on the Anderson campus. This campus/CBH partnership, crucial from the program's very beginning, has been a long and significant one in the church's life and outreach. The school's 1947 *Echoes* featured photos of the principals of the program, then brand new, including the "Radio Choir" of students directed by Cynthia Kane. It announced proudly: "Anderson College students are playing a large part in the success of the national Church of God radio program." They surely were, and so were key alumni and faculty members.

The campus was willing and eager to assist the church in this important new outreach effort. Young music professor Robert Nicholson was a central figure. Having returned to campus as a faculty member in the fall of 1945, he would go on to complete his master's degree in 1946 and doctorate in 1953. In the meantime, he was active in developing the choral program of the campus and providing leadership to the Christian Brotherhood Hour program. With Professor Clausen's retirement in 1945, the end had come for the first era of campus musical life. Nicholson had been asked to develop a

(Left) Christian Brotherhood choir and quartet, in the sanctuary
of Park Place Church of God
(Right) Professor Robert Nicholson leading the CBH choir

new and stronger choral program, not continuing the *a cappella* choir, which had known an intermittent existence, or the Glad Tidings Chorus, which had never been a true, touring college choir (see Table 15). So the mixed choral organization under Nicholson's direction became known as the Anderson College Choir and took the first of its many tours through the churches in the spring of 1947.

By the fall of 1947 Nicholson was music director of the church's national radio program. The college choir was its featured choral group. Nicholson also was music director for the church's international youth conventions in 1946, 1948, and 1950. He began teaching church music on campus and would be editor of the hymnals of the Church of God to be published in 1953 and 1971.[1] He was intentional in relating music closely to the practical life of the church, personally directing the sanctuary choir of Anderson's Park Place Church and leading the college choir on many tours of churches located west to Denver, south to Florida, and east to New York City. The campus choir by 1947-48 was one of the more active and prominent student organizations on campus. That year this forty-voice choir included members from sixteen different states. Particularly emphasizing religious music under Professor Nicholson, the group now sang regularly on the Christian Brotherhood Hour, was featured on campus at the annual May Festival, and sang occasionally in chapel and in the community.

In the spring of 1948 (March 25-April 4) the group made its annual concert tour to fourteen congregations of the Church of God located in New York City, Washington, D. C., Kentucky, West Virginia, Maryland, Pennsylvania, and Ohio. The choir that same year did special presentations of *The German Requiem* by Johannes Brahms in Anderson and nearby Yorktown. Joining the choir in the music ensembles of the campus were a men's and women's glee club, a modest college band, and an orchestra. The orchestra had been founded during 1946-47 as a string ensemble under the direction of Professor Ingyr Marie Lien.

Through the church's Board of Christian Education, Professor Nicholson also launched and edited, beginning in 1954, *Musical Ministry,* a mimeographed periodical for Church of God musicians and musical leaders. This was the first attempt at a formalized medium for music education in the church. The initial issue contained articles titled "Making Special Music Special," "Listen Accompanist!" and "This Changed My Choir." In addition, from his busy campus base, Nicholson edited two special-purpose books, a shaped note edition of *Select Hymns* in 1950 and *When Boys and Girls Sing* in 1957.

These various musical ministries of the college in support of the church's life were continuing evidence that the campus intended to serve effectively as a good citizen of the Church of God. A key means of service, of course, was the growing number of graduates who were filling pulpits and pews. In 1946 the director of Anderson's alumni association reported that half of all Church of God people in the United States then were being pastored by Anderson alumni, and that nearly all of the foreign missionaries then being sent by the American church were former Anderson students. Concluded sociologist Val Clear in his 1953 doctoral dissertation: "It seems to be the consensus among informed observers that the factor most responsible for the rapid rate and direction of change in the Church of God Movement had been Anderson College and Theological Seminary" (262).

Warming Up to the City

In the early years of its existence, the school had shared in Anderson, Indiana, the somewhat aloof and separated relationship which the Church of God had experienced with the general public. The tone had been set back in 1906 when the Gospel Trumpet Company first had arrived in town. According to Linfield Myers, local banker, "When the community discovered that the publishing house . . . was not an enterprise providing openings for an appreciable number of Anderson workers, but strictly an operation carried on by a colony of dedicated people who 'lived-in' on company premises and were not paid wages or salaries as other people were, the development gave rise to second thoughts. . . . The newcomers from West Virginia were regarded in Anderson as a group of religious fanatics" (21-22).

Speaking of the 1925-30 period, Robert H. Reardon recalled that "the town generally looked on us as a strange group of religious fanatics to be left quietly in peace. In the Church of God, however, Anderson was thought of as the Holy City and visitors coming to town for the yearly camp meeting were shocked to see people smoking openly in the streets."[2] Nonetheless, as he noted elsewhere, "The saints were well respected for industry and moral uprightness, particularly at Anderson Bank, presided over by its visionary president, Linfield Myers" (1991, 9). Key campus persons over the years also had a way of using humor and grace to good advantage.

One illustration makes clearer the tension sometimes encountered and the constructive way in which campus leaders increasingly turned such circumstances into bridges of understanding and friendship. As Anderson College pursued accreditation by North Central in the early 1940s, Father William Cunningham, faculty member of Notre Dame University and a member of North Central's Board of Review, was especially helpful. But his own Roman Catholic church tradition presented contrasts at points to that of the Church of God. He came to campus as an honored guest, spoke in chapel, and once was attending a luncheon with a group of College staff. President Morrison told what happened next.

"Thoughtlessly, our food service people served pork, even though it was the season of Lent. We were much embarrassed, and scurried around and cooked up something that he could eat with a clear conscience. When the meal was finished, he produced a long pipe from his pocket and filled its empty stomach with tobacco. From the first," continued Morrison, "Anderson College has maintained a tradition of no smoking in college buildings. Just how to handle a situation like this is anybody's guess. So I

(Top) Campus winter scene, looking westward "up the valley"
(Bottom) Warm greetings to returning alumni, Old Main

182

said loudly enough to be heard by all the group, 'Well, Father Cunningham, we offended you with our pork, and now you have offended us with your pipe. So we are even.' He saw the humor of it and returned his pipe to his pocket, all in good spirit" (1962, 187).

The cold, distant, church-city relationship eventually began to thaw also. Linfield Myers, for instance, had become a staunch friend of the campus and its inspiring leaders. From the perspective of 1973 he would be able to write, with particular reference to the long and effective presidential leadership of John Morrison, that he "elevated the struggling Bible school into one of Indiana's great liberal arts colleges and was one of the men who laid the foundation for Anderson's greatness" (25).

There obviously had been a slow but sure process, one leading from awkward aloofness to vital partnership. The warming up came from much relationship building and quality service rendered, including something as simple as high school student and local Church of God pastor's son, Robert Reardon, faithfully delivering the *Anderson Daily Bulletin* newspaper to 220 homes and to the downtown drugstores. One day, as college president, he would enjoy the benefit of some friends made because of such an ordinary job well done.

By the time of the school's accreditation in 1946, clearly a significant news story in the city, the college had planted many seeds of good community citizenship. There had been a few attempts to seek resources from the city, including the endowment campaign as the 1930s opened, the renovation of the old auditorium into a respectable gymnasium in the middle of that decade and, toward its end, dollars to build the library's meager book collection. Such attempts had been based on increasingly healthy and mutually beneficial relationships. These relationships were to become more numerous and mutually rewarding all the time.

The campus in its early years was primarily a community of Church of God persons. This was partly by design and partly because there was little to attract others when the school was small, unaccredited, and located somewhat off to itself out on the east side of town. President Morrison estimated that the student body of 1939-40 was about 90 percent Church of God, a figure that would drop to 80 percent by 1950 and to about 50 percent by the 1980s.

Just after accreditation he told the board of trustees in June, 1946, that one of the great tasks in the development of a church-related college is "the building and maintenance of a suitable faculty." His personal conviction, he said, was that, for Anderson College, a suitable faculty (beyond its academic credentials which Dean Olt monitored carefully) should be comprised of about 80 percent Church of God men and women.

One exception to this percentage was in the theological subjects where the president felt that "all the teachers should be Church of God." This exception, he insisted, "is not sectarian but only a means of obtaining certain desirous accomplishments."

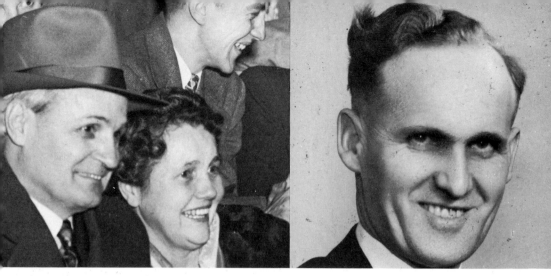

(Left) John and Eunice Morrison
(Right) Professor Ruthven Byrum, renouned artist

Morrison judged that a strong majority of Church of God people represented in all dimensions of campus life "will make for a certain unity of purpose and will reduce conflicting ideologies to a minimum." Nonetheless, he certainly did not mean for such concern about the maintenance of a distinctive Church of God identity to be a barrier to community relations. After all, a central thrust of the Church of God tradition was a bringing together in harmony, not a dividing of people.

What Morrison surely had meant, at least in part, was that never should there be an end to the sense of community, the distinctive feeling of togetherness for a common cause that had characterized the Church of God community from its 1906 beginning in Anderson.

Robert Reardon spoke of these early workers at the Gospel Trumpet Company as dedicated people "caught up in a cause and carried along in a sense of global mission. They were assured that God was working to restore the church, and this entire enterprise was the vehicle through which it was being carried out." Speaking of the Church of God people, of whom his own family was very much a part, Reardon said: "We knew who we were and what we were called to proclaim and do. We were dreamers of a great vision—a united, purified church, sanctified, empowered, global in purpose, reaching out, whatever the cost, to sound the trumpet of reformation before the end of the age" (1991, 2, 11).

The Anderson campus had emerged in that church community and visionary ethos and also came to value those cohesive and mission-laden strengths. Always the college would seek to remain an educational *community*. By its very nature as an educational institution, however, what the campus did not want to do was perpetuate the over-against-others attitude sometimes present in the church. One standard aspect of the mission of most institutions of higher education is community service.

Typically a college is expected to function in ways that enrich many dimensions of public life. This college's decision in the late 1920s to introduce the liberal arts into its curricular vision was, in part, a sign for the community of Anderson. It told the public that this young school was widening its horizon in ways that eventually would have great impact for good, not just in the educational and religious arenas, but also in the social, business, cultural, and recreational aspects of life locally. The school was in Anderson to stay, and it intended to be a good and an important local citizen.

As early as 1926 the East Side Community Club had been active in serving the betterment of the side of town where the College was located. Especially after its incorporation in 1950, this club worked to join religious and political forces in order to influence decisions about lights, sewers, streets, and bridges. Increasingly, Church of God leaders became involved with this club. Most of the time the club and the campus were in agreement on issues at hand. The Third Street and Truman Bridge project in the 1970s would be a major exception (see chapter eleven). In that instance, untypically, many city and community leaders were at odds with the campus view of what was best for the college and the city.

A key spearhead of the initial entry of the campus into community life was President Morrison himself. He was a likeable, community-minded man, a man with a remarkable sense of humor who moved easily among people. His humble background and lack of formal academic credentials probably avoided some barriers that otherwise might have been faced in an essentially blue-collar city. With strong religious convictions and always tenacious for the cause of the college, he nonetheless was tolerant of spirit and respectful of people who thought and acted differently. The Anderson Kiwanis Club soon became a key setting for such wholesome building of friendships. Organized in 1919, the year Morrison had first moved to town, this club met downtown in the Grand Hotel and became a focal point of fellowship and service for many city leaders.

Club historian Gene Bock later described Morrison as sincere and witty, "a minister, an educator, a mediator and peacemaker, and always the man with the crackling comeback," qualities that tended to endear him to all. "He always had an answer, something devastating," recalled Bock. The first time he was asked to speak to the club, Morrison rose to his feet and, before he could get started, the members got up in mass and began exiting the room (a group prank plotted in advance). "Dr. John," as he came to be known affectionately, immediately began speaking to their backs before they could reach the door. "Two thousand years ago," he announced judgmentally, "Christ told his

(Top) Robert H. Reardon, speaking at the fiftieth anniversary of General Motors
(Bottom) Charles E. Wilson, surrounded by (seated, left) John A. Morrison, Linfield Myers, and
(standing, left) Wilbur Schield, Robert H. Reardon, Russell Olt

disciples to drive out the devils. This they proceeded to do. But today they just walked out!" The crowd erupted in laughter and quickly returned to their seats" (Bock, vi-8). They listened appreciatively to a delightful friend whom they elected their club president in 1934.

Another member of this Kiwanis Club was Charles Erwin Wilson, "the man who arrived in Anderson from the East the same year that our club was founded, who helped emblazon the name of Anderson on the map of General Motors before climbing the main ladder to the vast corporation's presidency, thence to the even greater stage as our nation's Secretary of Defense" (Bock, I-8). Historian Bock spoke of the long friendship of Wilson, "the industrialist and world figure," and Morrison, "the moving spirit that brought us Anderson College," a friendship of great benefit to the city. Years later a beautiful new library would be built on the local campus. It would be the Charles E. Wilson Library, a wonderful liberal arts facility and also the official repository for many of the Wilson papers. So significant locally were these two men, so different and yet so close, that the 1973 book of Linfield Myers, which reflects historically on the life of the city, would be titled *As I Recall ... The Wilson-Morrison Years.*

Anderson's oldest service club is Rotary, started in Chicago in 1905 and with a local chapter organized in Anderson in 1917, the same year Anderson Bible Training School had begun. As John Morrison was beginning his term as president of Kiwanis in 1934, Dean Russell Olt was ending his year as elected president of the Rotary Club in Anderson. Among Olt's remarks to the club as he completed his presidential term was this: "Rotary is different from other service clubs. It is characterized by a practical idealism which transcends just horseplay so often found in some club meetings" (*Anderson Rotary Club*, 1964).

However one might judge the fairness of this remark as it reflects negatively on the shallowness of some other clubs, it unquestionably is true that, in matters of practical idealism and social justice, Olt himself excelled. His sensitive conscience helped shape the long-term character of the Anderson College campus. That conscience also had considerable influence on the city where he lived and served as an educational leader.

Compassionate Shadow of Dean Olt

A memorial service for outstanding campus leaders of the past was held during the fiftieth anniversary celebration of Anderson College in 1967. Among other things said then about the revered memory of Dean Olt (1895-1958) was this: "He was an innovator, an opener of windows, an advocate of minorities, a champion of the foreigner and the stranger, and a man to measure your life by." Robert Reardon noted that in one of Olt's personal papers this revered leader had mentioned his own deepest interests, apart from his obvious commitment to academic excellence. They were serving the church faithfully, working for peace, supporting racial equality, and improving the lot of working people through the labor movement (1979, 54).

Such frontiers of service in the name of Christ shared the rich tradition of the American holiness movement generally[3] and that of the Church of God movement particularly. The early Church of God "missionary homes" located in several urban centers had combined evangelism, education, and various forms of social service. Believing that the Christian gospel brought an end to traditional discrimination on the basis of nationality, race, or gender, the Church of God movement in its early years functioned quite "radically" and prophetically.

The Gospel Trumpet Company had supervised the construction of an Old Peoples' Home (1907) soon after it first had located in Anderson. In 1918, with many German-Americans under suspicion of potential disloyalty to the United States in the midst of the war in Europe, one day the Madison County Council of Defense visited the Gospel Trumpet Company. It wanted the company's German language publications stopped. The company was faced with a difficult dilemma. It decided to proceed with production of needed Christian materials for people wrongfully under suspicion. It also advertised on a full page in the college's 1927 *Echoes* its "Department for the Blind" which then was publishing books, the *Gospel Trumpet*, and the International Sunday School lessons for sightless people. In the midst of such compassionate and courageous Christian service, the college had been founded. It would find its own ways of carrying on the tradition.

Social tensions naturally worsened in the early 1930s as the young college struggled to survive and serve with dignity while the whole nation languished in economic crisis. Racial discrimination either worsened or at least became more painfully apparent across the land as competition for jobs intensified. The city of Anderson was one of many places where the Ku Klux Klan was present and influential. Unionization of workers in many places led to controversy and even violence. In 1932, for instance, efforts to unionize miners in Harlan County, Kentucky, brought intimidations and even death. After much publicity and many accusations of severe injustices, a carload of Anderson College faculty and students, including Dean Olt, was on its way to investigate. The Dean later recounted the fear and danger they faced just because they dared to ask questions.[4] Having finally seen more than enough, and being fortunate in managing to reach safety in Cincinnati, they read a front-page newspaper headline announcing, "Harlan County Vigilantes Beat Student Investigators." Those beaten had been from

Kansas Labor College, but they easily could have been from Anderson. Seeking justice often would have its risks.

In 1936 Dean Olt wrote in his personal memoirs that "a man should stand for what is believed to be right, regardless of the persuasion of the crowd or the cost, even if it means social ostracism, as sometimes it does." His own college experience, he said, had shown him that "blind subservience to any political party is a symbol of ignorance." He had become "committed to production for use and not for profit." So he was determined to aid in an equitable distribution of goods, to encourage collective bargaining in labor disputes, and to further the cause of pacifism. To be clear, however, he once wrote that he was a "relative pacifist." That meant that he would fight for a cause that is right, but "never when it inflicts pain on non-combatants." With all his power, Olt was prepared to champion equality for all races of people, while fostering in students the skills of critical thinking and a vision of academic excellence. Here was quite a combination of commitments, quite a Christian man. Here was a practical academic leader seeking to inspire a better world, and all the while helping to mold the very soul of a college campus.

Dean Olt, campus leader, also came to serve in the city of Anderson as chair of the mayor's Committee on Child Welfare, president of the Anderson Urban League, the Family Welfare Association, and the Anderson Council of Social Agencies. In 1948, in this latter capacity and through the department of race relations of the Federal Council of Churches, a successful clinic was established in Anderson. Soon it documented the southern cultural origins and patterns of the city and the many rights often denied to local persons of color. A resulting move for a fair employment practices ordinance emerged in 1949, but was opposed vigorously by the new leadership of the city's Chamber of Commerce. Dean Olt was labeled the guilty troublemaker in this matter. Economic pressure was put on President Morrison to control his dean and, for the first time, Olt was unsure of Morrison's full backing. So Olt quietly resigned all his positions at the college! Morrison couldn't sleep and would not accept the resignation. Finally, they resolved the difference and, even though the proposed ordinance had to be withdrawn because of widespread public opposition, the dean had stood his ground and had been affirmed in the campus community, despite considerable pressure to do otherwise. He would remain the dean until his death in 1958.

Tension with elements in the city was not limited to the struggle over this one proposed ordinance. Accusations of "communist" were directed on occasion toward the campus during the tense McCarthy era, with Dean Olt and campus social scientist Dr. Candace Stone the usual targets. But even writers in the *Andersonian*, the student newspaper, did not avoid some difficulty. Students Billy Joe Thomas and Don Wright found themselves needing to write to the board of trustees in December 1950, apologizing "for having placed Anderson College in an embarrassing position." What had they written in the November 15 issue that had been so troublesome in the larger public arena? Only that the use of the word "Communist," in their opinions, was often indiscriminate in the country at that time and that "few people would recognize a Communist if they saw one and fewer still know what a Communist is and what he stands for." To make the point, they had challenged any two students on campus to debate, themselves being willing to defend the Communist viewpoint. Now they explained to the board that "we erroneously gave the impression that we were Communist sympathizers." Their intent had been to expose the fallacy of labeling people, sometimes out of ignorance, and often for personal gain politically. They had misjudged public sensitivities at the time and that they now regretted.

Dr. Stone, a Quaker and social activist, was quoted in the February 10, 1948, *Andersonian* as saying about World War II: "I do not believe that Europe or the world will ever be restored physically or spiritually until we, the Christian people of America, are ready to take the blame for the holocaust caused by the war and set about to do all in our power to make amends in a spirit of love and self sacrifice." To her, this attitude reflected Christianity at its best. To some others it sounded weak and unpatriotic, an inappropriate accepting of guilt and responsibility that rightly belonged to others. Maybe, thought many people in the community, she and some others at Anderson College were themselves secret Communists!

Stone and Olt were kindred spirits. He chaired the executive committee of the Displaced Persons Commission of the Church of God, made some fifteen trips to Europe, and enabled the resettlement in America of many European Church of God and other families. Regarding the inclusion of families in desperate need but with no Church of God affiliation, Olt said: "We are on the spot . . . as a church in showing our broad sympathy and humanitarianism by so doing." To use Dr. Merle Strege's appreciative words about this attitude, the ethos of the Anderson campus was being shaped by a "broad sympathy, loving concern for the neighbor, a heart large enough to include the stranger and homeless" (1991, 13). But many others at the time were less than appreciative. When the local General Motors plants were unionized, Dean Olt walked at the head of a supportive parade downtown. Some community leaders never forgave him for this. Some also cried "communist" when Dr. Stone helped organize a local support rally to back the bus boycott in Montgomery, Alabama. So be it. These were causes seen to be just.

Dean Olt saw what he judged a major problem in the church. He wrote that "too many professing Christians have just been playing around with Christianity. Being a Christian has not made much difference" (132). He believed in action, in making a difference! Robert Reardon evaluated him this way: "Dean Olt was a man far ahead of his time. He nearly always was in some sort of trouble. Because of his support of the

Dean Russell Olt

unions, his pacifism, his support of black civil rights, and his rejection of narrow fundamentalism, he constantly was the object of criticism" (1991, 77). He also was a key source of the school's pride and inspiration.

One focus of that inspiration was on the elimination of racial discrimination. The Church of God from its beginning in the late nineteenth century had emphasized unity among all Christians. Many blacks became involved and were accepted readily. They began attending the annual Anderson Camp Meeting in rather large numbers, a fact causing some prejudice to surface in the local community.[5] For the first decades in the life of the Anderson campus, the number of black students was quite small, but Dean Olt was persistent in pressing the cause of equal opportunity for all. His pressing was in a context of some campus limitations on such practices as interracial dating, an accommodation reflecting social mores of the times.

One of the charter members of the campus board of trustees in 1925 was Sethard P. Dunn, a black Church of God pastor who served in Chicago beginning in 1920.[6] Serving on the board from 1925 until 1957, the college awarded him the honorary Doctor of Divinity degree in 1937 (see Appendix P). In 1960 the campus received a one hundred thousand dollar gift out of his estate from the Langley Avenue Church of God in Chicago and named a men's residence hall in his honor (see Appendix R). It was thought at the time that this was the first major building on any campus in the Midwest to be named for a black leader. President Robert Reardon wrote on that occasion that "in so doing, we pay tribute to the great common bonds which unite us and yearn for the dawning of a new day in good will, Christian concern, and mutual endeavor" (*Alumni News* January, 1960, 2). In part that new day would seem finally to be dawning in 1990 when, in that one year, black leaders would be very prominent on campus, with Dr. James Earl Massey installed as Dean of the School of Theology, Dr. Ronald Fowler of Akron, Ohio, serving as chair of the board of trustees, Dr. Benjamin Reid of Los Angeles, California, functioning as guest speaker for the fall Spiritual Emphasis Week, and Rudy Pyle III elected as president of the undergraduate student body.

That new day, however, faced obstacles even on the Anderson campus over the decades, in part because of the persistent influence of societal patterns of discrimination. Gabriel P. Dixon (B. Th., 1933) had been one of the first black students on campus. He was recognized in 1955 by the alumni association with its "Award of Achievement." Emery C. Williams (B. Th., 1946, 1947), a popular black student on campus, suffered a severe accident while working in March, 1945, as a part-time janitor at the YMCA in downtown Anderson. As he lay in a bed in the local St. John's Hickey Memorial Hospital fighting for his life, the sight in the hallway on his floor surely was not typical for the time. The floor was clogged with Anderson College faculty and students, nearly all white, singing and praying for the well-being of their beloved friend.

At the same time Jumpin' Johnny Wilson, college student and basketball star, was admired by the public, although at away games it was not unusual for a fan to yell racial slurs when Johnny was beginning to dominate a game. Once President and Mrs. Morrison, avid basketball fans, turned on such a rude fan and publicly reprimanded the blatant racism in no uncertain terms.

Early Anderson graduate Mack Caldwell had pioneered a short-lived effort to provide training for black leaders in the Church of God in the form of an extension of Anderson Bible Training School in the South (see chapter three).

Then, in 1937, Horace Germany (B. Th., 1944), a young white man from Mississippi, came to campus. Soon he was in a sociology class taught by Leona Nelson and found himself writing a paper on "The Negro Educational Problem in the South." In the process of research and writing, he became so convicted by the levels of injustice and need that, in a few years, he was home starting a college for blacks (now Bay Ridge Christian College in Kendleton, Texas), receiving help from Anderson and literally risking his life in the process.[7]

When the Supreme Court of the United States in 1954 ruled against segregation in the public schools, President Morrison wrote that "segregation has been a monstrous evil," that "when Christians read their New Testaments they don't find many props for segregation," and that "Anderson College has, from the very day of its beginning, not discriminated against any person or persons because of race or color" (*Alumni News* October, 1954, 2).[8]

Such an antisegregation stance soon was to go public locally, but not without some vigorous resistance in the city. On May 3, 1956, a community prayer service was held in Anderson's Central Christian Church on behalf of the nonviolent resistance movement in Montgomery, Alabama. The idea for this event had originated with the Anderson College International Relations Club and the Anderson chapter of Americans for Democratic Action. Professor Candace Stone also was a prime mover. She wrote after the event that "by our participation we acknowledged our own guilt of prejudice and asked to be forgiven." Even the campus was not without some guilt, but it intended to be in the vanguard of reconciliation.

Both Free and Responsible

A special kind of college had come into being in Anderson. It clearly was not one of those many church-related colleges that maintain their historic church ties as little as possible and more out of concern for public relations than true commitment. Neither was it one of those that rigidly perpetuate a particular tradition and discriminate against any faculty or students who dare think their own thoughts. *Nominal* was not a good adjective for the Anderson campus, nor was *fundamentalistic*. Anderson College, said Robert Reardon, "was not sheltered from ideas. Dean Olt and President Morrison saw to that. They were devoted to academic freedom, and so were spared the narrow, fundamentalist, dogmatic approach to learning" (1991, 90). Thus, the campus was prepared to carry on quality education with students, be self-critical when necessary, and engage in candid and constructive dialogue with a broadening range of constituencies.

The campus was evolving into a free and flexible place, but not at the expense of sturdy beliefs and genuine, relatively enduring roots in the ideals and perspectives of the Church of God movement. In fact, those ideals and perspectives themselves included something crucial for the effective functioning of a quality academic institution. T. E. Howard had put it well in the June, 1938, issue of *The Kansas Church Bulletin*, the Church of God state publication. The question was, "Shall we standardize the truth?" Howard's response was to recall that in Kansas there were Church of God ministers "of variant convictions and interpretations" who had expressed themselves freely and helpfully. "It has been demonstrated," said Howard, "that this can be done in a brotherly spirit and without sacrificing either sincere convictions or vital truths." In fact, such questing and candidness was said to be "as it should be and it contributes to the promotion of truth.... Truth thrives best in this kind of soil." This had been the early attitude and teaching style of Russell Byrum. Always it would be the firm position of Dean Olt. The Anderson campus tended to affirm in policy and practice the paradox of a rooted openness, a firm but flexible commitment, seeking to reflect the Church of God movement at its best in an academic setting.

Such also was the soil out of which President Morrison himself had grown. He was described as follows in the issue of *A. C. News* published in memorial to him (Feb. 1966): "He hated to live in a stuffy room. And whenever he thought the brethren were pulling the windows and blinds down so that there would be no more room for God's truth to pour through, he went to work with a vengeance. He wrestled and pulled and tugged and used his wit and wisdom and influence to pry those windows open so that a young man might have reason to breathe and think and pursue the truth and think his own thoughts before God." Implementing such a conviction, the Morrison-Olt leadership team sought to appoint faculty members truly compatible with the school's distinctively Christian mission. They also sought to encourage the candid creativity of those faculty members and to protect them from premature and unjust restraints originating from outside the academic community.

Inevitably some issues were awkward, and misunderstanding at times came easily. Nevertheless, when tension did develop and the faculty member involved was competent and responsible, the campus was prepared to be a leader, to test new frontiers, to keep the doors of learning open. Attacks against the Christian faith itself, of course, could not be tolerated if the distinctive religious nature of the school was to be maintained.[9] What was acceptable was the asking of any relevant question and the hearing of any responsible point of view. Very early the campus leaders had disagreed with (or at least were openly willing to consider alternative approaches to) aspects of F. G. Smith's interpretation of the New Testament book of Revelation. That was quite a volatile stance at the time since Smith's views were accepted widely in the Church of God movement, even considered by many ministers a crucial part of the movement's "standard literature."

Otto Linn had been a prominent Anderson faculty member in the first half of the 1930s, a consummate scholar selected as a member of the translation committee that produced the Revised Standard Version of the New Testament. As Merle Strege put it, Linn was one of the people in the Church of God movement "who have been captured by our notion that the truth may be pursued more than possessed. He firmly opposed authoritarian control of some minds by other minds" (1991, 56).

Val Clear was another such faculty member. He joined the Anderson faculty in 1947. Soon he was teaching in his sociology classes that intermarriage was the only real solution to the problem of racial discrimination. "I did that knowing that I was playing with fire," he admitted later, "but no one on campus raised any questions. Anderson College under J. A. Morrison and Dean Olt had the most enlightened policy of academic freedom of any institution in the country."

That enlightened policy, however, had its struggles and built-in dilemmas. President Morrison sometimes faced a difficult task when it seemed necessary both to protect the integrity of a responsible academic process and to reassure church and public constituencies that fundamental commitments were not being compromised. In the January, 1951, *Alumni News,* for instance, he said that "perhaps not since the years just before the Civil War has American society been so characterized by fear, conflict, confusion, and hatreds as now." Suspicious people were asking him if rumors were true that faculty members were teaching such outlandish things as communism, evolution, and premillennialism. His answer was No on these three subjects. He elaborated on the question of communism since the subject was so volatile nationally and locally. "There can never be at any time any fundamental agreement between the Christian philosophy and the atheistic philosophy of communism.... I wish to be very emphatic here in saying that there is no communist on our staff; and should we discover one, we should immediately oust him or her for the simple reason that a Christian college could not in consistency employ one whose belief stood in direct contradiction to the Christian faith."

As early as the publishing of the 1950-51 edition of the *Operating Manual of Anderson College,* the campus policy on academic freedom had been formalized and published. The primary justification for maintaining freedom of instruction, the official statement affirmed, arises from the learning needs of the student. "It is the student's right to learn the complete truth about the subjects he studies and his right to think without restraint about the problems that arise in such study. This freedom should never be denied the student" (34). The policy also said that "within the limitations imposed by the acknowledged purposes of an institution, it is the obligation of a college president and of a board of control to guarantee that liberty of teaching shall not be abridged.... Freedom is so precious an asset to an educational institution" (35). Limits to freedom, however, were recognized. They included "the universally accepted beliefs and mores of society," and restrictions clearly stated and firmly rooted in the commitments of a sponsoring religious body.

That balance of genuine freedom accompanied by understood limitations certainly was tested around 1950. There were the volatile issues of "socialism," "communism," and patriotism, including concern in the city of Anderson that Anderson College's Dr. Candace Stone, then a campus leader in the social sciences, might be a socialist sympathizer using her classrooms to push un-American propaganda. Dr. Stone, a Quaker who had come to love Anderson College and Park Place Church of God, wrote a long

196

letter of explanation to the campus administration and the chair of the board of trustees on December 18, 1950. In it she poured out her soul and described her philosophy of life and teaching.

She noted for campus leaders the statement in the 1950-51 *Operating Manual* about academic freedom, saying it was "a statement which does honor to a Christian college." She expressed her deep love for the school, said categorically that she was not a "socialist," and reported that she pointed out to students "what I believe to be fallacious, insidious and diabolical in the Communist philosophy." Nonetheless, she admitted that she openly entertained all relevant views and willingly ran the risk of being misunderstood, all in the cause of good education. "I have not prayed to save myself, for there are things more precious than one's job: such values as justice, respect for personality, academic freedom, [and] the responsibility of a Christian college in a darkened world."

The sociology department, which Dr. Stone launched on campus, seemed always on the cutting edge of social change and thus often in the center of controversy. "In the battles with the Curriculum Committee," recalled departmental member Val Clear, "we usually prevailed, probably because Dean Olt tended to support the positions we held. We were pacifists in a time of war and pro racial integration in a time of civil rights struggle. We performed the function of opening the eyes of students who had come from very protected environments." Other times of controversy yet lay ahead, particularly the one in 1971-72 involving the School of Theology and the Foundation for Religious Studies (see chapter ten) and the one in 1980-81 centering in part on the human sexuality course (see chapter ten). In all of these times of real tension, whatever the issue at hand, a sensitive social conscience and a commitment to academic integrity were part of the ethos out of which the campus sought to respond.

Truth, it was believed, is crucial and does set free. For truth to be well served, freedom was assumed to be an important prerequisite. But so was responsibility. In a school like Anderson, that responsibility was understood to include the prevailing context of Christian faith. Here is a difficult and yet an essential paradox. President Morrison said clearly in 1953 that a college should believe in academic freedom, although the exercise of such freedom can "cause college presidents bad dreams." Why? Because someone involved is likely to have difficulty with the truth that "all social benefits are had at the expense of social restraint" (Callen 1991, 113-114). Then in 1976 President Reardon would reaffirm a similar view of this paradox. "Difficult though it may be," he said, "the church college must bear the intellectual initiative, struggling to hold in balance the affirmations and the questions" (117-118).

In 1983 as the new dean of the undergraduate college, I completed a doctoral dissertation at Indiana University with the title "Faculty Academic Freedom in Member Institutions of the Christian College Coalition." This study explored the delicate balance

197

between faith and freedom in institutions like Anderson. Out of this study, and partly in the wake of a most painful time in 1979-1981 when there was major challenging by some church leaders of the appropriateness of a class, textbook, and professor (see chapter ten), there came about the development of a fresh policy statement for the *Faculty Handbook.* Titled "Academic Freedom and Responsibility," it was approved by the board of trustees in April 1984 (see Appendix E). This statement was followed by the board's approval in 1986 of a parallel policy relating to the acquisition of library materials and faculty and student access to them. In part it read: "The nature and mission of Anderson University encourages an open atmosphere in which faculty and student learning benefit from access to current and historical information representing all available points of view on any subject under examination."

With a curricular broadening in the years after the initial North Central accreditation in 1946, a concern for frontier social issues, and also a commitment to academic integrity, it was to be expected that the question would arise. On June 19, 1954, Dean Olt worded the question in the *Gospel Trumpet,* and then answered it his way for the whole church: "Always the question bobs up, Has the school lost any of its religion in its development? Unquestionably," wrote Olt, "the College is more wholesomely religious today than at any time in its history. That does not mean that the whole time is spent attending religious services or praying, engaging in religious activities, but it does mean that the religious impact is greater today than ever before.... Today testimonies are more effective because they come to the front where they should—that is, by living the Christian message among those not committed to Christ and his way of life" (5-6). He then proceeded to quote in full the college catalog statement, which detailed the specific philosophy of education, curricular focus, and particular meaning of what Anderson College meant by its being a "Christian" college (see Appendix B).

Students into the World Arena

The influence of Dean Olt's compassionate conscience and his inclination to redemptive action in the name of Christ found their way into the college's academic programs and faculty personnel, in fact, into the college's very character. Ministerial education always was crucial to institutional mission. The educating of teachers for the public schools was the first program to receive any kind of formal, outside recognition (1937). Knowing Dean Olt's own commitments, it seems only natural that the areas of sociology, social work, and criminal justice would have developed as predominantly as they did on this campus. In just this one segment of the faculty over the years would come outstanding teachers like Candace Stone (1945), Val Clear (1947), Lavern Norris (1958), and Joe Womack (1970), to name a few of the many who were to carry on the tradition of enabling students to be relevant, redemptive, and action-oriented in the personal and public arenas.

One day a "Center for Public Service" would emerge on campus (see chap. eleven) and a "Student Summer Service" (TRI-S) program (see chap. nine). These would seek to infuse the servant motive into the widest possible range of academic programs and to the farthest reaches of the planet. This intentional, pervasive program focus illustrated what in the 1980s would become a formally worded institutional mission statement. In part it would say that the campus existed to help students "experience what it means to love God and 'neighbor'" and, as a result, "to purposefully adopt a style of servanthood in all of life."

The motive of Christian mission was strong from the earliest days of the campus. Christian Volunteers, sponsored by the Board of Christian Education and the National Youth Fellowship of the Church of God, had developed specific avenues of service which were made available to Anderson College students. They included spending summers doing religious field work, teaching in vacation Bible schools, and functioning as apprentice pastors. Then, with the guiding inspiration of New Testament Professor Marie Strong, a new vehicle evolved for encouraging and organizing students to become involved in Christian service. Apparently the idea began in a Sunday school class at Park Place Church of God, became known as Christianity-in-Action, and soon was the largest and most active of all student organizations. It was said at one time to involve nearly one-third of the entire student body.[10] Students Gustav Jeeninga and Norman Beard were active leaders from the group's beginning in November, 1952, (Jeeninga later to become campus Professor of Old Testament and biblical archaeologist, while Beard became Dean of Students and then in 1964 director of one of the more prominent of all campus programs, TRI-S).

Beard, an accounting/business major, was asked by Professor Strong to be the first student director of this service organization (not a "social club" such as the others on campus). He led in contacting local institutions of the city to enable active student service in literacy assistance, nursing home and hospital visitation, community development, and jail ministry. Committees were set up to supervise these service activities, with a student heading each. One group accompanied Beard in going to local churches in six states to introduce the whole program and help laypersons begin similar ministries through their own congregations. The story of this innovative program of Christian witness and service was explained to the church in the June 19, 1954, issue of the *Gospel Trumpet*. Among the student testimonies was one by Delwin Brown, later to be a prominent professor of philosophy and religion on the Anderson campus and elsewhere. Reporting on the program of trailer court visitation, he said, "we have found that to be a Christian means more than just being a nice person. Christianity demands that we tell the world of the love of God, and the world includes hospitals, jails, shut-ins, underprivileged people" (9).

Of long-term significance was the jail ministry, soon being headed by Lloyd Lambert. He first came to campus as a student during the 1952-53 year as a young Christian, a former G. I. with a family, and a man with an alcohol problem now behind him. He found it natural to relate to socially and chemically troubled men, encouraging their faith in Christ and finding practical ways to get their lives back on track. With the help of campus professors like Marie Strong, Glenn Falls, and Milton Buettner, a place was found downtown for men to go after being released from jail. In November, 1956, this place was opened as a not-for-profit organization.

Called the "Christian Center," it still operates today in Anderson, and Lloyd Lambert, after investing a lifelong ministry of thirty-five years there, remains one of the most respected and loved citizens of the city. He said that "Anderson College had a profound effect on my life." Retiring from the center's executive leadership in 1990, a city-wide banquet in Lambert's honor was held as part of the fall meeting of the Midwestern District of the International Union of Gospel Missions. The banquet included the report that, during his thirty-five years of service, the center in Anderson had given direct assistance to 27,000 people. Robert Reardon, by then president-emeritus, spoke on this occasion of honor. He likened Lambert to the Apostle Paul, always a servant. Following Lambert in the center's leadership was his son Toby (B. A., 1985). The key program vehicle for the beginning of the Christian Center in Anderson was Christianity-in-Action.

As students found their way into youth camps, jails, and rest homes to serve and witness, and in the process to experience valuable dimensions of their own education, even more was happening on campus. There was a vision for the whole world. Several early graduates of Anderson Bible Training School had gone to serve on foreign mission fields. The international Student Volunteer movement had been a significant presence on the Anderson campus since the 1920s, stimulating a missionary interest and commitment among students. One of the many examples of this movement's influence was the experience of student Val Clear (B. A., 1941). The national director of the Student Volunteer movement came to campus in 1941, spoke in chapel, then talked to Val afterwards. Soon Clear was in Peru to teach for four years in a mission college, beginning a life-long teaching career that would feature being an active sociologist back on the Anderson campus. But always he would have an international focus, being influenced, especially by a strong interest in Latin America.

The campus not only sent graduates abroad to learn and serve, but also sought

(Top) Model United Nations Assembly, convened in the "Old Gym" (Byrum Hall)
(Bottom) Eleanor Roosevelt, guest of the Model United Nations,
with Professor Pichon Loh (left) and Dean Robert Nicholson

200

to bring international students to campus. Jamaica, for instance, was one nation to which Anderson graduates very early had gone in Christian service. Amy Lopez, a Jamaican, joined Anderson's faculty in 1927 as a professor of English and Dean of Women. She taught the "King's English" and made sure that her students gave attention to poise and grace, love and compassion. There was "the natural elegance of her warm spirituality" (Strege 1991, 67).

In the 1950s the campus was designating a significant proportion of its student aid dollars for international students. So in September, 1957, three freshmen arrived on campus from Jamaica, each with a four-year tuition scholarship and room/board assistance from the national women's organization of the Church of God. One was Melvyn Hester, an exceptional student who went on to graduate (B. A., 1961) with honors in history. He found the two-year general education program "broad and sound" and he encountered several highly credentialed and influential faculty members. He also found his Anderson education exceptional preparation for his coming life's work. First a teaching assistant at Indiana University, he later completed graduate degrees in the East in the fields of economics and public administration and functioned as the Executive Deputy Administrator/Commissioner of Human Resources of New York City. There he handled a budget of billions and hosted groups of students from Anderson in intense urban experiences. Here was one way that he could pass along a rich heritage.

Dr. Elaine Harper, who was said to teach English with a Southern accent, was judged by Hester to be "a humanist in the best possible sense of that word." There was Dr. Val Clear, Dr. John Carrington, and Dr. Fred Shoot "whose scholarly attitudes," said Hester, "were very influential for me." Most of all was Dr. Pichon P. Y. Loh, Chinese-born political scientist. Loh was a key force behind the ongoing Model United Nations program (see following), in which Hester became active. Loh accepted Hester as his special assistant. They joined during Hester's student days to research and write a scholarly paper on the communist parties in China and the Soviet Union, a pace-setting piece that Loh presented in several influential settings. Hester found the Anderson faculty to be one with two personalities. There still was an *in loco parentis* mentality. Dr. Adam Miller, Dean of Men, once called Hester in, for instance, to discuss the rumor that he was dating a white coed. But there also was in the faculty "a socially progressive crowd" with many doctorates from significant schools. These two personalities, in Hester's view, had a way of combining helpfully to form an excellent educational setting. He sensed quite rightly the school's "prophetic tension with the church," staying close, and yet staying meaningfully ahead.

The great commission of Christ increasingly was being explored in its social, economic, and political dimensions. Of particular educational significance was the "Model United Nations" program staged for the first time on the Anderson campus in the old gymnasium (now Byrum Hall) on April 25-26, 1947. It was sponsored by the International Relations Club, which had been founded in 1945 and chartered by the Carnegie Endowment for International Peace. That year, with W. Shirell Fox functioning as club president and Dr. Candace Stone as faculty adviser, more than seventy of the city's prominent citizens agreed to serve as sponsors. Participants were drawn from all nine of the high schools in Madison County. Here would be a joining of education and community citizenship, both at their best. The 1947 theme was "World Understanding: Your Job" and the guest keynote speaker was the Director of the Language Division, Secretariat of the United Nations. The three major sessions addressed the topics of atomic control, disarmament, and world government.

Beginning with this first Model United Nations in 1947, one was convened on the campus annually (in 1948 the event was a Model Security Council), with Dr. Stone providing active support until her retirement in 1957. By the eighteenth session, held in the new O. C. Lewis Gymnasium in April, 1964, twenty-eight high schools were participating from all over central Indiana, involving nearly six hundred students in 1964 alone. M. Jean Beliard, consul-general of the French consulate in Chicago, was the featured 1964 speaker. This program of experiential education was to continue on campus into the 1970s, with a highlight over its many years being the appearance in 1959 of Eleanor Roosevelt, former first lady of the United States and delegate to the United Nations. She represented effectively much that the whole program stood for, speaking at the final session that year, which was held in Anderson's Madison Heights High School gymnasium, with about two thousand appreciative persons present.

Enlightened citizenship was a maturing reality for Anderson College. The school had become a responsible and contributing member of the academic, church, city, and even world communities. It was on Christian mission "in the world," as it fully intended to be.

1. Robert Adams observed that Nicholson, an effective music educator, director and editor, was not a composer (no songs of his own appeared in the 1953 or 1971 hymnals he edited). See Adams, "The Hymnody of the Church of God (1885-1980) as a Reflection of That Church's Theological and Cultural Changes," doctoral dissertation, Southwestern Baptist Theological Seminary, 1980, 227.

2. In his final report as president to the board of trustees, April 22, 1983.

3. Timothy L. Smith, *Revivalism and Social Reform* (Abingdon Press, 1957).

4. "Little Journeys at Home and Abroad," (unpublished personal papers) written by Russell Olt, April, 1932.

5. In 1923 Indiana was reported to be the leading state both in membership and influence of the Ku Klux Klan. When carrying on membership drives in those years, the Klan would stage parades down the main streets of cities like Anderson, dressed in their ominous white garb, carrying a huge American flag and singing "Onward Christian Soldiers" and "Give Me That Old-Time Religion."

6. The Chicago congregation pastored by Rev. Dunn had emerged out of the racially integrated life of the Missionary Home in that city. E. A. Reardon, father of President Robert Reardon, was instrumental in bringing Rev. Dunn to Chicago as a local pastor. See Robert Reardon, *The Way it Was*, 84.

7. See Barry Callen, *Preparing for Service* (Anderson, Ind: Warner Press, 1988), 65ff.

8. Even though the campus never did practice racial discrimination in the sense of restricting admission or equal opportunity to any one race, still in the 1950s there were controversial campus restrictions against multiracial dating and marriage.

9. For many years and currently, the *Faculty Handbook* lists several causes for the potential dismissal of a faculty member on academic tenure. One such cause is "open, vocal, and sustained contempt for the Christian Faith or the customs generally held by the Church of God (Anderson, Ind.) community." For an extended discussion of the issues inherent in the exercise of academic freedom in church-related colleges, see Barry Callen, "Faculty Academic Freedom in Member Institutions of the Christian College Coalition," Ed. D. dissertation, Indiana University, 1983. Rarely, if ever, has this cause been invoked to justify the release of a faculty member.

10. An extensive recounting of the intent and organization of Christianity-in-Action is found in the B. D. thesis of Norman Beard, "Anderson College: Its Contribution to the Training of the Ministry of the Church of God," Anderson School of Theology, 1958, 72ff.

8 Looking Back and Moving Ahead

1950-1958

> **"**The mid-century call to the church and the challenge for the campus were both to celebrate the past and to 'find new vision and conviction to brace us and set us surging forward.'**"**
>
> (*Yearbook of the Church of God*, 1951)

Mid-century clearly was a crucial time of transition for the Church of God movement. Dating its life back to the years around 1880, the movement now was celebrating its diamond jubilee and reassessing both its past and future. The 1951 *Yearbook of the Church of God* recalled how God, so many years earlier, "was wondrously moving in the hearts of his people" (4-5). That moving was said to have enabled some Christian believers to recognize "the essential wrongness of divisions and ecclesiastical hierarchies." Even so, in the intervening years the Church of God movement had come to accept as appropriate some "necessary organization for service," including institutions such as the college in Anderson.

The call at this seventy-fifth year milestone of the church movement was to celebrate the past and "find new vision and conviction to brace us and set us surging forward." That spirit was shared fully at Anderson College. In fact, the campus took primary leadership in producing a historical film for the church in 1955. Called "From Heaven to Earth," it dramatized and celebrated the past and present of the Church of God movement as an instrument in God's hands. The soundtrack said in part: "Anderson in Indiana finally became the home of the publishing company and the home of the movement.... There from the blessed acres of another Galilee would arise the living quarters of the Gospel Trumpet family that would one day become Anderson College and Theological Seminary." That soundtrack continued, "Anderson in Indiana, a place to train and teach and inspire and inspirit the workers and the missionaries, the ministers, and all those going forth with God in whatever calling and whatever walk of life." [1]

Bulwark of a Courageous Spirit

President John Morrison, himself deeply immersed in the life and history of the Church of God movement, concluded his report to the college board of trustees in June, 1950, with a sober but bold look to the future. With specific reference to the Anderson campus, he said: "We shall start in again next year to work just as though it were the only year given us.... We shall be compassed about with uncertainties.... But God and truth are certain and this certainty keeps Christian colleges with this 'habitual vision of greatness,' and with that vision we go forward.

Many questions indeed were unanswered as the school faced the opening of the second half of the century. The 1940s had brought dramatic growth to the school, with more than a doubling of the student body and even more expansion of the faculty (thirteen full-time members in 1939-40 compared with forty-five in 1949-50). This growth had come for various reasons, particularly the influx of government-funded G. I.s after the war, the regional accreditation of the school in 1946, the large number of former students whose children had reached college age, and the growing feeling among Church of God people that higher education, especially Christian higher education, was appropriate and important for their children. With this institutional growth, however, new and pressing needs also had arisen for adequate facilities and a much broader base of financial support.

So the 1950s began with new campus ventures (the opening of the School of

Front row, (left): Paul Breitweiser, Walter Haldeman, Earl L. Martin, Dean Russell Olt, President John A. Morrison.
Second row, (left): Robert H. Reardon, Mattie Fry, Ann Baker, Ingyr Marie Lien, Mary Lou Barr, Lucille Willoughby, Ruth Ann Ramsay.
Third row, (left): Zylpha Hurlbut, Vila Deubach, Candace Stone, Anna Koglin, Elaine Harper, Betty Lindenschmidt.
Fourth row, (left): Marie Mayo, Cecil Hartselle, Leona Nelson, Valera Notley, Florence Eggert, Treva Gressman.
Fifth row, (left): Harold Linamen, Oliver Oesch, Elbridge Mac Kenzie, John Buehler, Robert Ramsay.
Sixth row, (left): Adam W. Miller, Carl Kardatzke, Robert A. Nicholson, Ross Ekstrom, Malcolm Gressman.
Top row, (left): Burt Coody, John Carrington, Lewis Hennigar, Myrl Ahrendt.

Anderson College Faculty

1950-1951

Theology, for instance—see below) and fresh determination to find the means to remain a viable operation in the face of so many new financial demands. A doubled student body may have increased tuition income, but, at the same time, it had raised many operating costs significantly, and at a time when inflation was eroding the real value of each dollar. President Morrison told the board of trustees in June, 1950, that this general situation was worsened by two other circumstances. First, Church of God World Service had failed for two years in a row to raise its full national budget, thus lessening planned allocations to the participating agencies, including the college. Also, the intended opening of the School of Theology the next fall would "lay an added burden of fifteen thousand dollars upon the college budget," an expenditure not yet accounted for, but still judged "positively necessary." Further, a new library now appeared necessary but expensive. While some twenty thousand dollars in cash and pledges already were in hand toward this dream, that was quite a small sum in relation to the estimated construction cost of about three hundred thousand dollars. Since a new library structure would not be a revenue producing building, the president felt that "we should not go in debt one dollar on the project." That left quite a challenge.

What was the solution? It was simple and painful. Cut operating expenses and raise more money. Help the church raise its budget and get more support from selected individuals. So the decade of the 1940s had ended with an intensified effort to broaden the school's financial base in the firm belief that there were "millions of dollars of untapped resources among Church of God people." [2] In the 1947-48 year a more systematic campaign of financial promotion had been launched to secure bequests, wills, annuities, and life loans. Thomas Ramsay and Charles Cheeks had been employed full time in this effort, Ramsay concentrating on securing wills and bequests while Cheeks was "seeking out persons in the church or those interested in the church who have met with more than average economic success ... and trying to interest them in the work the college is doing." [3]

In June, 1949, President Morrison shared some personal reflections with the board of trustees. It was the end of his thirtieth year with the school. Except for six months in 1938 and ten months in 1946 when he had been absent on leave because of illness (Earl Martin, his half brother, functioning in his place both times), he said that he had been "on duty every hour of every day." Some of the board members had served with him from the time the school first had been incorporated in 1925 until its accreditation in 1946 (S. P. Dunn, A. F. Gray, Earl Martin, and J. T. Wilson—see Appendix A). Now his current term as president was expiring and he wanted the board to know that it should feel free to chose whomever it judged best for the school's future, not being overly influenced "by what would be your natural wish to be considerate of me." Morrison struggled with health limitations and was keenly aware of the great challenges ahead for the school. The board proceeded to act as it thought best, electing Morrison to another term.

From the middle of October, 1951, through the middle of April, 1952, President Morrison was granted a sabbatical period for "general reading, study, writing, and relaxation." An administrative committee was appointed to carry on, chaired by Robert Reardon, the president's assistant. Morrison now had time to review all of his annual reports to the board since the dark financial days of 1932. Dollars, he observed, always had been a real problem over the years. Still, as he would tell the board in June, 1952, "even though the pages of our history have been darkened by this constant note of financial pessimism, they have also been lighted just as constantly by an optimistic note of idealism, spirituality, and consecration. Apparently the only sure bulwark against financial trouble is a brave and courageous spirit." That summer a sound film was completed by a Mr. Alberto Baldecchi and his assistant, Umberto Bonsunouri, of Los Angeles, California.[4] It sought to tell the school's story "in a simple and dynamic way." Now was the time to highlight a proud past and encourage fresh interest in a promising future.

Soon one sensitive and nostalgic event seemed to bring to an appropriate end a whole era in the college's life. In June, 1953, President Morrison, wishing to bring honor where honor was due, invited the J. T. Wilsons to be guests of the campus at the end of that school year. Round-trip train tickets were sent to Fredericksburg, Virginia, where Joseph Wilson, founding principal of the school, was living. He then was "a broken and discouraged man" who had come to feel that "the church did not appreciate what he had done" (Morrison 1962, 147). Very full of feeling, Wilson came and addressed the faculty and the board. He had not been in Anderson for several years and now was delighted at the school's obvious progress. He experienced a welcome sense of personal fulfillment on this special, nostalgic occasion. The following year he, one of the campus greats, would be dead.

The college now was old enough to have had a parade of great leaders march through its life. The quest for institutional maturity and regional accreditation had been long and demanding. By 1950 most of the people who would make the key difference in building the necessary and sturdy foundations for the future already had made their appearance in the school's life. Now, in various ways, they were being singled out and recognized with deep appreciation. One can learn much from the persons a campus identifies for special honor. For example, in most years during the college's first decades *Echoes*, the school yearbook, carried a formal dedication to someone who had had a

(Photos, next 2 pages)

Campus, about 1955: Morrison Hall (1); Kemp Hall (2); Gymnasium (3); *Barnitory* (4);
Old Main (5); Gospel Trumpet Co. (6).   (See page 262 for aerial view, about 1965)

209

(Left)   Russell R. Byrum   (Right)   John H. Kane

deeply appreciated influence on campus life. As would be expected because of their outstanding gifts of leadership and their unusually long tenures, President John A. Morrison
was so honored in 1927, 1939, and again in his retirement year of 1958. Dean George
Russell Olt received such recognition in 1928, 1933, 1943, and 1959 (in memoriam).

Less expected, but very reflective of campus values and church relatedness,
were the several *Echoes* dedicated to the influential pastors of Park Place Church of God
(H. A. Sherwood in 1924 and 1932, Albert F. Gray in 1929, E. A. Reardon in 1944, and
W. Dale Oldham in 1948). There also were the beloved teachers Bessie L. Byrum, honored in the 1923 and 1931 editions, Amy K. Lopez in the 1933 and 1936 editions, and
Earl L. Martin in the releases of 1934 and 1957. The distinguished list of dedications
even includes a loved field representative, W. E. Monk in the 1930 edition, and a school
janitor, Charles Kissell in 1951.

Greatness was an honored quality and usually was defined in relation to true
servanthood. Robert Reardon recalled that he went to his first footwashing service when
he was ten years old, an "ordinance" of humility and service practiced by Church of God
people because they understood Jesus to have directed his disciples that way. But foot-

washing took on its intended meaning for young Robert only in his high school years when once he saw President Morrison kneel and wash the feet of a janitor. That indeed was a powerful symbol of service, fellowship, the true church in action. For many years on the Anderson campus, it was a janitor who, in his own humble way, helped to show the way for generations of students and staff members.

Charlie Kissell had been born in 1892 as a Lithuanian in central Russia. In 1907 he was smuggled out of the country in a load of hay and made it to America where his sister was living. By 1924 he had found his way to Anderson College, a simple man with virtually no education and yet a man possessing an infectious spiritual vitality. The *Echoes* of 1951 was dedicated to him for his twenty-seven years of faithful service and Christian influence in the campus community. As one of many stories about him goes, he once was asked to offer the prayer in a college chapel service. He was both delighted and nervous. With all eyes closed, he began this way in all sincerity: "God bless the President, the Dean, and all other problems of life!" Many faces couldn't help but smile, knowing what this beloved man really meant. As the years would come and go, Charlie was joined by Galen "Coach" Smith (a son of F. G. Smith) and many others as campus personalities lacking in fancy titles and yet especially rich in human and Christlike qualities that went a long way to make the campus the special place it was.

Other persons were singled out to receive honorary doctoral degrees at the annual commencement ceremony or to have their revered names attached to magnificent new buildings on campus (see Appendices P and R). Russell R. Byrum finally would receive from the church a well-deserved recognition. Brought back by special invitation to a session of the General Assembly of the Church of God, he was called forward as a now elderly man separated for decades from his early leadership in the church and school by those sad events of the late 1920s. The whole Assembly stood to its feet and welcomed him with vigorous and long applause. So very much had happened since his resignation from the school's faculty in 1929. Both the school and the whole church were the poorer for his long absence from a place of significant church leadership. Honor seemed so little and so late in this case. At least it had been given shortly before his death in 1980.

There, however, were thousands of others less heralded and yet, in their own ways, no less important. Many alumni were so appreciative of their college experiences that their children and grandchildren began to follow in their paths to and from the beloved Anderson campus. Does Christian higher education run in families? By 1954 President Morrison was able to celebrate the presence on campus of a member of the third generation of students coming from one family. It was in the fall of 1925 that C. O. and Vernie Newman had arrived in Anderson, students they later said "as green as the farm we left." Then, in the fall of 1933, their daughter Frances had come. Now in 1954

213

freshman Don Hull arrived, a grandson, thought to be the first from a third generation of any family. Many other families soon would be represented on this campus by multiple generations.

An excellent example is a couple who, then retired in Anderson in 1990, would celebrate together their sixty-fifth wedding anniversary. At that time of celebration they had five children (four living), twenty grandchildren and eighteen great-grandchildren. Both John and Dora (Gerig) Batdorf had received diplomas from Anderson Bible Training School in 1924. By 1961, nine members of their immediate family had come to be part of the Anderson College scene since the early 1920s, and more were yet to come.[5] John would follow his years of pastoring with some time as a development officer back on campus. Dora would serve as a housemother of Martin Hall and continue her own collegiate studies at her *alma mater*, graduating in 1961 just before her youngest daughter completed her work in 1962.

John H. Kane worked for years to encourage alumni loyalty. Himself an alumnus (B. Th., 1921, 1939), he first had come to the campus in 1919 from Grand Junction, Colorado. He then had returned in 1944 to direct alumni activities after years of inspired pastoral leadership. A decade later, and for obvious reasons, the campus celebrated with him his effective, rewarding, and continuing alumni work. Repeatedly he had crisscrossed the country recruiting students, meeting with alumni, and spreading goodwill for the school. He was a spark plug, an editor (*Alumni News*), the "Jovial John" who would receive the honorary Doctor of Divinity degree in 1953 (see Appendix P) and after whom the Kane Dining Room would be named when the new Olt Student Center finally would be built (see Appendix R). His wife Cynthia also meant much to the community. Their son John attended the college in the 1940s and in 1946 married another student, Eunice Morrison, daughter of Gordon Morrison, who himself had graduated from the Training School in 1922 when his own brother, John, was assistant principal. Mark, son of John and Eunice, carried on the family tradition of relatedness to the campus (B. A., 1969; M. R. E., 1973; M. A., 1974).

Life in a Young Seminary

The board of trustees had taken the historic action back in June, 1949. Dr. Earl L. Martin, widely respected and loved in the Church of God, was named dean of the new School of Theology.[6] He had been a faculty member ever since 1930 when he had received the B. Th. degree. In 1936 Northwestern University had granted him the M. A. and Anderson the B. D.[7] The initial graduate school faculty for 1950-51, in addition to the dean, was comprised of only one full-time member, Dr. Gene W. Newberry, who taught Christian Theology, Church History, Philosophy of Religion, and Psychology of

Religion. The remainder of the first-year courses were taught on a part-time basis by campus persons Adam W. Miller (New Testament) and Robert H. Reardon (Pastoral Work and Leadership), and national church agency leaders Harold L. Phillips (Preaching), T. Franklin Miller (Christian Education), and Charles E. Brown, a special lecturer in Theology.

With one graduate degree offered, the 90 semester hour Bachelor of Divinity degree, the stated purpose of the School of Theology was to provide graduate courses of study for persons planning to enter the Christian ministry, including the roles of local church pastor, missionary, director of religious education, teacher of religion, and evangelistic and social worker.[8] The education was intended to be practical, with required field education, and theoretical, with a required thesis to be written by all potential graduates.[9] Classes were scheduled on a Tuesday-Wednesday and Thursday-Friday basis to accommodate persons driving from a distance. Standards of the Association of Theological Schools were in view in the development of all aspects of curriculum and community life. Clearly there would be a seeking of this professional accreditation at the earliest possible date.

From the beginning, seminary students were provided with a high level of financial aid. Tuition initially was set at $150 per semester but with $125 of that covered by scholarship. As President Morrison stated to the board in his report of June, 1950: "This new enterprise lays an added burden of $15,000 upon the college budget. But it is positively necessary, and we must find some way to finance it." It was a labor of love. There was no financial campaign and no increased giving from the church for the seminary project. The institutional operating budget for 1950-51 was $480,000, with the added seminary costs representing more than three percent of the total.

The relationship of the School of Theology to the larger institution had several dimensions. Adam Miller made clear that ministerial education courses would continue to be offered in the college with majors in Bible and Religious Education and minors in Practical Ministries and Christian Doctrine. It was important for the church to know that the undergraduate college was not abandoning ministerial education because of its opening of the seminary. Organizationally, the seminary, with its own dean and the beginnings of its own faculty, was administered by the institution's single president and board of trustees. While business and registrar support services were supplied to college and seminary by the same offices, recognition was made of the stance of the Association of Theological Schools that an accredited seminary should have significant and obvious independence, even if within a single school structure.[10]

That separation was seen in part by the facility arrangements. The seminary was given its own classrooms in the southeast wing of the third floor of Old Main. A new and fully separate library was established according to what was understood to be

ATS expectations. Three classrooms in that same wing were combined for this library (the college library with about 22,000 volumes was on the fourth floor). Even a different book classification system was introduced.[11] By November, 1950, 1,200 volumes were reported to have been given to the new seminary library by fifteen persons (especially members of the administration and faculty, one alumni chapter, and several of the church agencies in   Anderson).[12] A special graduate school book club was announced in 1952. Since more books were needed urgently, the appeal was for persons who would agree to buy two books per year for the seminary library, with the faculty selecting the appropriate titles. Harold Phillips helped greatly by using his travels for the Gospel Trumpet Company to visit used book stores in Kansas City, Chicago, New York City, and elsewhere, looking for key volumes that could be purchased inexpensively.

Before the seminary actually opened in October, 1950, the report was made that, despite the modest beginning resources, "the students of the first few years will carry away something never to be tasted by a later generation—the zest of a new venture, the close-knit fellowship of a small group." [13] Later testimony did substantiate this projection; nevertheless, the successful building of a sense of community in the new seminary was a difficult challenge. The student body was small, with some of the students attending only on a part-time basis and most of them pastoring or being otherwise employed and sometimes driving to classes from out of town. Classes were held in the midst of the college's life and most of the faculty had a range of other responsibilities competing for time. While the new seminary was a conscious and major commitment, some people found it easy to feel that the small seminary was a mere stepchild in the larger family of college life.

That first seminary class included thirty-five graduate students. Most of them were Church of God men who had graduated from the undergraduate college.[14] George Kufeldt, for instance, had graduated from the college with the B. A. in 1945 and the B.Th. in 1946. After having served most recently as pastor of his home church in Homestead, Florida, for two years, he learned of the seminary's beginning and made immediate plans to return. With him would come his wife, Kathryn, a local Anderson woman and Anderson College student whom he had married when an undergraduate, and their two small children. He soon was employed by Delco Remy in Anderson and worked there throughout his seminary years. Less typical was Kenneth Prunty, who had never been to Anderson prior to the summer of 1950. He came to the seminary that first year immediately after graduating from South Dakota State University with a major in

(Top) Gene Newberry, Robert Reardon, Adam Miller
(Bottom) First School of Theology faculty, 1950, (left): Harold Phillips, T. Franklin Miller, Gene Newberry, Robert Reardon, Adam Miller, Earl Martin

217

sociology. Influenced to come to the seminary by his Church of God pastor, Kenneth brought his wife Florene. She found employment at the campus business office and Kenneth, like George, went to work at Delco Remy.

In June, 1953, eight of those first thirty-five students received their Bachelor of Divinity degrees.[15] Their three years had been busy and fulfilling Those not pastoring had been encouraged to be on call for ministerial service in the area on weekends. Seminary chapel services each Wednesday and Friday had brought inspiration and helped mold a diverse group of individuals into a worshiping community of young ministers and scholars. By April of that first year Dr. Newberry had guided the organizing of the seminary student body along the lines of the Oberlin Student Union Plan.[16] Every student was to serve on one of the various commissions, including Christian service, athletics, publications, social life, social action, and interseminary. Dewayne Bell was elected first president of the seminary' s executive council and Lonnie Swan edited a little publication called *The Seminarian.*

Of the first thirty-five students in 1950, only three were women, and they took only one course each. Of the seventy-two different persons enrolled in 1953-54, still only two were women. Later the enrollment of women would rise to as high as 20 percent of the total. Never to date, however, have women been present in the School of Theology to the degree that now has come to be common in American theological education. Over the years only three women would be members of the full-time faculty.[17] Since nearly all students were male and most were married, there was obvious need for their spouses to have fellowship opportunities and address together their common concerns. They faced a life of ministry with their husbands and often felt unprepared and unclear about their future roles.

As the seminary began, one club on campus called the DAMES Club promoted friendliness and understanding among the married women of the college. At first the seminary wives sought to participate in the life of this club. By 1951, however, it was obvious that a separate group was needed for women of the seminary. Initially it was known as Divinity Dames, later Grad Wives, and then *Kalim* (meaning "vessel" in Hebrew).

With the significant and varied seminary backgrounds of the faculty and the Christian unity focus of the Church of God heritage, an ecumenical emphasis in seminary life was inevitable. In the fall of 1951 three seminary students attended and then expressed sincere appreciation for an interseminary conference that had convened at Winebrenner Graduate School of Divinity in Findlay, Ohio.[18] By 1952 there was formal participation in the national Interseminary Movement and participation in meetings at Earlham College in Richmond, Indiana, Bexley Hal in Gambier, Ohio, and Butler University School of Religion in Indianapolis, Indiana. Donald Courtney, later to return to the seminary as professor of Christian Education, chaired Anderson's Interseminary Commission in 1952.

An important new program thrust was initiated in 1952, in part to enhance this ecumenical concern. Robert Reardon, then identified in the college catalog as Coordinator of Public Relations, initiated the concept of "Vocations Days" on campus. The grand idea was to bring to campus large numbers of high school juniors and seniors and then guide them as they sought opportunities for Christian service in many walks of life. The numerous pastors and youth counselors who would accompany them, beginning that first time in May, 1952, were to be treated to special programming, including the first of the seminary-related Laymen Lecture Series.[19] These functions, happening simultaneously, represented a service to the church's young people, an effective new student recruitment tool, a good way to promote the young School of Theology, and a means for the exposure of Church of God leaders and seminary students to the stimulating thinking of some of the best Christian minds of the time. Lecturers in those early years included Dr. Paul S. Rees, Minister of the Covenant Church, Dr. Walter M. Horton of Oberlin Graduate School of Theology, Dr. Charles Templeton, Evangelist of the National Council of Churches, Dr. Wayne Oates of Southern Baptist Seminary, Dean Elmer Homrighausen of Princeton Theological Seminary, and Dean Floyd V. Filson of McCormick Theological Seminary.[20]

Genuine expansion was experienced by the seminary as it began its third year in the fall of 1952. There now were over fifty students originating from twenty-three different states, Canada and China. The southwest wing of Old Main's third floor was acquired for increased library and classroom space, and two full-time additions were made to the faculty. John W. V. Smith, a doctoral candidate at the University of Southern California, came from Pacific Bible College in Portland, Oregon, to teach church history, and Delena Goodman, graduate of Oberlin College, came from Decatur, Illinois, to be seminary librarian. Now the staff was adequate to implement the full three-year program. Dean Earl Martin, having suffered a heart attack and then seeking relief from administrative burdens, returned to teaching and writing in 1953 (primarily in the college). Dr. Adam W. Miller assumed the seminary's administrative leadership. Good foundations already had been laid for the future.

Sidney Johnson, later to become a beloved career missionary in the Church of God, recalls his three years at the School of Theology (1952-55) as "the best three years of my life as far as my ministry is concerned." The seminary was like "a big family." The faculty members were deeply committed to the life of the church, and they conveyed to Johnson and many other students a sense "that something really important was happening." So it was.

Dollars, Bricks, and Books

The decade of the 1950s witnessed more than the founding and maturing of a seminary on campus. President Morrison reported that the 1953-54 year saw total enrollment reach 1,076 (college and seminary, 883 full time). This was the largest enrollment in the institution's history and, said Morrison, made Anderson the sixth largest in size among twenty private schools in the state. Two years later the number would rise to 1,139 (college) and 81 (seminary), a total of 1,220, which was exactly double the number of students on campus a decade earlier when accreditation first had been achieved. Student recruitment now was being done by the offices of the president and the director of alumni, with Robert Reardon, John Kane, and a campus committee taking the lead.

Reardon coordinated these increasingly successful recruitment efforts. There were mailings, alumni rallies, showings of the college film, the college choir tours directed by Robert Nicholson, drama tours directed by Malcolm Gressman, and summer tours of a men's quartet and a women's trio. The spring Vocation Days program in 1953 brought to campus 473 high school juniors and seniors and 116 pastors. Focused particularly on high school students in Madison County, there also was a Science Day on campus and, of course, the annual Model United Nations.

Although such activities, which focused on local high school students, certainly had increased in recent years, the president told the board of trustees in June, 1954, that "the primary function of this institution is to serve the educational interests of the Church. With this in mind," he said, "our recruiting program is beamed in the direction of the young people throughout our movement."

The college graduating class of 1953 included eighty-nine people who initially were placed as follows: thirty-two ministerial students (eighteen to pastorates, fourteen to seminary—eleven of these to the School of Theology), thirty-one teachers, eleven to graduate schools other than seminary, ten to business, two to religious education, and three "special." That also was the year that the young School of Theology on campus graduated its first class (see detail above).

What was the general financial environment in which the school was living as it sought to educate more and more students? The picture painted by President Morrison in June, 1951, was hardly encouraging. Looking at recent trends, he said, "The cost of instruction, supplies and maintenance of facilities has more than doubled, while income from endowment has gone down and down. Tuition and fees have been raised again until the traffic will bear no more." "Teachers," he continued, "have been unable to exist on the salaries offered them."

Many colleges were finding themselves operating in the red. In 1954-55, for instance, about 70 percent of the Anderson College's total operating budget of some seven hundred thousand dollars was coming directly from student tuition and fees. The president spoke of moving that percentage down to 50 where it belonged, but as yet he could not see how to get that done. Over the years that percentage would be brought down somewhat, but not as low as his goal of 50 percent.

If the school intended to remain distinctive and serve primarily the church's young people, then the college assumed that the church must provide increasing support. Morrison spared no words as this point was made to the board of trustees in June, 1951. His argument went like this: "The Church of God is just as much duty-bound to support Christian higher education as . . . home and foreign missions or any other aspect of church work. I am dead certain that the Church of God today owes its existence as a wide-awake, aggressive, spiritual, progressive, intelligent religious movement to the fact that a third of a century ago she entered upon a positive program of education." To be fair, the president was not scolding the church for any serious lack of support. He was highlighting the magnitude of the challenge at hand. In fact, he would tell the board with pride in 1957 both that, apart from student tuition, most of the remaining income for operating expenses was coming from Church of God World Service and that the college ranked first among the church-related colleges of Indiana in the proportion of its income that came from the church.

But church support, however generous, would not be adequate. New sources of income had to be found. Soon these sources were to include wills, private corporations, committed business and professional friends, foundations, even the state and federal governments through student aid and low-interest loans. Since the late 1940s Thomas Ramsay had been working to secure the writing of wills that included the college. Although it cost the college several thousand dollars each year to fund this effort, often with little immediate cash flow result, Ramsay's work was viewed as a long-term investment, a calculated venture of faith. By 1954 he had secured 803 wills, to add to a few other wills and estates that had been arranged through the development work of his colleague, Charles Cheeks.

Then a relatively new idea came along. The industrial community was coming to realize that it had a social responsibility to help support higher education. Institutions of higher education in many states were considering banding together to further encourage this realization and to seek funding from this source. The first example was the Associated Colleges of Indiana. In the 1951-52 year, Anderson College joined this effort as a charter member, committing the college president to twenty days a year of personal solicitation on behalf of the association. About $250,000 was raised in 1952-53, with Anderson getting $12,000. There was hope for more in years to come. By 1956-57 total receipts exceeded $600,000 and Anderson's share was about $40,000. It was a modest, although an important new source of revenue. Soon even the new seminary would

221

engage in such an effort for a few years, in this case with the Associated Theological Schools of Ohio and Indiana (ATSOI). The case made by ATSOI to private corporations was that quality theological education raises the moral level of the society in which they seek to do business.

President Morrison informed the board of trustees in June, 1957, that during the previous two or three years a deep concern had been felt on the part of some Church of God business people for the financial well-being of the college. "Already several thousand dollars had been given as these persons began addressing their concern," and, said the president, "preliminary steps have been taken to implement this movement." In 1957 a small group of business and professional men met in the home of Wilbur Schield in Waverly, Iowa, and there brought into being the "Anderson College Business and Professional Men's Foundation." Early members included Adam Macholtz, who was Vice-President of Pemco, Inc., in St. Joseph, Michigan, and father of two sons educated at Anderson College (James and Robert). Vern Schield, founder of Schield Bantam Corporation of Waverly, Iowa, became involved because, as he was quoted in a 1964 booklet on the Foundation, "honesty and integrity are still great requirements to successful business. Anderson College provides a Christian education which is so much needed in our business world today."

In that same publication Charles M. Schulz of California, creator of the "Peanuts" cartoon, said that he believed in the school "because it holds for me the hope for a continuing educated ministry. The air-waves of today carry enough false prophecy. We need the assurance," said Schulz, "that young Church of God ministers will receive an education from an institution that will teach them faith in a reasonable doctrine for reasonable men."

There were many others who felt much like Lowell J. Williamson, then president of Plaza Oil and Gas, Ltd., Calgary, Alberta, Canada. He said: "In an age of planned obsolescence and a penchant for change, it gives me great satisfaction to keep my ties with Anderson College, which has continuously offered a unique blend of academic, spiritual, and social values."

So the financial base of the college was broadening. With such growing resources, there was much to be done. During the 1950s the first stage in the construction of many new facilities had begun. Leading the way, of course, had been Morrison Hall, dedicated in October, 1949. At that time the new facility had been designated for the proper housing of women. Now something had to be provided for men. In June, 1952, the board of trustees took steps to authorize the possible securing of a low-interest

(Top) Kemp Music Hall
(Bottom) President Morrison sets cornerstone for new Wilson Library

TABLE 14

College Degrees Conferred
1943-1957

Year	B.A.	B. S.	B. Th.
1942-43	12	10	17
1943-44	1	12	14
1944-45	5	22	22
1945-46	18	25	20
1946-47	16	25	29
1947-48	24	21	11
1948-49	42	31	14
1949-50	49	72	30
1950-51	41	49	15
1951-52	37	51	11
1952-53	35	45	9
1953-54	32	32	9
1954-55	35	40	3
1955-56	42	37	13
1956-57	30	43	6

loan from the federal government. Already an excellent site for the location of a new residence hall had been purchased from Maplewood Cemetery, lying just to the north across from the main campus. The following spring, after considerable effort on the part of Robert Reardon and Chester Edwards (business manager and treasurer), a loan of $550,000 was approved. That summer, through a contract with Associated Builders, Inc. of Anderson, the construction began. Dedication came in October, 1954. Then in June 1960 this new men's residence hall was given the name Dunn Hall in honor of long-term and now deceased trustee and church leader Sethard P. Dunn (see Appendix R).[21]

As early as 1953, concurrent with efforts to fund and build adequate student housing, there were vigorous efforts to gather the resources necessary to build a new library on the site of Kemp Music Hall. After all, how much longer could a college with about one thousand students and expanding programs function with a library cramped on

(Top) Dedication of Wilson Library
(Bottom) President Morrison, Charles E. Wilson, Dean Olt

the fourth floor of Old Main and able to seat no more than two hundred? About $125,000 of pledges already were in hand for this purpose, including gifts from Charles E. Wilson and others, and about $100,000 of the church's Mid-Century Campaign goal earmarked for a new library on the Anderson campus. More, however, was needed before beginning and a fund drive in the city of Anderson soon was envisioned. Locally the ground was laid by a public relations program directed by twenty leading citizens. The public was told about the value of Anderson College to the community. Then the firm of Marts and Lundy, Inc., of New York City guided many local workers in seeking $250,000 for the new library, seen by the school as an "absolute necessity to the ongoing of the institution."

The school had worked from its beginning to establish and enrich its relevance to the life of the Church of God movement. With the library project and the local campaign to raise $250,000 in Anderson came the opportunity and the need to do the same establishing of relevance in relation to the city. A fine booklet was produced with a picture of Old Main superimposed on a view of the downtown area of Anderson. Titled "Enriched by Cooperation," this key campaign piece reviewed briefly the history of Anderson College. That history was called a "magnificent record of growth and vitality," a record "in which every citizen of the city of Anderson can take pride, for it reflects the virility of a growing city in a great state."

The relevance of the campus to the public locally was emphasized in all ways possible. In 1954 about 300 students were preparing to be teachers in the public schools. While the college was national in scope, that year 246 students were enrolled from Madison County, and the total student body was estimated to be contributing annually about $1,100,000 to the economic life of the city. Thus the campaign goal of $250,000 represented only about one-quarter of the amount that students were giving to the city each year. A letter from President Morrison addressed to "Fellow Andersonians" was reproduced in the booklet. It began by saying: "At the turn of the century when the founding fathers of the Church of God selected Anderson as a site to locate their headquarters, they chose well. Anderson College is proud to be a part of this thriving industrial community."

As funding efforts proceeded and construction preparations were made, a welcome breakthrough on another front came in the spring of 1956. The Lilly Endowment of Indianapolis, solicited for years by the campus without success, pledged $50,000 to the library fund if the school raised a matching $50,000.

Soon there would be a "Lilly Lounge" in a new library. This was the beginning of a long list of generous grants that the Lilly Endowment would make to the campus in years to come (see Appendix S). Linfield Myers and Judge Harold Achor, as well as H. E. Hastings of the Associated Colleges of Indiana, had been helpful in securing this first

Prominent campus women. (Standing, left): Blanche Martin,
Cynthia Kane, Eva Clare Kardatzke.
(Seated, left): Adeline Olt, Eunice Morrison

and vital grant from the Endowment. Also in 1955-56 funding help for the first time came from a national foundation. The Ford Foundation made a large gift to education, with Anderson College receiving about $170,000. This money was to be considered endowment, with earnings used to increase faculty salaries. While not usable directly for the library, it was academically related and of great encouragement.

The long dream became reality when the library itself was built during the 1956-57 year. With the impressive structure completed, the 30,000 books were moved in special boxes that went out a window on the fourth floor of Old Main, traveled on a cable that was elevated on poles across the ravine, and went into a second floor window of the new library. What a sight! The fourth floor of the library was developed into the "Little Theatre," an intimate place for many memorable productions in the years to come. Dedication was scheduled for October 26, 1957, during the annual Harvest Festival and Homecoming (see Appendix R). This would be an occasion with more media attention focused on it than any other occasion to date in the school's history.

Charles Wilson, former industrial leader in Anderson and then Secretary of Defense under President Dwight Eisenhower, agreed to be present and give the main address. The proud new library building would carry Wilson's name and a wall would carry his portrait, given by his family. Total cost of the structure had risen to $620,000, an amount fully covered by gifts, grants, and pledges by dedication day. It would be a day of real celebration!

As the president recalled for the board of trustees the following June, "Some 5,000 friends from the church and from the city attended the dedication. National coverage was given the affair by newspapers, radio, and television. This new library building is regarded as one of Indiana's most beautiful buildings. A picture of the library appeared in an issue of *Life Magazine*." Campus staff person Shirell Fox spoke over a national radio network. Never before had the morning and evening newspapers of Anderson devoted so much space to any college-related story. Thousands gathered along Third Street on the north side of the new library for the dedication ceremonies. It was a very cold, windy day, but there was considerable warmth in what was happening. The campus, the city, and scores of key college friends had joined to accomplish something significant.

The ceremonies began with an organ processional played by the minister of music at Park Place Church of God and soon to be a professor of English, Milton Buettner. Following were an invocation offered by President-Elect Robert Reardon and two musical selections by the Anderson College Choir directed by Professor Robert Nicholson, soon to be the new college dean. Appropriately, the two selections were "Hallelujah" and "I Hear America Singing."

Even with the two new student residence halls and a magnificent new library, the facility needs of this growing campus were far from met. During the years of the library's funding and construction, efforts were made to secure another low-interest (2.7%) government loan for yet another residence hall. They finally were successful and construction was underway on a second new hall for women. It would be located along Third Street, occupied for the second semester of 1958-59, and named in honor of Earl L. Martin (see Appendix R).

So the decade was ending with four fine new buildings on campus, three residence halls and a library. More was needed rather urgently, however, particularly a student center with food service facilities and a new gymnasium. They would become reality in the decade to follow.

President Morrison with his beloved autobiography

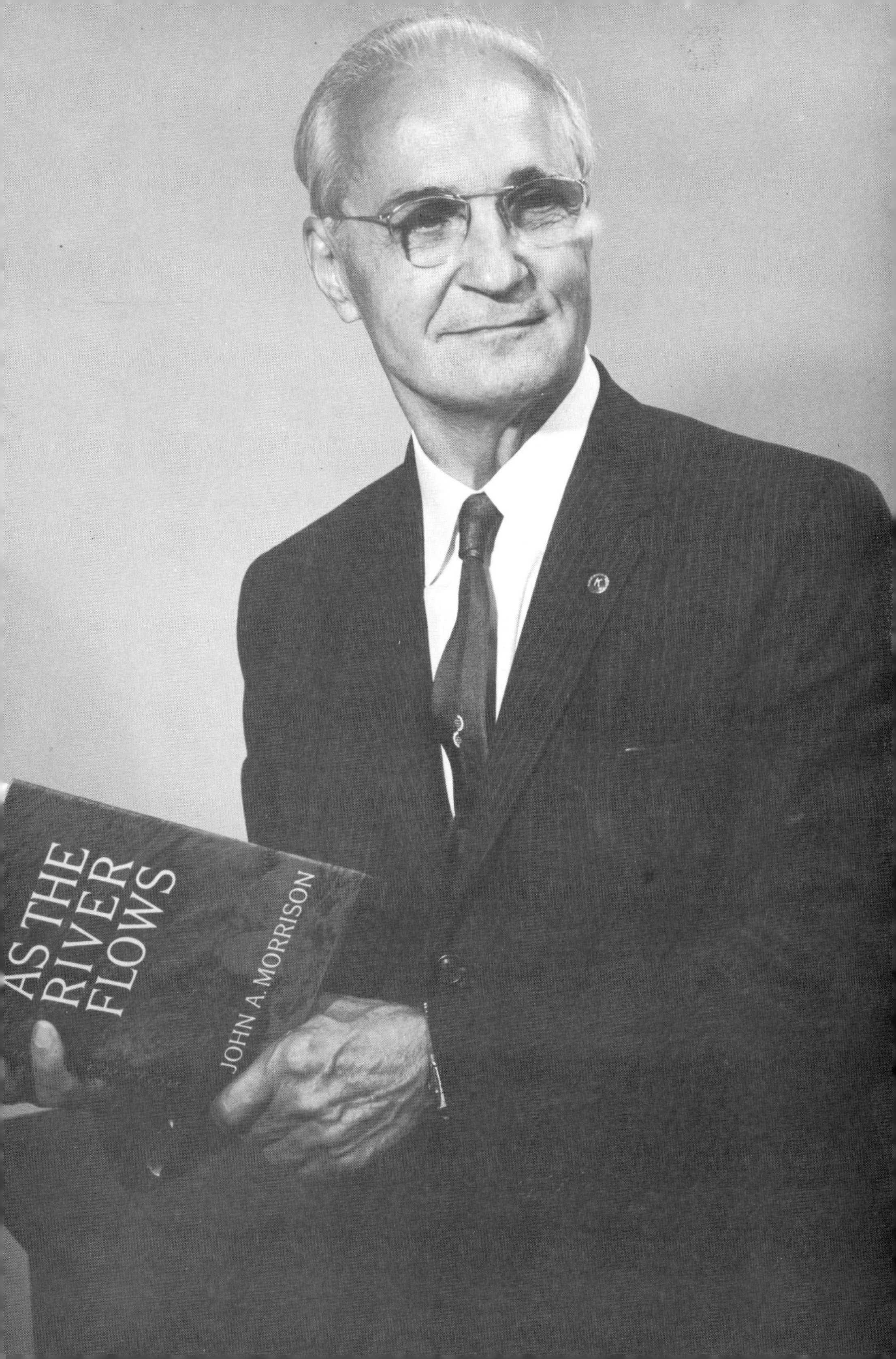

AS THE RIVER FLOWS

JOHN A. MORRISON

Dean Olt and student Carl Erskine

Changing Curriculum, Changing Times

In 1959-60 the first formal review occurred by North Central of the institutional accreditation first achieved in 1946. As one of his early tasks, Dr. Robert A. Nicholson, by then the new college dean, led in the preparation of a self-study that leaned heavily on the extensive work accomplished by the President's Study and Planning Commission in 1955-57 (see following and chapter nine). The examination team that came to campus

230

was impressed with the goals set by this Commission and were convinced that likely they would get accomplished. The visitors called Anderson a "dynamic institution" and added: "The new administration is aware of its responsibilities. There is over-all faculty support. Apparently the congregations of the Church are sympathetic to the tasks that Anderson has undertaken." [22]

Anderson College, said the team, "has a highly qualified faculty." Of its reported fifty members, twenty-five held the doctor's degree and twenty-three others the master's, placing the campus "well above the 75th percentile ranking established in the 'Trends' report of 1958." Faculty salaries, however, "appear to be the central problem facing Anderson.... If it is true that almost every male member ... receives supplementary income from outside work, the need for increased faculty salaries is apparent."

But President Reardon contested this team impression of "almost every male member" and its suggestion that existing outside employment was primarily for additional income. While he did not want to defend the salaries as adequate, he did report to North Central the findings of a careful survey of the faculty. Only twelve full-time faculty members, in fact, were employed outside regular teaching duties. In no case was such work unrelated to the teacher's professional field, and often, he insisted, such involvement enriched rather than detracted from classroom effectiveness. The administration did address the legitimate concern about faculty salaries (see chapter nine), but over a period of years and with a cautious eye on related issues that had an effect on the stewardship of over-all operations

The new library, of course, was a significant advancement for the academic program in general. It, however, was supplemented by other developments during the 1950s. For instance, in 1956-57 the college received a $15,000 grant from Lilly Endowment for improving methods of instruction.

Dr. Robert Nicholson (soon to become college dean) chaired a committee that decided how best to use these funds. A group of Anderson professors spent a few weeks at the University of Michigan under the guidance of specialists, and then a master teacher of national reputation was invited to the Anderson campus.

Academic curriculum always received faculty attention. Table 14 shows the undergraduate degrees conferred over a fifteen-year period, with the most striking change being the lessening number of Bachelor of Theology degrees following the opening of the School of Theology in 1950. This trend was not away from theological education, but toward the graduate level for specialization, typically based upon the B. A. program. The Bachelor of Arts curriculum was designed around a traditional liberal arts program emphasizing a breadth of general education and restricted specialization. The Bachelor of Science, first introduced on campus in 1942, provided for greater specialization in teacher education, music, and business. Appendix L groups the 881 undergraduate students in 1956-57 by the fields or special programs in which they were majoring.

In 1947-48 the faculty had introduced an integrated, two-year, general education program "to provide a unified body of knowledge before specialization in the junior and senior years." It assumed that there are "basic principles and concepts to the Good Life and Christian Citizenship which all students should hold in common." This program was a voluntary set of core courses in the humanities, social studies, and sciences that operated until 1961 when it was discontinued for lack of student appeal. According to the "Institutional Profile" written for the North Central Association in 1970, this curriculum's primary weakness was "its failure to align properly with professional and other vocationally-oriented programs." The faculty then decided to move to a single degree program, the B. A., beginning in 1961 (see chapter nine). Within this curriculum was one program of distribution requirements established for all students regardless of career goal. About half of this 124-hour degree was to be devoted to general studies.

A review of the annual reports of Dean Olt to the board of trustees during the 1950s reflects several important aspects of the academic life of the college. Inter-institutional cooperation was pioneered with an evening program of courses beginning in September 1953 and offered jointly by the college and Purdue University.[23] This relationship would be renewed in the 1980s on an even larger scale. The faculty was loyal and stable generally, with only two to four resignations each year. The dean explained each departure to the board of trustees, as well as the successes in new faculty recruitment. Professional growth was an important consideration, including an active program of sabbatical leaves. As Olt told the board in June, 1953: "We confidently believe that by 1960 our faculty will be unsurpassed in strength by that of any church-related college in the country. Plans are under way to have everyone except those near retirement age fully qualified professionally by holding the doctor's degree."

Academic roles other than teaching also were being valued. In 1952-53, for instance, President Morrison's seventh book was out and Dr. Adam Miller's *Introduction to the Old Testament* soon would be released. Dr. Lewis Hennigar was the elected secretary of the Indiana Philosophical Association, and Dr. Vila Deubach was chosen president of the College English Association. While Dr. Candace Stone was on leave studying social conditions in Europe, Dr. John Buehler's "Synthesis of Amino Acids" study was published in the *Journal of the American Chemical Society*. These are only representative illustrations of the many professional roles being filled and the research and writing projects being completed by faculty members.

Responsibilities other than being the supervisor of traditional academics were prominent on Dean Olt's agenda. He tracked carefully student enrollment patterns, worried about the impact of excessive student employment off campus, and kept a watchful eye on a range of evolving student personnel services. In June, 1956, he summarized these services for that school year. "A number of behavior problems cropped up; serious ones were dealt with severely.... The Director (Vila Deubach) reports a total of 191 students were granted scholarships, grants-in-aid, remitted tuition, railroad refunds, vocational rehabilitation, and loans from college funds.... The total amount expended in this program was $32,764." All of these activities received at least general supervision from Dean Olt. Then in the summer of 1958, which saw the death of Dean Olt, Norman Beard assumed the role of director of student affairs as Dr. Deubach, while remaining chair of the Department of English, became librarian.

Much about campus life was changing, usually in the direction of crossing new frontiers in the pursuit of long-term goals. In physical education, for instance, the "golden age" of athletics and physical education sometimes is said to have begun in 1953 when brothers James and Robert Macholtz joined the faculty. There had been quality leadership earlier, especially with Ernie Rangazas, who remained as department chair until 1959. But finally there was a strong Church of God presence in athletics and, especially with James Macholtz, a long-term person with academic strength who would help integrate physical education and athletics into the larger academic and religious mission of the campus. Winning years were ahead with James Macholtz coaching football and his brother Robert coaching basketball (see Appendix J).

Much of campus social life for students revolved around the social clubs.[24] In 1952-53, Triad staged its annual All-School Amateur Hour in October. Then in November Rowenna Dodge was crowned homecoming queen (see Appendix K) during the Harvest Festival activities, the initial meeting of Christianity-in-Action was held in the cafeteria, and a capacity crowd jammed the college gym to enjoy the Booster Club's musical, "American Tribute." During semester two, Dr. Samuel Moffett made six presentations as a feature of the annual World Mission Days services, the Sachem Club presented "Quiet Please," and Camarada staged the operetta "Hansel and Gretel." The May Festival that year featured the crowning of Velma Van Hoose (see Appendix K) and the traditional ceremony of winding the Maypole was produced by Phyllis Long's Rhythmics class. By 1955 student F. Dale Bengtson (B. S., 1957) was directing a band of thirty-six members. This exciting group made its initial appearance in halftime ceremonies at a game between Anderson College and Taylor University.

Organized in 1951 and very active through 1957 was a traveling drama group known as "The Christian Thespians." The purpose of these gifted students was to encourage, through demonstration, the use of drama in the teaching, preaching, worship, and recreational life of local congregations. In just these few years participants traveled some 50,000 miles in at least thirty-five states, presenting more than 350 performances of various plays like "The Terrible Meek" by Charles Rann Kennedy. School of Theology student Donald Brumfield (B. A., 1952; M. Div., 1958) was very active and functioned as executive director for some years. All this activity supplemented the ongoing spring tour plays.

One certainly could sense changing times when President Morrison spoke a personal word to the board of trustees in June, 1954. That year his current term as president would end, marking his thirty-fifth year of service (four as assistant principal, two as principal, and the rest as president). Some years earlier the board had adopted a retirement plan calling for the active service of full-time personnel to conclude at age sixty-five. Morrison's age now would allow only four more years of service if he were elected to another five-year term. He was willing to serve the final four years, but he also was open to the board's wisdom on the next step. He encouraged the board to "discuss this matter frankly in my absence." It was discussed and he was reelected. So, with only four years left for his executive leadership, Morrison determined that they, like all the others, would be vigorous ones that looked creatively to the future.

The following June the president laid before the board a major issue that called for the most careful study. Representatives of all the state and private colleges and universities of Indiana had convened a few months earlier to discuss the implications of the great influx of new students expected to flood the campuses in the coming ten to fifteen years. The baby-boom enrollment growth would peak about 1970 when approximately a doubling of total enrollment over the 1955 level likely would have occurred. Morrison said that growth in the Church of God movement could be even more rapid and "Anderson College naturally is primarily concerned with the education of Church of God youth."

So, by the fall of 1965, some two thousand people likely would be enrolled on the campus in Anderson! Many new teachers and buildings, more equipment, and much more money would be required. It was time to prepare. Morrison proposed the immediate establishment of a President's Study and Planning Commission, to be chaired by Robert Reardon, then the school's executive vice president.[25] The Commission's agenda would include a comprehensive look at all aspects of campus life as the campus sought to position itself for the challenge to come. The board readily agreed.

The Commission went to work, the decade neared its end, and the president's retirement approached. The 1950s had witnessed an increase of about fifty acres of campus land, the construction of four major campus buildings (three student residence halls and the library, see Appendix R) and what seemed like a never-ending process of remodeling Old Main. In a short period these years also had witnessed the deaths of a series of the greats of Anderson College. Dean Olt had fallen gravely ill with cancer. In 1958 the president spoke with emotion to the board about this man with whom he had worked so closely for thirty-three years. He said that he had never even suspected the dean of "one low or unworthy act." "For integrity of purpose and for selfless devotion to chosen ideals," he confessed, "I think I have not known his equal." Morrison also said he doubt-ed that the dean's worth to the institution would be appreciated fully "until many years hence when the history of the institution ... is being written up." Well, now is that time and here is that writing!

Olt died in June, 1958. During his illness and forced absence from the office, music professor Dr. Robert A. Nicholson, who also had been assistant to the dean since 1956,[26] had been asked to sit in and do whatever was necessary. These were awkward and unwelcome months, prelude to the coming of a major transition. Not only the dean, however, but others also had died. Art Professor Ruthven Byrum, son of church pioneer Noah Byrum, died in March, 1958.[27] Only weeks later it was Dr. Herman Reichenbach, professor of physics and math. Soon it would be the beloved Dr. Carl Kardatzke[28] who had been chair of the college's Department of Education since 1933. Suddenly it seemed the end of an era.

The retirement of Walter S. Haldeman in 1958 tended to symbolize the best of the past that had prepared for an even better future. Professor Haldeman had served as faculty member in Christian education since 1933, after having graduated from Anderson's ministerial course in 1924 and then having completed his B. Th. in 1929 and B. D. in 1934. He had been responsible for the college library in some of its earliest years, was elected president of the alumni association in 1927, and now in 1958 was being honored by that association with the Outstanding Alumni Award. Haldeman had built many bridges to the church and city. Serving for years in leadership roles in the national Board of Christian Education, Board of Church Extension and Home Missions, and Associated Budgets Committee of the Church of God, he also had been a moving force behind the weekday religious education program in the city of Anderson. He had served as president of the East Side Community Club, the Optimist Club, and the Anderson Association of Churches. Dedication, service, and widening horizons described both Walter S. Haldeman and Anderson College itself.[29]

Leaders of the past were passing from the scene, but new ones were becoming available to carry on. Important additions were being made to the faculty. Val Clear had returned to campus in 1947 in the field of sociology. In 1949 Harold Linamen arrived from California to teach business, coming at personal sacrifice because "it was my church school."

The next year Elaine Harper left her teaching of Latin in Bessemer, Alabama, to teach English. Fredrick Shoot arrived in 1953 to teach Bible and Greek, and three years later Peter Tjart (B. A., 1949), of Canadian background, returned to teach German. Such persons each would enjoy long and significant tenures in Anderson. Their commitments to the campus and the church were equally strong. They and their colleagues would carry on effectively.

235

John Morrison and Russell Olt had been a great executive team. Now two more men had emerged and the many years yet to come would show them to be a quality leadership team also. They would be Robert Reardon, already chairing the commission that had been preparing for the institution's future, and Robert Nicholson, already functioning in the dean's office because of Olt's illness and then death. Morrison's retirement finally had come and to the board he said: "I take delight in the fact that the administrative affairs of the school are being given into the hands of so capable a man as Dr. Robert H. Reardon. Of his dedication and his ability I am not in doubt. He is young enough to have physical energy and old enough to have had experience, both of which he will need."

President Morrison had been a marvelous mixture of qualities. Although lacking in formal education, he always had sound educational instincts. His heart was in the church and his passion was to wed good religion and good education so that each could be at its best. He had wisdom, was very practical, and possessed the perseverance and humor necessary to be patient until dreams could come to be shared by others. He could be a fighter, although he tended to choose with care the battles worth fighting. He was also a sensitive, reflective, sometimes poetic man. He would write in his autobiography about how he loved to fish and how fishing was good for a man's soul. He preferred "a small clear stream that goes laughing down the mountainside and crooning through the deep and silent woods. To fish alone along such a stream brings to one's spirit the strength that only solitude affords. One's soul is washed in the riffles of clear water and in the pure mountain air. The grandeur and wonder of nature mocks the pride of man and speaks to him when he is alone and inclined to listen" (211).

Morrison cared deeply about the Church of God movement, its treasured vision of Christian unity, and the importance of its vital relationship to the Anderson campus. Through all the struggles of getting the college and seminary established, understood, and accepted in the life of the church, the president had remained steadfast in his conviction that the church was the school's home and that the school was vital to the well-being of the church's future. If he did relish a good scrap, his "fights" tended to be about important matters—and he respected his opponents, sometimes his dearest brothers and sisters in the fellowship of faith.

As church historian Merle Strege summarized, "He fought for space in the church so that Anderson College might have room to grow intellectually and theologically. He fought in the church for a vision of Christian unity that would transcend the bonds of narrow sectarian interest." And further, concluded Strege, "his vision for the institution ... was that it might become a school of wisdom—coupling the wisdom of the Scriptures with the wisdom of the Western intellectual tradition. Such an institution might offer young women and men more than narrow training for careers. It could make available the time and space, the human and material resources, to explore ancient questions about the meaning and purpose of life in the sight of God" [30]

1. See Barry Callen, *The First Century,* Vol. 1, 64-65.

2. President's report to the board, June, 1948, 7.

3. President's report to the board, June, 1950, 3-4.

4. Titled "A Campus Sketch," this film now is available on videotape in the University Archives.

5. See *Alumni News,* July/August, 1961, 6. Louis Gerig, Dora's nephew, would become a significant trustee in 1988.

6. T. Franklin Miller of the Church of God's national Board of Christian Education had been appointed by President Morrison as the first dean and had been approved by the board of trustees in February 1949. He chose not to accept this appointment, however, in part because of his sensitivity about not holding an earned doctorate.

7. He also was granted an honorary D. D. by Anderson in 1937. The first catalog of the School of Theology does not list his Anderson B. D., possibly because of its questionable nature as a true graduate program when seen in relation to the B. D. now to be offered.

8. *Bulletin of the School of Theology,* 1950-51, 7.

9. In the first years, the full titles of all theses were printed with author names in the commencement programs and seminary catalogs.

10. This stance was altered later by the Association. Though costly for the campus, eventually some of the duplication of personnel, materials, and services, resulting from the initial stance, were eliminated. Of particular note was the complete merging of libraries in 1989.

11. The college used the Dewey Decimal system and the seminary the Union system designed particularly for seminary libraries.

12. *Alumni News,* November 1950, 2.

13. Harold Phillips, *Alumni News,* June 1950, 3.

14. Three of the thirty-five were female, all part-time. The Anderson College graduating class of 1951 was comprised of 105 (83 were men!), 43 being ministerial students. Of the 43, 14 accepted pastorates, 13 went directly to the new School of Theology, while five went to other seminaries (with the other eleven miscellaneous or unknown). By 1953-54, of the 70 seminary students, 18 held degrees from institutions other than Anderson (two from Pacific Bible College, the remainder from a range of church-related colleges not associated with the Church of God and from state institutions).

15. They were Charles Alford, Jerry Hamon, John Holeman, George Kufeldt, Kenneth Prunty, Wilbur Qualman, Donald Smith, and Lynn Smith.

16. *Alumni News,* July/August, 1951, 8.

17. They were Delena Goodman (librarian, 1952-1983), Irene Caldwell (Christian education, 1966-1973), and Juanita Leonard (church and society, 1987 to the present). See Appendix G for a cumulative listing of all full-time School of Theology faculty members. A persistent problem over the years has been the relative inability of the seminary to recruit and then place in the ministry significant numbers of women. This is in spite of the stance of the Church of God movement

that there are no biblical or theological obstacles to ordaining women. Some critics have suggested that higher priority should have been placed on efforts to recruit and place women. The rapid growth of the student body in the 1970s did see a rise in the enrollment of women from 9 percent of the total in 1974-75 to 20 percent in 1979-80. That trend did not increase further in later years.

18. *Alumni News*, December, 1951, 8.

19. This series was so named because of the sponsorship of Laymen Life Insurance Company under the leadership of Everett Hartung.

20. This particular lectureship continued through 1972. Then several other programs of similar purpose replaced it.

21. Following Dr. Dunn's death in November, 1959, the campus received a $100,000 gift from the Langley Avenue Church of God in Chicago to memorialize their pastor of nearly forty years. When he retired as a campus trustee in 1957, Dunn had served the campus for thirty-two years. This was believed to be the first building on a predominantly white campus in Indiana named for a black person.

22. Report dated April, 1960, by team members W. C. Buthman of Hendrix College and E. H. Kleinpell of Wisconsin State College at River Falls.

23. See *Andersonian*, September 30, 1953.

24. Officers of the Booster Club for 1956-57 were Delwin Brown, president, Gary Ausbun, vice-president, David Coolidge, secretary, and Jack Samuels, treasurer. All of these men became leaders in their fields in later years. Many students gained their initial leadership experience as officers of the campus social clubs.

25. Robert Reardon had urged the establishment of this study and planning process. Once approved by the board, the president turned to him for personal leadership in its design and implementation.

26. Robert Reardon had become an admiring friend of Robert Nicholson and had urged Dean Olt to name him as the dean's assistant in 1956.

27. He had become one of the best known painters in the Midwest. See the thesis titled "A Study of the Life of Ruthven H. Byrum, Indiana Artist, As It Is Connected With His Contribution to Indiana Art." by Clarence Robert Farlow, Ball State University, 1960.

28. In a class taught by Kardatzke, Lavern Norris first became interested in marriage and family life. Norris returned to Anderson and joined the faculty in 1958, teaching in this field until his retirement in 1992.

29. See chapter four, note one.

30. *Signatures*, Fall 1988, 9.

9 Rapidly Widening Horizons
1958-1969

"Colleges which are either unable or unwilling to change, modify and face the new day with courage and imagination will be left behind like the village gas station deserted beneath the new interstate highway."

(President Robert H. Reardon)

In 1958 President John A. Morrison retired after thirty-nine years of administrative leadership. He had been the school's only president to that time (see Table 1) and had seen many struggles and dramatic developments over the decades. Now a new era of leadership was beginning with Robert H. Reardon at the helm. This new, young executive was well prepared and would ensure significant continuity with the school's past. Big new challenges lay just ahead.

Reardon had a dream in his heart, and a plan was already in place (work of the President's Study and Planning Commission). This dream and plan would prove adequate to guide the institution through tumultuous times that lay just ahead for America and the world.

The dream rested on more than mere future aspirations. Reardon told the board of trustees in June, 1961, that already the result of the young institution's life was clear. Graduates of Anderson College were filling a thousand pulpits each Sunday, guiding most of the national enterprises of the Church of God movement, carrying a large share of the lay leadership in the local churches, and serving in numerous mission stations around the world. "It is this record … which has earned for our Institution the love, respect and devotion of the Church.… It is my unshakable conviction," Reardon con-

239

cluded, "that this enterprise has been our church's most productive investment." Still, many of the largest dividends were yet to be received.

A Dream and a Dean

Robert Reardon was highly conscious of following in the presidential footsteps of a great and respected friend. He knew that he could not and should not try to replace Dr. Morrison, only follow him. Then there was the untimely death of Dean Russell Olt, who, said Reardon, "for thirty-three years worked with John Morrison in an educational partnership unique in the annals of higher education."[1] What could be said about the future? "Are we," asked Reardon, "on the threshold of a bright golden age where vast new buildings will spring up overnight, funds will pour in Niagara-like, faculty salaries double, utopian relationships exist among students, and defeat become unknown on the gridiron? Obviously, no. The Olt-Morrison years were never anything but struggle. The struggles will continue."[2]

But a good foundation had been laid. The school's lot had been cast with the church, and in that there would be no wavering. The school's range of influence and friends had begun to widen, a trend that would only accelerate in the years to come.

By the middle of the 1960s it would become obvious that higher education was in the midst of a revolution. The upheaval, in part, would be initiated by the Soviet Union's launch of Sputnik and the resulting race into space, accompanied shortly by a knowledge and technological explosion. There would be a doubling during the decade of the 1960s of the number of students in American higher education, along with the turmoil of the civil rights movement and the bitter controversies surrounding the Vietnam war. It surely would be a time of tension, expansion, and change. Said Reardon in the midst of all this: "Many sacred academic cows will be slaughtered in the field. . . . Colleges which are either unable or unwilling to change, modify and face the new day with courage and imagination will be left behind like the village gas station deserted beneath the new interstate highway. *Anderson College has no such destiny in mind.*"[3]

To the contrary, President Reardon had assumed his executive office in 1958 armed with some deep convictions and a sturdy dream. He had listed his central convictions in his inaugural address, reproduced in *Alumni News*, November, 1958. He began his administration by announcing that he believed:

—That the youth of the church and the nation are our greatest wealth, deserving our best, since what happens to them will happen to the future;
—That the heart of a Christian liberal arts college is a qualified and inspired faculty;
—That there is an essential unity in the truth and no honest Christian student

Robert Reardon (left) and Robert Nicholson, neighbors, friends,
an effective leadership team

need repudiate his or her faith to maintain integrity;
—That without the claims and insights of religion, education loses its way and may easily turn into a sort of Frankenstein monster, destroying human freedom and dignity and perhaps ultimately bringing destruction to the human race;
—That learning is neither for wealth nor prestige, but for responsible Christian citizenship;
—That a church that will take a college and seminary to heart, fostering growth, pouring into her sons and daughters its wealth, will reap rewards in enrichment of its own life far greater than it can ever know; and finally,
—That our confused, bleeding world desperately needs what we have to offer.

When retiring from the presidency twenty-five years later he would look back on the dream that had been formed by these beginning convictions. He would describe to the board of trustees in his final presidential report of April 22, 1983, the dream with

241

Music Hall in old Park Place Church of God

which he had begun. He had wanted "a strong, thriving academic environment, marked by quality and excellence, in which the student would be challenged to move upward toward his or her potential." That potential would be reached in part by expanding cultural horizons and by enhancing the international dimension of an education that was "deeply rooted in Christian faith" and that encouraged lives of service. He had looked into the future from his 1958 vantage point and was confident that he could see in Anderson, Indiana, "one of the truly great Christian colleges in America." This was the vision that had nerved and inspired his many years of leadership. He wanted always to

TABLE 15

Directors, University (Choir) Chorale

The mixed campus choir was known as the
Glad Tidings Chorus from 1928 until 1945, then
the Anderson College Choir from 1945-198 , and
since then the Anderson University Chorale.
Directors are listed below.

Henry C. Clausen	1928-1945
Robert A. Nicholson	1945-1959
Charles R. Stanley	1959-1963
F. Dale Bengtson	1963-1973
M. Eugene Miller	1973-1980
Paul B. Smith	1980-1984
Richard L. Sowers	1984 to present

be remembered "as one who tried to keep the dream alive."

As Russell Olt had been at John Morrison's side, Robert A. Nicholson was chosen to stand by Robert Reardon as the quest proceeded for the dream's fulfillment. In all of Reardon's years as president (1958-1983), he would seek to follow the admonishment he received early from Dr. Ralph Noyer: "If you hire small-minded people, soon you will be knee-deep in midgets." This caution surely was heeded in the crucial choice of a new dean for the undergraduate college. Reardon was thirty-eight years old when elected president and Nicholson became his dean when only thirty-four. They had become neighbors and close friends soon after the Reardons had moved back to Anderson in 1947. Reardon was attracted to Nicholson because "of his bright mind, his love for the church, and the sterling quality of the Anderson College Choir which he had established."[4]

By 1956 Reardon had watched this energetic, young professor handle some sensitive problems in the music department and show an unusual capacity for carrying administrative responsibility, including his chairing of the academic and curriculum sections of the President's Study and Planning Commission of 1955-57. He had encouraged Dean Olt to name Dr. Nicholson as the dean's assistant. Then, because of Olt's terminal illness beginning in 1957, Nicholson began carrying most of the daily responsibilities of the dean's office. Olt died in June, 1958, and Reardon, then the new president, knew

243

what he wanted to do—nominate Nicholson to be the next college dean. "Of the decisions in which I played a part during my years as president," Reardon would report decades later after his own retirement, "none was more crucial for me, for the institution, or for our constituents."[5]

Despite the range of administrative and teaching roles he already had fulfilled, this was a difficult transition for Nicholson. He had graduated from the Anderson campus in 1944. By the following year he had found himself back on campus, twenty-one years old, having only begun his own graduate education, and now teaching a full load in

(Left) Professor Paul Breitweiser
(Right) Student Band, with director Malcolm Gressman standing, front left

music, a field in which he had not majored in college. Naturally there were professional insecurities and uneasy feelings that soon were conquered through experience and the completion of his doctorate in 1953. But the feelings returned when he was asked to fill the shoes of a man who for decades had been the revered academic leader of the campus. "I was not the traditional liberal arts based person typical of other deans I soon met. It took me years," he admitted, "before I felt at home in deanly circles, but finally I did" (Callen 1991, 17-18). He was held steady by "the power of high purpose," the title of a book Dr. William Mikesell would dedicate to him (1961).

The Reardon-Nicholson team brought to campus a new leadership style. Morrison and Olt had been a dominating pair, totally committed, very much in charge. Now the new team, while strong personalities and leaders, were by comparison more process and collegial persons. Reardon had taught part time for a decade and he knew how sensitive faculty members can be when regarded as "employees" and perceived to be generally disregarded in the larger decision-making process of the institution. He continued Morrison's pattern of not presiding at faculty meetings, for instance. Rather, he would sit with the faculty, seeking to avoid being in an adversarial role. The responsibility of the chair, he said, "I gladly have left in the adroit and highly skilled hands of Dean Nicholson who, more than any other, has shielded me from many an arrow."[6]

Reardon saw Nicholson as having "the uncanny ability to lead, but still maintain a collegial relationship with the faculty."[7] Nicholson, in turn, saw Reardon as a strong institutional leader, a critical characteristic during those volatile years of challenge and change soon to come, but one lacking a strong self-perception as an academic leader. While his academic instincts were excellent, the new president preferred to give his dean wide latitude in shaping academic policy and curriculum. In administrative style, this young president and even younger dean tended to carry on processes similar to those of the President's Study and Planning Commission of 1955-57 (see detail below). That Commission had been conceived and chaired by Reardon, had included Nicholson significantly, and had functioned in ways not typical of Dean Olt's approach to faculty committees and decision making. The various dialogue groups of the Commission had been given ample opportunity for candid dialogue and genuine influence on future directions.

Nicholson especially was viewed as representative of this more open process. In his first year as dean he attempted to maintain the many administrative mechanisms of Olt, such as signing all class schedules personally and meeting periodically with all students on probation. But this was hardly practical (he remained choir director for one year, for instance, leading his last tour in the spring of 1959—see Table 15). Neither did his personality fit Olt's ability "to put the fear of the Lord into a student" with a quick and often intimidating meeting. Nicholson's view of the office was moving another way. He sought as quickly as possible to change the deanship from full authority and even hands-on supervision of almost everything not immediately under the president's control to the more restricted arena of chief academic officer. The new dean intended to be an active, more focused, more delegating academic leader.

The Ten-Year Plan: Goal One

So the new leadership team was in place. The president had a dream, the administration had a new style, and the institution had a clear plan to guide it. The plan had evolved from the President's Study and Planning Commission which had been established by the board of trustees in June, 1955, with the charge "to study and project under the direction of the board a program for the college extending over the period 1955-65." Robert Reardon was Commission leader, with the help of special consultant Dr. Ralph Noyer, then Dean Emeritus of nearby Ball State Teachers College (now Ball State University). Commission membership included selected faculty, students, trustees, pastors, alumni, and parents.

Reardon, then executive vice president, had encouraged this planning process, the most open and comprehensive ever attempted. Looking ahead from the year 1955, it was realized that a new administration would be in place soon. Some form of careful planning was needed both to ensure crucial stability and to enable strategic change in the face of the dramatic enrollment growth expected. So this cluster of committees was designed to focus around all major aspects of campus life. It would "stir the pot of participation," as Nicholson put it, help prepare a systematic self-study such as North Central would expect in a formal accreditation review process soon to come, and provide a framework for addressing the many issues related to what was expected to be a rapidly growing college and seminary.

Based largely on the Commission's work, the new administration in 1958 had ready for implementation six specific goals to guide a ten-year development plan. Nicholson, from the much later perspective of 1990, said that they proved to be "as effective a set of goals as we have ever had." They were stated very simply, reflecting the guidance, style, and even authoring of Robert Reardon. They tended to be practical and measurable. They were as follows:

Goal One: Exalt the spiritual and train for responsible Christian
citizenship.

(Top, left) Ronald W. Moore, student, 1963
(Bottom, left) Dr.Valorous B. Clear, sociology professor
(Right) Civil rights march, from campus to downtown Anderson,
led by President Reardon (front center)

Goal Two: Improve instruction.
Goal Three: Increase faculty salaries.
Goal Four: Recruit, enroll, and retain qualified students.
Goal Five: Build and conserve the physical plant.[8]
Goal Six: Increase and broaden the base of financial support.

In several of his early annual reports to the board of trustees, President Reardon organized major institutional developments by these goal areas and thus sought to show serious and successful addressing of them over the years. A special issue of *A. C. News*, the campus alumni publication, was released in May, 1967, to commemorate a "jubilee of commemoration" for the school's half century of existence and service. This publication also focused on the ten-year development plan and highlighted the advances of 1958-67 under the same six goal areas.

Then in 1968 came a report on the evaluation of the ten-year program by a faculty committee comprised of Professors John Carrington, Val Clear, Vila Deubach, and Elbridge MacKenzie. A brief summarization of this highlighting and evaluation gives a broad picture of institutional initiatives and progress during much of the 1960s.

Goal One. Exalt the spiritual and train for citizenship. President Reardon made his view clear in his 1962 report to the board of trustees. "It is better to say that Anderson College does not *have* a religious program, but that it *is* a religious program." Professor Marie Strong was now director of religious life. Christianity-in-Action remained the core of student involvement in direct Christian witness and service, with Professor Milton Buettner as adviser, Larry Brown as student director, and about one third of the student body active through just this one campus organization. An organization of Christian athletes also was inspired by the presence on campus of new baseball coach Carl Erskine, a native of Anderson who had become one of the greats of professional baseball.[9]

But addressing this first goal went beyond effective campus programming. As the president went on to say, the contribution of the pastors in the Anderson churches was important. Also of vital, possibly primary importance was the quality of human interaction experienced every day in the routines of campus life. Dean Nicholson made this very point in his 1961 report to the board of trustees. "Probably faculty recruitment and development is the most crucial task for the College in the years ahead," he judged. Why were these seen as so crucial? Because, to meet goal one, the faculty members

(Top, left) Norman Beard
(Top, right) Commissioning TRI-S students, 1966
(Bottom) Karen Johnson (B.A.'89), right, and Lori Salierno, left,
  meet with Mother Teresa in Calcutta, India

themselves would have to go well beyond "passing observations on religious matters" to the challenges of "a deep personal piety, an evident concern for the individual student, a belief in Christian commitment, and devotion to Christian nurture."

Faculty recruitment, then, was understood as identifying people with excellent academic credentials who also would be inspiring teachers and who were "devout and contagious Christians whose own personal lives were in keeping with the high behavioral standards of the Church of God." The dean's success here was remarkable. To begin the 1969-70 year, for instance, seven new faculty members came in just that one year, all destined to make long-term contributions to the accomplishment of goal one. They were Duane Hoak in education, Robert Smith in drama and speech, James Rouintree in music, Patricia Miller in physical education, Larry Osnes in political science, James Massey, and myself in religious studies. By 1969, 70 percent of the faculty had been recruited during the first eleven years of Nicholson's deanship. In the midst of rapid student enrollment growth and many faculty retirements, he was building a new faculty with Goal One always in mind.

At the opening of the decade of the 1960s, Park Place Church of God built a magnificent new facility on the edge of campus and then gave the beloved old church three blocks away to the college. The regular and required chapel sessions were relocated to that historic sanctuary and Shirell Fox, in addition to directing campus publicity, was asked to assist the president by assuming full responsibility for chapel programming. Here was the very pulpit where President Reardon's father had preached and the seats where many prominent national leaders in the Church of God movement had sat and worshiped over the decades. Now it belonged to the campus and hosted chapel and the music program.

Pressure soon grew among students for the elimination of required chapel, a pressure typical of the times that overwhelmed many other church-related colleges. But Reardon was not flexible on this issue. The campus community as a whole, in his firm opinion, still needed to be together regularly, to experience and learn together, and to worship often together.[10] Fox would work hard to program effectively for the meeting of these needs and Reardon himself, possessing considerable communication skill, frequently made significant contributions. Many well-known guests ministered to the student body, like Dr. E. Stanley Jones in 1963 and again in 1966.

Exalting the spiritual in students, as Goal One said, necessarily included nurturing responsible Christian citizenship. What a challenge and opportunity the decade of the 1960s was in this regard! Its beginning was symbolized well by the Alumni Association choosing as its Outstanding Alumnus for 1961 Dr. Val Clear, graduate in 1941 and sociology faculty member since 1947. Active locally in leadership of the Urban League, a juvenile detention home, the county welfare program, and other interests, he had been in Cuba in 1957 during an anti-Communist revolt. In 1960 he had been serving as visiting professor in Puerto Rico and became involved there in disaster relief during a devastating flood and also in the planting of new churches. He represented well on campus and in the world a continuation of the sensitive and activistic social conscience of the now deceased Dean Olt.

These were the volatile years of the civil rights movement in the United States. The Church of God, especially in its early years, had been a pacesetter as a multiracial fellowship. Now its General Assembly, meeting annually in Anderson, spoke vigorously and often during this decade about civil rights and racial justice.[11] In 1968 President Reardon himself told that year's Assembly that its previous action, which had declared an open-door policy for all races (1964), now needed more positive action. He introduced a new and forthright open-door policy statement that included a call for each congregation of the Church of God movement to ratify it, with their names then being made public. The Assembly so ordered.

Reardon already had taken some direct action of his own on the campus. In March, 1965, President Lyndon Johnson had proposed legislation to guarantee voting rights to every qualified citizen. Events in places like Selma, Alabama, had highlighted deep racial problems in the nation. In college chapel on March 16, Reardon announced that he planned to lead a peaceful demonstration march from the campus to the Anderson downtown center after chapel that Thursday. There was mixed reaction among students. The question on all minds was whether or not to march. Direct social action of this kind was new to many students. There were many black persons in the Church of God movement in the United States, and always there had been ethnic and racial diversity on the campus. But some students were troubled by the idea of a public demonstration in favor of racial equality.

Ronald Moore was one such student. He was from a Church of God family in Florida and had graduated there in 1961 from a segregated high school. A very insecure young man, he majored in accounting, graduated in 1966, judging his Anderson College experience "a long process of tremendous growth." He was most active in SAM Enterprises, a campus organization through which business students got involved in the free enterprise system. For instance, the group promoted concerts on campus like the New Christy Minstrels and Peter Nero. It was a valuable, real-world experience. Moore also had what he called "my Damascus road experience" when his accounting professor, Glenn Falls, took an interest in him, confronted his insecurity, and expressed a life-changing confidence in his worth and potential.[12]

But it was Reardon's march in 1965 that forced the segregation issue for several students like Moore. As a new student, Moore was uncomfortable when a black student routinely sat next to him in the school cafeteria. That always had been unacceptable at home. It seemed no issue on this campus. Now the president was going public aggressively and asking the student body to join him. Many did. (See photo, p.247) But a group of students from the South held a competing prayer meeting, praying for the misguided marchers. Fred Burnett[13] already had moved a considerable distance in his own racial attitude and decided to march. Ron Moore was caught between opinions and neither marched nor attended the opposing prayer meeting. Later, wishing he had marched back in 1965, he became an outspoken advocate for racial justice and equality. As Goal One sought, here was an example of real student growth in both spirituality and responsible Christian citizenship.

Now expressions of meaningful Christian citizenship were happening in places of special need around the country and on the international scene. TRI-S (Student Summer Service) had been launched in 1964 with Norman Beard as founding and longterm director. This "grand experiment" began "with good intentions, modest goals, pass-the-plate funding and no model."[14] Students needed a way to express their concerns and fulfill their Christian callings. They needed some program to bring together vision, learning, and service.

Larry Brown and other student leaders joined with President Reardon in this concern. John F. Kennedy's Peace Corps was bringing a new sense of idealism. Could there be a vehicle for a Christian version of this idealism, only short-term in nature to fit academic calendars? The answer was yes! As Reardon told the board of trustees in June, 1965: "Students cannot grow spiritually without activity and involvement. The answers to our questions about God, man, life, death, and human destiny cannot be found in the library alone." Many colleges offered programs of travel and cultural exposure and learning. TRI-S was to feature service and over the years would become one of the more distinctive and significant of all institutional programs, one President Reardon would be proud had begun in his administration.

In the last chapel before the summer vacation of 1966, with TRI-S only two years old, more than one hundred students were commissioned to serve instead of vacation. That fall Reardon told alumni that already TRI-S had opened a new world of learning for students. The returning volunteers "have made the campus come alive with the ferment created by first-hand encounter with the great issues of our time.... These TRI-S volunteers have built bridges of understanding out into a world hitherto unknown except as a student comes to know it in books, lectures, and visuals." The president predicted that this program "will mark the beginning of a whole new epoch in the life of this college and will have a renewing effect on the church we seek to serve."[15]

The coming years would prove him right. Many young women and men would travel and serve abroad for the first time through TRI-S, some then returning to campus to prepare for lives of missionary service in the name and style of Christ. Over the com-

Religion professors. Standing (left): Gene Newberry, George Ramsey, George Kufeldt
Seated (left): Frederick Shoot, Marie Strong, Gustav Jeeninga, Boyce Blackwelder

ing years TRI-S "alumni" would be a major source for new, career missionaries sent out by the Missionary Board of the Church of God (see Table 33). Also, the proportion of Anderson graduates entering service vocations would increased markedly.

Goals Two and Three

That first goal, calling for exalting the spiritual and nurturing responsible Christian citizenship, was pervasive in campus life. It lay at the very heart of campus mission. The other five goals in the ten-year plan comprised a series of ways by which this central goal could be accomplished most effectively. Goals two and three centered in improving instruction and increasing faculty salaries.

Goal Two. Goal two had been stated simply: "Improve instruction." Its accomplishment, however, was complex, expensive, and somehow, by its very nature, never fully completed. But during the 1960s much advancement was made in this crucial area. As Dean Nicholson told the board of trustees at the opening of the decade:

"We are not simply another college; we are a *quality institution* dedicated to the cause of providing the finest possible liberal arts education within a framework of the Christian faith. In this task there is no resting place, no maintenance of the status quo."

The dean was an activist and there was much to be done. Help came in 1959-60 when Dr. Frederick Shoot was named director of summer school and began work on expanding the summer and evening programs. The following year he also was named counselor for academic affairs, giving attention particularly to students with academic problems. In 1965 Dr. Glenn Falls was appointed associate dean, working principally in the development of academic programs and projects. Dr. Shoot also was named an associate dean in 1967.

Possibly the central accomplishment of the college dean's office during the 1960s was a careful managing of the curricular operation in order to maximize both its efficiency and effectiveness. This management was seen especially in the attention given to class sizes, teaching loads, and the relative numbers of faculty and students. At the opening of the 1960s the teacher-student ratio was 1 to 16.8. Through the conscious enlargement of some class sizes in an effort to contain rising costs, this ratio was moved to 1 to 20 by 1965-66 and remained there throughout the balance of the decade. The average number of student credit hours generated by a faculty member rose from 240 in 1960-61 to 305 in 1969-70, although the average number of class preparations dropped from 3.52 to 2.91. This drop was the result of conscious administrative effort, increasing the number of four-hour courses and the multiple sectioning of some courses, usually taught by the same instructor.

Two years of curriculum review by the undergraduate faculty resulted in some major changes, effective September, 1961. Now there would be only one undergraduate degree, the Bachelor of Arts, with a doubling of the required hours in religion, a first-time requirement in philosophy, at least one year of a foreign language, and a new requirement in the creative arts. This revised curriculum was supported by a series of new instructional resources. In 1961-62 alone, a well-equipped language laboratory was installed and an instructional materials laboratory begun (currently known as the Instructional Materials Center). A computing center started operation in 1965 with the gift of an IBM 1620 computer and a full complement of supporting data processing equipment. A room on the third floor of the new science building (see below) was selected as the computing center. More than fifty students enrolled in the new field of computer science. As Professor Thomas Harbron, director of the new center, put it: "We are living in the dawn of the 'Second Industrial Revolution.' As the first . . . freed man from dependence upon muscle power, the second is freeing him from dependence on his mental abilities in routine tasks."[16] Anderson College had entered early and eagerly into this developing new field.

TABLE 16

Undergraduate Departmental
Organization and Chairs: 1960-61

<u>Div. of Humanities</u>   Vila Deubach, Chair

Art	Robert Youngman
English/Speech	Vila Deubach
Foreign Languages	Nancy Osborne
Philosophy	Lewis Hennigar

<u>Div. of Sciences</u>   John Buehler, Chair

Biology	Zylpha Hurlbut
Chemistry	John Buehler
Mathematics/Physics	Gloria Olive

<u>Div. of Social Sciences</u>   Glenn Falls, Chair

Business/Economics	Glenn Falls
Education	Elbridge MacKenzie
History/Political Science	Pichon Loh
Physical Education	James Macholtz
Sociology/Social Work	Valorous Clear

<u>Div. of Religion</u>   Adam Miller, Chair

Biblical Studies	Adam Miller
Theology	Ronald Joiner (acting)
Religious Education	Donald Courtney

<u>Div. of Music</u>   Robert Nicholson, Chair

Music, Theory/ Literature	Cecil Hartselle
Music, Education	Robert Nicholson
Music, Applied	Cecil Hartselle

<u>Note</u>: For a comparable presentation for the year
1992-93, see Appendix H.

Soon there were specialized laboratories in Christian education, reading skills, curriculum, music, psychology, business, and accounting. There also was the founding of the Museum of Bible and Near Eastern Studies, the dream and largely the work of Dr. Gustav Jeeninga, after whom it later would be named. Jeeninga's own archaeological interest was awakened by a trip to the Holy Land in 1952 and by Dr. James Muilenburg at Union Theological Seminary in New York. The primary intention of the museum was to enrich biblical instruction in the classroom. The museum began modestly in Jeeninga's office on the fourth floor of Old Main soon after he joined the faculty in 1960. It was recognized formally by the board of trustees as an educational research center in 1963. Soon it grew into a hallway display, and in 1975, after several moves, settled in its present location in the lower level of the School of Theology building. Funded mostly by the gifts of interested friends, this museum came to house many well-displayed items viewed frequently by students, groups from the city, and others. There were regular newsletters and an annual lectureship featuring prominent archaeologists, with Dr. Jeeninga always the guiding light and director.

Meanwhile, the library was expanding its holdings and services in its fine new facility. Under the leadership of Dr. Vila Deubach, and after only fours years in the Wilson Library facility, a professional reference librarian was available at all times and book holdings had reached more than 46,000. A $30,000 grant from the Lilly Endowment had been of great assistance (see Appendix S). By 1969 book holdings had surpassed 90,000, a tripling over the previous decade. In 1964 Byrd Library was completed in the lower level of the new School of Theology building, giving much added space and convenience for graduate students. Because of the understood accreditation expectations of the Association of Theological Schools, the seminary library was independent of the college library in space, staffing, funding, and even most technical services, even though the libraries were immediately adjacent to each other. In the 1980s this cumbersome and expensive circumstance finally would be changed.

So instruction was being improved by a revised curriculum, staff assistance to the college dean, and a range of new instructional resources, including a much strengthened library. But there was much more. Soon to be a significant distinctive of the campus would be its achieving of professional accreditations in a range of programs providing both advantages to graduates and stimulation to faculty for constant program improvement (see Table 1). The first was achieved in 1963 for the program of teacher education through the National Council for the Accreditation of Teacher Education (NCATE). This difficult and important program advance gave graduates licensing reciprocity then existing among thirty-five of the states. Other program accreditations were to follow, including that of the Association of Theological Schools (ATS), which granted accreditation to the School of Theology in 1965 (see below).

Table 16 details the organization and leadership of the undergraduate academic program in 1960-61. The "divisional" structure did not play a significant role in directing academic operations. That direction tended to reside with the individual department chairs and the college's centralized academic administration.

Coordinate with program advance was continued emphasis on the credentials and professional growth of faculty members. President Reardon alerted the board of trustees in 1962 that competition for qualified faculty members was growing and would get even more intense. He was proud that Anderson College had been able to remain in the top ten percent of all North Central institutions when measured by faculty credentials. Senior faculty members were retiring, like music professor Cecil Hartselle in 1963 after his thirty-nine years of service. Younger ones such as myself were being enabled to gain professional credentials through a special campus loan program. A religious studies professor, I graduated from the School of Theology in 1966, taught at the college one year, and was assisted in obtaining a second master's and a doctorate before returning for long-term service beginning in 1969. Many received fellowships and research grants. For instance, Dr. James Macholtz was a Fulbright lecturer in the Philippines, Dr. Gustav Jeeninga was a Fellow of the American Schools of Oriental Research in Jerusalem, Nilah Meier studied in Latin America under the sponsorship of the U. S. State Department, and the entire religion faculty (college and seminary) spent much of the summer of 1968 in the Middle East through a grant from the Lilly Endowment.

This international dimension of professional growth was evident elsewhere. Increasingly, of course, after 1964 students were traveling abroad through the TRI-S program to serve and learn. Often faculty members traveled as leaders and learners. By 1967 there were interdisciplinary courses on campus in Africa, the Balkans, the Far East, the Middle East, Latin America, and the Soviet Union. There were language studies in French, German, Greek, Hebrew, Russian and Spanish, and non-Western units built into courses like World Literature, World Civilization, Anthropology, and Archaeology. The campus now was an active member of the Cincinnati Council on World Affairs, a consortium of colleges and universities in Ohio, Indiana, and Kentucky that brought significant international guests to the campuses, stimulated international program development, and arranged high-level faculty growth opportunities. Anderson College first joined in 1964 and remains active to this day.

One might even speak of the "Kenya connection." A large mission field for the Church of God movement, this nation in East Africa had gained independence in 1963 and developed many relationships with the Anderson campus over the years. Nearly every year a few Kenyan church leaders came to Anderson to study. In 1977-78, for instance, fourteen of the college's fifty-five international students were Kenyans, far more than from any other foreign country. A series of faculty members beginning in the

1950s invested sabbatical leaves in addressing various needs of the church in Kenya (Carl Kardatzke,[17] Paul Saltzman, Harold Linamen, Gene Newberry, and others). Numerous TRI-S groups of students visited and served.

Beginning in 1973 and with the financial support of the Lilly Endowment, Inc. (see Appendix S), Dean Nicholson gave key leadership to a "Volunteer Teachers to Kenya" program, which saw Anderson and Earlham Colleges cooperating in sending teachers to be assigned work in government and *harambee* schools. While several School of Theology graduates have served terms of missionary service in Kenya, long-term Canadian missionary to Kenya, Dr. Douglas Welch, returned in 1978 to teach missiology in the School of Theology. As dean of the college, I traveled to Kima Theological College in Kenya in 1985 to assist with that school's accreditation efforts. In 1983 the World Conference of the Church of God convened in Nairobi, Kenya. Then in 1990 a film crew from Covenant Productions on the Anderson campus traveled across Africa to produce a contemporary documentary for use by the Missionary Board of the Church of God. Instruction was being enriched on the home campus and being useful worldwide.

Dean Nicholson established himself early as a true servant of the whole church. Many ministers of the Church of God pastoring in the southeastern states had come to feel the need for higher education opportunities in their area, particularly education for church leaders. In his first years as college dean, Nicholson made several trips south as a consultant and assisted in arranging for an experimental "Southeastern Extension Center" of Anderson College. This Center met for six weeks in the summer of 1958 in Columbia, South Carolina, and then again in Birmingham, Alabama, in the summer of 1959. Soon this effort evolved beyond an extension service of Anderson College and became the present Warner Southern College in Lake Wales, Florida.[18]

So, as seen from the vantage point of 1970, three broad objectives characterized Anderson's undergraduate instructional program. They were breadth in studies prescribed and range offered, emphasis on student self-discovery, and a highlighting of the professional and vocational. These general curricular emphases all were infused by the pervasive theme of *service*. As the 1970 North Central self-study said: "To a considerable degree the student who chooses Anderson College does so out of a conviction, usually religious in its basis, that his life and lifework can be useful to other persons and to society generally" (63). This combination of religious conviction and service motive was seen clearly in the 1963 self-study application submitted for NCATE accreditation of the teacher education program. The leading objective stated for this program at Anderson College was "an attitude of Christian stewardship toward his profession."

(Top) Anderson College Choir, 1968-69
(Bottom) Homecoming parade, Meridian Street, downtown Anderson

Row: Janet Armey, Rena Elkins, Chris Reinhardt, Kathy
ey, Shelly Ramsbarger, Carol Richardson, Kathy Buck,
Helbling, Barbara Ratliff, Marsha Friermood, Marian
r, Antha Merriman, Rose Marlowe, Sharon Davis, Hope
ns. Second Row: Esther Beason, Rena Taylor, Janet
r, Joan Merrill, Christine Clay, Cheryl Hurst, Eunice
way, Cozette Beach, Kay Pylate, Barbara Starkey, Jeanette
r, Jeannie Cook, Chris Densmore, Karen Strege, Carol
eton, Diane Mundy, Imy Tate, Linda Thornburg, Vonda

Germany, Carolyn Morgan. Third Row: David Doty, Cal
Bloom, Daryl Smith, Don Secrest, John Sutherland, Mark
Haskins, Allen Lucas, Ron Fritts, Dave Irwin, Doug Shearer,
Mike Parker, Gary Powell, John Rountree, Bill Taylor, Merle
Strege, Tony Wolfe, Rick Reinhardt, Ken Ward, George Ram-
sey, Dan Miller, Drew Helvey, Mike McDonald, Terry Carroll,
Jeff Nielsen, Henry Layne, Terry Jones, Dan Rinker, Gary Jones,
Steve Reinhardt, Fred Harting, Joe Cookston, Nolan Young,
Rick Cox, Jim Dodson, Ren Baldwin

TABLE 17

Comparative Faculty Salary Scales: 1958-1962

	1958-59		1959-60		1960-61		1961-62	
	Doctors	Masters	Doctors	Masters	Doctors	Masters	Doctors	Masters
Professor	4,800		5,600		6,000		6,500	
Associate	4,800	4,000	5,400	4,700	5,700	5,000	6,100	5,400
Assistant	4,800	3,800	5,000	4,600	5,200	4,900	5,600	5,200
Instructor		3,800		4,200		4,400		4,900

Note: All of the above figures are contracts for nine months of service, with any summer instruction compensated separately. Modest variations existed for some persons and were based on seniority of service and other than teaching assignments, such as being chair of a department. By way of comparison, the Anderson public schools in 1958-59 paid $5,150 to a teacher with a masters degree and five years experience.

Teaching was said to be "a sacred responsibility" and "the selection of a teaching position will be based on the opportunity for service rather than on purely selfish motives."[19]

This curricular orientation also was reflected in student perceptions of campus climate. In May, 1969, the College and University Environmental Scales (CUES) instrument was administered. Results of student perception were reported in the 1970 North Central self-study (35, 65). They showed comparatively high levels of campus emphasis on "awareness" (self, aesthetic, and societal understandings), "community" (friendliness, cohesiveness, group orientation), "propriety" (considerateness, thoughtfulness, and group standards of decorum) and "practicality" (vocational preparation, enterprise, school spirit, and activities). There was a lesser student perception of "scholarship," defined by the instrument as "emphasis on competitively high academic achievement and serious interest in intellectual speculation, knowledge, philosophical theories and ideas." Students saw their professors as "dedicated scholars in their fields" (88 percent) who "go out of their way to help you" (92 percent) more than as persons who "really push the students' capacities to the limits" (26 percent), or who stimulate "a lot of interest in philosophy and methods of science" (26 percent). Such was reflective of the school's history, close church relationship, and person-centered, service orientation.

Goal Three. Increase faculty salaries. This goal also was straightforward and practical. If quality faculty members were to be recruited and retained, faculty salaries had to be increased. It was a matter both of being fair to teachers and their families and of facing realistically the competition in the faculty marketplace. Being a member of this special campus family certainly offered many compensations other than salaries. But dollars were a problem. Dean Nicholson told the board of trustees in 1967 that the campus still was managing to withstand outside offers of $13,000-$17,000 being made to faculty members receiving $7,500 at Anderson College. This gap, however, was widening, a trend that somehow had to be stopped and reversed.

Progress began slowly. In the spring of 1958 the administration found it impossible, in its view, to grant any salary increases for the following year. Morrison was about to retire and gave Robert Reardon, soon to succeed him, the task of announcing this painful circumstance to the faculty. Professor Val Clear over the years was both a close friend of Reardon's away from campus and occasionally a "leader of the loyal opposition" on campus. He and others were conscious of the comparatively low salaries, the general need for spouses also to be employed, and the sometimes perceived willingness of the administration to spend money for things like campus vehicles when salaries were frozen, a willingness seen by some people as real and not justified. Clear tended to think that his loyalty to the Church of God movement might be used by the administration to rationalize a more modest salary. Ironically, some other faculty members assumed that their nonassociation with the Church of God movement might be causing salary discrimination against them. This complex of often negative perceptions was worsened by the administrative practice of not making public any salaries.[20]

For a few years there appeared on campus a small chapter of the American Association of University Professors, in part to keep pressure on the administration to give priority to faculty benefits. But such pressure was also a self-imposed goal of the new administration. Success would not be easy. In that first awkward year of 1958-59, the president and dean received salaries of $10,000 and $8,500, separated on principle but always intended to be kept close. All faculty members holding the doctorate received $4,800 and most others received $3,800 (rank was largely irrelevant to salary level and obviously Dean Olt had designed this two-tier system as leverage for faculty members to complete their doctoral programs).

In the years 1958-61, however, more of a formula was developed to reflect credentials, experience, teaching excellence, and rank. President Reardon presented this new approach in his June, 1962, report to the board of trustees to remove "faculty salaries from the suspicious unknown to the point where each faculty member can easily establish his own salary rate through application of the published formula." Effort was made to develop a "considerable range" between the Instructor and Professor ranks (see Table 17).

There was obvious progress in both salary and fringe benefit programs, although levels remained below the national average. The North Central visiting team had judged in 1960 that faculty salaries was a crucial problem area. In the 1970 self-study later to be prepared for North Central, the report would be made with pleasure that nearly all continuing faculty members had experienced a doubling of salary between

1959-60 and 1969-70, while cost-of-living had risen only 27.4 percent (consumer price index). That would be real progress.

Goals Four, Five, and Six

Compensating faculty more adequately and improving instruction generally were contingent upon the accomplishment of goals four, five, and six. They centered in recruiting, enrolling, and retaining qualified students, improving campus facilities, and broadening the institution's base of financial support.

Goal Four. Recruit, enroll, retain students. The decade beginning in 1958 saw considerable change and progress in the number and qualifications of college students enrolled and in the range of vital support services made available to them. Strong national trends were responsible in part for much of this. The freshman class entering in the fall of 1961 was composed of 192 full-time women and 159 full-time men, a total of 351 and a 25 percent increase over the preceding fall's new class. The long anticipated growth now was much in evidence. This class came from thirty-six states (Indiana 108, Ohio 43, Michigan 35, Pennsylvania 26) and five other countries. It was served by the expanding programs of the office of Dean of Students.

Called "Coordinator of Student Personnel" during the 1950s when it was staffed by Vila Deubach, this key role early in the new administration became known as the Dean of Students. Norman Beard, recent graduate of the School of Theology and employed in the campus business office, assumed the role and Dr. Deubach became head librarian of the new Wilson Library. Dean Olt had supervised closely such student support programs previously, but Dean Nicholson now encouraged decentralization and specialization.[21] Student recruitment and financial aid, for instance, were in Beard's growing area of responsibility. Beginning in 1964, the new TRI-S program also was operated by Beard. In the following decade this one program was to become so successful and time consuming that eventually Beard would give to it his full time. In 1958, however, the focus tended to be on an effective plan for student recruitment and major advances in student retention, partly through a growing program of financial aid.

Beard himself was the first director of a formalized financial aid program. In 1961 he brought H. L. Baker (B. S., 1961) to this particular role. Its rapid expansion was assisted greatly by the federal government's significant entrance into higher education. The National Defense Education Act, first through loans in 1960-61 and then through work grants in 1964-65, was most helpful. In 1961-62 Anderson college awarded

Expanded campus, about 1965: O. C. Lewis Gymnasium (1); Warner Auditorium (2); Olt Student Center (3); School of Theology (4); Hartung Hall (5); Park Place Church of God (6); Charles E. Wilson Library (7); (See page 210 for aerial view, about 1955)

$250,514 in student financial aid, $35,773 of which went to School of Theology students. Of the remaining $214,741, $144,475 were National Defense Loans. By 1968-69 more than 1,000 students were receiving annual aid of more than $1,000,000. Such funds clearly improved the picture of student retention.

Goal Five. Build and conserve physical plant. With more and more students being recruited and retained, the problem of adequate campus facilities again became acute. This need was addressed aggressively. On June 20, 1962, the new School of Theology building was dedicated with the hope that soon its intended chapel and library would be completed (see detail that follows). Even while this dedication was proceeding, the new O. C. Lewis Gymnasium was under construction (as was the architecturally unique Warner Auditorium being built on the adjacent campgrounds of the Church of God, an impressive setting for many campus commencement ceremonies yet to come). The new gym was ready for use in the fall of 1962. Very modern in design, it would seat 2,600 people and was said to be the world's largest cross-vault laminated wood structure.[22] See Appendix R.

Among the gymnasium's dedication speakers were Adam Macholtz, member of the board of trustees and officer of the A. C. Business and Professional Men's Foundation, and his two sons, Dr. James Macholtz, chair of the Physical Education Department, and Professor Robert Macholtz, director of intercollegiate athletics. This proud new facility replaced the old "Roundhouse" originally built in 1908 as the auditorium for the main services of the Anderson Camp Meeting and then remodeled in 1936 for campus athletic use (see chapter six). Soon to be razed, the old gym suddenly was pressed into new service when a fire at the old Park Place Church of God in 1966 (then the campus music hall and chapel auditorium) forced a change of plans. Later the old gym would be remodeled again with major assistance from Lilly Endowment, now into a quality theater auditorium that yet continues the long-term service of this most historic of all remaining campus buildings.

But more was to follow. That same June a construction contract was awarded to build the Olt Student Center. In addition, plans already were drawn for another men's residence hall (Smith Hall), with financing temporarily held up by the need first to conclude successfully the financial campaign underway for a new science building (Hartung

(Photos on preceding pages):

(Left page, top): School of Theology
(bottom): O. C. Lewis Gymnasium

(Right page, top): Olt Student Center
(bottom) Hartung Hall

TABLE 18

Large Gifts: July 1958--May 1966

Contributors	Amounts
World Service (Church of God)	$1,181,814
Associated Colleges of Indiana	355,880
Park Place Church of God (Music Hall Building)	250,000
C. C. Mansfield (Annuity)	250,000
Computer (Anonymous)	200,000
Myra Smoak (Orange Grove)	189,500
Lilly Endowment, Inc.	182,000
Everett Hartung	168,400
Donald Boyes (Boyes House, president's home)	142,073
National Women's Missionary Society (Church of God)	136,455
Arthur Betts	130,750
Wilbur and Eileen Schield	114,074
Langley Avenue Church of God (Dunn Memorial)	102,500
General Motors Corporation	100,000

Hall). That campaign was a key aspect of the accomplishment of Goal Six. Dramatic growth in the physical plant clearly was underway. See Appendix R for a summary of new buildings and dedications.

April 16, 1963, was to witness an emotionally moving event on campus. The new Olt Memorial Student Center was opened. First through the doors was Mrs. Olt, widow of the late and beloved dean. Following her were Dr. and Mrs. John Morrison and about seven hundred students. Somehow it seemed like the proper closing of an era of foundation building and, at the same time, the launching of much that soon would come in a broadened future for an expanding campus.

On that opening evening in April, the first event was a lovely candlelight dinner for all students and served in Wilbur Schield Dining Room, named for the first president of the Anderson College Business and Professional Men's Foundation and a campus trustee of many years (see Appendix A). Later that evening President Reardon found himself where he loved to be, among students. He sat on the floor during an all-campus sing and later told the board of trustees, "I was reassured again that these splendid young people are worthy of whatever efforts we can make in their behalf."

Goal Six. Increase and broaden financial support. Nothing symbolized better and was more responsible for making possible that broadened future than "Project 62." The general goal was to expand the institution's financial base. In this instance, the specific objective was the construction of a major new science building financed in part by a campaign in the city of Anderson. This campaign was to raise $750,000 for what would be called Hartung Hall. Project 62 had the guiding support of a campaign cabinet comprised of leading civic and industrial leaders of Anderson and headed by Elmo A. Funk. Shirell Fox led a public relations effort intended to inform the public about the purpose and goal of the campaign.

Then on October 25, 1964, came the dedication of the completed Hartung Hall,[23] with President-Emeritus John Morrison saying in his invocation prayer that this building would house the search for the truth of science, which of course is God's truth. The address was given by Louis C. Goad, executive vice-president of the General Motors Corporation, with Mayor Frank Allis of Anderson pledging in his prayer of dedication: "We are determined to use this building for the glory of God and for the benefit of mankind." The campus, the city, and local industry now were closer partners than ever before. Something important had been accomplished. It was more than a fine building. It was a symbol of what could be done together.

Such a broadening of the financial base was supplemented by the continuing development of what in the early 1960s was called the Anderson College Business and Professional Men's Foundation. It recognized great gift potential in the growing number of campus friends who were leaders in business and the professions. President Reardon was anxious that such persons be encouraged to become involved more deeply in the ongoing work of the institution. Now significant gift assistance was coming from the church, government, corporations, foundations, and individuals. Large gifts between 1958 and 1966 are listed in Table 18. Of particular and continuing significance, of course, was the Church of God.

A summary of total gifts and grants at five-year intervals makes clear how significantly goal six was achieved. For 1955-56 the total was $181,169. For 1960-61 it was $666,434, and by 1965-66 the total had risen sharply to $1,200,000. For the many years yet to come, and to enable what would be ever-widening program aspirations, much, much more yet would be needed. But the necessary process had begun. Anderson College now was attracting the attention and support of many new people who were seeing great value and potential in the campus. They were being identified, organized, and encouraged to get involved.

At the kickoff dinner for "Project 62" held at Anderson's YMCA on April 10, 1962, two major gifts were announced. They were $75,000 from the Lilly Endowment,

Inc. and $32,000 from the faculty of the campus. Soon the $600,000 level was passed on the way to the $750,000 goal, the largest amount to that time ever committed in the city to any campaign except for a hospital. A gift of $100,000 was received from the General Motors Corporation, a major employer in Anderson. The days were gone when the city of Anderson seemed to have little awareness that a college even existed in its midst.

Support for the ongoing operations of the campus continued, of course, from the Church of God. There were, however, many changes in church funding needs and available resources. As President Reardon told the board of trustees in June, 1962, Anderson College's share of the national church budget had declined steadily from 1951-52, when it was 17.04 percent of the total, to 1961-62 when it was only 12.82 percent. That decline occurred despite the addition to the campus of the School of Theology, an expansion that only later would be recognized formally and funded in part through Church of God World Service.

Even while the six goals of the Ten Year Plan (1958-1967) were being pursued vigorously, also being addressed by the institution were the challenges of managing effectively the needs of a rapidly growing student body and the complexities of growing, annual operating budgets. Chester Edwards and Gilbert Fritzler were handling budget control competently through the Business Office. More was needed, however, than a good system of budget control. It would take a thoughtful, strategic plan to determine wisely the interrelated tasks of estimating enrollment, establishing student costs, and projecting income as the new decade approached.

Such a planning process was initiated and called "Battle of the Budget." The president, college and seminary deans, leaders of the business office, respected faculty members Glenn Falls and Harold Linamen, and the statistical and analytical skills of Norman Beard combined in this crucial effort. In 1968 Paul E. Sago came to campus in the new position of vice president for financial affairs. He would coordinate all business, fund-raising and development programs, with priority on augmenting income. Dramatic institutional strides had been made in the years just past. More of the same was just ahead.

Seminary: Accreditation, Church Acceptance

The aspiration for North Central's regional accreditation of the seminary program, while expressed at the seminary's beginning by Dean Earl Martin, never was sought actively. Perceived to be of primary importance was eventual accreditation of the graduate program by the (American) Association of Theological Schools. Such recognition, leaders hoped, would confer a higher level of institutional status, thus strengthening student recruitment and transfer potential, opening new avenues of financial support, and giving a stable and respectable platform for program development and maintenance.

Of particular concern was the need to help the Church of God in North America view the School of Theology as a new educational ministry deserving of recognition and strong support. There was virtually no tradition of seminary education in this church movement and certainly no requirement of it in the ministerial credentialling process.[24] The challenge was obvious and substantial. By December, 1955, associate membership status with ATS had been sought and gained. A long and demanding process toward full accreditation had begun.

Dr. Walter Roberts, then president of ATS, was invited to give the seminary's baccalaureate address in June, 1958, followed by a conference with school officials on a review of progress toward accreditation. Results were then available from the seminary portion of the final report of the President's Study and Planning Commission (1955-57). The charge to an eight-member seminary committee of that Commission had been to

> make a study of the School of Theology as a whole, look at its development since its organization in 1950, evaluate its standing in relation to the AATS, work out a blueprint for accreditation as soon as possible, and make such recommendations as would make the School as effective an instrument in the training of young people for the Christian ministry as possible.

Clearly the study results indicated that significant progress had been made, with careful attention having been directed to all aspects of accreditation standards. But the need for more faculty and better facilities also was obvious.

Then came 1960, which was designated by the General Ministerial Assembly as the "Year of the Seminary" in the Church of God. A $100,000 campaign was launched across the church to help build a School of Theology building, with the promotional brochures stating that "full accreditation for work at the graduate school level cannot be obtained without it." The National Woman's Missionary Society[25] pledged $75,000 beyond the campaign's $100,000 goal to help reach the $250,000 actual cost of the first unit (the chapel portion not to be built initially). The church was informed with pride that there were 134 former School of Theology students then serving as pastors and associates, and 21 others serving as missionaries outside the United States.

Reported also by Dean Adam Miller was the visit in February, 1960, of a team from ATS.[26] This team's members had been pleased to find a "clarity and unanimity of understanding of the purpose of the School of Theology," which, as reported by Dean Miller, was

> to produce well-prepared Church of God pastors, who would be full-orbed [persons], loving, learning, exalting the ministry of the Church and Word,

and exhibiting a high level of responsibility not alone in ministering to a local congregation, but also in meeting the needs of the wider community.

These ATS representatives saw the plans for a new School of Theology building and noted that ATS accreditation would "insist on a high degree of separation between college and seminary. This is to insure that there be no danger that the interests of the college could damage those of the seminary." Concerns were registered about the level of faculty salaries and the diversion of students from their educational pursuits caused by the common student need for substantial secular employment while seeking a seminary education. This latter problem made community building outside the classroom, as well as weekend and other field education assignments, difficult at best to schedule.

Campus resolve was clear and the needed support came. Construction of the new seminary building began in 1960-61 and on January 15, 1962, with deep gratitude and much enthusiasm, the seminary moved its home from the third floor of Old Main to a beautiful new $307,000 facility adjacent to the college library and facing Third Street. It was announced that the seminary faculty would be brought to full strength by 1963-64, thus meeting a crucial standard for accreditation. In part, this plan was assisted by a three-year, $30,000 grant from the Lilly Endowment that helped greatly in making possible the coming of George Kufeldt in 1961 (Old Testament), Hollis Pistole in 1962 (Pastoral Work and Field Education), and Boyce Blackwelder in 1963 (New Testament). By 1963-64, then, the faculty was at full strength. The seminary had its own home and appeared ready to achieve its accreditation goal. Dr. Adam Miller concluded his deanship in 1962, and Dr. Gene Newberry, the original full-time seminary faculty member in 1950, assumed leadership. He had the credentials and the teaching experience, was loved across the church, and had a strong sense of call to this responsibility. The accreditation goal now was in sight.

Another ATS team came in November, 1964, and then reported that the seminary's "progress is impressive"; however, ATS decided to postpone action on accreditation status for another year in light of a series of lingering concerns. As summarized in a long letter to President Reardon, the central issues continued to be the diversion of students by secular employment, assistance to the dean to allow the time for proper administration, support for the faculty's professional development, the tightening of admissions standards, and the enhancement of library holdings and services. Such issues, while identified as concerns, nonetheless were intended to be seen in the context of the team's concluding statement: "Your advance has been steady and rapid and deserves high praise."[27]

That advance continued as the seminary soon was able to move its library from the basement of Wilson Library to the lower level of the new School of Theology building. This was made possible during 1964-65 in part by a gift from the Byrd family, thus the name Byrd Memorial Library honoring G. M. Byrd, pioneer minister, and his son, Chaplain Wendell Byrd, who had been killed in Korea. Wendell's brother, Cecil, had a long and distinguished career as a professional librarian at Indiana University and the American University of Cairo, Egypt, and later would be the speaker in May 1989 when the Byrd Library was to be united with Wilson Library to form a united University Library. In addition to library progress, a study-work formula was created to limit excessive student employment, and Professor George Kufeldt was named seminary registrar to lighten Dean Newberry's load.

Then in December, 1965, following another ATS visit, the decision finally was made by the association that full accreditation should be granted. There was celebration in the seminary. While there were three "notations" associated with continuing concerns in relation to particular ATS standards, these did not hinder the seminary from now functioning fully in the arena of accredited theological schools.[28] Progress reports would be made in relation to these notations and by February, 1976, the last one was removed officially. Vital assistance had come from outside sources to help make possible a substantial addressing of these continuing growth needs. Dean Newberry, for instance, reported to the board of trustees in April, 1967, that the Seatlantic Fund had joined with the Lilly Endowment in providing $28,000 over three years for the seminary's library expansion. For faculty development, the Lilly Endowment also had awarded the religion faculties of the Anderson campus the necessary funds for a five-week historical and archaeological seminar in the Middle East, which occurred in the summer of 1968 (see Appendix S).

Accreditation of the School of Theology by ATS has been maintained without interruption since 1965. In addition, however, program developments and trends in theological education during the 1970s raised again that earlier aspiration for the seminary to be included in North Central's regional accreditation of the programs of the undergraduate college. There was prejudice in some graduate school circles against students from "theological" schools with only professional accreditation, particularly in relation to a graduate program with a discipline specialization. Such regional accreditation status was first granted to the School of Theology during 1974-75. Therefore, when the time came in 1978-79 for the periodic review and reaffirmation by North Central of the college, all parties agreed that the self-study would include the entire institution and the visiting team would be a combination of North Central and ATS representatives. The result was wholly favorable, with North Central continuing its formal recognition through "the first professional degree" (the three-year graduate program by then called the Master of Divinity—the former Bachelor of Divinity). That joint process of review and reaffirmation was repeated successfully in 1988-89.

What did the achieving of accreditation really mean for the seminary? Dr.

Pistole had been impressed as a faculty member by the responsibility it tended to place on the seminary for serious theological scholarship. The curriculum should be more than a ministerial training program emphasizing ready information and relevant practical skills. Students should be enabled to be disciplined scholars as well as equipped practitioners. As Dean Newberry stated to the board of trustees: "It means that we have been able to keep faith with scores of students over these sixteen years in our pledge that their ministerial training would have an integrity, a depth and quality, worthy of their high calling."[29] Choosing the path of formal accreditation had been a conscious choice to open the seminary to the scrutiny and standards of the wider community of theological education. It represented a commitment to avoid a highly sectarian form of ministerial education, surely an appropriate implementation of a central burden of the Church of God movement.

Walking the long and demanding path to accreditation had tended to set much of the seminary's agenda in its early years. But in the years to follow there would be other challenges to face that would require equal commitment and creativity. Accreditation had brought the desired recognition in the world of theological education. Soon the need for recognition within the Church of God itself would come to involve a series of dramatic, sometimes painful, and finally very productive changes in the School of Theology and in its relationship to the Church of God movement.

The final years of the decade of the 1960s were volatile, dynamic, and difficult ones in the United States and on its campuses. The cry for human rights was loud and no national consensus on the war in Vietnam had been reached. Was the church relevant to all of this conflict and change? How could the seminary react to a new breed of student? Many young seminarians now were eager to sharpen their critical skills, and then often were prepared to turn them on the perceived irrelevance of the typical local congregation and the traditionalism they felt existed in the School of Theology curriculum. Candid dialogue was insisted upon in the classrooms, and new emphasis on clinical, urban, and counseling opportunities was necessary. Dean Newberry cautioned the board of trustees in 1968 that "the historical complexities of our time are indescribably acute. We must learn how to make the timeless gospel timely in our age."[30] President Reardon told the board the following year that "many of our students have lost confidence in the Church, in the nation, in things, and in that cornerstone of our modern tower of Babel—the university itself."[31] Dean Newberry stood in this gap, both believing in the academic enterprise and honestly loving the church, despite its obvious shortcomings.

During 1967 the old "B. D." name of the standard seminary degree program was changed to Master of Divinity. This was in response to criticism throughout the world of theological education that the word "bachelor" misrepresented and demeaned a seminary's program by implying a mere extension of undergraduate-level work. A new degree, the Master of Religious Education, was launched at Anderson, in part to address the widening range of student interests and professional goals. Unable to mount alone the kinds of experiential educational opportunities now being called for, the School of Theology capitalized on its accredited status to find vital linkages to new educational and financial resources for students.

A new organization now had emerged, the Accredited Theological Seminaries of Ohio and Indiana (ATSOI), to raise funds for seminaries by approaching together the business community. The association's appeal was that seminaries prepare spiritual leaders who impact a community's moral climate which, if strong, enables effective business activity. The School of Theology not only joined the ATSOI effort in 1967, hoping for new operating support, but in 1969 became partners with Christian Theological Seminary in Indianapolis. This partnership was a sharing of a grant from the National Institute of Mental Health intended to create workshop opportunities focusing on the pastor as counselor. Anderson's Dr. John Vayhinger was the key liaison person. Then in 1970 the seminary joined several other seminaries in an experimental effort in Chicago funded by Lilly Endowment (Urban Ministries Program for Seminarians—UMPS). Somehow a young seminary in a small city in Indiana had to develop preparation opportunities for ministry in an urban environment.

The School of Theology was trying to meet rising student expectations and sometimes even demands in an increasingly complex and troubled culture. The resulting pressures on the school had become heavy indeed. A full faculty had been assembled, accreditation standards met, programs expanded, and relationships developed. But student enrollment in the seminary had changed little over the years. Operating with only 70-80 students was viewed increasingly by the campus administration as unrealistic without some changes being made. There were significant student retention problems and questions about the attractiveness of traditional programs and their practical relevance in the life of the church. The time had come for fresh thinking about the future.

The financial burden of operating the School of Theology had been carried willingly by the college from the beginning. But that burden had increased. As early as 1961, President Reardon referred to the operating deficit of the seminary that was being absorbed on an institution-wide basis. "The parents of college students and students themselves," he said, "are paying the bill for a sizable share of graduate ministerial training in the Church of God. This is an institutional policy which ought to change."[32]

In June 1964 the president noted that, whereas the seminary in 1958 had brought in 0.7% of the institution's operating budget through student charges while requiring 4.9% for instructional expenses, in 1964 it was 1.0% of such income to support 5.8% of such expense. Seminary tuition had been kept relatively low by design. But low tuition, coupled with plateaued enrollments and sharply rising costs, were posing questions that could hardly be ignored for long.[33]

Given the distinctive character of the Church of God movement and all the turmoil of the time, President Reardon was prepared to ask the most basic question: "What is the best way to educate ministers for the Church of God?" Pursuing that question seriously and courageously soon would bring major changes, considerable controversy, and a new and stronger foundation for the seminary's future. In that process there would be some pain and some new vision. Out of that process would emerge a sense of providential guidance, a new lease on life for the seminary.

During the Christmas vacation of 1965, Dr. John Morrison, the beloved president-emeritus, was stricken with a heart attack and soon died. It was a time of sorrow, gratitude for a marvelous past, and fresh determination for others to carry on. The horizons of the campus were widening rapidly, and President Reardon was committed to keeping the dream alive. He reflected to the board of trustees his own judgment about the great debt owed to Morrison. "When we were with him," he said, "all the good things in our lives seemed to emerge." At the alumni banquet in June, 1963, six oil portraits were unveiled, done by the famous James Wills of Houston, Texas. They would help future generations to keep some touch with a legacy of leadership now passing from the active scene. To be hung in honored locations on the campus were the portraits of John A. Morrison, George Russell Olt, Earl L. Martin, Carl Kardatzke, John H. Kane, and Adam W. Miller. Later a portrait of Gene W. Newberry would join the group.

1. In Barry Callen, *Faith, Learning, and Life*, 91. Originally appeared in *Alumni News*, July-August, 1958.
2. Callen, *Faith, Learning, and Life*, 92.
3. *A.C. News*, special issue, 1964.
4. *Signatures*, Summer 1990.
5. *Signatures*, Summer 1990.
6. Final president's report to the board of trustees, April 22, 1983.
7. *Signatures*, Summer 1990.
8. In May, 1959, the executive committee of the board of trustees approved "The Ten Year Building Program," a detailed statement of major facility needs and planned action steps. It projected a Russell Olt Memorial Union, a School of Theology building, a gymnasium, and major remodeling of Old Main and of old Park Place Church (for a fine arts center). Additional student residence halls also would be needed. The intent, beyond meeting the primary and urgent needs of campus people and programs, also was to proceed "in such a manner as will make available to the camp meeting on a permanent basis the facilities of housing, food services and classrooms."
9. During his career with the Brooklyn Dodgers (1946-1959) Erskine threw two no-hit-

ters and pitched in five World Series. He was to bring stature to Anderson's baseball program and become a key trustee of the campus and a leading community citizen in Anderson.

10. See Reardon, *This is the Way It Was*, 78-79.

11. See Barry Callen, *Thinking and Acting Together* (1992).

12. The potential was real. Moore worked in the business office while a student. He stayed on after graduation, then with a wife and two children. President Reardon and later Presidents Nicholson and Edwards showed great faith in him. Soon he was controller, then assistant treasurer when Chester Edwards retired, then treasurer when Paul Sago left in 1976, and eventually senior vice president for finance/advancement and treasurer of the university.

13. Graduating in 1967, he would return in 1976 as a professor of New Testament.

14. Holly G. Miller in *Signatures* (Winter 1989-90).

15. *A. C. News,* October, 1966.

16. *A. C. News*, December , 1965, 10.

17. Dr. Kardatzke wrote a major article published in the *Indiana Teacher* magazine (December 1954) titled "Education in the Land of the Mau Maus." According to the *Alumni News* (January, 1955, 5), "this is the first time an Anderson College professor has filled four pages of such a far-reaching and influential magazine."

18. For a brief history of this extension effort and the new college, see Barry Callen, *Preparing for Service* (Warner Press, 1988), chap. 10.

19. NCATE self-study, Appendix A, August 1963.

20. Dr. Clear maintained one practice that surely was annoying to a young administration under substantial financial pressure. About two weeks before contracts came out each year, he would predict the level of average salary increase, always putting it a little above what likely was possible and thus making even a good raise less than his widely announced expectation. Clear referred to himself as Reardon's "biblical visitor," a thorn in the flesh!

21. President Reardon always chose to stay as close as possible to student life, partly because he genuinely loved students and partly because some student achievements and problems had public and church relations implications, matters about which he cared very much. Dean Nicholson's relationships increasingly were more with faculty than students. He moved more toward certain functions of the president's office than toward the arena of student discipline and support programs. Beard had several specialized skills, including his reputation of knowing all students on campus by name.

22. *Andersonian,* October 19, 1962, 1.

23. Everett A. Hartung had been a business and community leader in Anderson since 1935. A prominent Church of God layperson and loyal friend of the school, in 1965 he and his wife gave stocks valued at $175,000 to help build the college's modest endowment portfolio at a time of rapid enrollment growth and program development. During the excavation for the construction of Hartung Hall, there were an unexpected few moments of fear. A worker encountered a large pipe below ground, could not identify it, and proceeded to cut it off. Flames suddenly shot twenty feet into the air! Apparently it was part of one of those many old gas wells that earlier had been so common in Madison County (see chapter one).

24. In 1973, after twenty School of Theology graduating classes, twenty-three percent of the seventy-seven persons newly ordained that year in the Church of God were seminary graduates (thirteen percent from the School of Theology). In 1983 the pattern was similar, with 157 ordained, 20 percent seminary graduates (16 percent from the School of Theology).

25. Currently known as Women of the Church of God.

26. *Gospel Trumpet*, September 11, 1960, 8.

27. Letter from Charles L. Taylor of ATS to President Robert H. Reardon, January 7, 1965, 3.

28. Those notations related to adequacy of faculty, opportunity for enrichment of faculty, and diversion of students from academic pursuit by employment. A fourth, related to level of library support, emerged later, but was satisfied and removed in 1976.

29. Report to the board, June 1966, 1.

30. Report to the board, May 9, 1968, 1.

31. Report to the board, May 1, 1969, 2.

32. President's annual report to the board, June 15, 1961, 5.

33. In 1977-78, after a series of changes had been made and enrollment had increased significantly, tuitional income had risen to 2.9 percent of the institution's total and seminary expense had remained rather level at 5.6 percent.

10 Keeping on Course
1970-1983

**"There is a shaking in the foundations which inspires both hope and fear....
This is no time to abandon our mission. It is time for obedience."**
(President Robert H. Reardon)

The Vietnam war years had brought turmoil to the nation and considerable tension to the Anderson college campus and most others. President Reardon, a strong leader determined to retain the distinctives and integrity of the campus, had both applauded the sensitive consciences of students and held the line when, in his judgment, they wanted to go too far (such as objecting to the continuation of mandatory chapel/convocation attendance).

He said in 1972 that he hoped "the turbulent 1960s, with their rebellious, impatient, tuned-in, turned-on, tell-it-like-it-is, revolutionary approach to the world," were over. He now wished that the college would "recover something of the quiet thoughtfulness and balanced judgment which are marks of civil and refined people."[1]

The Anderson campus had not been forcibly disrupted or even burned as some had been, but neither had it escaped the strain of those difficult years of civil unrest and world disorder. While life on campus had not been radically changed as in many places, increasingly it had grown diverse, stimulating, full of opportunity for each student to grow in all ways.

Many Dimensions of Student Life

In the midst of it all, a central task was to manage rapid growth and change, keeping the institution on its distinctive course. The school year 1963-64 provides an example of the increased richness of student life on campus, the complex context for the mission challenges of the 1970s. The spiritual had been enriched that year by thirty-one ordained ministers on the faculty and staff, the enthusiastic reception of E. Stanley Jones as Religious Emphasis Week speaker, and the continuing service involvement of many students through Christianity-in-Action. Shirell Fox worked hard to provide the best of

TABLE 19

Annual Musical Productions
1964-1992
Produced Jointly by the Drama and Music Departments

Annie Get Your Gun	1969
Brigadoon	1976, 1986
Call Me Madam	1991
Fiddler on the Roof	1972, 1979, 1988
Finian's Rainbow	1982
Funny Girl	1981
Hello Dolly	1971, 1980
Kismet	1977
Kiss Me Kate	1989
My Fair Lady	1965, 1974, 1983
No, No Nanette	1990
Oliver	1970
Oklahoma	1975, 1985
Pirates of Penzance	1992
South Pacific	1968, 1978
The Music Man	1973, 1987
The Sound of Music	1966, 1984
Where's Charlie	1964

Note: No production in 1967.

chapel programming, always with a worship emphasis even when major lecturers or cultural events were featured. The Music Department saw a total of 211 students participate in choir, orchestra, band, glee clubs, Oratorio Society, and small ensembles.

About 260 undergraduate students in 1963-64 were involved in dramatic presentations, either on stage or behind the scenes. Two religious plays, "Christ in the Concrete City" and "The People Versus Christ," were presented in churches in several states. That same year, beginning the annual tradition of a major musical being presented jointly by the Drama and Music Departments, "Where's Charlie" was staged. See Table 19 for all of the musicals presented since 1964.

The Hoosier College Conference provided stiff competition in the seven intercollegiate sports in which a total of 104 Ravens participated in 1963-64. Football struggled with two wins, five losses, and one tie. Basketball had a 10-10 year, while success was experienced in cross country (4-1), tennis (5-2), baseball (13-4), golf, and track. Anderson College won the conference championship in tennis that year and initiated a wrestling program for future competition (see Table 27).

The previous year Ken Strawn had concluded one of the most outstanding basketball careers that would ever be seen on the Anderson hardwood. When he scored his two thousandth point against Franklin College on February 9, 1963, coach Robert Macholtz remarked, "It'll be a long time before that one's topped." In the years to come Anderson often would capture the all-sports trophy in the conference because of quality performance spread across the several sports. It also would maintain a substantial intramurals program.

Then there were the many student organizations. In 1963-64, for example, Norman Beard, dean of students, reported to the board of trustees that there were ten campus social clubs involving 320 students in formals, picnics, service projects, Homecoming float construction, all-school entertainment programs, and more. Also, 250 students were active in fourteen special interest clubs, ranging from business and international relations to radio and photography (see Appendix I for a complete listing of student organizations in later years). The campus was busy, varied, and full of pride, with quality performance the intended end product of whatever was being attempted. In fact, President Reardon told the trustees in 1965 that the church's growing pride in the campus might grow so great that pride itself could become something of a concern.

"There was a day," he said, "when most of us went out into the church . . . and much of our energy was spent carrying on a battle with the 'saints.' One of the most difficult things we have had to adjust to in the last decade has been the general love, trust and acceptance with which the institution has been accepted by the church. . . .

(Top) David Armstrong, Rhonda Rothman, in "My Fair Lady", 1984
(Bottom) Thomas Harp, David Rinker, in "The Music Man", 1973

However, beneath that smile I think I sometimes detect a pride in size, status and an over enthusiasm for what education can do. The college now must change its stance," he concluded. "It must abhor the prospect of becoming a denominational status symbol." Much of the anti-intellectualism of the church's past now appeared gone and, Reardon observed, "among us there is an amazing unity within diversity."

The world and the church were changing, and the campus had become responsible to provide leadership as a new day dawned. The president feared the abortion of mission by a settling for business-as-usual methods, a drifting into "salvation by organization, structure, and bylaws" and the unconscious attempt "to bring in the Kingdom of God by architects, fund raisers and lawyers." The church and campus needed each other, maybe more than ever before.

Student life, with all its fun, diversity, drive, and occasional experimentation, needed to be kept in balance and congruent with institutional mission. Intercollegiate athletics, for instance, was put in perspective by Professor James Macholtz, then chair of the Department of Physical Education. Anderson College teams had experienced their share of success over the years, but success was to be measured by more than a win-loss record. The athletic program, said Macholtz, "should seek to be primarily educative and Christian in nature. The temptations to gain prestige, acquire publicity, provide entertainment, and make money should be avoided."[2] The task, Macholtz insisted, was to focus on mission and the highest well-being of all participants.

Such an emphasis on the well-being of persons also was underscored by President Reardon's own tradition, dating back to the 1950s, of sharing with the college student body in the annual Christmas Chapel the "Uncle Barney" story.[3] This heartwarming story combined sentimentality, traditional family values, and a call for expressions of human compassion. Reardon tended to transmit institutional heritage and mission effectively by personal presence and storytelling.

Our Mission Stands Firm

The maintenance of institutional integrity had remained high on President Reardon's agenda during the volatile 1960s. His working assumptions had been made public and he was willing to act on them. In April, 1967, for instance, he had shared with the board of trustees these key perspectives on the future:

1. Our fundamental commitment is to a high quality liberal arts undergraduate college, with its ultimate objectives being identical to those of the Church—the redemption of the individual and the redemption of society. Central in this commitment is primary responsibility to the Church of God through ownership, operation, and control.

2. American society will continue its gradual secularization and the spiritual and moral base of the nation will continue to erode. This will eventuate in a paradoxical posture for Anderson College, one of involvement in the world and withdrawal from the world.

3. One of our greatest battles will be to maintain the sense of community—knowing, caring, learning, sharing with each other, and nearly everything in our secular society today militates against this. . . .

Then, as the decade of the 1970s opened, the president acted boldly on these assumptions. He intended to make clear that Anderson College was and would remain a special place. So, on July 15, 1970, he sent a candid letter to the homes of all new and returning students. It said that it was intended to "contribute to the strengthening of our common life in the institution with which you have decided to cast your lot." These pointed lines emphasized the standards of conduct of the campus, including a rejection of discrimination based on color, race, or creed. One key sentence read: "Students advocating racial separatism, unnegotiable demands supported by threats of violence, or hostility toward Christian teaching on brotherhood should seek their education elsewhere."

In June, 1970, President Reardon had told the board of trustees that "there is something apocalyptic about these times." Campus life across the nation, he said, had been "politicized, radicalized, and in many cases immobilized." None would soon forget the spring of 1970 when President Richard Nixon had sent American troops into Cambodia. The reaction on some campuses had been violent. What would follow on the Kent State University campus, for instance, only deepened a widespread anger.

Students at Anderson College tended to be troubled, but without reacting in destructive ways. Certainly helpful was the "Asbury/Anderson Revival," which Reardon identified as "the most outstanding event of the 1970-71 year." For fifty consecutive days beginning February 22, 1970, there was a daily celebration of repentance, joy, and praise convening spontaneously at the South Meridian Church of God in Anderson. It had begun with students coming from Asbury College in Kentucky to witness about what had happened in that school's chapel on February 3. Scheduled for the usual fifty minutes, that Asbury chapel had lasted for more than seven days (!) and then had spread to many other campuses, including Anderson.[4] Nearly half of the Anderson student body became involved, some students receiving important spiritual help and some losing perspective by ceasing to attend classes altogether. Several faculty members were key participants and gave valuable guidance. Campus pastor James Earl Massey spoke in chapel to give counsel on the higher wisdom of combining spiritual experience and disciplined intellectual pursuit. Times were volatile and perspective was crucial.

Said Reardon in 1970: "There is a shaking in the foundations which inspires both hope and fear. . . . This is no time to abandon our mission. It is time for obedi-

President Reardon, Wilson Library in background

ence." Then he added in his 1971 annual report to the trustees what was at the heart of his concern. "My main concern is not whether Anderson College will survive; the overriding concern is what *kind* of institution we are becoming, or ought to become. . . . If we are true to our Christian heritage," he cautioned, "we most certainly will find ourselves swimming hard against the current. The great moral and spiritual foundations of this nation and of our society are eroding. . . . The great unchanging ground upon which we stand, it seems to me, as a Christian community is the historic event of the Incarnation and the Bible as the fundamental and essential rootage from which our faith must spring." The president knew well the school's religious, moral, and intellectual tradition, and he intended to keep it on course, whatever the challenges.

It was not a time when maintaining a strong sense of campus community or holding steady in the pursuit of an unchanging mission would be easy. Despite the positive effects of the Asbury/Anderson revival, the student body at Anderson College was increasingly diverse denominationally, racially, and economically. Automobiles now were common, making it easy for many students to leave the campus altogether on weekends. A certain impersonality came subtly with the much increased size.[5] The times themselves tended to nurture among students a hostility to almost anything that could be seen as institutional regimentation. Student costs were kept relatively low at Anderson in an attempt to stay affordable for the youth of the church. In part through particularly low residence hall and board fees, the attempt was made to encourage a significant residential experience on campus.[6] While students around the nation seemed finally to be backing away from the tactic of physically disrupting life on many campuses, now thinking this radical approach counterproductive, there were a few tense situations on the Anderson campus. They were not violent, but emotions ran deep nonetheless.

From some church leaders, for instance, came vigorous criticism of the school's choice of Theodore Hesburgh, president of Notre Dame University, as the 1970 commencement speaker (see Appendix Q) because of his being a prominent Roman Catholic. Hesburgh, a true statesman in higher education, delivered an outstanding address and the threatened withholding of World Service dollars by a few pastors did not materialize. From college students there was a considerable effort to make chapel attendance voluntary, something many church-related colleges, under pressure, agreed to do in these years. The Anderson administration finally did increase the number of excused absences per semester and expressed increased sensitivity to the call for a greater breadth of programming; but there was no yielding on the importance and necessity of chapel/convocation.[7]

From seminary students there developed a strong opposition to the concept of a "seven-year track" which had been introduced by the administration as a way of coordinating the college and seminary ministerial education programs on campus, even merging selected undergraduate and graduate classes for efficiency of operation. Graduate students tended to view this as a weakening of their seminary experience and resisted openly (see below for larger perspective and related events). Finally there came a compromise on the implementation of the seven-year track, one that defined with care which college students were eligible to enroll in certain seminary classes.

But, whatever the compromises on some issues, there was administrative insistence that the seminary and the whole institution learn to live, as Reardon humorously put it to the board of trustees in June, 1972, "by the rigid application of a simple formula which vanished from the scene in government years ago. It was rediscovered," he said with a little smile, "on an ancient Sumerian tablet, inscribed as the distilled wisdom of a bankrupt merchant. It reads: 'Live within your income.'" Finances would continue to be an annual struggle, but already a pattern had begun that would be unbroken for decades. Budget control always would be tight and student enrollment and income projections conservative, with small annual surpluses planned and somehow achieved year after year. Here was a determined stability in the midst of dynamic and sometimes controversial times.

President Reardon already had presided over the construction of several new facilities on campus. But he did not wish to be known merely as the leader who built a fine new campus. He made clear to alumni that a campus builds because it must serve effectively its growing enrollments and programs. He warned, however, that "it is the Spirit that gives life. An institution is not an end to be served, and it is only as we are able to become a servant educational community that our corporate life will be found."[8]

The fulfillment of Anderson's corporate life always would be related closely to that of the Church of God movement. The administration in 1981 developed a brochure distributed widely on campus and in the church. Titled "Anderson College: In Partnership with the Church," it said clearly and without reserve that being church-related was essential and vital to the nature and mission of this college. In part, it said this about the Anderson campus:

> [It] values the church relationship in which the thought and practices of the church and the methods and perspectives of the academic disciplines are enabled to probe and inform each other. The College assumes that the theology and life of the whole Christian community, and of the Church of God Reformation Movement in particular, is worthy of orienting and enriching the educational process. It is equally aware of its responsibility to be a source of research, rethinking, and renewal in the church. Formulations of theology are never fixed or finished, and church traditions lose their significance apart from fresh analysis and an understanding of contemporary relevance.

The essential paradoxes within this statement were judged vital and indispensable, and on occasion were lived out with an inevitable tension. As the president told the trustees in his May 1968 report: "Given a compelling cause, a cadre of bright minds tempered by experience, a disposition to venture and risk failure, and a continuing climate of trust and openness, there is a powerful thrust in this combination that propels institutions forward to meet the demands of the new day."

Reardon earlier had written to the body of alumni to announce his view of what the college could not and should not be expected to do for its students. What tasks were beyond the intention or ability of Anderson College? It could not "build walls high enough to wall in all the good and wall out all the evil." It could not "keep an honest student protected from those ideas which challenge the validity of faith." Nor could it "distill truth into a neat series of vaccines and inoculate its students in such a way that they will all think alike, believe alike, and have neat little formulae and answers for all the questions of life."[9]

But, the president had continued, the campus was full of crucial abilities. There was a distinctive and demanding mission for which it would give its best and should be held accountable. It could: "fan the spark of faith; give its students vast resources with which to grow in mind and spirit; provide teachers of great skill and Christian devotion whose maturity and vision draws out these qualities in their students; demand high standards of conduct and responsibility of its students; foster and nourish that 'heavenly encounter' which enables the student to develop those God-given faculties which will lead to useful Christian citizenship" (23).

How Best to Educate Church Leaders

Soon an irony befell the campus. In an effort to identify the best way to educate future ministers for the church's life in troubled times, the campus found itself in the deep waters of church controversy. Persons who then were School of Theology faculty members recalled vividly a day in 1971 when they were summoned as a group to the president's office for what seemed to them a dramatic announcement.

On that occasion, President Reardon had placed in question the continuance of the Master of Divinity program, at least offered independently on campus. He suggested rather that wisdom lay with new, versatile, and shorter master's programs (forty-five instead of ninety semester hours), more coordination with the undergraduate college's religion faculty and curriculum, a new Center for Pastoral Studies to facilitate practical and continuing ministerial education, and cooperative relationships with seminaries like Christian in Indianapolis and Asbury in Kentucky. Reportedly, he even hinted (or at least, in their anxiety, some faculty members thought he might have meant) that, depending on the outcome of such changes, all current seminary faculty members might not be needed in the future. The immediate result of this meeting, not surprisingly, was confusion.

The intent behind such announcements was to dare to embrace innovation in the face of persistent problems and to put programmatic specifics to the thinking that already had been done by a Joint Committee on Theological Education[10] appointed in 1969 by the administration. The group had been charged to look at the entire campus program of ministerial education, break down old walls between college and seminary, and deploy teaching resources interchangeably to best advantage. The president's goals were to appeal to a wider range of students with the new degree programs, eliminate duplication and use resources wisely, draw qualified pastors into the educational process, and take the lead in interdenominational cooperation. The Association of Theological Schools was said to be supportive of this effort, at least as a three-year experiment.

After the president's meeting in 1971, seminary graduate Jerry Grubbs,[11] then pastoring in Tennessee, was one of many pastors who received contacts from the seminary announcing that his *alma mater* was in danger "of being closed." Some seminary students wore black arm bands. The strategy of a seven-year track on campus had been intended to identify ministerial students early, accelerate their professional education at the undergraduate level, and retain them for the seminary, with introductory graduate courses already satisfied, the potential for electives increased, and the length of time required in seminary shortened for many. But some people perceived this strategy very differently. The seminary community, while appreciative of the desired goals, resisted what it judged the inevitable watering down of graduate courses to accommodate under-prepared college students. Particularly offensive to some was a feared dilution or even deletion of the standard M. Div. program, which they considered the heart of a true seminary. Some innovations, such as beginning use of the January Term calendar in 1969 to enhance field education opportunities, seemed most desirable. But a threat to the integrity or even continuation of the M. Div. program was judged intolerable.[12]

The volatile situation intensified even more when President Buford Norris of Christian Theological Seminary pressed to finalize the formation of the "Foundation for Religious Studies," a proposed ecumenical enterprise to be based in Indianapolis. Major foundation funding was anticipated for realizing the significant cooperation of several seminaries of differing theological traditions, each enriching the other's students. The School of Theology was urged by FRS officials to participate through cross-registration of students, open library access, limited faculty sharing, and even relocation to Indianapolis.[13] A special meeting of the board of trustees in March, 1972, considered the matter further, hearing the strong support of President Reardon and Dean Newberry for a limited FRS relationship, a new Center for Pastoral Studies, and other program innovations. The trustees also heard strong objections from seminary faculty and student representatives who feared that a standard seminary program (the M. Div. degree) was about to be compromised and thus the possible closing of the seminary could be at hand.

Finally the decision was made, not for physical relocation of the seminary, never a serious consideration, but for a Foundation for Religious Studies relationship, a new Center for Pastoral Studies, and the new forty-five hour Master of Ministry and Master of Arts in Religion degree programs (with continuation of the M. Div.). Having begun to plan initial implementation, negative reaction surfaced in the Church of God. Some church leaders felt that the seminary was being compromised, especially because of a Catholic seminary involved in the Indianapolis relationship (they pictured future Church of God ministers being educated by Roman Catholic priests). After vigorous debate in the 1972 General Assembly, a 499-422 vote rejected the appropriateness of the Foundation for Religious Studies involvement and called for a quick end to it. A one-year study committee was authorized to bring a report to the 1973 General Assembly containing "recommendations for the continuation of a Church of God seminary, responsible to the General Assembly." Out of the pain of this conflict, the Church of God was beginning to claim real ownership of "its" seminary.

As these called-for recommendations were being formulated, constructive attitudes were taken in the seminary. New programs not being debated were implemented with enthusiasm. Student internships in "covenant" churches multiplied and "ministers-in-residence" began coming to campus to share their experiences. Leadership change also came to the School of Theology. As chair of the college's department of religious studies, I became the founding director of the new Center for Pastoral Studies and immediately became involved in the final design and initial implementation of the new forty-five hour graduate degree programs. Also functioning as acting dean of the School of Theology during Dean Newberry's 1973-74 sabbatical in Kenya, East Africa, I was elected and ratified in June, 1974, as the new dean of the significantly new School of Theology.[14] During Newberry's deanship (see Table 1) I had been involved in a great effort to foster a sense of community, to provide quality scholarship, and to oversee the seminary's accreditation; and always he had been respected by the church.

The 1973 General Assembly received and approved twelve recommendations designed to affirm and strengthen the School of Theology and to set continuing strategy for achieving increased support for the seminary and its students.[15] That strategy yielded real fruit when the 1974 Assembly approved a five-year plan of direct support for the School of Theology through the World Service budget, initially to total $200,000. That same Assembly proceeded to adopt a proposal for the national church to join with the Anderson campus in raising an annual fund to defray the tuition costs of Church of God seminarians.

This fund, soon to be known as the Boyce W. Blackwelder Seminary Tuition Fund, would be the vehicle for raising and distributing directly to seminary students, from its beginning to the present, well in excess of one million dollars. Particularly in its early years, the actual raising of the funds (see Table 20) was done largely by the inspired work of Dr. Hillery C. Rice (B. Th., 1940, 1942), retired pastor and now a campus development officer who loved ministerial students and was on the road as a salesman for support of their education.

Never had such attention and support come to the School of Theology from the Church of God. Although the process had generated considerable controversy, the campus goal of being willing to risk nontraditional innovation to find more productive and viable ways to educate ministers had brought excellent results. The general outcome, in fact, created the programmatic and financial framework in which the School of Theology has operated from then until the present day. As dean I summarized the process for the board of trustees in 1974:

TABLE 20

Blackwelder Fund: Seminary Financial Aid

	1974-75	1975-76	1976-77	1977-78
Amount Available for Distribution to Eligible Students	0	$51,647	$72,703	$101,464
Annual Tuition for Full-Time Students	$840	$840	$960	$1,060
Average Percent of Tuition Underwritten by This Fund	0	40%	45%	45%
Number of Graduate Students Aided for Part or All of the Year	0	143	161	185

The Church of God in general and this board of trustees in particular have found it necessary to search relentlessly for the most appropriate and feasible model for educating ministers in a context of excellence, without destroying meaningful bridges to the sponsoring church, and without compromising the integrity of the school itself. This process to date has proven time-consuming, painful, and profitable in ways often unanticipated.

The outcomes were several. Now clarified was the necessary working premise that seminary education should proceed within the organizational framework of the Church of God movement. A cooperative, ecumenical enterprise, such as the earlier proposed Foundation of Religious Studies, was not acceptable to the church. The School of Theology should function with much greater direct accountability to and financial support from the Church of God than had been the case in the seminary's first decades of existence. Its dean, once elected by the board of trustees, should stand for General Assembly ratification, a seminary line item separate from that of the college should appear in the World Service budget of the church, and the several undergraduate colleges of the church should work toward curricular coordination with the School of Theology. Further, the School of Theology was to be recognized as the church's only seminary. In fact, the church's Commission on Christian Higher Education, in its major report on "Theological Education and Ministerial Training in the Church of God," successfully proposed to the following 1976 General Assembly:

We propose that the General Assembly recognize seminary training as the normal, the ideal level of initial preparation for the future young minister, and that the Assembly continue to authorize an annual appropriation of funds whereby this level of ministerial training can be made available to eligible students who give evidence that they will use their educational experiences for the good of the church.

It had been a long road from places like Oberlin in the 1930s and 1940s, where a few Church of God persons were experiencing seminary education for the first time, to a formal recognition that such education should be made available within the life of the Church of God movement and even recognized as "normal" and "ideal." While it is granted that such recognition was aspirational, in no way mandatory, and had several qualifications associated with it, nonetheless it now was an approved statement of principle for the future.

The recent program changes in the seminary, particularly the new emphasis on internships, preaching, evangelism, ministers-in-residence, and the founding of the Center for Pastoral Studies, were applauded widely. While the M.Div. program was retained, masters programs requiring only half the number of hours now were in place to serve persons who otherwise might not have been able to attempt seminary at all or who had ministerial goals other than pastoring. A beautiful new chapel and, beneath it, much needed library expansion space were constructed in 1974 (completion of the original seminary building plan), with the chapel named for the beloved former dean, Adam W. Miller (see Table 1). This chapel featured the Willhardt Window[16] highlighting chosen theological symbols in stained glass and was linked to the new Wrather Communication Laboratory now on the completed upper floor.

Worship now enjoyed a prominent architectural statement right in the midst of seminary academic life. Soon missionary service did also as the M.A. Rel.: Christian Mission degree program was launched in 1976 in partnership with the Missionary Board of the Church of God (Lester Crose the initial mission professor and program director). Meanwhile, the new Center for Pastoral Studies was developing rapidly under my direction. By 1981 the Center had enrolled 781 church leaders (including 205 black ministers and 141 women) and had awarded thirty-seven Diplomas in Ministerial Studies (fifty CEUs) and five Advanced Diplomas (one hundred CEUs).[17] President Reardon spoke this way to the trustees in June, 1974, about the Center for Pastoral Studies:

> It is an ingenious vehicle which, if managed carefully, can bear an enormous amount of freight. The impulse to tradition is strong—perhaps nowhere so strong as in academia. It would be easy for us to lapse back into traditional separatist concepts—with the college and the seminary each rebuilding its own walls. I think such a direction would be not only cowardly, but would be to turn away from one of the most promising developments anywhere on the horizon.

With the School of Theology's quarter of a century of service celebrated in 1975, a new era had begun for the seminary. Student enrollment began to rise significantly, moving from a first semester headcount enrollment of 68 in 1972 to 188 by 1977. Major new student-aid dollars now were available, the seminary's visibility in the Church of God was high, and its programs had a new vitality and flexibility. The Blackwelder Fund's contribution in those first years was significant, as Table 20 makes clear. Throughout, however, one question persisted. How independent should the seminary be? How separate should it be from the Anderson campus itself, from the ministerial education program of the college, and from the university model of a graduate school of religion? These were critical and perennial questions for the entire campus and for the church at large.

From its beginning the seminary had been primarily a project of Anderson College. This institution almost singularly had provided the vision, funds, facilities, and administrative leadership. One board of trustees and one president always have governed and administered jointly both the college and seminary. All presidents to date have shown clear interest in and definite support for the School of Theology. They have seen it, not as an incidental and costly extension of the much larger and more significant undergraduate college, but as a central aspect of the institution's mission.

Also from nearly the seminary's beginning in 1950, however, there had been a few voices saying that, because the School of Theology was to be the seminary of the whole Church of God movement, it should be independent of the sole control of the Anderson administration. All the national church attention focused on the seminary during the 1971-1974 period, combined with new church funding then dedicated specifically to the School of Theology, naturally raised this question more formally. Should the School of Theology be a separate corporation serving the whole church, and in that way should it be more immediately accountable to it?

One of the 1973 recommendations of the church's General Assembly study committee on the seminary was that, by June of 1977, the General Assembly test the thesis of a "free-standing seminary." However, by June of 1976 the Assembly's Special Advisory Committee on the seminary was ready to report on this issue.

The campus administration and board of trustees were seen as having acted in good faith and set excellent new directions for the seminary. They were said to have acted responsibly on behalf of the whole church. Therefore, with appreciation for this good stewardship and given the unmanageable costs apparently involved in any alternative, the committee was joined by the church's Commission of Christian Higher Education in commending the Anderson campus. They called on the Assembly to "grant its approval, for the present time, for the seminary . . . to remain in coordinate relationship to, and under the administrative guidance of, the Anderson College board of trustees and its administrative officers."[18] It was done.

This decision has been in place and unchallenged ever since. In fact, campus developments in recent years have solidified this integrated arrangement even more. In the 1970s as dean I developed a seminary faculty handbook which, while containing material relevant only to the seminary, attempted to clarify that basic personnel and policy procedures were intended to be the same campus-wide.

Faculty committees in the seminary were separate from those of the college, except for the Faculty Affairs Committee (recognizing the commonality of personnel policies and procedures). When Robert A. Nicholson assumed the presidency in 1983, he encouraged a restructuring of the committee system of the board of trustees, for the first time bringing about a board committee focusing specifically on the School of Theology. Then in 1987 the institutional name was changed to "Anderson University" (see Table 1) in part to clarify to various publics the structural relationship of the seminary to the larger campus.[19]

In 1989 three more unifying steps were taken (detail in chapter twelve). The previously separate college and seminary alumni bodies were merged into one, and a significant trustee development grant was sought and received from the Lilly Endowment to enable the board of trustees to become more effective as the governing body of a seminary as well as of a college. Also, a process of many years finally was completed when the campus libraries, Wilson and Byrd, were fully merged into one spacious and automated University Library, now served by a common cataloging system and professional staff.[20] Obviously Anderson University valued the School of Theology, saw it as crucial to its own identity and mission, and continued to be prepared to operate it as effectively as possible on behalf of the whole church.

While there has been no serious consideration of a free-standing seminary since 1976, and recent developments have further consolidated the seminary's existence on the Anderson campus and integrated into its life, issues have persisted related to the seminary's distinctive integrity within the larger Anderson University structure. Occasionally the complaint has been heard that the seminary appeared to be treated as a campus stepchild in the face of a much larger college. Nevertheless, administrative attention, budget allocations, and facility development argue convincingly that the seminary's joint structural relationship on the Anderson campus has been the best stewardship available to the Church of God in the quality operation of its seminary.

Coordinating Ministerial Education

As highlighted above, of particular concern has been the School of Theology's relationship to programs of ministerial education on the Anderson campus. A major philosophic stance was stated by President Robert Reardon as early as 1960. He said:

> It so happens that, in our case, the college and seminary can operate with a degree of separateness and yet make an excellent contribution one to the other in our total framework. I think there is a tendency for Christian liberal arts colleges, as they progress through the years, to become secular. On the other hand, I think there is a genuine tendency on the part of theological seminaries to become remote and iconoclastic. At our institution we feel that a great deal is to be gained in the fruitful relationship of these two "coordinate parts" of our total institution.[21]

But exactly what constitutes a fruitful relationship between college and seminary ministerial education programs on the same campus has not always been clear or consistent. Over the years, significant separation has been the rule, keynoted initially by the general expectation of the Association of Theological Schools. Student organizations of ministerial students on campus have functioned with relative independence from one another, although the current college organization is staffed by a selected seminarian who seeks ways to build bridges of understanding, appreciation, and cooperation. The seminary's "Theo Week" newsletter focuses on seminary news and its chapel programming, and attendance typically involves the seminary community exclusively. Academic calendars have tended to duplicate those of the college, although the pattern and timing of class offerings sometimes have varied widely. Seminary students have participated in some all-campus intramural programs, once fielding a team known as "Yahweh's Finest"! Commencement ceremonies have been common with the college, but in the first years the seminary planned its own baccalaureate services.

In the first years of the seminary's existence, there remained a strong ministerial education program in the college. The preference seemed to grow, however, for an undergraduate ministerial student to emphasize the liberal arts aspect of the college curriculum and delay concentrating on the professional emphasis of ministerial education until seminary. About 80 percent of the seminary student body came from Anderson College in those years. Following the seminary's founding, the B. Th. program in the college declined to the point of elimination.[22] Seminary dean Adam Miller noted in 1958 that the high percentage of seminarians coming from Anderson College meant that "the seven year program of training is becoming an accepted pattern for the students of the College."[23]

Later years were to see decreasing emphasis on the professional aspects of ministerial education at the college level, with occasional criticism from the church that Anderson College was no longer the school to attend for the aspiring young minister. This seeming capitulation to the seminary, judged by some as hardly a "fruitful relationship of coordinate parts," took quite a turn in that turmoil period of the early seventies.

As detailed above, President Reardon had appointed in 1969 a Joint Committee on Theological Education involving all college and seminary leaders in ministerial education. Significant changes were called for and implemented not only in the seminary, but in the direction of reemphasizing the role of the college faculty and earlier involvement of the undergraduate ministerial students in both the academic and practical aspects of Christian ministry. The wall between college and seminary faculties and the campus ministerial education curricula was lowered, in fact nearly removed for a brief time. Dean Newberry of the seminary reported in 1969:

> One important result of the new program is to make the young ministerial student the responsibility of both faculties, undergraduate and graduate, for his seven years on campus. Both faculties would be deployed in new ways to take advantage of special competencies. Four four-hour courses in the Seminary will be taught in alternate years by College and Seminary teachers, with the courses open to both undergraduate and graduate students.[24]

When the Center for Pastoral Studies was established in 1972, it was used for a time as the structural home of both seminary and college religion faculty members on campus. Jerry C. Grubbs, for instance, when appointed in April, 1973, to replace Dr. Irene Caldwell in the seminary's Christian education chair, was "to become a member of the Center faculty, with [his] primary base of operation being the School of Theology."[25] Faculty governance of the seminary's curriculum had been broadened to include religion faculty. Before long, however, a more traditional division between these faculties developed. Each faculty was to be considered adjunct to the other, and the seminary dean and college departmental chair each held joint appointments to assure constant communication and the hoped-for coordination.[26]

Pressure for this "normalization" had come in part from rising seminary enrollments in the 1970s, with the resulting need for the School of Theology faculty to devote its time more exclusively to the seminary. There also was concern that the earliest possible nurturing of an undergraduate student's commitment to ministerial education should not be allowed to so blur the perceived difference between college and seminary that students would not be motivated to go to the School of Theology because, they might say, "I've already had all those teachers." A particular question eventually was raised about the frequent classes that for some years admitted both undergraduate and graduate students. Was this an erosion of academic integrity and was this the best way to function together on a common campus?

All of this activity and questioning had been a bold experiment in new and better ways to offer programs of ministerial education. Some aspects of the experiment had durability and some did not. The eventual result was a significant structural separateness not unlike the basic circumstance back in 1950. The hope, however, was that a few frontiers of cooperation had been crossed permanently (the library and alumni organizations being significant examples). Meanwhile, in 1990 the college's Department of Bible and Religion initiated a new major in Christian Ministries. Clearly the college intended to remain a place for ministerial education either in preparation for or, when appropriate, for students not intending to attend seminary.

Normalization also included a constant sensitivity to the personnel and curricula of the collegiate ministerial education programs on other campuses affiliated with the Church of God movement. They too needed some level of involvement and a sense of ownership in the church's one seminary, even though there was not available to them any participation in its governance. While typically there has been genuine goodwill in this ongoing process, there also have been somewhat differing philosophies of ministerial education and even programs that occasionally have functioned as competitive to the School of Theology.[27]

There has been one other front on which the question "How separate should we be?" has persisted. The seminary clearly is a professional school functioning at the graduate level. But, along with the obvious emphasis on the practical dimensions of ministerial preparation, there has been some question regarding the extent to which the seminary also should function as a graduate school of religion. To what extent should emphasis be placed on academic research skills, theoretical explorations into various aspects of religious topics, and opportunity for students to specialize in given academic disciplines within the seminary's curriculum?

Accreditation certainly had been an influence in ensuring quality student scholarship, whatever the curricular emphasis. Dramatic growth in library resources over the years had helped to enable increasing levels of academic activity. From the seminary's very beginning a thesis had been required of all degree students and the titles of these research efforts were published in the commencement programs. Nonetheless, the seminary's clear mission has been centered in the preparation of ministers, especially pastors, and not scholars of religion. Eventually the thesis requirement was dropped in favor of comprehensive examinations that stressed integration of the goals of the whole curriculum. In the 1980s, replacing the comprehensives, a sequence of required courses, covering all three years of the M. Div. program, was introduced to highlight, integrate, and evaluate the professional as well as academic goals of the curriculum.

One of the new degree programs launched in the early 1970s, however, had been the Master of Arts in Religion. The intent of this program was to serve the student who had primary interest in content specialization, sometimes in preparation for a teaching career in the religion field. Students had a wide range of interests and needs and the seminary attempted to be versatile in addressing as many as possible. But, since the school remains a seminary and not a school of religion, a core of courses central to the mainstream of the curriculum was required whatever the program or specialization. This core, plus the assumption that all courses in the seminary reflected the school's professional orientation, allowed even the M. A. Rel. program to be seen by North Central's regional accreditation as a professional program.

The formally stated goals that have guided the School of Theology in recent years highlight an emphasis on the academic, but clearly in the context of the spiritual development of the student and professional preparation for practical service in the life of the church. Identifying itself as aspiring to be "biblical in orientation, evangelical in emphasis, and ecumenical in spirit," the seminary's goals, intended for all seminary graduates regardless of degree programs, are the following:

> **Scholarship**: Encouraging and equipping persons in their quest for knowledge of the Bible's content and meaning and of the historical development of the Christian church and its faith, always seeking in the process to promote academic excellence in the pursuit of truth;
> **Fellowship**: Stimulating spiritual growth, enabling personal discovery and discipline, and exploring the meanings of individual faith and life together;
> **Service**: Enabling persons to develop competency in the skills and use of resources necessary for fulfilling the call to ministry; and
> **The Church-at-Large**: Providing for the continuing education of those engaged in ministry, encouraging them in professional growth; serving as a center for research and writing, providing resources and incentives for creative leadership in the church.[28]

Such goals make clear how complex and demanding is the mission of a seminary.

Partners with the Church of God

From its beginnings, the School of Theology was an ecumenically minded educational community. Clear examples include the early desire for it to be accredited by the Association of Theological Schools, its participation actively in the interseminary movement, the Accredited Theological Schools of Ohio and Indiana (ATSOI), and the Urban Ministries Program for Seminarians (UMPS), and the bringing to campus of leading voices from the larger Christian community. Two full-time faculty members from other than the Church of God tradition were appointed over the years in the field of pastoral care and counseling, Dr. John Vayhinger (1968-1981) and Dr. Theodore Stoneberg (1981 to present). Various faculty members have been active in a range of professional and ecumenical organizations and have sought to bring to the seminary classrooms the fruits of such enriching involvements. Dr. John W. V. Smith, church historian, was a pioneer in these efforts and others, such as Dr. Gilbert Stafford and Dean James Earl Massey, continue the tradition. Many secular and religious agencies of social service in the city of Anderson and within driving distance have provided staff assistance and practicum settings for the seminary's students.

In a few instances the ecumenical vision took on or nearly took on more institutionalized forms. In the late 1960s, for instance, Winebrenner Theological Seminary in Findlay, Ohio, was experiencing low enrollment and financial problems. Given the close historical linkage of its sponsoring body and the Church of God,[29] discussion was initiated with the School of Theology in Anderson about the possibility of a foundation on the edge of the Anderson campus that could assist future students from that church body if Winebrenner were to close and its students directed to the School of Theology. The idea was welcomed, but leadership and circumstances soon changed at Winebrenner and no foundation ever developed.

What did develop for a few years beginning in 1972 was a "Wesley Center for Biblical Studies." The Evangelical Church of North America established a house on the edge of campus, brought to the campus at its expense faculty member Dr. Eldon Fuhrman, and sought to recruit its students to the Anderson campus. There they would be regular students supported and nurtured in supplemental ways by this Center. This experiment worked rather well but for only a few years. Also, beginning in 1981 and following a careful examination of the seminary, the United Methodist Church formally recognized the School of Theology as an acceptable seminary for the education of United Methodist ministers. In some years there have been as many as twelve students from this particular denomination in the seminary's student body. Specialized instruction in United Methodist history and polity has been provided by appropriate church leaders available locally.

As explained earlier, however, the aborted attempt in the early 1970s at establishing the seminary's formal participation in the envisioned experiment of a multi-seminary "Foundation for Religious Studies" in Indianapolis keynoted a trend in another direction. By the end of the 1970s, ecumenical experiments had fallen on hard times. The Urban Ministries Program for Seminarians in Chicago had been drastically reorganized after its foundation funding ran out, making it unaffordable for the School of Theology. The Association of Theological Schools in Ohio and Indiana had proven not worth the major investment of time required, so the seminary became inactive in this program.

From the seminary's beginnings, the primary constituency to be related to and served was the Church of God movement. Particularly after 1974, the Church of God had become conscious that the School of Theology was "its" seminary and accordingly began providing significant support. The major new financial aid resources, restricted to

Church of God students, stimulated a rise in the percentage of Church of God students from 74 percent in 1973-74 to 90 percent in 1977-78. While not eliminating ecumenical involvements and emphasis,[30] the partnership with the Church of God movement clearly came to receive primary attention.

Out of that dynamic period of innovation in the early 1970s came programs like the Center for Pastoral Studies, "covenant" churches, and ministers-in-residence. All of these School of Theology programs emphasized the practical and continuing dimensions of theological education, and all of them were substantial bridge builders and avenues of service to the Church of God ministry in particular. As dean I became active in visiting annually all of the Church of God colleges in the United States and Canada to nurture relationships, coordinate curricula, and recruit seminarians. This was included in a report to the board of trustees in 1975:

> It is administered by persons who love and seek to be a meaningful part of the church community being served. It is staffed by a faculty committed to students and to standards that range beyond the sterilities of many academic ghettoes. While it is true that its curriculum is in flux, that movement is less a loss of direction and more an honest experimentation in meeting the educational and spiritual needs of young church leaders preparing to serve. The Seminary is a community of real Christian conviction with a clear church home.[31]

When I joined the seminary faculty as the dean in 1974, I was the youngest member of a senior faculty. A major challenge faced was the rebuilding of this faculty as a series of retirements came along. This task was compounded by the sudden death of Boyce W. Blackwelder in 1976. In the one year of 1980, for instance, both Gene W. Newberry and John W. V. Smith retired, one having served since the seminary's founding and the other since the opening of its third year. Such rebuilding needed both to bring academic and professional strength to the classroom and to heighten the church's confidence level in the theological commitments and practical relevance of its seminary. The coming of Dr. Blackwelder in 1963, for instance, certainly had assisted greatly in such confidence building since he had been a successful pastor, a widely respected preacher, and also held strong academic credentials. The faculty appointments of Jerry Grubbs in 1973 and Fredrick Shively in 1974 were conscious attempts to enrich the seminary classrooms with fresh pastoral perspective.

Helpful also in the eyes of many church leaders was a change in the general mood and priorities of most seminary students. As average scores would show from the annual administration of the *Theological School Inventory*, part of the seminary's orientation of all new students, the emphasis in student minds shifted from the social action of

299

President Reardon addressing college student body

the radical sixties to the evangelism of the more conservative and introspective eighties. Student respect returned for the institutional church. Church planting and church growth became major concerns. Students also seemed more serious about their time in seminary as increasingly they were not coming right from college, but from years of pastoral experience or in a process of career change to Christian ministry. The average age of a School of Theology student began to rise until it was well over thirty years.

This partnership with the Church of God movement included significant financial support flowing from the church to the seminary. In 1980, for instance, World Service allocations to the School of Theology for general operational support included 5.79 percent of the total national budget, with another 2.69 percent for the Blackwelder Seminary Tuition Fund. Support also was received in the forms of general goodwill and a modest stream of graduates coming to the seminary from the colleges of the Church of God. A few laypersons gave generously to make possible major student fellowships. Of particular note were the Daniel and Betty Schemmer Fellowship in Christian education, begun in 1974-75, and the Leonard and Zella Warren Fellowship in Church of God history established in 1975-76. Results of the Campaign for Anderson University in the late 1980s (see chapter twelve), would include the establishment of a large number of new scholarship funds for seminarians.

In response to such support, the School of Theology sought actively to provide service to the church. Of primary importance were the graduates themselves. The first graduating class in 1953 was comprised of eight men, all of whom were placed as Church of God pastors.[32] By 1959 a cumulative total of seventy-four had graduated. Fifty-four were pastoring, seven were missionaries, two teachers, two chaplains, and nine in other forms of service. As the number of alumni continued to grow in all categories, the centrality of the seminary in the life of the church became increasingly obvious. During the years 1978-1988, 470 graduated, with 200 going into the pastoral leadership of local congregations, 49 proceeding to additional graduate study, 36 going to the mission field, 21 into chaplaincies, and 15 into teaching, etc. In recent years it has been the practice in each annual meeting of the General Assembly of the Church of God to present the whole seminary graduating class to the Assembly, with the seminary dean introducing them individually so that the Assembly could celebrate God's continuing provision of leadership for the church.

A goal of the seminary has been to instill in graduates a thirst for lifelong learning and then provide various means to assist that ongoing process. An early effort, beginning in 1958 and lasting about ten years, was a program called "Ministers Week" which convened for several days before school opened each fall. As many as seventy-five ministers would come to campus for short courses taught by seminary professors. This kind of effort was expanded in 1972 into the Center for Pastoral Studies, which now has evolved an elaborate system of standardized courses, workshops, and diplomas for the continuing education of ministers, ranging from those with no college education to those already holding seminary degrees. Over one thousand persons are participating currently, including large numbers of black and female ministers not otherwise served by the seminary. Cooperative efforts have multiplied, notably with the Board of Church Extension and Home Missions of the Church of God in the areas of church growth, urban ministries, and Hispanic leadership development.

In 1983-84, under the leadership of Dean Jerry Grubbs, a specialist in adult education, a twenty-four hour "Theological Studies Certificate" program was launched for laypersons and other nontraditional seminarians. Research continued about the possibility of offering the Doctor of Ministry program for M. Div. graduates. Dean Grubbs implemented an extension campus program, offering the Master of Arts in Religion degree with specialization in pastoral ministries in cooperation with the Warner Southern College in Lake Wales, Florida.

But the seminary's service to the church has gone far beyond its graduates, extension, and continuing education programs. Dr. James Earl Massey and then Dr. Gilbert W. Stafford, for example, have combined an academic base in the School of Theology with being speakers on the Christian Brotherhood Hour radio broadcast of the Church of God. Senior leaders in the Church of God, following their retirements, have been invited into the seminary's life to make valuable contributions. These have included T. Franklin Miller (pastoral ministries and Center for Pastoral Studies), Harold L. Phillips (New Testament and homiletics), Marie Strong (New Testament), Lester Crose (Christian mission), and Hillery Rice (field representative). Lectureships continued to bring key Christian leaders into the church's life. Of particular significance was the beginning of the Newell Lectureship in Biblical Studies in 1982, and the seminary sponsorship of the International Dialogues on Doctrinal Issues initiated in 1980 and coordinated initially by Dr. Gilbert Stafford for doctrinal leaders of the Church of God movement worldwide.

One central service to the Church of God movement has been the seminary's preserving, analyzing, and recording of the history and thought of the Church of God. Beginning as early as 1953, the seminary library began a "Warner Collection." Eventually a major assortment of materials accumulated both by and about Church of God authors and subjects. Dr. John W. V. Smith and later Dr. Merle Strege would combine their seminary academic roles with functioning officially as the historian of the Church of God movement and campus archivist. The seminary's archives became recognized formally as a national depository for the church's historical materials.

Quite apart from all such services to the church, the period 1979-1981 emerged as one of the more tense and difficult times of church relations ever experienced by the campus. An evangelical resurgence was prominent in the nation as the Reagan era approached. Some students, parents, and pastors began to ask whether the radical 1960s and the growing pluralism and toleration of the 1970s had tainted even the faculty and classrooms of Anderson College. There was a mood of suspicion in some of the church's circles. It focused mostly on two or three professors and, according to some reports, their alleged violation of biblical teachings in relation to issues like pornography and homosexuality.

One pastor acted dramatically in May, 1980, by mailing to all Church of God ministers an "open letter" to President Reardon. The letter was accompanied by exhibits, transcripts of student interviews, even a series of line drawings and quotations from a textbook currently in use in the college's human sexuality course. The material was thrust on the church public with accusations of substantial impropriety on the part of given faculty members and tolerant inactivity on the part of the campus administration. Issues of morality, school governance, and academic freedom thus were raised in a most inflammatory manner, a manner judged necessary and justified by the "open letter" author and viewed as highly unfair and inappropriate by many others on and off the campus.

In part, the struggle that followed, the low point in all of Reardon's years, came to the Anderson campus because of its visibility, its strategic influence, its many contact points in the church's life, and its traditional willingness to address difficult issues and risk new thinking. In this case, some persons thought that particular examples of classroom attitudes, materials, and processes had gone too far.

In the May, 1980, issue of the *Anderson College News*, President Reardon himself, prior to the open letter, had lamented the severe moral disintegration in the nation, with students increasingly finding themselves "awash in a completely permissive society." He had called for church-related colleges to stand in the gap, to "draw their faculties and administrators from the ranks of professionals who are committed Christian men and women," to avoid "the deadly sin of accommodation—the reflection of the values and attitudes of the world around us." But he also had cautioned that "church leaders must resist the temptation to enforce narrowness, creedalism and watchdog surveillance" so that the "ancient partnership of faith and learning can be restored." Now, with the appearance of the open letter, the issue was being joined, with some insisting very openly that Reardon's analysis was exactly right and that the Anderson campus should be the first to repent and measure up to it.

The centennial of the Church of God movement was celebrated in Anderson that June with an unusually large and international gathering at the annual camp meeting. The issues and accusations against Anderson College erupted on the floor of the General Assembly in the midst of this celebration. Some professors, it was said, believed and taught that the Bible is not infallible. Major focus was on a range of complaints about aspects of the college course in human sexuality, including the beliefs and methods of its instructor and the content of the main textbook then in use. The immediate handling of the matter was the naming of a study group of respected national leaders to review these troublesome matters and make recommendations.

The board of trustees, caught unprepared at the General Assembly, determined to address the whole situation forthrightly. The national press moved quickly with stories centering around the college's course in human sexuality and reports that the Church of God movement was facing a split.[33] Paul Tanner, executive secretary of the Executive Council of the Church of God, responded to the "church split reports." He charged "faulty reporting and from unofficial sources" and assured that "consensus among responsible leaders in the church who are acquainted with all the facts is that our problems are not festering, but rather healing."[34] The intent was not to cover over real problems, but to emphasize that there now was a responsible process in place and a reasonable outcome likely.

While there was some real pain in the process, Tanner's analysis proved correct. The fabric of college-church relations was stretched almost to the point of breaking, but cooler heads and constructive effort soon would reestablish it. The matter came to a conclusion in the 1981 General Assembly when the board of trustees presented a major report of its analysis, stance, and intent in relation to the full range of concerns at issue.[35] It was one of the more important documents of educational philosophy produced at Anderson College in many years.

In part, this report was organized around five specific recommendations that had been made to the board of trustees in October, 1980, by the Select Committee which had been named jointly by the board and the chair of the General Assembly. These recommendations addressed issues from faculty personnel policies to specifics about the course on human sexuality. The board's report noted constructive steps already taken in regard to each of the recommendations.[36] It also made a series of crucial observations on several questions. "What about humanism at Anderson College?" "What is at the heart of a Christian liberal arts college?" "Does Anderson College require members of its faculty and staff to sign a belief statement or creed?" "What kind of faculty and staff does Anderson College intend to employ?" (See Appendix C for a sampling of the board's key answers to these questions.) The 1981 General Assembly received this extensive report of the board with appreciation and a difficult year finally had ended on a constructive note. Both the church and the campus had sought to speak and listen with care. Both would work effectively to bring long-term good out of it all.

As the church's centennial arrived in 1980, it was natural for campus personnel to play key roles in providing pivotal materials of the church's heritage, even in the midst of a time of tension. These included my 1979 multi-volume anthology of the church's heritage titled *A Time to Remember* (later revised edition titled *The First Century*) and Professor John W. V. Smith's major narrative history of the Church of God movement titled *The Quest for Holiness and Unity* (1980). The whole seminary faculty in 1979 joined to produce the crucial booklet titled *We Believe: A Statement of Conviction on the Occasion of the Centennial of the Church of God Reformation Movement*.[37] The Center for Pastoral Studies of the School of Theology had been publishing its quarterly journal *Centering on Ministry* since the spring of 1976. The spring 1981 issue was particularly crucial to the church since it focused on the subject of biblical inspiration and authority at a time when "inerrancy" was a topic of vigorous and potentially divisive discussion among ministers across the church.

Clearly the School of Theology knew that it should be and increasingly was functioning as a major center for reflection and writing in the church's life. Both the campus and the church had faced some hard times; but they both had matured and still were key partners. In 1981, for instance, Anderson College granted honorary doctoral degrees to four of its own graduates of earlier years, persons who had gone on to make major leadership contributions to sister Church of God colleges. They were Milo Chapman (B. Th., 1939) from Warner Pacific College; Walter Doty (B. S., 1939) from Mid-America Bible College; Leslie Ratzlaff (B. A., 1940, B. Th., 1941) from Warner

Southern College; and Horace Germany (B. Th., 1944) from Bay Ridge Christian College. The campus had reviewed its mission, had been tested on its fundamental commitments, continued to honor what it valued most, and was still on course.

1. As quoted by John W. V. Smith, *The Quest for Holiness and Unity* (Anderson, Indiana: Warner Press, 1980), 389.

2. *A. C. News*, April, 1966,. 24.

3. This little story originally appeared under the title "Let's Go Neighboring" by Leah Neustadt, in *Guideposts*, Guideposts Associates, 1954. In recent years an audiotape has been available of Reardon reading this story.

4. For detail and interpretation, see Charles Tarr (who was South Meridian's pastor at the time), *A New Wind Blowing!* (Warner Press, 1972), and Paul Prather, "Asbury's Sweet, Sweet Spirit" in *The Asbury Herald* (Summer, 1991), 3-6.

5. Enrollments by decade had increased as follows: 1920-21, 117; 1930-31, 232; 1940-41, 342; 1950-51, 824; 1960-61, 1,335; and 1970-71, 2,003. From 1967-68 to 1971-72 the undergraduate enrollment of Afro-American students had risen from 39 to 122.

6. In 1970-71, for instance, annual tuition and fees at Anderson College were $1,405 for a full-time student compared to $1,650 at Butler University, $2,150 at DePauw University, $1,710 at Franklin College, $2,060 at Hanover College, and $1,600 at Manchester College. Room and board charges at Anderson that year were $790, lower than nearly all other colleges in Indiana.

7. The very phrase "chapel/convocation" reflected the broadened approach to programming. Nonetheless, at least the reading of the Bible and prayer were present in nearly all sessions.

8. *A. C. News*, December, 1965.

9. *A. C. News*, October, 1964, p. 23.

10. This Joint Committee was a large group, including all seminary and college religion faculty members, two pastors, four ministerial students, and selected campus staff persons.

11. Dr. Grubbs later would serve as a professor of Christian education in the seminary, and then as its dean (see Table 1), and since 1988 the institution's vice president for student life.

12. At the seminary's annual spring banquet in 1972, student cynicism was expressed by the presentation of a master's degree hood that was only one inch wide and had its traditional scarlet color reduced to a pale pink!

13. Some discussion also had involved area seminaries of the "free church" tradition, Earlham School of Religion, North Park Theological Seminary, Mennonite Biblical Seminary, and Goshen Biblical Seminary. President Reardon told the board of trustees in June, 1971, that "it seems strange that schools . . . with such striking theological affinities should be running duplicate programs on separate campuses." But nothing came of this conversation, and Reardon was not willing to consider moving the Anderson seminary to Indianapolis.

14. While away on sabbatical leave in Africa, Dean Newberry had asked to be relieved of the heavy responsibility of the deanship so that he could return to teaching and writing.

15. See Barry L. Callen, *The Assembly Speaks* (Warner Press, 1985), 47.

16. The window is in memory of Mr. and Mrs. Ed Willhardt, Toledo, Ohio, who lost their lives in an airplane crash in October 1975.

17. Rather than standard academic credits, this program granted CEU's, continuing education *u*nits (a standard in many professions for measuring professional growth).

18. The full text of this June, 1976, action of the General Assembly is found in Barry L. Callen's *The Assembly Speaks* (Warner Press, 1985), 48-49.

19. Having been the graduate professional school of a "college" often seemed awkward and unclear as long as the institutional name was "Anderson College."

20. The seminary's Union and the college's Dewey classification systems were abandoned in favor of the more commonly serviceable Library of Congress system.

21. Letter to President Carl H. Lundquist of Bethel College and Seminary, December 29, 1960.

22. The President's Study and Planning Commission's final report in May, 1957, noted that the most striking curricular change during the period 1942-1957 was the declining B. Th. degree. While there had been thirty B. Th. graduates in 1950, there were only six in 1957. The reason was not a decline in campus emphasis on theological education but the new role of the School of Theology. "An increasing number of ministerial students are taking a B. A. degree in preparation for graduate training in theology" (pp. H 4-5).

23. Report to the board of trustees, June, 1958.

24. Report to the board of trustees, May 1, 1969, 2-3.

25. Letter of appointment dated April 17, 1973. Significantly, the letter was not written by the seminary administration specifically, but by Robert A. Nicholson, identified as "vice president" rather than the college dean. This initiative of Dr. Nicholson, not reflective of any long-term administrative arrangement, did reflect the structural fluidity of that time.

26. This arrangement continues to the present. At an earlier time Adam Miller had been seminary dean and college department chair at the same time.

27. One school, Mid-America Bible College, has not emphasized as typical and ideal an undergraduate liberal arts education en route to seminary. Another, Warner Pacific College, is a liberal arts college that has maintained in recent years a master's program in ministerial education (not the equivalent of the M. Div. , with small enrollments, and at least not intended to be competitive with the School of Theology).

28. As stated most recently in the 1989-1991 School of Theology catalog, p. 16.

29. Daniel S. Warner, a leading pioneer Church of God figure, had been a minister in the church body associated with the earlier ministry of John Winebrenner, sometimes known as the Winebrennarian Church of God or the Churches of God in North America.

30. In 1980 the School of Theology became a charter member of the Wesleyan Urban Coalition in Chicago. In recent years the seminary has sponsored on campus a series of regional ecumenical workshops on aging, church growth, and other topics of widespread interest. Also in 1980 the seminary hosted the annual meeting of The American Society of Church History on the theme "The Restorationist Vision" and then, in 1983, co-hosted with Warner Press the annual meeting of the Wesleyan Theological Society.

31. Annual report to the board of trustees, June, 1975, p. 1.

32. Included was George Kufeldt who went to pastor in Cassopolis, Michigan, later to return as a Professor of Old Testament in the School of Theology. He retired in 1990.

33. For example, *Houston Chronicle*, Saturday, July 19, 1980, Sec. 5, p. 3 and

Christianity Today, November 21, 1980, pp. 52-55.

34. In *Vital Christianity*, October 19, 1980, p. 18.

35. One day before this June 16 presentation, the board sent all faculty members a statement of its confidence in their being "persons of exemplary integrity and ability." It included advance copies of the significant report about to be made public.

36. These steps, after elaboration, were summarized briefly as follows:

1. A clearer definition of the relationship between the church
and this Christian liberal arts college has been stated.

2. New programs are in place that support the integration of
biblical theology and the academic disciplines.

3. Hiring policies and procedures are in place that now make explicit the
nature of Christian commitment expected of faculty and administration.

4. A new standing committee of the Board of Trustees, the
Committeeon Educational Policy and Personnel, has been established to
affirm, validate and oversee personnel policies and practices.

5. The course Human Sexuality has been thoroughly reviewed.
There has been a change of instructor, a realignment of course material,
and a redesignation of the course for upper division students.

6. Beginning in 1981, no faculty member will be tenured
without approval of the Board of Trustees.

37. In January 1979 President Robert Reardon had assigned the task of writing this statement to the School of Theology faculty. He said in his January 17 letter to the faculty that "reformation theology—as articulated by F. G. Smith and others—is dead. During its heyday its radical ideas drove the engine of our movement and gave it the cohesiveness and toughness born out of deeply held convictions. There are some fairly serious matters facing the movement today, but none more serious than the need of a clear articulation of those central views which yet remain as a time-tested part of our heritage." The resulting statement was printed by Warner Press and enjoyed wide circulation in the years to follow.

11 Enriching the Journey
1970-1983

> **"**This is a very yeasty time in our history. There is a determination among us not to go with the 'drift of things' . . . but, with the quiet confidence, maturity, and sensitivity born of years of experience, to shape our own destiny as a vital Christian college . . . . It is a time of high adventure. **"**
>
> (President Robert H. Reardon)

The essential paradox was clearer now than ever before. A campus such as the one in Anderson has to be both *in* and *other than* the world. That is, to be true to itself, its acknowledgment of divine revelation, and its valued church relationship as a crucial context for the academic enterprise, there always was necessity for this school to keep on a distinctive course. Clarity of mission was central. Some clash with popular societal values would be inevitable along the way. Influential presence in a widening range of settings was intended and was happening. Anderson College, however, was committed to being a different place. That difference somehow had to be evident in institutional purpose and in the nature and quality of campus programs and people. Trends on campus and especially those in the surrounding culture would necessitate a constant vigilance and creativity—and provide numerous new opportunities.

A Time of High Adventure

The mission of the college and seminary, while providing stability and crucial differentiation, also stimulated a reaching outward. It would abhor artificial boundaries to its vision. It would not abide any abortive isolation from "the world," even while seeking to make a difference in that larger arena. In fact, as that key partnership-with-the-church document of 1981 said in part, the college

> exists as a *vital link* between the church and the literary, political, religious and scientific worlds of the day. It strives to stimulate student awareness of these worlds through the community's life, creative teaching, experiential learning and service experiences at home and abroad.... In this way the College functions as a catalyst: (1) to assist students in finding their role in the world as responsible Christians; (2) to further enable the church to proclaim a message and present a ministry that is culturally and intellectually pertinent to the times; and (3) to be an agency which builds bridges of meaning, hope and social responsibility in today's world.

Chapter ten of this work concentrated on the quest during the 1970s to reexamine institutional mission and keep the campus on course. Concurrent with that quest for maintaining mission clarity and faithfulness was an enrichment of the programming that increasingly could fulfill the call for the campus to be a vital link to the complexities and crying needs of a contemporary world. While being firm about some unchanging essentials of institutional mission, President Robert Reardon was not lacking in willingness to be flexible, even innovative and risking in finding the best ways for its fulfillment. As he said to the board of trustees in June 1976: "There is some pain in this.... We are making some mistakes, but dead and unresponsive we are not. This is no 'steady state' for us. It is a time of high adventure." In fact, the year before he had sought to identify for the board some characteristics of the church community that first came to Anderson just after the turn of this century, the community out of which the campus had been born. Those characteristics, he suggested, had enduring meaning and the potential "to create a thriving, innovative, educational community unique in the annals of higher education in America." Obviously they still held excitement for him, so much so that, he concluded, "if it can be properly engineered, we may be on the threshold of the most exciting development in our sixty-year history."

What were these pivotal characteristics of community vitality? Among those who established the Church of God movement in Anderson, there was "a centrality of faith and purpose. . . which gave meaning to their lives and to those who came to join the community." There was, said Reardon "a deep sense of destiny" accompanied by a strong sense of stewardship of life in response to God's love. There was "a fundamental feeling about the dignity of labor." All members worked for the good of the whole community, with the apprentice method common for the learning of necessary skills. Nor was life mundane and colorless. The arts flourished. There were active poets and painters

TABLE 21

Full-Time Equivalent Enrollment
Fall Semesters, 1968-1979

	College	School of Theology	Total
1968-69	1422	65	1487
1969-70	1529	69	1598
1970-71	1622	74	1696
1971-72	1591	67	1658
1972-73	1459	59	1518
1973-74	1505	55	1560
1974-75	1616	68	1684
1975-76	1695	123	1818
1976-77	1790	130	1920
1977-78	1769	155	1924
1978-79	1777	145	1922
1979-80	1782	141	1923

Basis: End of the third week of first semester; each full-time student counted once, with part-time students equated to full-time at 12 hours.

and an outpouring of new musical literature. It was a cohesive and creative community of faith and learning. It just may be, wrote Reardon to the board in 1975, "that God is at this time calling us out of the educational lockstep to a higher level of activity more compatible with the Christian faith and with the aspirations of the Church which brought us into being."

Such inspired activity would not be easy, particularly in the undergraduate college where functioning as a true educational community was increasingly difficult. The sense of community certainly had been a distinctive mark of the school's history. Structural lines were not drawn tightly on this primarily residential campus. Personal acquaintance was prized and obvious gifts tended to guide the functioning of individuals. But size of the student body and diversity of student backgrounds and goals now were having an impact. The college was feeling the tension of its dual commitment to the values of community and diversity. Times were dynamic. Achieving high aspirations would

TABLE 22

College Faculty and Student Sizes, Ratio: 1974-1979

	1974-75	1975-76	1976-77	1977-78	1978-79
Full-time Faculty (FTE)	74.61	74.48	75.21	80.25	80.09
Part-time Faculty (FTE)	15.64	19.74	22.90	23.11	26.57
Part-time Faculty Percent of Total Faculty	17.3	21.0	23.3	22.4	24.9
FTE Students (Sem. One)	1616	1695	1790	1769	1777
FTE Faculty	90.25	94.25	98.11	103.36	106.66
Ratio 1:	17.9	18.0	18.3	17.1	16.7

Note: All figures for full-time equivalent faculty exclude library or Instructional Materials Center members of the faculty, and count administrative persons only to the extent of their teaching assignments.

involve vigorous adventure and experimentation. Such challenges came easily to an administration prepared to cross new frontiers, although without abandonment of the traditional and distinctive mission.

Student enrollment growth had been substantial (see Table 21). Within that growth, however, the presence of students in the undergraduate college who were affiliated with the Church of God movement declined to about sixty percent during the 1970s. Partly because of rising student costs and state-based financial aid programs that encouraged college-bound students to stay within their home states, there also was a localizing trend in higher education. A national college like Anderson recruited students from its church constituency across the nation with increasing difficulty. While in 1978-79 the percentage of Anderson's matriculating first-year students who were from Indiana was 38, that percent had risen to 51 by 1982-83.

With this enrollment growth had come many forms of student diversity. President Reardon reflected on the contrast with the school's opening years. Students, he said, had much in common in 1917. All were committed to Christian ministry through the Church of God movement, all were under the jurisdiction of the Trumpet Family, and all "ate, slept, studied, prayed, courted, fought, recited, worked, loafed largely in one place, under one roof later called Old Main." Hostility or indifference from city and church further drove them together in a community of their own. But by the 1970s it was different. How, asked Reardon, "does one build a common tie between a Church of God female freshman from California in the nursing program living in Morrison Hall and a married male senior living in an off-campus apartment, doing his professional semester teaching in the high school within the walls of Pendleton Reformatory?"[1] It surely was a demanding challenge for a campus that prized community building as an essential aspect of the educational experience.

There also came with this enrollment growth heavy new instructional loads for the faculty to carry. Much of the additional load was assumed by part-time faculty persons, secured both to meet the unexpected and not necessarily long-term enrollment growth and to enrich the classroom with effective practitioners. Some of these persons were competent teachers and some were not. A needed goal now was to avoid a major shift in the traditional full-time-equivalent ratio of faculty to students and of full-time to part-time faculty, while also maintaining consistently high instructional quality. During the 1960s a teacher-student ratio of about 1:20 had been maintained in the college as a matter of conscious administrative intention. This ratio understandably dropped to about 1:19 in 1972-73 with the introduction of an associate degree in nursing, a faculty-intensive program. A lowering also was encouraged by changes in the general education requirements which now deemphasized a few large-enrollment classes like World Civilization. In 1978-79 the ratio had dropped to 1:16.7 (see Table 22).

This yeasty time of high adventure, however, was not limited to the tensions resulting from growth in student enrollments and faculty loads. The world was a troubled place. One campus event was shared widely when President Reardon highlighted it as the centerpiece of his 1973 institutional Christmas card. There had been no press coverage, only quiet emotion and substantial significance. College students and the whole nation had struggled through the Vietnam war and were gripped with new anger and frustration when American bombs had begun to fall in Cambodia. With mounting tension, a simple idea was put forward—plant a tree on campus as a symbolic act.

About a thousand students, faculty, and staff persons soon were gathered in a great circle in the "ravine." They listened to the wisdom of the biblical text, sang songs of peace and, as Reardon put it, "prayed for forgiveness and strength to help bind up the wounds of the world." The life and mission of the campus were on display in those few, sacred moments. Lowered carefully into a hole was a Ginkgo tree, representing the ancient tree of life. Students filed by to help pack in the dirt, putting their hands lovingly, servingly, right into the soil. Neither Reardon nor anyone else there, would ever forget "the faces of those wonderful kids, shining with idealism, distressed by the course events had taken, but determined somehow to relate their young lives to the pain and agony of the world." It was time to broaden the base for learning and hold high the need for serving.

Expanding the Base for Learning

Early in this decade the college faculty gave extensive study to the program of distribution requirements mandated for all undergraduate students. Dean Nicholson's perspective expressed in 1972 was that, with few exceptions, the academic program of the college had been "static in scope" for some fifteen years. The creative energy had been invested mainly in handling the doubling of student enrollment and upgrading the professional competence and personal commitment of the faculty. Now the time had come, he said, "to refine and broaden the base of our academic programs" while, of course, "avoiding proliferation and mere expansionism." [2] In this spirit the college faculty voted a revised program of distribution requirements, effective September 1973. Total hours were reduced, academic skills were emphasized (reading, writing, oral expression, mathematics, and foreign language), and lists of courses were grouped under six "Areas." Requirements were stated as objectives rather than academic disciplines or specific courses, focusing more on outcomes, student development, and choice.

The decade of the 1970s also had opened with a change in academic calendar intended to enable new flexibility and creativity in the curriculum offered by faculty and elected by students. The primary innovation was the introduction in 1970-71 of a 4-1-4 calendar featuring a new January Term. One course was made available to regularly enrolled students without additional cost. About ninety percent participated from the beginning, taking advantage of new interdepartmental and international opportunities.[3] Dr. Frederick Shoot was named Dean of Instruction (college) to help carry the increasing operational aspects of this curriculum. The following year (1971) Dr. Duane Hoak was named Dean of the Faculty (college) to give fresh impetus to the equally crucial management of faculty growth and evaluation programs.

Beginning with the freshman class entering in the fall of 1976, a plan was introduced over the next four years that at first was called the "Big Idea." Dean Nicholson explained to the board of trustees in June 1975 that this "Big Idea" was actually a "redefinition of education at Anderson College.... Using the historic liberal arts as the basic curricular structure, the learning experience is infused with four fundamental, supportive elements: (1) the continuous experience of labor, both menial and vocationally related; (2) the discipline of training (personal and interpersonal skills); (3) a strengthened academic competence; and (4) the experiential and value elements of the Christian faith." The hope was that such infusion would clarify institutional mission and ethos, revitalize and improve the public image of higher education, and redefine both the meaning of a "liber-

ally educated person" and the role of the faculty member in the process. A network of educational partnerships in the private and public sectors was envisioned, linkages which might even "rid private colleges of dependence upon government sources of income." It indeed was a big idea.

Assisted by a $300,000 implementation grant from Lilly Endowment in 1976 (see Appendix S), this "Big Idea" evolved into a series of coordinated program thrusts known as "The Anderson College Plan: Expanding the Base for Learning." Here was a long-term and multifaceted program design intended to emphasize the following distinctive characteristics of the Anderson College experience:

—A value-oriented educational experience;
—A liberal arts basis for intellectual inquiry;
—Experiential learning related to academic study;
—Career education based on the philosophy of the stewardship of life;
—Various approaches to educating the "total person";
—Institutional flexibility in meeting the changing needs of students.

These characteristics were to be fostered in students through a new (1) Student Support System (helping students assess their capabilities, interests, and motivations), (2) Personal Effectiveness Training (developing self-awareness, communication skills, social and decision-making skills through four one-hour modular courses), and (3) Work-Learning: Partnership in the Educational Enterprise (broadening the base of learning through cooperative relationships with business, industry, labor, and government). Together these three frontiers of coordinated new initiatives constituted the "Plan." The central aspiration was that students in the college would take advantage of the richness of these new educational support services and thereby come closer to the ideal of what a college experience can mean intellectually, spiritually, and vocationally. The intent was not another program located in one office, but an attempt to impact institutional philosophy, permeate all aspects of campus life, and address critical problems facing private higher education generally (finance, poor public image, student retention, unclear understanding of what it means to be a liberally educated person).

The new "Plan" was directed by Dr. Larry Osnes (B. S., 1963), recently appointed Dean for Academic Development, chair of the Department of History/Philosophy/Government, and founding director of the Center for Public Service that had been launched in 1973 by an earlier $300,000 grant from Lilly Endowment (see Appendix S).[4]CThis Center, like the TRI-S program before it, already had made a perva-

(Top) Dr.Duane C. Hoak, as dean of the college faculty
(Bottom, left) Frederick Shoot, as dean of college instruction
(Bottom, right) Dr.Larry Osnes, as dean for academic development

315

sive influence on campus. This influence was in the direction of experiential education, providing effective vehicles for select students from a wide range of majors to engage the public arena with the motive of serving, not merely "servicing" people. In 1977 Dr. Douglas Nelson assumed leadership of the center. By that time the Center for Pastoral Studies was implementing effectively a similar educational philosophy in the School of Theology, only focused entirely on the field dimensions of ministerial preparation and the continuing education of Christian ministers (see chapter ten).

Now the newly developed team of undergraduate academic administration was functioning effectively and in considerably expanded circumstances. Dr. Frederick Shoot, Dean of Instruction, was handling undergraduate academic operations.[5] Dr. Duane Hoak, Dean of the Faculty, was focusing on faculty recruitment, evaluation, and development, and Dr. Larry Osnes, Dean for Academic Development, was guiding frontier thinking and academic planning. I was playing similar roles as dean of the School of Theology. Of course, behind all of this was Dr. Robert A. Nicholson, dean of the College and after 1971 also Vice President for Academic Affairs. He was the engineer, strong as a process person, specializing in curriculum management while enabling others to be at their visionary, administrative, and instructional best. It surely was a time of real innovation, even while a broad-based and quite traditional program of liberal arts and pre-professional education was being maintained. Key words were relevance, service, and growth.

The college's academic departments and their graduates reflected much of the school's traditional and continuing program emphases. For 1977-78 they were as follows, with 3:10, for instance, meaning three full-time departmental faculty members and an average of ten graduating majors over each of the previous three years: Art (2:8, primarily art education); Biology (5:18, primarily teacher education, premedical and nursing support); Business and Economics (6:55, primarily accounting, with marketing a new strength); Chemistry (2:5); Computer Science (2:4, joint majors with business and mathematics); Education (6:30, elementary, secondary, early childhood); English/Speech (6:7 and 2:8); Foreign Languages (4:5,Spanish, French, German); History/Philosophy/Government (6:11); Mathematics (3:8); Music (8:19, vocal, instrumental, music education, music industry, church music); Nursing (6 plus clinical: 68 total associate degree graduates); Psychology (4:23); Physical Education (7:15, teacher education, community recreation, athletic training); Physics (3:3, preengineering, environmental science, nursing support); Religious Studies (6:46, Bible, theology, Christian education); Sociology and Social Work (7:92, sociology, social work, criminal justice, marriage and family).

New within this large group of academic departments was Nursing. St. John's Hospital in Anderson terminated its three-year diploma program and then had worked out with Anderson College a new associate degree program in nursing. St. John's became the principal clinical setting for these students (often local and nontraditional) and in the initial years provided an annual grant of seventy-five thousand dollars to assist the campus with the heavy costs of such a demanding, faculty-intensive program. Richard Hakes was the founding program director beginning in 1972-73, with Louise Spall and the current Patricia Bennett later to follow as directors.

The first nursing students entered in 1973 and, in June 1975, the first associate degrees (seventy-five) were awarded. Although most students in this program over the years would be women, the very first to graduate was a man. John Lee Ackerman came from Newton Falls, Ohio, and later would be a medical missionary to Haiti. An associate degree program in criminal justice was approved to begin in 1974, with others soon to

TABLE 23

A Tribute to Old Main
May 9, 1968

We gather before Thee, O God, in gratitude and thanksgiving for this building, which has served us across many years. We thank Thee for the minds that conceived it, for the dedicated hands that built it, and for the people who have maintained it. We thank Thee for the families who have lived here, the students who have learned here, the teachers who have taught here, the lovers who have courted here, the artists, the musicians, the scientists, theologians, poets, philosophers, and all scholars who have labored together here, having many gifts, yet being one in Thee.

We thank Thee for this roof that has sheltered us from the storm, for these walls that have enclosed us in their protective arms, for the halls and rooms that have known joy and sorrow, and resounded with the sweet, sad music of the years. We thank Thee for these windows which have opened outward on the world, and through which the light has continued to shine across the lengthening shadows of the years.

We praise Thee, O God, on this day, for our forefathers, many of whom now sleep, but whose memory rests upon us like a heavenly benediction.

Grant, we pray, that the memory of this building always will stir us to greater service, more noble living, and become an everlasting landmark to call us back to those things which are eternal.

Through Jesus Christ our Lord.

TABLE 24

Capital Addition Summary: 1971-1978

Building	Completion Date	Total Project $ Cost	Purposes Served
Decker Hall	1970	3,220,845	Faculty and Administrative offices, Classrooms, Instructional Materials Center
Myers Hall	1971	628, 629	Single student housing for 110
Olt Student Center addition	1971	441,556	Enlarge student dining room, add private dining rooms and student recreational space
Natatorium	1973	508,234	Olympic size pool, locker facility
Seminary Chapel	1975	542,012	Chapel addition, library expansion, air conditioning, remodeling
Byrum Hall	1975	586,712	Renovation of oldest campus building; 533 seat auditorium
West Campus Housing	1977	323,350	Two apartment style buildings for 88 single students
Byers Hall	1977	126,904	Purchase and remodeling of building to house nursing department, house single students on 2nd floor
Athletic Field Complex	1978	497,000	Football and baseball fields, all-weather track, stadium seating, tennis courts, practice fields
Krannert Fine Arts Building	1978	3,750,000	Facilities for art, music, a gallery, and classrooms for general use

follow in secretarial studies and early childhood education.

Of particular significance alongside these new associate degree programs was continued success in the achievement of the professional accreditation of particular programs. Teacher education and graduate-level ministerial education had been accredited in the 1960s (by NCATE and ATS respectively). Now the 1970s saw the addition of music in 1974 (NASM), nursing at the associate degree level in 1975 (NLN), and social work in 1979 (CSWA), with athletic training yet to come in the 1980s (see Table 1). Anderson was distinctive in the community of Indiana's many church-related colleges in its seeking and successfully achieving such a broad cluster of professional program accreditations. These now widely recognized centers of excellence on campus went a long way in defining and distinguishing the campus as a home of quality education. This education was strong experientially, had a public service focus and, as the 1978 self-study for North Central summarized, it was "derived from the notion of Christian stewardship and the long-term relationship of the life of learning, the life of work, and the life of faith" (17).

Razing Old Main

Such educational aspirations, innovations, and recognitions could not have been accomplished without significant development of campus facilities and increased utilization of new educational technology. The physical appearance of the campus already had changed considerably in the 1950s and 1960s (compare photos, pp.209, 263) but much more change was just ahead. By the fiftieth anniversary of the campus in 1967, an important and in some ways sad consensus had become clear. Old Main must go! The massive old structure, so full of history and sentiment, already had been remodeled many, many times. It had served nearly every function in the college's life. Now, however, to alter it enough to serve the needs of the school's future and meet fire codes at the same time was impractical. Soon its razing would symbolize a major ending and a major beginning.

W. Sherrill Fox, with campus guest "Sparky" Schulz

Even the thought of razing Old Main made President Reardon reflect. "When I think of the great foresight and phenomenal dedication of our forefathers who worked out under these trees to form the concrete blocks by hand and to build this building themselves, something always stirs inside me." He then concluded: "I would like to believe that those of us in the present generation could be inspired by their example to put something here in place of Old Main which will reflect well on our generation." [6] On May 9, 1968, the old cornerstone was removed and a corporate prayer of thanks and praise was offered (see Table 23).

A new campus development plan was underway. While program frontiers were being crossed by such bold innovations as the Center for Pastoral Studies, the Center for Public Service, indeed, the whole A. C. Plan, also being launched was a projected ten-year, twenty million dollar campus expansion program. Featuring in part a concern to build the meager institutional endowment to insure long-term support of a distinct mission and quality programs, this expansion would include many dramatic facility improvements. Between 1971 and 1978, for instance, ten major facility projects were completed at a total cost of $10,625,242 (see Table 24). Of this amount about seventy-five percent came from gifts and twenty-five percent from low-interest loans from the federal government.

The earliest of this cluster of capital projects was replacing Old Main with the impressive new Decker Hall.[7] In 1968 a government grant in excess of one million dollars was approved under the 1963 Higher Education Facilities Act. It was the largest ever received by the campus. With about twice that amount raised among Church of God congregations, alumni, and friends around the nation, plans were finalized for a four-level, ultra-modern structure with nearly fifty percent more floor space than Old Main. A group of house trailers was set up on campus to house many of the administrative and faculty offices during the process of construction. The offices for business and registrar functions, for instance, squeezed into classrooms in Hartung Hall. This process was difficult, but it would be worth the inconvenience.

Occupying the central core of the top floor of Decker Hall was the newly expanded Instructional Materials Center. Dr. Darlene Miller, its director since her own graduation in 1962, had seen much progress in this instructional support program. What

(Top) Razing Old Main
(Middle, left) W. Sherrill Fox removes Old Main cornerstone
(Charles E. Brown in background)
(Middle, right) Contents of Old Main time jar examined
by (left) Robert Reardon, T. Franklin Miller,
Russell Byrum, Harold Phillips
(Bottom) Dorothy Morrison (Blevins-Dicus) with President Reardon

OLD MAIN

Old Main was constructed in 1905 by workers of the Gospel Trumpet Company to provide housing for their families. Timbers came from the St. Louis World's Fair. Building blocks were made by hand on the site. It became the birthplace of Anderson College in 1917, providing offices, classrooms, laboratories, living quarters for faculty and students, a chapel, library, laundry, dining room, and post office. It was replaced in 1970 by Decker Hall.

ERECTED BY THE FAMILY OF DR. JOHN A. MORRISON
FIRST PRESIDENT OF ANDERSON COLLEGE

earlier had been the Anderson Instructional Materials Service (AIMS) in two rooms on the second floor of Old Main now had matured beyond merely projecting films and providing a practical work setting for teacher education students.

In the middle 1960s its directorship was professionalized with full faculty status. Many departments now called for its services and advancing technology was expanding its horizons.[8] Primary space was dedicated to it with suites of faculty offices and classrooms surrounding it. Occupying prime space on the lower level was a new computing center featuring the installation of a Hewlett Packard 3000 system (the IBM 1620 system that had served since 1965 was sold to a college in Iowa).

The last of this group of capital projects was the Krannert Fine Arts building in 1978. By then music and art were the only instructional units not occupying modern facilities designed for their particular needs, and these, particularly music, had been special emphases of the church and college. An art program had begun rather modestly in 1936 with the work of Ruthven Byrum, famous Indiana painter.[9] and now the program was poised for major development. Music had been central from the school's beginning in 1917 and had evolved into one of the finest programs among private schools in the Midwest. The Anderson College Choir now had received international recognition.[10] Vocal student Sandi Patti (B. A., 1979, D. Mus., 1991) soon would be judged year after year as the best female vocalist in all of gospel music.

Since 1971 the music program had been housed by renting space in the educational wing of Park Place Church of God adjacent to campus. It, of course, had been accredited in 1974 by the National Association of Schools of Music, but on condition that new facilities were forthcoming. Special credit belongs to Dr. F. Dale Bengtson for leadership in planning both for this accreditation and the new facilities soon to come. A magnificent new fine arts center was constructed and dedicated in the spring of 1979, with the Krannert Charitable Trust contributing $1,250,000. It was named the Ellnora Decker Krannert Fine Arts Center (Decker Hall having been named in honor of her parents) and consisted of five connected units housing offices, studios, galleries, and choral and instrumental rehearsal and recital halls.

The choice of persons to be honored in the naming of these various structures said much about campus appreciation for its church heritage and for its widening circle of long-term and faithful friends (see Appendix R). Linfield Meyers and Dr. Rollie Bennett had been local community leaders and campus friends for many years and now had named in their honor a residence hall and a natatorium. Adam W. Miller, for whom the new seminary chapel was named, was a beloved missionary, church leader, and cam-

(Top) Decker Hall
(Bottom) Krannert Fine Arts Center

322

pus staff and faculty member during crucial years of campus development. Andrew L. Byers was a pioneer minister, song writer, and managing editor of the *Gospel Trumpet* for many years. Now his former home, located immediately west of Morrison Hall, was remodeled into a facility for the temporary home of the nursing department

The Krannert Fine Arts Center consisted of several wings honoring Bill and Gloria Gaither, Wilbur and Eileen Schield, and Rev. Marvin L. Forbes (funded in his honor by a personally appreciative Charles "Sparky" Schulz, artist of "Peanuts" fame).[11] Included also in that building was the Jessie C. Wilson Galleries, named in her honor by various members of the Charles E. Wilson family, and the Marjorie Austin and Ruth Heaton Performance Halls. At the dedication ceremony of this magnificent fine arts facility on April 26, 1979, an honorary doctoral degree was awarded to Charles H. Webb, then dean of the School of Music, Indiana University. In a moving litany of dedication led by Dean Robert Nicholson were these words: "There are alleluiahs within us that can only be unlocked by some yet unwritten strain of music, by some yet uncreated work of art.... Amidst the many activities that will characterize these buildings across the years, may their finest fruits ever be the strain of music, the work of art that stirs human hearts, that unties human tongues to glorify Him who gave us the gift of creativity."

Naming the renovated old auditorium-gymnasium was an opportunity to honor six pioneer Byrums. Brothers Enoch and Noah had been early leaders in the church's publishing work. Father and son, Robert and Russell, had been early campus builders, and Russell and his wife Bessie were early and influential faculty members and authors. Ruthven, of course, had been the artist who launched the campus art program.[12] These six gifted and diverse pioneers from one extended family had given and now represented so much that the campus wished to preserve and build upon. The 1975 litany of dedication of this renovated facility sought to put this into words of gratitude and resolve (see Table 25).

Preserved in the process was this only remaining historic building on campus, now to serve primarily as a small (533 seat) theater for the dramatic and musical arts. Crucial funding was secured from the Lilly Endowment (see Appendix S). While at the time the Endowment was not inclined to support bricks and mortar projects, this was an exception since it preserved a historic building and avoided new construction.

Conservatism and Cash Flow

One possible impression should be eliminated from the reader's mind. It could be inferred from the extensive program innovation and campus expansion discussed above that key administrative leaders were being less than careful stewards of relatively scarce financial resources and even may have been inclined to be speculative and opportunistic to a fault. But, in fact, there had been no cavalier abandonment of traditional values and relationships in order to advance a fast-paced change. There actually was a steadying conservatism that had balanced the wave of growth, experimentation, and innovation. Such caution and patience were seen clearly in studies and actions in church relations (see chapter ten). It also was clear in relation to the faculty tenure policy, the

---

TABLE 25

Litany of Dedication
Byrum Hall--June 17, 1975

Leader: Almighty God, we thank Thee for the flood of memories which this occasion revives within us--memories of people, of strong faith, compassionate services and Christlike character. We thank Thee for the great host of unseen witnesses who surround us here today. We pray that the courage and zeal for truth which motivated their lives may burn within us.

People: We pause, O God, to remember from whence we have come and those who laid the foundations upon which we build.

Leader: Deepen our gratitude for the sacrifices of those who made the pilgrimage before us; those who found restoration and peace within Thy Church and not only the challenge for service, but the strength to render it.

People: Deepen within all of us today a new love for Thy Church, a new joy in Thy service and a new hope for the future.

Leader: O Thou, who didst in former times, lead our fathers and grandfathers forth into new truth, give Thy grace to us, their children, and their grandchildren, that we may prove ourselves a people who are mindful of Thy favor and aware of Thy direction.

People: Save us in our day, O God, from apathy, from despair, from confusion, from self-righteousness, from arrogance of spirit, and from walking in any evil way.

Leader: Blessed be Thy name, O God, for showering our lives with the blessing of people like Noah Byrum, Enoch Byrum, Russell Byrum, Bessie Byrum, Robert Byrum, and Ruthven Byrum.

People: We thank Thee, O God, for blessing our lives with the Byrums. We are inspired and led by their strong love for the church. May such love be reborn in us today.

Leader: Forgive us, O God, if we have taken our heritage for granted. Lead us to a new appreciation and awareness of that heritage as we build and plan for the future.

People: We join together here at this point to dedicate Byrum Hall to Thy glory and purposes. Amen.

---

future of campus library relationships, the philosophy of budgeting and funding building projects, the bridge issue, and the "university" question.

The campus had evolved a traditional, seven-year up-or-out faculty tenure policy dating back to the policies of Dean Russell Olt in the 1950s. In 1975, however, the board of trustees asked Dean Nicholson to lead a process reviewing this policy. Higher education then was in flux. The Faculty Affairs Committee on campus had been discussing some dilemmas and options regarding the current policy. This campus needed to maintain its academic program at maximum strength while preserving its flexibility and distinctive nature. There were features of the tenure policy that were perceived by both the faculty and administration to be disadvantageous on occasion. Thus, a year-long study proceeded, with a general moratorium in the meantime on the granting of tenure to additional persons. The task force (a trustee, faculty members, and students) worked deliberately on the complex and delicate issues and then reported its findings and recommendations to the board of trustees the following June.

The board approved the judgment of the task force that, in balancing the strengths and weaknesses of the current policy and in reviewing alternatives, the general policy should continue, with the weaknesses addressed. Two weaknesses highlighted were the lack of specific expectation of continuing professional growth of tenured faculty members and the up-or-out mandate at the end of the seventh year (sometimes forcing premature and unwise decisions).

Much now was to be said in the revised policy about growth expectations, and some flexibility was added in the required timing of tenure decisions. But the basic policy stood firm, along with its perceived features of stabilizing personnel decisions and protecting the faculty's freedom to engage in quality instruction, research, and publishing (see Appendix E for a later statement of policy on academic freedom and responsibility). Problems had been addressed constructively and without radical and potentially disruptive action.

By 1978 the board of trustees also was supporting a concern of the administration that the library situation on campus be carefully reviewed. In neighboring buildings were two separate collections and operations, the college and seminary libraries, with a related Instructional Materials Center housed in yet another location (Decker Hall) and functioning with partial independence from these libraries. Obviously, all of this raised major questions about how campus library and other resource centers should relate to each other. The concerns were for stewardship of dollar resources and the most effective provision of services to students and faculty

Said President Reardon rather bluntly to the board of trustees in 1978: "In the establishment of the Seminary we were given poor counsel by the leadership of ATS, which mandated a complete separation of the two libraries and urged the adoption of the

TABLE 26

Assets, Liabilities, Net
Worth, Endowment: 1957-1977

Balances	1957-58 $		1967-68 $		1976-77 $	
Total Assets	3,383,971	100.0%	12,474,360	100.0%	26,290,793	100.0%
Total Liabilities	1,582,310	46.8%	5,671,729	45.5%	7,271,583	27.7%
Total Fund (Net Worth)	1,801,661	53.2%	6,802,631	54.5%	19,019,210	72.3%
Endowments						
Endowment	44,614		291,319		1,662,194	
Term-Endowment	-------		--------		39,662	
Quasi Endowment	178,511		243,262		1,140,524	
Totals	223,125		534,581		2,842,380	

Note: See Table 29 and Chapter 13 for updating of this information.

Union cataloging system—a different system than Dewey Decimal used in Wilson Library." His view of the road ahead was that "we must now give thought to what can be done to correct our mistakes and draw together the resources of the two libraries for the total student body. Ideally," in his view, "there ought to be a single library administration, a single cataloging system, single purchasing, and a joining of the two buildings to facilitate use." After all, Wilson Library had joined an automated, shared bibliographic data base system in 1976-77 (Ohio College Library Center—OCLC). Surely the relatively modest libraries sitting side by side on the Anderson campus[13] could accomplish their own coordination.

In 1979-80 a major self-study of campus libraries was directed by librarian Richard E. Snyder, with outside consultant assistance.[14] The charge given was to identify points of commonality among the Charles Wilson Library, the Byrd Memorial Library, and the Instructional Materials Center, and make carefully researched recommendations for capitalizing on them. The factors pressing for change included urgent need for increased library space and concern for lessening all needless duplication of staff and technical services. Library technology was shifting the focus of library services from local self-sufficiency to area and even national cooperation. The apparent philosophic shift of the Association of Theological Schools now permitted flexibility in the

327

School of Theology's participation in more of a campus-wide library system.

By April 1980 the study task force was near consensus on such crucial points as (1) a change of classification system to Library of Congress for both libraries; (2) a combined periodicals collection; and (3) a major space addition somehow physically linking Wilson and Byrd Libraries (adjacent buildings), thus enabling further merging of collections, staffs, services, and general library administration. The administration and then board of trustees soon endorsed such consensus as right directions for the future, with an immediate beginning of the long process of shifting to the Library of Congress classification system. Addressing the full implications of these recommendations would be a major challenge of the 1980s. Actions, while guarded and thoroughly researched, nevertheless would bring substantial change.

With this concern for effectiveness and efficiency in faculty tenure policy and library operations was a continuing campus philosophy of fiscal conservatism generally. Attention to detail and stewardship consciousness, seen both as good business and important Christian ministry, was symbolized by Chester L. Edwards. It is understandable that an honorary doctorate was awarded him in 1970 just prior to his retirement in 1971 (see Appendix P) and that the Edwards Room is so prominent a place in Olt Student Center. Edwards had been converted in a Church of God tent meeting in 1922 in Loxley, Alabama. Pursuing an accounting career with the Santa Fe Railway until 1943, he moved that year to Anderson, Indiana, to become the bookkeeper for Anderson College (then maintaining essentially a one-person business operation). Over his twenty-eight years with the school, he became comptroller, business manager, and treasurer, seeing annual operating budgets grow from a few hundred thousand dollars to several million. He was stable, particular, conservative, an honest and straightforward Christian gentleman. Current treasurer and senior vice-president, Ronald W. Moore (B. A., 1966), began his work in the business office under Chester Edwards and absorbed his admirable qualities.

Within such a committed, yet cautious campus environment had come much change indeed. Yes, there was extensive program enrichment and building construction. No, this aggressive campus advancement had not been accomplished by an inordinate increase of institutional debt. To the contrary, a quite conservative financial philosophy had been followed. Since a large percentage of annual institutional income came from undergraduate tuition (about 70 percent), student enrollment projections were made with care. Operational budgets were set realistically in light of likely income, and building projects were not contracted until much or all of the cost was covered by special gifts, grants, or low-interest government loans.

It was the consistent board and administrative stance that capital expansion would be accomplished in a way that would serve, not throttle the flow of funds available for quality educational programs. Faculty salaries and departmental budgets were increased as support was available. Budget control always was tight. While student charges were kept as low as possible, rising operational costs had to be addressed annually. Tuition (annual, full-time college students) was $410 in 1956-57, $850 in 1966-67 and $2,200 in 1976-77. While this rise in cost to students was substantial, it was matched with considerable growth in financial aid programs. Tuition levels in the college remained at or below the average for private colleges in the region. Seminary tuition levels were kept especially low.

It became a matter of school pride to report year after year that again the fiscal year had ended in the black, although sometimes just barely. A commonly heard phrase was "black is beautiful!" The alternative seemed irresponsible and was avoided consistently by whatever planning and belt-tightening was necessary. Comparison of total institutional assets, liabilities, and fund balances (net worth) demonstrates a dramatic growth in assets combined with a significant percentage *decrease* in liabilities (see Table 26). The continuing concerns were the heavy and potentially volatile reliance on income from student tuition and a relatively small base of endowment that could enrich and stabilize operations in years that might experience an enrollment downturn.[15]

The joint accreditation team (NCA/ATS) that visited the campus in 1978 analyzed the general institutional circumstance as "a strong fiscal position." Occasionally campus officials would describe Anderson College as "not wealthy, but healthy." The evaluation team agreed, putting it this way (5):

> No college as substantially dependent (70 percent of educational and general) upon tuition and with as slender an endowment as Anderson (2.8 million in 1976-77) can be content. But its books are in order, it has had no operating deficit in its unrestricted current fund for the past ten years, and its several new and relatively new buildings have been so handled as to constitute a very manageable debt-service drain on its operating revenues (about 3 percent). Over the past ten years, assets have increased 111 percent, liabilities only 32 percent.

Much was said in chapter ten about consistent commitment to meaningful church-relatedness. The Church of God movement was a primary campus partner and would remain so by deliberate campus choice. The very membership of the board of trustees, prescribed by the Articles of Association to be a majority of ordained, Church of God ministers, and the personal determination of campus administrative leadership joined in the maintenance of this key partnership. But also determined to be of key importance was fostering a growing relationship with the local community of Anderson.

(Top) Male Chorus, in Rotunda, Russell Se[nate]
Office Bldg., Washington, D. C.

(Left) Dr. F. Dale Bengston, with student L[...]
Ferguson

This now was happening in many ways, including through the experiential dimensions of the "A. C. Plan." One issue of city relations proved negative and quite troublesome, however. It had to do with the city's proposal of a major street-bridge project.

In February 1975 a letter was sent locally on campus letterhead to "all friends of Anderson College." It was an urgent call for awareness and united action against the proposal to build another new bridge across the White River and link to it a widened traffic corridor down Third Street right through the campus. Here, it was said, was "a serious and crippling threat" which would create two campuses and endanger both. On March 11, 1975, the campus and Executive Council of the Church of God organized a march to the courthouse downtown to stage a press conference, highlight vigorous opposition, and insist that there were viable alternatives. Legal action was begun, leading in August 1975 to the signing of a memorandum of agreement. This set of compromises cleared the way for the project, with at least a few city concessions for the sake of student safety (some 1,200 students were estimated to cross Third Street six times each per day). The struggle had been for maintenance of the cohesion, integrity, and security of a residential campus community. Progress, as judged by the city, prevailed for the most part and had forced campus agreement to some unwelcome changes, including the loss of all faculty, student, and guest parking along Third Street.

One final issue in the 1970s represented symbolically the intersecting of program/plant/enrollment expansion and the cautious conservatism of the campus itself. Should the institution's name be changed again? It had been "Anderson College" (including the seminary) since 1964 (see Table 1). During 1978-79 the possibility of a change to "Anderson University" was discussed widely on campus. The faculty, by a narrow margin, voted to favor the change, although there were many issues and strong dissenting voices.[16] In April 1979 the board of trustees discussed the possibility at length, looked with favor on the proposed change, but, being cautious, delayed the decision. Finally it would be made when the time seemed more right (1987). The institution, surely prepared to be innovative, looked at such a change of image and identity with hesitation and reserve. Claiming higher ground was part of campus ethos. Appearing premature and pretentious, however, was not a stance to take.

Such caution did not prevent the campus from seeking to dramatize its own economic significance to the city. Back in 1954, in preparation for a campaign in the city on behalf of the Wilson Library building project, an Anderson College Citizens Committee had staged the "silver dollar game." A total of $50,000 in silver dollar coins had been secured for faculty, staff, and students to use in all local financial dealings to dramatize the direct financial contribution of the campus community to the local economy. In 1954 that annual contribution was estimated to be 1.1 million dollars (an amount increased to 9.9 million for 1979).

During the 1970s the campus had awarded many construction contracts to local firms. The general public had become much better informed about the campus and now tended to be proud of its attractive facilities and appreciative of the quality academic programs—some of which had obvious local benefits (nursing, accounting internships, teacher education, and others). Beyond the academic programs were such crucial facts as the campus having been central in the founding of the Anderson Symphony Orchestra[17] and having hosted the annual Special Olympics of Madison County beginning in 1977. Gifted area musicians and handicapped young persons and many other local citizens now were finding some common cause with the visible, varied, and locally meaningful life of this campus.

Taking Institutional Inventory

As the decade of the 1970s neared its end, several circumstances encouraged a careful inventory of the institution's status and future. Recent years had witnessed rapid growth in student enrollment and educational programs. The years ahead likely would see student enrollment decline because of a national drop in the number of available people of traditional college age. That projection raised important questions. What had the Anderson campus already become and what might it—must it—yet become if the next decade were to be encountered successfully? The year 1978 was the regular time for another self-study to be completed for the North Central Association and the Association of Theological Schools and early in the 1980s President Reardon's time of retirement would arrive.[18] It was a good time to take careful stock.

The "Institutional Goals Inventory" was administered to a randomly selected group of faculty, administrators, and students in the spring of 1978. The instrument's emphasis was on determining perceptions of the "is" and the "should be" of eight general goal areas relating to academic programming. Rated highest by campus respondents in the "is" category was individual personal development, defined as "identification by students of personal goals and development of means for achieving them, enhancement of a sense of self-worth and self-confidence."

This was followed closely by "academic development" and "traditional religiousness." Personal development was being supported by a wide range of advising and counseling services, planned social activities, a staff of residence hall directors and assistants, and the like. Development of the individual was a prized goal of campus life.

(Top) Ravens football team in Macholtz Stadium
(Inset, top) Robert and James Macholtz, coaches of champions
(Bottom) Women's basketball team, 1981-82

Names like those of Norman Beard, Cleda Anderson, and H. L. Baker were prized on campus and would always be remembered appreciatively by most students.

Rated lowest in perception of current reality was off-campus learning, including work-study, multi-campus study, and awarding degrees for supervised study off campus. The closest agreement between "is" and "should be" was on traditional religiousness and the largest gap was on intellectual orientation. On most goals the campus community was quite united in judgments about the is and should be. Anderson College was residential, person-centered, faith-oriented, rather traditional despite all of the innovation noted above. There was, however, a particular desire for improvement in intellectual attitudes and skills.

The campus self-study team, which I chaired as dean of the School of Theology, concluded its 1978 report to NCA/ATS with a Prospectus section. It identified ten "broader institutional concerns" known to be significant challenges for the immediate

TABLE 27
Intercollegiate Athletics
Beginnings of All Men's and Women's Sports

Sport	Initial Year
Men's Basketball	1930-31
Men's Track and Field	1931-32
Women's Basketball	1933-34*
Men's Tennis	1933-34
Men's Cross-Country	1939-40
Men's Baseball	1940-41
Men's Football	1947-48
Men's Golf	1947-48
Men's Wrestling	1963-64**
Women's Volleyball	1975-76
Women's Tennis	1975-76
Women's Softball	1977-78
Women's Track and Field	1977-78
Women's Cross-Country	1980-81
Men's Soccer	1989-90

*Did not play every year until 1951-52
**Dropped in 1984-85

future. The list was led by noting the task of somehow maintaining current student enrollment levels in light of the national projections for decline. Central to this task was managing to appeal to increasing numbers of Church of God students (said to be a "historic responsibility" of the campus) while also broadening the appeal to other student constituencies that were compatible with campus standards and goals. To appeal effectively to old and new constituencies, somehow the campus would have to remain affordable in the face of severe and increasing financial pressures on all private higher education.

Then, concluded this Prospectus, there was the fact that "each passing year brings more troublesome government regulations and bureaucratic tangle" (301). Clearly a more effective, long-range planning model would have to be employed on campus. The past reliance on "the prophetic perceptions of individuals," excellent as that had been in most cases, now would have to yield to "a different combination of episodic and systematic planning, research and evaluation" (302). That planning model would need to be based on a clearer view of what the institution hoped to become, especially in balancing a maintenance of the integrity of the liberal arts with the social and economic realities of "vocationalism." Here were large issues indeed.

In October, 1980 President Reardon echoed the concern over finances. The gap in student costs between those of Anderson College and those of publicly funded institutions somehow had to be lessened.[19] "Church of God students," he insisted, "need a Christian alternative which does not bankrupt their parents nor saddle them with impossible debts upon graduation." Reardon estimated that it would take an endowment of thirty-five million dollars to "equalize" student charges, a tremendous challenge indeed (one that would not be met satisfactorily in the years just ahead despite vigorous effort).

There, of course, was another major area of challenge on the president's mind as he addressed the board of trustees that October. The spring and summer of 1980 had been an especially volatile and painful period of church relations (see chapter ten). The president attributed the problem in part to "the rise of neo-fundamentalism across the nation," which had helped to create "an atmosphere of fear and suspicion." The years ahead would require special wisdom and skill in "building a sense of brotherly diversity without embarking on an internecine conflict."

Obviously, Reardon reflected, closer attention would have to be given to "the selection and retention of faculty, policies by which this process is carried forward, and the maintaining of sensitive balances between the board, the administration, and the traditional canons of academic freedom." There was not the first thought of breaking the primary partnership with the Church of God movement; however, the president issued this warning to the board in light of recent events: "Just as the board of trustees stood firm against the imposition of Dr. Smith's (F. G. Smith) 'standard literature' in the early

335

30s, so we must be careful to seek persons with Christian commitment who are dedicated to the mission of the College and Seminary, while resisting efforts of the Judaizers to foster educational sectarianism in an institution which has a long tradition of freedom to think and explore." See Appendices C and E for policy statements that were developed in this regard.

"Educational sectarianism" surely did not describe the Anderson College of the early 1980s after all of the philosophic and program enrichment and alumni achievement experienced during the 1970s. William (Bill) Gaither (B. S., 1959) had been voted 1969s "Gospel Songwriter of the Year" by the Gospel Music Association of America ("He Touched Me" was one his most successful songs). In 1968 Malcolm Gressman suddenly died, ending his tenure as the campus Director of Drama since 1951. His successor, Robert Smith, later judged that, in addition to the religious tour plays, there had been "a persistent effort to move toward valid drama of a secular sort" (40). In athletics, Terry Murawski, record-setting quarterback of Coach Richard Young's 1969 championship football team, accepted an offer to turn professional with the Miami Dolphins of the National Football League. Such trends and persons symbolized a campus opening to the wider world and having an increasing effect on it.

Student life beyond the academic reflected everything from the ridiculous to the sublime (see Appendix I for a complete listing of student organizations in 1977-78). The ridiculous included the periodic, student-produced programs called "Cheap Thrills," which began their outlandish and popular life in 1970 and ever since have persisted in their humorous parodies of campus life.[20] These programs were sponsored and produced by the Dativus social club. Student "talent" was evident throughout the productions as pie-eating contests got out of hand, Thomas Harp (B. A., 1975) did hilarious pantomimes, Aldean Miles (B. A., 1973; M. Div., 1979) produced outrageous little movies, and many others set aside traditional dignity and joined the fun.

The sublime tended to be seen on other fronts. "God Squad" was organized by Coach Robert Bloom as a vehicle through which athletes could encourage each other, sing, and share their faith in Christ. Then on February 5, 1981, the sixty-two voice Male Chorus, under the skilled direction of Dr. M. Eugene Miller, sang at the National Congressional Prayer Breakfast in Washington, D. C. Among the three thousand people present on this occasion were President Ronald Reagan (seated immediately in front of the chorus), Justices of the Supreme Court, and many members of the Senate and House of Representatives. It was a long way from the school's being an isolated Bible training venture in the 1920s to now having the opportunity, through these gifted young men, to move the leaders of the United States with an inspired rendition of "Precious Lord, Take My Hand"! Featured for this particular song was gifted black soloist Milton Hines.

Intercollegiate athletics had come to involve scores of women and men in a wide range of sports by this time in the institution's life. Appendix J identifies the head coaches, most valuable players, and selected records in men's football, basketball, and baseball since 1947. Table 27 lists all intercollegiate sports and the time of their beginnings.

In 1975 Norman Beard concluded seventeen years as Dean of Students to begin giving major attention to continued development of the TRI-S program. His successor was Cleda Anderson who had joined the staff as Dean of Women in 1967. She would be a significant and loved presence on campus until her retirement in 1988, being responsible for student health, counseling, discipline, residence halls, and organizations. Her sincere commitment to holistic student development, integrating the personal, spiritual, physical and academic, tended to represent campus ideals at their best. Here was a person who listened carefully and cared deeply about the dilemmas many students faced in their personal and intellectual lives.

What, then, should this distinctive and yet diverse institution be in the future? The administration took the initiative to develop a proposed set of "projections for the eighties." They were presented to and approved by the board of trustees in April 1979. Leading this extensive report was an innovative device, a visionary paragraph of what "an experienced and perceptive educator summarizing a joint North Central Association/Association of Theological Schools visit in 1989" should be able to write about the campus those ten years hence. That paragraph, according to the intentional envisioning of campus leaders, ideally would read:

> Anderson College is a healthy place. During the past decade, when colleges and seminaries were declining in enrollment, struggling to maintain fiscal strength, and compromising their educational and spiritual commitments for the sake of expediency, this institution has raised its standards, increased its enrollment, improved its physical plant, heightened its national influence, disciplined itself to a balanced budget, strengthened its endowment, addressed its problems with ingenuity and goodwill, and come to the fore in American higher education as a leading Christian community of education and faith. Its ideals of Christian character and service are increasingly evident in the 4,500 graduates who, during these past ten years, have moved into the mainstream of national and international life.

In order to realize such a vision during what promised to be a difficult decade ahead for higher education in the United States, six general goals were established, along with a range of more specific objectives. As the 1980s approached, then, the campus was committed to these broad goals:

1. As an institution of the Church of God we shall seek to broaden and deepen our involvement in its mission. New and serious efforts will be made to exalt the Word in our common life, to understand it more fully, and to live more freely in its light as a practicing community of love, obedience, discipline, and concern. We shall strive to prepare more competent, more dedicated leadership for the Church;

2. We shall fashion an aggressive recruitment program, seeking to increase the number of high quality students, compatible with our aims and objectives, nurturing them with the finest student support systems in financial aid, academics, work experiences, recreation, health, and spiritual development;

3. We shall embark on a program of rigorous stewardship to eliminate waste, conserve energy, and maintain all physical assets in first-class condition, adding to the physical plant only those facilities essential to our primary needs;

4. A program will be devised to stimulate interaction between the College and its various constituents, increasing the flow of services outward and maximizing the inflow of financial resources. Special emphasis will be given to a major upgrading of planned giving for endowment, and the strengthening of support for the operating budget;

5. There will be a relentless pursuit of quality, refinement, and excellence in the educational program, and in every phase of institutional life;

6. We shall place high priority on the recruitment, strengthening and rewarding of people—faculty, staff and all employees; it is through them that these institutional goals will be achieved.

So the stage was set. The last surviving teacher from the original faculty of Anderson Bible Training School, Russell R. Byrum, was now dead in 1980 at age ninety-one. By then, through the TRI-S program alone, nearly four thousand persons had traveled, studied, and served all around the world. Here was no ordinary, no provincial campus. While full accomplishment of such a vision as now was being projected would be demanding and sometimes elusive, it would be addressed seriously and in substantial ways. The eventual level of success, while admittedly partial, would be gratifying and even enviable.

1. Report to the board of trustees, June, 1974, 3.

2. Report to the board of trustees, June, 1972, 5.

3. Although this new calendar was much appreciated, issues and perceptions changed during the decade. Students, for instance, needed to enter the summer employment arena earlier than a 4-1-4 calendar would allow. So the January Term was eliminated beginning in 1980-81.

4. Robert Greenleaf came to campus on behalf of the Endowment to trouble-shoot the school's proposal for this center. He was impressed by the insights, motives, and apparent implementation skills of the people involved and recommended that the proposal be funded. His book, *Servant Leadership* (1977), highlighted many of the same values as did this center and came to be quoted often on campus. The honorary board of directors for the new center included the governor of Indiana, all United States Senate and House representatives from Indiana, and the mayors of Anderson and Indianapolis.

5. Occasionally Dr. Shoot would take the initiative to assist quality students in special circumstances to find legitimate and yet accessible ways to complete their degree programs. An example was Ronald Patty (B. A., 1975), prominent music evangelist and father of well-known graduate Sandi Patti (Helvering) (B. A., 1979; D. Mus., 1991).

6. *Andersonian*, May 11, 1967, 3.

7. The name *Decker* came from the launching gift for this project in 1966. It was from the Decker Real Estate Company in Anderson whose owners included Mr. and Mrs. Herman J. Krannert of Indianapolis. The building was named for pioneer Andersonians Philip and Phoebe Katherine (Spencer) Decker.

8. Dr. Miller directed this center from 1962 until 1981 when she assumed the chair of the Department of Education. She was succeeded by the current Instructional Materials Center director, Shelby Cantley, who oversees a more technologically sophisticated operation—including two microcomputer laboratories.

9. See note 25, chap. 8. Recently St. Johns Hospital in Anderson has gathered and begun a prominent display of several Byrum paintings of early scenes in the city of Anderson.

10. Climaxing a European tour in the summer of 1973, for instance, the choir, directed by Dr. F. Dale Bengtson, received a number one rating among participants in a two-week international music symposium at the world-famous Vienna School of Music in Austria.

11. See *Anderson College News*, March 1979 for the story of the way the ministry of Rev. Forbes had had a crucial effect on the personal and professional life of Charles Schulz.

12. See *Anderson College News*, July 1974 for the story of the Byrum family and its many contributions to church and campus.

13. In 1976-77 Wilson Library housed about 92,000 volumes and 604 current periodicals. The School of Theology's Byrd Library housed about 48,000 volumes and 340 periodicals, with many duplications between them. In addition, the Instructional Materials Center housed some 2,500 curriculum lab books along with much audio-visual material.

14. The study was expedited by a grant from the Office of Management Studies, a division of the Association of Research Libraries. In part to insure continuing recognition of the appropriate and distinctive needs of the School of Theology, the consultants were Dr. Raymond Morris, librarian emeritus of Yale Divinity School Library and Dr. Ray Suput, former head librarian at Garrett Theological Seminary and then head librarian at nearby Ball State University.

15. For instance, in 1967-68 revenue from undergraduate student tuition was 71.0 percent of total revenue. In 1979-80 it was 71.4 percent. In those same years income from endowment

was only 1.3 percent and 2.1 percent respectively.

16. The issues included the commonly understood and secular meaning of university in the public arena, concern about church perceptions of motive for such a change, the confusion of the graduate-level seminary being part of a college, concern that maybe such a significant move should have the benefit of more research and decision time.

17. In 1967-68 Howard Lowe of the college faculty took initiative to get formed, with campus financial support, the "Anderson Community Orchestra," following years of occasional performance under the leadership of Professor Ingyr Marie Lien. A presentation of Haydn's *Creation* with the College Choir in May 1968 was a significant beginning. The name "Anderson Symphony Orchestra" dates from May 1970.

18. On May 11, 1978, there was a community celebration in recognition of President Reardon's twenty years as the chief executive of Anderson College. A special letter from President Jimmy Carter was read and an unveiling of a special cartoon of "Ol' Reardon" drawn by his friend Charles Shultz. Among the public statements of admiration and gratitude were the ones by Dr. James Macholtz, representing the campus faculty and staff, and President Blair Helman of Manchester College, representing the community of higher education in Indiana. A few months earlier the sixtieth anniversary of the campus (1917 to 1977) had been celebrated with a huge birth-day party on campus. It featured a "happy birthday" concert in O. C. Lewis Gymnasium played by the Indianapolis Symphony Orchestra under the direction of John Nelson.

19. For 1980-81 the annual tuition charge for a full-time student at Anderson College was $3,200, with Anderson being one of the least expensive of the many private colleges in Indiana. The comparable figure that year at nearby Ball State University, for instance, was $975.

20. See "Cheap Thrills: Twenty Years of Yucks" in *Signatures*, Spring, 1991, 14-15.

12 Diversity with Distinctiveness
1983-1990

"What have I cared about most over my forty-five years on the Anderson campus, particularly my presidential years? Number one is mission. . . . The second is servanthood. . . . The third is the delicate relationship between governance and accountability. . . . Finally, I have cared deeply about moving us closer to a God-directed, great future. . . . "

(President Robert A. Nicholson)

The 1980s promised to be different and demanding years for American higher education. As never before, institutions would be pressed to demonstrate their worth to supporting publics. The years of rapid expansion in higher education were ending. Student enrollments probably would drop. Schools would have to recruit more aggressively, market themselves more attractively run their complex operations more efficiently, and nurture relationships with those who really cared about them.

Keen awareness of all these trends and related demands was evident on the Anderson campus. An early response was the decision in 1981 to become involved in the program of the Higher Education Management Institute (HEMI) of the American Council on Education. The prompting campus concerns were needs, felt widely in the institution, for improved management skills and structures, better means to accomplish long-range planning, and increased faculty and staff ownership of the whole enterprise. The HEMI participation began with a major needs assessment survey and was to be followed by targeted training, all built on a value system featuring open communication, teamwork, participation in decision making, encouragement of initiative, mutual support, high standards, and careful use of formal goals and objectives. There was not, in fact, widespread use of the HEMI training modules, partly because the survey and feedback

Presidents Reardon (left) and Nicholson, at Nicholson's inauguration as third president

process themselves consumed so much time and energy during 1981 and 1982. But the needs identified and the values highlighted would be influential in the years just ahead. The needs all would be addressed in a variety of ways. The values would be highlighted repeatedly.

Changing of the Guard

Only once before had a new president assumed office on the Anderson campus, and that one occasion already was nearly twenty-five years in the past. But retirement was coming for President Robert Reardon. Having been elected to a new five-year term in 1978, he informed the board of trustees that October that he would not serve beyond the conclusion of that term (1983). By then he would have reached the age of sixty-four, including thirty-six years with the campus, and twenty-five of those as its president. He had no intent of encouraging any search process for his successor to begin prematurely, leaving him a lame duck. "The changing of the guard in the halls of ivy," he said, "is often a painful and debilitating experience for the institution and those most centrally involved. We must not let this be our experience here." He was a strong and respected leader. His wishes were honored.

Reardon suggested a broad process and timetable for this crucial transition of executive leadership. The board of trustees saw wisdom in them and it was done. The time through 1980-81 would be a steady state, a presidential search committee would be appointed in June, 1981, the candidate chosen would be elected by the board and ratified by the General Assembly of the Church of God in June, 1982, and then would serve alongside President Reardon as president-elect for the transitional year 1982-83. Concern had been expressed by some faculty to the 1978 NCA/ATS visitation team about the coming selection of a new president (then still four or five years away). Said the team in its final report: "The office of the president is a powerful one and it appears to deserve the authority it exercises. Over the years the College's progress has been considerable ... and attributable to the strength and continuity of this office. The prospect of change in the office, however distant, obviously prompts some uneasiness" (15).

But the process went well and the candidate chosen symbolized trusting relationships and institutional continuity. The choice turned out to be Dean Robert A. Nicholson. Certainly the challenges ahead would require all of his considerable relational, process, and organizational engineering skills. He was aware of the institutional needs recently identified in the HEMI study and committed to the management values emphasized there (see above). He was an activist and would seek to embody those values in every aspect of his new administration.

So the 1982-83 year was a planned transitional time, with the president-elect and the president functioning side by side. Their offices in Decker Hall already were side by side, and they were close colleagues and friends who, while quite different in several ways, nonetheless understood, appreciated, and trusted each other. Admittedly, a whole year was a long and potentially awkward time for such an arrangement. But it was used to the full in laying a foundation for the future. Once it was over, in his first report to the board of trustees in September, 1983, President Nicholson reflected: "At the beginning of this period President Reardon and I made a commitment to each other and to the board that we would do everything in our power to make the transition a constructive one for the College and for each of us. I believe, under God, we both have been able to say, 'We did it and did it well.'" Future challenges were great and would demand the best from all parties. Fortunately, the new administration got off to a good start.

Part of the accomplishment of the transitional year was organizing a new administrative team. Nicholson introduced a new vice-presidential structure. I was asked to move from the deanship of the School of Theology to replace Dr. Nicholson as Vice President for Academic Affairs and Dean of the College. Dr. Jerry Grubbs, seminary professor of Christian Education and Director of the Center for Pastoral Studies, assumed deanship in the graduate school.[2] Ronald W. Moore became Vice President for Finance, Cleda A. Anderson Vice President for Student Life and Human Resources, and Duane C. Hoak Vice President for Business and Administrative Services.

The resulting team became known as the President's Executive Staff (PES). This group began meeting regularly. In the new administration PES became a primary setting in which a wide range of immediate and long-range institutional issues were reviewed candidly and with the balancing perspectives of these members who represented all phases of institutional life. The work of PES soon was supplemented by Dr. Michael Collette, named as the first Planning Officer in the institution's history, and often was enriched by wisdom from the deans of the three new undergraduate schools (Drs. F. Dale Bengtson, James Macholtz, and Darlene Miller). See below concerning the establishing of these school structures.

Dr. Lewis B. Mayhew, noted scholar of the complex and dynamic arena of higher education in the United States, released a crucial book in 1979 titled *Surviving the Eighties*. This sober writing was based on the belief that American higher education, "after a century of gradual and then rapid expansion, must now anticipate several decades of no growth or even decline" (ix). The number of eighteen-year olds had about doubled from 1950 to 1980, with rapid growth in the 1960s and slower growth in the 1970s. But, counting actual births, there would be a sharp drop between 1979 (peak year) and 1994 (valley year). Mayhew noted a predicted drop of about a million students, assuming that any new, nontraditional market for new students would prove limited (4).

One class of institution Mayhew saw as particularly vulnerable, even at risk of seeing multiple closings, was the "small, little-known liberal arts college" with enroll-

Mort Crim (left) and Ronald J. Fowler, board chair,
join President Nicholson at his inaugural dinner

ments of one thousand or less, little endowment base, and substantial debt-service oblig-ations. Chaos could be avoided, however, if a school had a "dedicated and committed constituency" instead of "an ill-defined, declining, or ambivalent base of support." Mayhew had in mind those fortunate instances where church bodies valued and support-ed their own schools (2, 4). His central thesis was this: "Institutional vitality, viability, and even survival depend on the timely interaction of established and tested procedures and processes, wise human skills and abilities, and fortunate vagaries of history" (27). It would be an uncomfortable time for church-related institutions, a time not even surviv-able for some.

Anderson College had moved beyond the endangered category by the opening of the 1980s. It was relatively unknown, to be sure, sometimes said to be "the best kept secret in the Midwest." But it enjoyed a church constituency that valued and supported it (sometimes evidenced by the intensity with which there was conflict over a matter between church and campus). It now had grown in student enrollment well beyond the one thousand level, although maintaining that enrollment always had and would continue to take constant creativity and vigorous effort. Operating budgets still received very little help from any meaningful endowment, but at least they were established realistically and were not being strangled by an inordinate level of necessary debt service. Quality execu-tive leadership was in place and there was continuing confidence that, in spite of whatev-er would be the coming "vagaries of history," the hand of God remained on this special institution.

The issues for Anderson College now were less those of mere survival and more ones of: (1) clarifying and communicating institutional mission; (2) structuring for effec-tive governance and accountability; and (3) somehow accumulating the many new resources needed to enable the campus to shape and control its own destiny. The chal-lenge was not managing to keep the doors open; it was to maintain the integrity of the institution, to nurture its distinctiveness in the midst of growing diversity. One measure of the challenge ahead was the fact that Anderson, a relatively young institution, had amassed an institutional endowment considerably lower than most private colleges. Its endowment as of June 30, 1985, was $2,259 per full-time equivalent student, compared to DePauw's $27,083, Hanover's $26,450, Franklin's $29,940, Earlham's $71,370, and Wabash's $106,880.

The Heart of the Heritage

Of immediate importance to the president-elect was the desire to clarify the dis-tinctive nature of institutional mission in the midst of all the growth and change. This desire was accompanied by the intent to be more systematic in directing institutional life

through formalized planning processes in light of a newly clarified mission. The Nicholson administration soon would be characterized by significant attention to our mission statement (see below) and the crucial interrelatedness of body-mind-spirit, faith-learning, servanthood, restructuring, and strategic planning through published goals and objectives. The years ahead would be busy ones indeed.

During his president-elect year, Robert Nicholson developed a proposed institutional mission statement intended to enable the campus community to focus more sharply on its special nature and vocation. He recalled for the board of trustees the extensive use of the brochure "Anderson College: In Partnership with the Church" (1981) as a statement of *who we are*. Now the proposed mission statement, said to be crucial as a basis for long-range planning, focused on *what we are to be*. Formally adopted by the board in October, 1982, this mission statement read:

> Our mission is to be an institution of Christian higher education at its best. We understand this to mean building that quality program which will enable each member of the campus community to become stronger in body, mind and spirit; to experience what it means to love God and "neighbor"; to purposefully adopt a style of servanthood in all of life.

In the months that followed, guided in part by this mission statement, Nicholson worked with a campus-wide task force to evolve a set of proposed four-year institutional goals that also received board approval in April 1983 and again in October 1987 (seen then as still adequate as a framework in which to continue establishing annual objectives). These future-directing goals were as follows:

1. To Strengthen Key Distinctives. These distinctives are:
   a) A commitment to Christian servanthood;
   b) A striving for academic excellence;
   c) A genuinely caring atmosphere;
   d) An active concern for wholeness and human development;
   e) A breadth of international and intercultural experiences;
   f) An interdependence with the life of the whole Christian community and with the Church of God in particular, in light of the Bible as resource and authority.

(Top) Opening college chapel, fall, 1983, sanctuary of Park Place Church of God; procession led by Robert Nicholson, new president, Barry Callen, new dean, and Donald Collins, campus pastor

(Bottom, left) President Robert A. Nicholson
(Bottom, right) Dean Barry L. Callen

2. To Provide a Stimulating Educational Environment. To enhance the development of the intellectual, cultural, physical, relational, vocational, spiritual—for students, faculty, and staff.

3. To Strengthen Faculty, Administration and Staff. To attract individuals who personally and professionally embody the values of the institution; to nurture and reward them; to be fair in our operating practices; to increase minority presence.

4. To Enhance Institutional Planning and Participation. To develop a comprehensive planning/budget/evaluation program; to move increasingly toward a style of participation and shared values, accountability, and open communication.

5. To Maintain or Increase Enrollment. To retain and strengthen our present student base; to strengthen our minority, international, and non-traditional student presence.

6. To Increase Student Financial Aid. To make a quality educational experience financially attainable.

7. To Enhance and Energize Relationships with Our Constituents—the Church of God and the wider Christian community, the community of Anderson, our alumni, friends, parents, and the broader public; to increase public awareness of the institution and its members.

8. To Increase Endowment and Other Resources. To bring endowment, including irrevocable trusts and annuities that will become endowment, to a total of $30 million within ten years through doubling in each succeeding three-year period, while concurrently increasing program gift support; to preserve, enhance, and utilize effectively our physical facilities; to continue sound fiscal management.

The new administration, then, was able to begin its tenure in July 1983 with fresh and concise statements of institutional mission and goals. Soon, however, it became obvious that more flesh was needed on this directional skeleton if it could be expected realistically to inspire an appreciative understanding of the heart of campus heritage and lead clearly to a series of specific action steps. Accordingly, there were various attempts to explore what really was meant by servanthood. In 1988 the trustees approved a commentary on the mission statement, one evolved by the President's Executive Staff that began the process of identifying both central sources and essential *implications* of the mission (see Appendix D).

Then a task force of faculty and staff persons labored to develop by 1987 what would be called the "Community of Character" document. Obviously appreciative of the concerns that Warren Bryan Martin had expressed in his 1982 book titled *College of Character*,[3] this new campus document sought descriptively, not prescriptively, to identify a few qualities vital to the distinctive character of this particular campus community. The Anderson campus, so this document affirmed and described at some length, had been and continued to be shaped by the biblical, church, and liberal arts traditions. It also affirmed as the community's heritage and continuing aspiration certain qualities. They were as follows:

1. *Love of God, Self, and Neighbor.* Life at its best is the embodiment of love—love of God, self, and neighbor. This quality of character is experienced through such practices as prayer, gathering for worship both in word (not fearing the truth) and celebration (not fearing the witness), welcoming strangers, patience, forgiveness, reconciliation, peaceableness, and giving care. Life at its best involves a healthy self-regard, as one receives and shares God's love.

2. *Respect for Persons.* Each member of the community is created in the image of God. Persons can expect to be treated fairly and with dignity.

Servant Sculpture, prominent image of campus mission, created by Esther Augsburger

Persons who manipulate, abuse, or harass others will be held accountable by the community.

3. *Honesty and Integrity.* Sound ethical principles and moral practices are expected of each member of the community. In the classroom, office, and residence hall, or on the campus or athletic field, persons should conduct themselves with uprightness, honesty and sincerity. Academic dishonesty is not tolerated. Violation or abuse of another person's property will not be tolerated. Anderson College, as an institution, in all its relationships is called to demonstrate the qualities of honesty and integrity.

4. *Reconciliation.* This ought to be a community where one can find support in the pain and struggle of life and where God's redemption can come to bear. A community of faith in God and love for neighbor is a community of reconciliation, providing the opportunity for a second chance. This will be demonstrated in the shaping of a community judicial code. The first act of discipline need not necessarily be expulsion from the community. Rather, a community of reconciliation will reprove, counsel, instruct, guide, and support in the process of positive change.

5. *Freedom with Restraint.* Persons must be free to pursue life with enthusiasm and creativity. The liberal arts tradition informs this quest to become a freely thinking and thus freely acting individual; however, both the biblical and church traditions inform freedom in that not all humanly contrived ideas and actions are moral. Truth and practice must always come under the scrutiny of divine wisdom. It is at times appropriate to exclude or modify certain beliefs and practices that threaten the fiber of community character. Critical thinking and creative conflict skills are needed to deal with such situations.

6. *Health and Wellness.* A community of Christian character values health and wellness, which are understood to mean the optimal well-being of each individual given their capacities to develop. This is viewed as a fitting response to God as Creator. Anderson College takes seriously the stewardship of the body and is committed to physical exercise, proper diet and nutrition, and provision for sleep and relaxation as evidences of this stewardship. Persons are challenged to maintain a balanced life of exercise, food, and rest. Illegal drugs, alcohol, and tobacco are forbidden on campus and at any function under the sponsorship or supervision of any individual or group related in any way to the college.

7. *Spiritual Maturity.* Spiritual maturity is evidenced best by a presence that energizes all of life. Spirituality is a mode of being in the world; it is a pilgrimage along which path people may be redeemed and grow in the spirit of Christ. Increasingly a person in the Anderson College community should acknowledge God in Christ as the companion on the journey, become a lover of all of life, welcome and affirm life in all it brings, move with grace and hospitality rather than fear and hostility, combine gentleness with strength,

and feel at home in the Spirit.

8. *Joy and Pleasure.* Life can be filled with joy and pleasure. This is particularly apparent in a community formed by relationship to Jesus Christ. That which is joyful and brings wholesome pleasure is to be enjoyed. Where one's own pleasure is at the expense of another, through manipulation or denigration, it is totally inappropriate. The community must cultivate wholesome ways to be together, while confronting the behavior of those who seek joy and pleasure at the expense of others.

Putting into words such a rich treasury of mission statement, sources, implications, resulting goals, and qualities of this campus community was a systematic way that the new administration attempted to identify, preserve, and freshly appropriate the heart and calling of a particular heritage. The statement of mission itself, for instance (see above), focused on five central themes crucial to campus life and reflective of the Church of God movement to which the campus always had been related closely. These themes were as follows:

1. Christian Unity	"*we* understand ... campus *community*";
2. Christian Freedom	"*stronger* in body, mind and spirit";
3. Christian Wholeness	"stronger in *body, mind and spirit*";
4. Christian Competence	"building that *quality* program";
5. Christian Service	"*love* God and neighbor ... adopt a style of *servanthood* in all of life."[4]

The eight qualities identified above were seen as the appropriate motivations and standards, the ideal ethos in which to bring such mission themes to life. Around such qualities revolved many community-forming stories, some of which are told in earlier chapters. Together these qualities and very real stories tell the tale of a distinctive campus community shaped over the decades by the commitments and pioneering visions of tradition creators like Joseph T. Wilson, Russell R. Byrum, John A. Morrison, George Russell Olt, Carl Kardatzke, Amy Lopez, Otto F. Linn, Adam Miller, Vila Deubach, Candace Stone, Val Clear, Robert H. Reardon, and now Robert A. Nicholson.

One little story emphasizes the assumed importance of dedication to the campus as a *cause* to which, it traditionally has been assumed, all community members should be committed. It was a humorous incident with a serious point behind it. As President Reardon once prefaced the story, "Dr. Morrison's remarkable political skills included the subtle, the persuasive and at times the hammer and tong approach."[5] The campus bookstore used to be in the basement of Old Main, just below the president's office. One particular faculty member, Dr. John Carrington, often was cynical about various actions of the school's administration. He would do his complaining to a friend downstairs, not aware that the radiator and hot water pipe carried sound upward rather well.

What happened next was reported this way. One day Morrison had had enough of the cynical sounds from below. He called the man in, leaned back in his presidential chair, and told him straightforwardly to get happy or get out! As the story goes, the faculty member somehow found it possible to get happy, and he stayed for many years. The serious point was that the campus was a community, a shared and even sacred cause. While all members never would agree about this or that, and certainly the administration was not always right on every issue, all community leaders at least should share the same basic values and pull constructively in the same missional direction.

Design for Strategic Planning

That Anderson city newspaper headline back in 1946, when the campus announced its initial accreditation by North Central (see chapter 6), had been overstated. It had declared that the "institution takes its place among academic leaders in the country." But the 1980s represented a time when such a claim could gain real credibility. The conditions for achieving this high level of institutional maturity appeared to be four in number. First, the vision had to be clear, unwavering, and compelling (thus all the mission emphasis as stated above). Second, the board of trustees and the institution's academic administration required structural revisions to enable their most informed and effective functioning. Next, the necessary financial resources had to be gathered. Finally, the right educational partnerships had to be developed.

With mission statement and goals in place, attention was turned to the needed restructuring. Richard Doney, Professor of Comparative Literature at Northwestern University, had chaired the evaluation team sent to campus in November 1978 by NCA/ATS. The team's final report contained this observation. "The strength and success of present (and past) administration has undoubtedly had its effect on the board of trustees which, traditionally, has played a much less active role than expected." Wrote the team, "the origin of this relatively quiescent role may go back to the very first board who were essentially clerical 'watchdogs' for the interests of the Church and not necessarily readied for participation in normal corporate responsibilities" (5).

Even if such an observation was somewhat overstated, it had its point. The critical problem in campus-church relations in 1980-81 (see chapter ten) certainly had shown that the members of the board of trustees, at least in that instance, had not been adequately involved and informed in advance about related campus policies and practices to have enabled an early and effective response to the challenge. Future challenges of several kinds likely lay ahead and President-Elect Nicholson believed in a strong board. So, in

1982, the campus affiliated formally for the first time with the Christian College Coalition and the Association of Governing Boards, both anxious and able to assist in the orientation and support of board members. Nicholson immediately began a close and crucial relationship with the board chair, Ronald J. Fowler. Together they planned a restructuring of the board, bringing into being a series of standing committees designed to enable members to function more knowledgeably and effectively.[6] In 1989 a grant was sought and received from the Lilly Endowment to make possible the special preparation necessary for the board to govern effectively the theological seminary (see Appendix S).

Institutional restructuring also occurred in the college's academic administration. That effective 1970s academic leadership team of Nicholson-Hoak-Osnes-Shoot no longer was in place (Osnes left the institution in 1983 and Shoot retired in 1980). During the spring of 1983 President-Elect Nicholson asked me, then dean of the School of Theology, to replace himself as dean of the College and Vice-President for Academic Affairs. Together they designed and put in place by that fall a new school structure, gathering the academic departments into natural groupings. Each school would have its own dean, all reporting to the dean of the college. From the faculty I recruited Dr. F. Dale Bengtson (B. S., 1957), Dr. James Macholtz (B. S., 1951), and Dr. Darlene Miller (B. S., 1962) for these key leadership posts. Altered modestly in design in 1991, this structural arrangement remains to this date (see Appendix H), with the addition of Dr. Blake Janutolo to replace Dr. Macholtz who died in 1985, and Dr. Kenneth Armstrong (see below).

As the new president explained to the board of trustees in September, 1983, this restructuring into schools "creates a framework in which such institutional goals as academic excellence, a stimulating educational environment, and the integration of faith and learning can be approached creatively and consistently." The intent was not to raise more and higher walls within the college, which would have allowed the new schools to go their own independent ways, even setting their own admission and general education requirements. Instead, the schools were to function as implementers of standards, policies, and requirements common to the whole college and remaining under the control of the college's unified faculty.

A key example of this intended unity, even within increased structural diversity, was the liberal arts program of requirements for all baccalaureate degree candidates. The pattern of the early 1980s dated back to 1973 and had been reviewed extensively by a curriculum coordinating committee during the years immediately preceding 1983. In 1980 the college faculty had reaffirmed the conceptual design of this general education curriculum, but called for a few key adjustments—like the introduction of a "freshman seminar" and a "senior capstone." For the balance of the decade, implementation of the freshman seminar proceeded, with review and refinement all along the way. Senior capstone, however, suffered from a continuing lack of agreement on conceptual clarity and implementational viability. Finally, having never been launched successfully, the college faculty in 1991 voted to drop it altogether. But the program in general stood. It had been approved by the college faculty in November 1982 with a conscious tie to the emerging new articulation of institutional mission.

Soon the school planners realized that more than a general sense of direction and revised structures were required to better enable the institution to travel along the right path. Well-informed and systematic planning also was judged necessary.[7] Early experiments at a comprehensive planning process were attempted and proved both useful and frustrating. Progress and partial deadends were experienced, but without dampening the desire to move on. The engineering skills of this president would not yield easily in pursuit of what was judged an important goal.

Somehow, the president insisted, better ways had to be found to translate general goals into specific operational priorities and to tie more directly the results of the planning process to the annual budgeting process. Somehow the institution had to equip itself to handle in a regularized and efficient manner the implications of potentially declining student enrollment, significant shifts in student attitudes, values, and interests, and the decreasing levels of federal student financial assistance. One way to accomplish all of this was to "become proactive in management approach," thus avoiding being "doomed to drift aimlessly toward contraction or demise."[8] So, when the opportunity arose in 1986 to seek a Lilly Endowment grant focused on "Institutional Development" (see Appendix S), it was seized quickly as needed assistance in moving from the early experiments to "the design of a strategic planning process, ongoing and comprehensive in nature" (6). The request was funded.

Part of the institutional development grant was used to support the potential of Anderson's involvement with the Coalition for the Advancement of Private Higher Education and through it the quality consulting help available from NCHEMS consulting services.[9] A particular focus was on identifying and then measuring intended student outcomes of the educational process. Included in the process was the administration in March 1988 of the "Institutional Performance Survey." Responses from trustees, faculty, and administrative leaders gave a helpful picture of commonly held affirmations and concerns about the functioning and future of the institution (see below for some of the key findings).

Another new feature of the emerging process of planning was the campus Committee on Strategic Planning appointed by the president. In February, 1988, this committee of sixteen faculty, staff, and students, chaired by Professor Douglas Nelson, produced a major report for the president. It identified six strategic issue areas emerging

William and Gloria Gaither, Campaign co-chairs, with Presidents
Reardon and Nicholson (right)

from the interaction of institutional mission, goals, and current analyses of the institution's internal and external environments. The president soon concurred with the committee's work and affirmed the six issues as now his own "priorities for reflection and action."[10] These strategic issue areas were servanthood, student clientele, involved community, quality education, enhancing institutional assets, and relations with the Church of God movement. Each was elaborated at length by the committee, along with listings of related evidence, implications, and recommendations.[11] The overall health of the institution was judged to be quite good, some obvious problems notwithstanding. This view was similar to the picture seen in the results of the Institutional Performance Survey.

The IPS picture of campus status, while recognizing a dynamic and challenging environment being faced, expressed no panic. The institution, according to common perception, was known by experience to be resilient and likely would find a way to accommodate almost any eventuality. A strong majority of faculty members were thought to be reasonably well satisfied with their employment. Some dissatisfaction was seen in the

355

level of appropriate recognition and rewards received by faculty and staff from their supervisors and administrators, and in the level of participation in some decision making (although most key decisions that had been made were seen as sound). There was a general sense that the institution had a distinctive purpose, even if a common definition of that purpose was not clear to all community members—especially the meaning of *servanthood* and the precise implications of the special relationship to the Church of God movement.

A general description of the campus community was offered by IPS results from among several campus types tested by the instrument. Respondents saw the campus as traditionally a clan-like community, one, however, less so than in the past since now it also was exhibiting some definite "hierarchy-like" characteristics. Clan-like was defined as being like a family, highly personal, bound together by loyalty and tradition, and led by a strong father or mother figure. Hierarchy-like was defined as formalized, tightly structured, governed by formal rules and procedures, emphasizing well-oiled processes, and led by organizers and coordinators. The Morrison, Reardon, and Nicholson administrations had functioned in different times and had exhibited their own distinctive styles. But, in each instance, central administration had been strong and had shaped significantly the ethos of campus life. Now, in Nicholson's case, while the positive aspects of clan life still were treasured (exceptionally prominent being mission and heritage rhetoric), the perception was that they were being pressed by certain internal and external factors and were being accompanied by the increased presence of formalized structures and procedures (in part a reflection of the president himself).

Campaigning for the Cause

So, with formal statements of mission, goals, and annual objectives in place, the general education curriculum rethought, and board and administrative structures revised, attention turned to the next major challenge. There had to be a gathering of necessary resources to make possible the fulfillment of all these high aspirations. Soon into the time of President Nicholson's administration, he and his skilled chief financial and development officer, Ronald W. Moore, formed the outline of a five-year plan. Moore in particular would provide the needed leadership. The decision was made not to employ the services of a fund-raising organization, but to enhance and rely on in-house staff and a network of volunteers. This would avoid a drain on funds raised and increase the institution's own development expertise that would remain in place after the campaign.

The central goal was seeking a way to provide the context for highlighting a range of key institutional needs and stimulating greatly increased financial giving to the institution that would undergird the specialness, not merely the survival of the school.

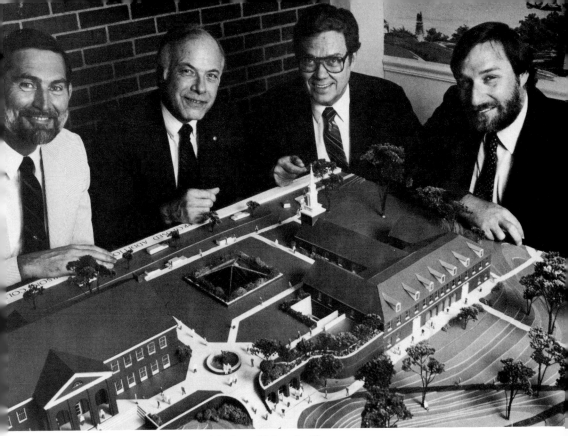

Model of new University library
(Left) Barry Callen, Duane Hoak, Robert Nicholson, Ronald Moore

The way that emerged was a high-profile financial campaign. It would not be focused primarily on constructing this building or establishing that program, but a "Campaign for Anderson College" (updated to "University" in 1987—see below). It was time to campaign for *the cause*. It was time to broaden the base of financial support and to increase the circle of campus friends who were giving something for this significant educational enterprise.

In 1985 the board of trustees enthusiastically joined the administration in launching a five-year "Campaign for Anderson College" that sought $25 million for the heart of the institution, primarily its students, faculty, and educational programs. Ronald Moore joined President Nicholson in assuming campaign leadership, along with alumni Bill and Gloria Gaither who co-chaired a national campaign cabinet. Significant funding was sought for endowment of student financial aid, faculty development, key educational programs, and a major expansion of library space, including computer automated modernization of library services. The stress on endowment was seen as essential if the future

357

Ronald W. Moore

was to be marked by stability, excellence, and the institution retaining significant ability to control its own destiny.

This campaign had a much larger goal than had ever been attempted before. Unlike others in the past, it was not focused primarily on a major building project. Keynoted instead was an emphasis on the urgent need for endowment, for the identifying and long-term support of a range of key ideas and central programs. Admitted the campaign co-chairs: "It always seems easier to get people excited about giving money for tangible edifices.... But for this campaign we were looking for donors who cared about ideas, who were willing to invest in programs and visions."[12] And such people were found. Early in the five-year process, good campus friends LaRita and Leland Boren emerged with the idea of a million-dollar challenge. Then the retiring business department faculty member Dr. Glenn Falls, joined by his wife Ruth, presented another gift of one million dollars to endow, among other things, faculty growth programs.

Ronald Moore, functioning as campaign director, and President Nicholson worked tirelessly in the effort. The goal was to reach the $25 million level by December 31, 1990. President Nicholson, however, announced his retirement effective in June 1990. Accomplishing the full goal by his retirement time appeared possible and, with special effort, was accomplished especially in his honor. In fact, the board of trustees revised the goal upward to $28 million and that too was surpassed by December of 1990! This campaign was by far the most successful such effort in the institution's history. Final totals are seen in Table 28.

During this five-year effort 8,542 donors had made a charitable contribution. A total of 114 endowed student scholarship funds had been established, 92 college and 22 seminary. Two funds of $250,000 each were funded to assist faculty members in obtaining terminal degrees and for general faculty development activities (the Glenn and Ruth

TABLE 28

The Campaign for Anderson University
1985-1990

	Goal	Gifts/Commitments to 12/31/90
Gifts for Current Use		
Annual Fund (Unrestricted)		$ 2,777,161
Scholarship Funds		2,884,956
Educational Program		1,067,695
	$6.5 million	$ 6,729,812
Endowment		
Scholarship Funds		$ 4,405,080
Educational Program		818,861
Unrestricted		3,550,766
Deferred Gift Agreements		8,295, 871
Loan Fund Principal		12,670
	$13.5 million	$17,083,248
Facilities and Equipment		
Library Expansion Project		$ 3,284,551
Other Projects		706,731
Land, Equipment, Art		1,504,355
	$5.0 million	$ 5,495,637
Total	$25.0 million	
Revised Goal	$28.0 million	$29,308,697

Falls gift). The Herbert J. and Eloise M. Contos Business School Memorial Fund of $135,000 now existed and would provide major support to the college's largest academic department. Before the campaign, the institution's working endowment was approximately $3.8 million. When it had concluded, that number had risen beyond $12 million, with $8.3 million more in irrevocable deferred gift agreements committed to endowment.

Buildings and educational equipment had not been the primary focus of this

TABLE 29

Key Financial Statistics:1967-1988

	1967	1977	1988	% Increase 1967 to 1988
Total Assets	$12,010,790	$26,290,793	$52,378,050	336.1
Total Liabilities	5,487,024	7,271,583	12,922,900	135.5
Total Fund Balances (Net Worth)	6,523,766	19,019,210	39,455,150	504.8
Total Plant Assets	8,060,651	16,717,322	32,721,856	305.9
Total Plant Net Worth	3,877,125	11,989,608	24,594,239	534.3
Total Endowment Funds	511,410	2,842,380	8,584,559	1,578.6
Total Gifts, Grants & Bequests	957,386	1,662,713	3,785,396	295.4
Total Current Funds	2,336,888	9,063,011	20,842,379	791.9

Note: Selected updating of this information is found in chapter thirteen.

campaign effort, but certain pressing needs of this kind were not ignored. A Broadcasting Center had been opened with 2,400 square feet of space for television and radio studios (soon to house the new campus radio station, WQME—see below). The Kissinger Learning Center now existed with space, staff, and specialized resources for learning disabled students.[13] About $1.5 million had been expended on a wide range of educational equipment, especially microcomputers. Most prominent of all was the University Library. The library study in the late 1970s had set the agenda (see chapter eleven) and now major financial assistance from the Kresge Foundation, Lilly Endowment, and General Motors Foundation helped make high aspirations become present reality.

In 1986 the board of trustees had approved a library expansion project. It would involve a projected $3 million to physically connect Wilson and Byrd Libraries by the underground construction of 30,000 square feet of new library space. When associated remodeling was complete in the existing buildings, the overall result would be a new facility enabling substantial integration of holdings and services and prime new space for a greatly expanded church and campus archives (including the Charles E. Wilson papers). While funding for the construction costs was being sought as part of the $25 million Campaign and I was chairing the library committee that shaped the particulars of all the programmatic needs, a "Dream of Distinction" grant was sought successfully from Lilly Endowment (see Appendix S).

The grant proposal, dated June 1987, explained to the Endowment: "Our dream is that the library become not only a modern, attractive physical structure, but also a sparkling symbol of what Anderson College wishes for each of its students: access to all print and nonprint resources through the best of library technology and, in addition the opportunity to employ microcomputers in the full range of learning."

In view was a fully integrated, on-line library computer system readied for use by completion of the decade-long process of reclassification of all holdings to the Library of Congress system. This "dream of distinction" became a full reality on October 7, 1989, dedication day for the new University Library. The address was given by Cecil K. Byrd, Professor and Librarian Emeritus of Indiana University, whose own mind had first "come alive" in the simpler beginnings of the library's earlier years (see chap. five). Dr. Kevin Radaker, Professor of English, responded for the Anderson faculty on this historic occasion, saying: "I am excited and encouraged by these improvements and by what they signify about our institution's aspirations for the future."

The funding of this project had continued the campus policy of requiring the assurance of major gift funding before any large building project was begun. The project finally required about $3.2 million. By September 1988 this full amount had been committed, including the institution's having qualified for a $400,000 challenge grant from the Kresge Foundation. Such an avoidance of accumulating heavy institutional indebtedness, which would have to be carried by the operating budget, was one important reason why each fiscal year would continue to function with a net surplus from current operations. That meant that the aspirations for the future, to which Dr. Radaker had pointed, had a real chance to become increasing reality.

By every measure, the Campaign for Anderson College (University) was a resounding success. Cautioning, however, against the temptation to lose perspective in the midst of big numbers and rows of new microcomputers, campaign director Ronald W. Moore summarized it all this way: "The real story of the Campaign is people—the students we are privileged to serve, a faculty dedicated to teaching and scholarship, a caring and supportive staff, and the thousands of donors who have joined in unique partnership with this campus community. All of the large financial numbers," he concluded, "are only important when viewed as direct benefits to the learning process."[14]

There had been much direct benefit indeed! Although many of the benefits of the Campaign still lay in the future, some could be seen even before it had concluded in

School of Theology deans, (seated, left): Gene Newberry, Adam Miller
(Standing, left): Barry Callen, Jerry Grubbs, James Earl Massey
Earl Martin, not pictured

1990. Table 29 summarizes key financial statistics, showing especially the large growth in endowment funds (admittedly having begun on a small base).

Beyond the gratifying numbers, however, President Nicholson emphasized another significant outcome of this campaign. A vision for the university's future was evolving, one far more extensive than mere survival. Would the school's many alumni and friends step forward as never before with strong support for the heart of that vision? The answer was yes!

Partnership in Servanthood

Clearly the campus had quality leadership, a rich heritage, an evolving model for strategic planning, and many generous friends who helped make possible a successful financial campaign for the cause. But the challenges were great and many of them could only be met by an intentional nurturing of a range of vital partnerships. Some objectives would never be possible if they were approached by this campus alone.

The Church of God movement, of course, always had been a key partner. The decade of the 1980s, unfortunately, had begun awkwardly in church relations. But the genuineness of this relationship and the fact of essential integrity on both sides soon prevailed. President Nicholson, as an immediate priority of his young administration, took to the road to convene open roundtables with a wide range of pastors. With him went Dr. William E. Reed, highly respected national church leader now retired and serving as campus director of church relations.[15] Exchanges were candid and most constructive. Nicholson was a genuine Christian man who valued highly the church relationship and was willing to make himself available and vulnerable. He stated it this way in his September 1983 report to the board of trustees: "It is *from* the Church that the College draws the majority of its student body and a sizable amount of its financial support. It is *for* the Church that the College strives to provide quality educational opportunities, properly balanced with the spiritual values to which the Church holds."

At the undergraduate level, there were at least three significant developments in church partnership, one financial and two curricular. The financial involved the establishment and substantial growth of the "Matching Church Scholarships" program. Beginning in 1980, the College soon had agreed to match up to $750 any scholarship provided to a student by his or her local church. That first year forty local congregations provided $37,017 to 97 students, matched by $13,224 from the College. By 1985-86 more than 530 students received close to $250,000 from 350 congregations, totaling nearly $490,000 when the campus match was added. A major church partnership in student financial aid had taken hold, enhancing admissions, retention, and church relations.

The positive curricular development was that the undergraduate college became more active again in ministerial education. Since the beginning of the seminary in 1950 and the soon demise of the Bachelor of Theology degree, the college had done little in professional ministerial courses other than in Christian Education. Toward the end of the decade of the 1980s, however, several factors led to the launching of a new major in Christian ministries in 1989. More older students were in school, the other Church of God colleges were emphasizing ministerial education as grounds for church support, and the curriculum developers realized that many such students never would go to seminary unless they were challenged and professionally involved during their college years. Early student response to the Christian ministries major was encouraging and was nurtured through Dr. Fredrick Shively's direction of AUCME (Anderson University Center for Ministry Education).

The negative development in church relations came at the end of the decade. In 1980 the class that had attracted church criticism had been Human Sexuality. Now, in 1990, it was the art class in Life Drawing, which was restricted to a specialized student clientele and at times employed undraped, professional models in highly controlled circumstances. With pornography a major problem in the society and little understanding outside the Art Department about why such a seemingly questionable practice as "nude models" was being justified as crucial for art majors, it was difficult to satisfy critics who soon were out to eliminate from their church college this appearance of immorality in the classroom.

At the president's lead, the board of trustees gave considerable attention to this difficult matter. The trustees understood why "outsiders" had difficulty appreciating the legitimacy of this course, especially the use of an undraped model. But it became equally clear that art and pornography are different things and that the art faculty members involved were committed Christians who always had conducted themselves and this class in a sensitive and professional manner. Finally, in May 1990 with considerable reluctance, the board decided that "we will voluntarily cease the use of totally undraped models ... [and] will continue to work seriously at providing the students a strong art education, well suited to their academic, professional and spiritual needs." It seemed a struggle the campus could not win under the circumstances. To some faculty members it seemed an unfortunate and not well-informed church intrusion into educational affairs, even a violation of academic freedom. But the board fulfilled its role and had made a difficult judgment.

At the seminary level, always a central part of campus-church partnerships, the decade of the 1980s was an eventful one for the leadership. In 1983 President Robert H. Reardon had retired and his college dean of many years, Robert A. Nicholson, had assumed the presidency. Nicholson then requested that I, then dean of the School of Theology, fill the vacancy of college Dean and Vice President for Academic Affairs, with Dr. Jerry C. Grubbs of the seminary faculty assuming the deanship of the School of Theology. Then in 1988, at the retirement of Cleda Anderson, Dean Grubbs became Vice President for Student Life at the college and I was asked to provide interim leadership at the seminary for eighteen months to enable a search process that eventually brought back to the seminary as dean one of its former faculty members, Dr. James Earl Massey. So, to begin the fresh decade in January 1990 a new seminary dean was in residence and soon there also would be a new president (a graduate of the seminary).

On the negative side, the significant enrollment decline that had begun some

(Top) Robert Nicholson leading ceremony of cornerstone laying, Reardon Auditorium
(Bottom) Reardon Auditorium

years earlier in the seminary continued. The 1983 fall headcount enrollment of 189 had slipped steadily to a low of 100 by decade's end. One obvious reason was a sharp drop, almost an ending of new seminarians coming directly from the graduating classes of Church of God colleges other than Anderson. This decline resulted primarily from fewer young, seminary-bound and other ministerial candidates in these church colleges. This circumstance, with its obvious impact on the School of Theology, also presented a potential leadership problem for the church in the years ahead. Further, the presence of seminary graduates entering the ministry of the Church of God movement had not grown over the years. Of the 432 ministers ordained between 1968 and 1972, fourteen percent had seminary education, nine percent of these from the School of Theology. The more recent year of 1987 showed only thirteen percent for that year with seminary preparation, and only five percent of those from the School of Theology. Even though the cumulative presence of seminary-educated men and women now was significant indeed, obviously much progress yet was needed in achieving an adequately prepared ministry for the Church of God.

Late in 1989 a special grant program in trustee development was announced by Lilly Endowment. Given the coming of a new seminary dean (James Earl Massey), the major enrollment-related issues at hand, and the clear commitment of the campus to continue its responsibility for operating the seminary on behalf of the whole Church of God movement, a grant was sought and received (see Appendix S). Its specific purpose was to prepare the university's board of trustees to become increasingly effective in its role of governing a seminary. The fact that half of the board's membership was made up of Church of God ministers was not in itself a guarantee of the board's capacity to govern with maximum wisdom.

For the School of Theology, the year 1990 was similar to 1970 in at least one important way. The time appeared to have come again for daring thought and innovative action. Another period of turmoil was not inevitable if insightful leadership emerged to clarify the vision and gather support for thoughtful action. The university told its alumni and friends through *Signatures* magazine that the seminary was entering "the James Massey era" and that "the Dean is in." Many celebrated Dr. Massey's coming and, so alumni were told, his bringing with him a "freshness and a new sense of innovation and hope. That's important because this is a building time."[16]

In 1990 Dr. George Kufeldt, member of the seminary's first graduating class in 1953, retired after twenty-nine years as seminary professor of Old Testament. Successful progress in the years ahead would require the seminary to maintain Dr. Kufeldt's distinguished example of combining loyalty to the church tradition, dedicated scholarship, and commitment to the highest standards of theological education. It was a time of historic transition. The approach of the 1990-91 school year, in fact, marked the completion of forty years of distinguished service by the School of Theology. Release of the volume *Listening to the Word of God*,[17] a joint publication of Anderson University and Warner

President Nicholson and Robert Orr, Governor of Indiana,
celebrate the new "University" name

Press, was intended in part to honor the teaching ministry of a beloved seminary faculty member of the past, Boyce W. Blackwelder (see Appendix R). This book also intended to highlight again the biblical orientation, the educational vision, and the communication responsibilities central to the mission of the School of Theology.

Now joining the Church of God as vital campus partners were new relationships focused on the city of Anderson. By the end of the 1980s the people in leadership of all aspects of city life, and increasingly even the general public, were thinking more and more of Anderson as a university town. Pride in the presence of the campus was replacing apathy.

While remaining national, private, and church-related, the campus intentionally had become significant to the local scene. Nearly four thousand former students had remained in Madison County,[18] many as public school teachers, accountants and nurses (see Table 33 for detail). At President Nicholson's inauguration in October, 1983, for instance, official greetings were brought on behalf of state government by alumnus Julian Ridlen (B. A., 1963), then Treasurer of the State of Indiana.

TABLE 30

Graduates by Degree Programs: 1981-1991

The following records the numbers of graduates of formal degree programs offered by the University's college and seminary during selected years. The year 1981, for instance, means the graduating class of June-August 1981.

	1981	1983	1985	1987	1989	1991
College						
B.A.	272	291	256	285	272	292
B.S.N.	0	0	4	3	12	0
A.A.	21	26	26	20	11	15
A.S.	40	52	40	39	40	21
Seminary						
M.Div.	27	28	27	19	21	13
M.R.E.	3	1	2	2	4	0
M.A.Rel.	9	10	11	14	6	8
M.Min.	0	0	1	0	0	0
Annual Totals:	372	408	367	382	366	349

President Nicholson soon would preside over the county-wide United Way campaign. Since 1980 the campus had co-sponsored with the Anderson Area Chamber of Commerce the "Anderson Leadership Academy," developing leaders for promoting the city's growth. A Speaker's Bureau channeled faculty and staff persons into resource roles in nearly all community organizations. Robert and Dorothy Nicholson became active in hosting in the president's home on campus a wide range of community leaders. They built many friendships, increasing the public's awareness and appreciation for the programs and people on campus. The personal warmth and credibility of the Nicholson as educational leaders and community-minded people made a real difference.

Thousands of local residents now visited the campus. On an annual basis, nearly all of the fifth graders from the local public school system came for a special promotional day. Sports fans arrived during the summer to watch training camp practices of the National Football League's Indianapolis Colts.[19] Adults were taking advantage of classes designed and priced for their needs (see below), and some fifteen thousand annually were attending a range of musical, dramatic, religious, and other events in Reardon Auditorium. In 1985 the campus was chosen to receive the Community Image Award. The downtown Anderson Rotary Club, in presenting this award, cited the cultural influence of Reardon Auditorium on the community and the campus contribution annually of some $10 million to the local economy.

Reardon Auditorium obviously had become a centerpiece of both campus and community. Even funding its construction had been a sample of vital partnership. Since this auditorium would fill a major public need in the community, including becoming the permanent home of the Anderson Symphony Orchestra and Anderson Community Concerts, a public campaign was mounted. The importance of this project was seen widely and, even though the early 1980s was a time of significant economic recession in Anderson (an unemployment rate of about 20 percent), $1.7 million toward the $5.5 million project total came from General Motors and other community supporters. The name *Reardon*, of course, was in honor of the retiring president who had maintained that both worship and the arts were central to campus mission and community enrichment. Now the college's chapel-convocations could be moved across the street from the crowded sanctuary of Park Place Church of God (the first convened in the new auditorium on January 10, 1984). Now the city had a new point of pride, a very visible and functional symbol of a mutually beneficial partnership between campus and community.

While the new auditorium was beginning to enrich the community as a cultural and entertainment center, the campus was broadening its partnership with the city through two new academic thrusts into adult education. The first had begun in 1982-83 when president-elect Nicholson and Dr. Larry Osnes approached local officials of General Motors to inquire about the educational needs of their employees. The automotive industry was in transition and many workers would need retraining or risk facing unemployment. How might the local campus help within the limits of its mission and educational expertise? The officials were anxious for help, and an excellent way to address the question of the campus' technical competency was close at hand. Purdue University recently had received public funding for a statewide technology program to meet just such a need as existed in Anderson's industry-based work force.

A unique and widely admired new partnership developed by 1984 between Anderson College and Purdue University (located in north-central Indiana). This institutional alliance was encouraged by President Nicholson, guided on Anderson's part by myself as dean, and implemented especially by Dr. Michael Collette. Purdue, at the invitation of Anderson College, would establish a base of operations in Anderson, offer aca-

Campus mascot, the Raven, celebrates at Macholtz Stadium

demic work in appropriate technical fields at the associate degree level, and contract with Anderson College for the faculty to teach all "general" course work in their programs. The associate degree in applied science began in 1985, marking the first time in Indiana that a state-supported university had contracted in this way with a private college. But in this case it was the least expensive and most effective way to meet a real public need. The institutions genuinely respected each other and they both were involved for the right, servant reasons.

The other thrust into adult education was launched by Anderson College (now University) in 1987 by establishment of the "Division of Adult and Continuing Education." For persons at least twenty-five years old, the intent was to provide quality, convenient, and affordable[20] education for primarily part-time, local, adult students.

TABLE 31

Summa Cum Laude Graduates: 1988-1992

The following are graduates of the college listed in the commencement programs of 1988-1992 as having completed their Bachelor of Arts degrees summa cum laude (a cummulative gradepoint average of 3.90 or above on a 4-point scale). Those designated * graduated with a perfect 4.0 average.

June, 1988
Matthew Dwayne Baugher*
Kristi Benay Bengtson
Gerald Anthony Considine

Rachel Annette Deal*
Susan Duncan Nightingale*
Pricilla Ridgway Wacaster*

June, 1989
Wendy Suanne Hanna
Sherri Sipe Massengale
Beatrice Frost Ormond*

Nancy Sue Sowers
Donna Marie Stackhouse
Kevin Lee Wilson

June, 1990
Kim Rader Bender
Laura Lee Campbell
Dawn Marie Claussen*
William Bradley Colwell*
Heidi Jo Hansel*
Charla Jeanne Hazen
Cheryl Ann Huffman
Christin Michelle Jones

Kelli Jene Kirkpatrick
Angela Denise Marsh
Ginger Eileen McFarland
Timothy Allen Mosher
Charnjit Singh Pabla*
Kelli Lynn Pennell*
Terisa Anne Tennison*
Derek Eugene Wilder*

June, 1991
Todd O'Neil Callen*
Linda Lee Chandler
Joyce Michelle Cullison
Richard Charles Fairbanks
Deena Denise Fitch*
Jennifer Lee Frasure*
Kandi Jo Gallant

Lucille MacMillan Helping
Eric Jason Houchin
Anita Jo Hunt*
Mark Aaron Lashbrook
Amy Jo Moore
Linda Ann Timmerman*

June, 1992
Jennifer Lanette Alwine*
David Andrew Arvin
Angela Michele Bates
Kimberly Lois Gahr*
Elizabeth Joy Guetschow*
Lisa Delores Heaton
Paul Carlson Holm
Darla Nanette Perry

Andrea Lynne Peters
Amy Louise Richards
Jill Christine Schickedanz*
Jennifer Lee Segessenman*
Janet Sue Southern
Mary Kay Steffey
Paula Marie Wensel
Melissa Joy Wilkie

Initially the Associate of Arts degree was offered, with concentrations available in general business and secretarial studies. This was soon followed by "general studies," a good base for an eventual four-year program for selected students. Under founding director Myrnie Richman, soon a wide range of noncredit workshops and other opportunities for area adults was being offered.

Another institutional intent, beyond functioning in new ways as servant to the local community, was to address that significant national decline in eighteen year olds that had been foreseen before the decade had opened. Total fall headcount enrollment in the college, a record 1,881 in 1983-84, had dropped to 1,763 by 1986-87. This negative trend now was reversed by the influx of an enthusiastic adult student constituency. There were risks to be run, but the judgment was made that strengthened student enrollment and community service were adequate compensating factors. That judgment would prove sound on both counts. By 1990-91, four years into the adult education program, the college's enrollment had risen to 2,030, with 310 of these being adult education students.[21] The number of graduates for each of the university's degree programs during the years 1981-1991 is reported in Table 30.

Something else had begun in 1987 in addition to an adult education program. From then on the entire institution would be known officially as Anderson University (see Table 1). This change, of course, had been given consideration before (see chap. ten). Now it had come up again at a new point in the institution's life. On May 15, 1987, after months of opinion gathering, President Nicholson formalized his recommendation to the board of trustees. "To me," he said, "much rides on definition." He suggested action to effect the name change. The trustees agreed that beginning on September 1, 1987, the corporation name (including the college, seminary, and new adult education division) would be Anderson University. On May 26 President Nicholson and Ronald J. Fowler, board chair, jointly wrote to all members of the General Assembly of the Church of God about this change. Clarification of context and intent were judged crucial.[22] In part, they said:

> The Church of God, with its several colleges, deserves a university in its midst which incorporates its largest undergraduate college, its Seminary, a growing graduate program, and thrusts of service and research which minister to the whole Church and "into all the world." We have desired increasingly to be that institution in program and outlook. We now propose to move to that name which best describes our existing structure and programmatic aspirations for the future.

Nicholson had shared with the board of trustees, who confirmed some commitments that he saw as basic to an adequate and distinctive definition of "university" in the

Anderson setting. Teaching would remain a central function, although faculty research, community service, and additional graduate programs likely would get new emphasis. There would be continuation of the "special wedding of the liberal arts, professional studies and a concern for serving," and there would be persistence in the struggle "to maintain community and intimacy, in spite of all societal forces to the contrary." Possibly most basic of all, the president and board had affirmed the following: "Acknowledging God as the source of truth and wisdom, we seek unification in a Christian faith perspective. We seek 'university'—unity in the midst of diversity—and not 'multiversity' as is often seen today in higher education."

Part of this was reality, part aspiration. Institutional mission was essentially unchanged. It was just that there now seemed to be a bigger arena in which that mission was being challenged to extend. Somehow the new name, assumed with no arrogance, was a visible catalyst gently prodding the campus on to important new frontiers. One such frontier was the arrival in 1988 of Dr. A. Patrick Allen to become dean of the undergraduate college. I concentrated for a year on continuing tasks as Vice President for Academic Affairs and Corporate Secretary, served for eighteen months as acting dean of the School of Theology, then plunged into fresh opportunities when named by the president and board of trustees as the first faculty member to attain the new rank of "University Professor."[23] Dean Allen began exploring future developments for undergraduate academic administration and curriculum. He brought fresh energy and new expertise to the expanding challenges and opportunities.

Much was happening on campus. Better ways to communicate were needed. In the spring of 1987 the alumni publication, *A. C. News*, was enhanced significantly and given the new name *Signatures*. Why this unusual name? Said the editors in the first issue, "Anderson College students are urged to do something with their skills—to advance a profession, to promote scholarship, to humanize bureaucracies, to pursue solutions to human problems, to live as thoughtful, compassionate Christians, to make their creative mark on society." So the publication would feature both news and names, highlighting those creative marks being made in the world. That first issue of *Signatures* in 1987 profiled professors from several disciplines, including Glenn Falls and Harold Linamen in business, Lawrence Shaffer, prominent in physics research, Patricia Bennett, a leading nursing educator, and Barbara Jones, active on the frontiers of teacher education. These women and men and their many colleagues and former students were doing things worth announcing widely. They were placing their distinctive and redemptive "signatures" on at least a few of the pages of today's troubled world. A listing of selected honor graduates from 1988-1992 is found in Table 31.

One way to summarize the 1980s on campus is to recall that President Nicholson's favorite hymn was well-known to be "Great Is Thy Faithfulness." The president really believed this hymn's message and lived accordingly. Perhaps the best way to highlight the decade is to review the experience of two students. Much expansion, resource gathering, strategic planning, and partnership in building programs, structures, and vital relationships had taken place. But it all was intended to enhance the quality of the educational experience of each student.

Michael Little left his home in Iowa to become a freshman at Anderson College in September 1979. Even though his father was a Church of God pastor, Mike came with a rebellious attitude toward the church and soon began to enjoy beating the system on campus. As he admitted years later, "I had my own little crusade breaking all the rules." During the last three of his five collegiate years he lived near campus. Much of that time he helped organize student dances at the local National Guard Armory (events not permitted on campus or to be sponsored by any campus organization). He acted as a middle man between students wanting to purchase alcoholic beverages and city people happy to sell. He even made money selling classroom tests, research papers written by ghost writers, and fraudulent chapel attendance cards. He was an underground leader, a deliberate trial to many of the school's standards and traditions.

Campus officials over the years, special people like Cleda Anderson, H. L. Baker, Donald Collins, and Jerry Grubbs, sought to be patient and redemptive with those occasional students like Mike who chose awkward paths in search of their own identity and faith. Anderson College proved for many such students to be the place where a testing of the past finally would lead to a constructive future. During his fourth year in college Mike Little realized that the church was a vital reality despite its imperfections. His conversion came primarily through his relationships with caring people on campus, including mathematics professor Paul Saltzmann and campus pastor Donald Collins.

Mike began visiting people in nursing homes with Professor Saltzmann and later would venture to India on a TRI-S trip with Donald and Gloria Collins. He began attending worship services again, easing back toward the established church by beginning to relate to the Christian Center in downtown Anderson (see chapter seven). Graduation came in June 1984 (B.A., business management). Now what Mike cared about the most was ministering to needy persons, much in the tradition of the former Dean Olt (see chapter seven). Located in Washington, D. C. since 1987, Little has become a member of the Church of the Saviour and in 1990 began directing Lazarus House, a nationally acclaimed housing community for recovering alcoholics and drug addicts. How grateful he had become that the Anderson campus had been patient and redemptive with him. He would continue that wonderful tradition for other people in other places, extending the mission and ministry of the campus.

Glynis Gordon, a young woman from South Africa, was in the college's graduating class in June 1990. She was asked to share with the large audience gathered in

Reardon Auditorium for the Baccalaureate service that year some personal reflections on her Anderson experience. It was an exciting day for her, partly because her mother, whom she had not seen for two years, had arrived from South Africa to help celebrate the occasion. Celebrate what? Not just a ceremony concluding a college career, but a truly changed life. Miss Gordon's comments speak for themselves and represent similar growth experiences enjoyed by hundreds of other students. She said:

> As you can imagine, my freshman year was filled with adjustments. Because I am from South Africa I have been asked all kinds of questions, like "do you have a pet lion?" or "what tribe are you from?" My all-time favorite question was, "Where did you find clothes to wear when you came to America?" Did they think I'd arrive in a grass skirt with a bone in my hair! But I guess I had lessons to learn too. When I studied about the principle of checks and balances in my American National Government class, I was embarrassed when I found out that Dr. Nelson was not referring to a huge government banking system.

> Anderson University has provided many learning experiences for me away from the classroom. During Spring break my junior year, I went with six of my friends from Anderson to Hope Hill Children's Home in Hope, Kentucky. I met children of all ages from broken homes. I was amazed at how loving these children were and how they made the most of their lives. I reevaluated my priorities and found there were a lot of changes to be made.

> During Christmas break my senior year I traveled with a TRI-S group to a Church of God Navajo reservation in Klagatoh, Arizona. I was fascinated by the Navajo lifestyle—no running water, no electricity, no telephones. In a place that seemed to have only the basic necessities for living, I discovered I could live. I learned in those two weeks how worthless is our overabundance of material possessions. I realized how uncomplicated life can be when our relationship with Jesus is free from preoccupation with those things. It was a well-timed lesson right before graduation.

> Probably the biggest learning experience for me happened my freshman year. I went to Chicago on a social problems trip and there I met a man by the name of Richard who challenged every aspect of my political views. I realized how narrow-minded I had been and how prejudiced I was. One thing that Richard said that has stuck with me was that there was more to taking a stand against racism than just admitting apartheid was wrong. God's timing is perfect because that summer when I went home I got the opportunity to work at a kindergarten in one of the black townships. It was only then that

my eyes were opened to the political injustice in South Africa. God tore down my old political structures and began rebuilding.

It also has been at Anderson that I have formed friendships that will last a lifetime. I have had the same roommate for three years, and sometimes I think that without Lynn and my other special friends I never would have made it. I have grown in my leadership abilities by being a resident assistant as well as vice president for L'amifidel social club. I have lived through "Rush Week," participated in "Airband" and humiliated myself in "Cheap Thrills." I've had hands-on experience at the campus radio and TV station and experienced snow for the first time — and I hope the last. I have gone home with students over the holidays and have seen all parts of America. And, to top it all off, in a few hours I will receive a diploma with a degree in Mass Communications. I could not ask for anything more from Anderson University. Thank you for this wonderful opportunity!

When Glynis had concluded these remarks, President Emeritus Robert Reardon, robed and seated with the faculty, was overheard saying to those sitting next to him, "That makes it all worthwhile!"

1. Prominent among the institutional perceptions identified in that 1981-82 "HEMI" survey were that: (1) increased clarity was needed in the institution's central goals and objectives; (2) "top administration" was strong and, while desirable in many ways, had too much direct influence on educational activities; and (3) the "downward" flow of information within the institution was not adequate to enable many members to enjoy optimal levels of "ownership" and effective participation in campus life.

2. This election by the board of trustees required and received official ratification by the General Assembly of the Church of God as, of course, had Dr. Nicholson's as president.

3. Martin was the guest leader in Anderson's 1984 Fall Faculty Sessions. The book was published by Jossey-Bass, San Francisco.

4. The 1988 self-study prepared for NCA/ATS offered a brief commentary on the mission statement. It listed five emphases inherent in the statement that were central aspirations for the functional operation of the institution. They were as follows:

1. *Community.* We desire that whatever strengths we have may be realized in each faculty or staff member or employee—as well as in students, who are the

primary focus of our efforts.

2. *Wholeness.* We see ourselves not only as an institution of the mind, but also of the spirit and body. We tend to distrust the segregation of these three, although we have not become adept at dealing with them in an equal or an integrated fashion;

3. *The Experiential.* We have believed for more than twenty years that`experiential learning, when placed alongside of traditional learning styles, reinforces understanding, and brings earlier maturity;

4. *God and Man.* We seek to develop understanding, worship, and compassion within the individual;

5. *Servanthood.* The questions "life to what end?" and "education to what end?" deserve an answer, we have believed; that answer is found in the Christian understanding of servanthood, which we attempt to pursue.

5. His final president's annual report to the board of trustees, April 22, 1983.

6. These committees, in addition to the continuing Executive Committee, were: Educational Policy and Personnel; School of Theology; Finance and Development; Student Life; Buildings and Grounds; and Trusteeship.

7. While the Anderson campus was engaged in its early efforts at strategic planning, the Church of God movement was making a similar attempt for itself on a national level. The "Consultation on Mission and Ministry" convened in Indianapolis in April 1984 and evolved "five areas of concern," nineteen related goals, and many objectives to address these goals. The assumption was that each general agency of the church, including Anderson College, would take seriously these concerns and goals and would find their own ways of addressing them. As dean of the College, I functioned as chair of the design committee for this national consultation of the church.

8. Proposal to Lilly Endowment for the Institutional Development grant, April 1986, 4.

9. In 1986 Anderson was selected as one of eleven colleges nationally to participate with CAPHE in a special project. The goal was to assist these schools in defining and assessing institutional effectiveness. Each school was scheduled for reaccreditation review in 1989-90, was deemed not at risk in this process, and was being encouraged to demonstrate to its accrediting body that "student outcomes" could be documented and were appropriate to its educational mission.

10. President's letter to all faculty and staff, dated April 26, 1988. It was accompanied by the full report of the Committee.

11. See the full report of February 1988 and the story on it titled "Report Assesses Health of the University" in *Signatures*, Fall 1988, 11-12.

12. *The Campaign Journal*, April 1991.

13. Named for and made possible by Glen and Connie Frederick of Tucson, Arizona. Student Maggie Campbell of Indianapolis was one of the first students to benefit directly (A. A., 1991). Infected with encephalitis as a child, with damage to eyes, hands, and central nervous system, she nonetheless now had the help she needed on the Anderson campus.

14. *The Campaign Journal*, April 1991.

15. At Dr. Reed's death in 1985, he was replaced by Ann Smith (B. S., 1958), formerly a career missionary with her husband Nathan in Japan and Korea. Supporting effectively the work of church relations was Rev. Donald Collins, campus pastor, and scores of faculty and staff members.

16. *Signatures*, Spring, 1990, 6.

17. Published in 1990 in honor of Dr. Boyce W. Blackwelder who taught New Testament in the School of Theology from 1963 until his death in 1976. I was editor of this vol-

ume. Chapters were contributed by several of Blackwelder's teaching colleagues and former students in the School of Theology who themselves now teach in the biblical field at various institutions across the Church of God. Six of them were on the faculty of Anderson University, both college and seminary.

18. Dennis Carroll is one of the many alumni now providing distinguished service in the community. Having graduated in 1969 and then completing a graduate law degree, he was elected in 1980 to his first term as Judge of Madison County Superior Court 1. In 1990 he also was elected a member of the campus board of trustees. See Appendix O for the identity of some other distinguished alumni.

19. This team chose the Anderson campus beginning in the summer of 1984 because of its general location, excellent facilities, and supportive ethos. Also in the summers the campus now was hosting numerous high school band and sports camps.

20. That first year tuition was set at $75 per credit hour, far below the level being charged traditional students and consciously comparable to the fee level of nearby Ball State University (a state institution about twenty miles away to which many Madison County adults had commuted for years because, it often was said, "Anderson College is too expensive"). The intent was to eliminate that cost problem and offer such persons the real opportunity to have needs and interests met much closer to home.

21. In 1990-91, adding in the 94 seminary students, the institutional total was 2,124 in the fall semester.

22. Approval of this change of name was required by the General Assembly since a change in the school's Articles of Association was involved. The concurrence was given readily that June. There was much church pride in this maturing institution that now had widened horizons, and yet roots remaining in a vital church partnership.

23. One aspect of this special appointment was provision of the time and resources required to research and write volumes such as this present one and its earlier companion, *Faith, Learning and Life* (1991). The establishment of this rank in April 1989 was called by the president a "maturing of our university model." It was defined as "a senior and distinguished scholar/teacher-in-residence honored for particular potential to combine publication and teaching in the service of the mission of the university."

13 Kindle the Flame

1990 and Beyond

"These are our moments to serve the young, to search for our community's new generation of leaders, to confirm and support the preparation of the newly called servants of the church, to walk with those new and courageous persons who will mark the paths in still unknown frontiers of discovery.**"**

(President James L. Edwards)

Somehow it seemed like a new beginning, one that had close ties to things past. The church's Gospel Trumpet Company had mothered the campus in 1917 and had shared with the new school its own leaders, including its president, Joseph T. Wilson. Now, in 1990, Robert Nicholson retired after an unprecedented career of forty-five years on campus beyond his student days. That year he was named "Man of the Year" in the city of Anderson and the Anderson University Student Association established the annual "Robert Nicholson Award" to honor outstanding faculty and staff members selected by the students.[1] Again, then, from Warner Press across the street would come the chief executive officer of the publishing house. This time it was Dr. James L. Edwards who had been called to be only the fourth president of Anderson University.[2]

Typical of the history of this campus, the resulting transition would be smooth, there would be a great outpouring of love for the retiring leader, and the new president would represent considerable continuity with the past. The focus, however, clearly was on the future. There were trends of significant proportions to be addressed. The university's Committee on Strategic Planning, back in February 1988, had identified several such trends, some of which had the potential of threatening the traditional value system and distinctive mission of the campus itself.

For instance, the university in 1987-88 was receiving eighty-five percent of its new undergraduate students from only six states (54 percent from Indiana, up from 41 percent in 1979-80). The number of new college students affirming affiliation with the Church of God movement had declined to about forty percent. Despite the obvious pride and continuing support of the Anderson campus by the Church of God, a national trend toward lessened loyalty of church families to particular church institutions was being experienced by most church bodies, the Church of God included. The consumerism mentality in the culture struggled with the servanthood emphasis on campus. With most student homes closer to campus and automobiles now common, the institution increasingly was being vacated on weekends, making more difficult the building of community. Large numbers of Christian young people were electing to seek their higher education close to home, usually in a publicly supported and presumably more affordable institution than a private school like Anderson.

The Seeds of Greatness

With only a few months of his presidency remaining, Robert Nicholson had shared a few of his considered perspectives with the Alumni Council of the campus in a relaxed retreat setting. He posed what he judged the key question: "Do we possess the seeds of real greatness as a Christian university of the future?" The then almost concluded Campaign for Anderson University was building for the future, he said, primarily by expanding the institution's endowment base (see Table 28). The new name *university* certainly provided an expansive self-image. A rich heritage, a clarified mission, and the strongest faculty ever were identified with pride as vital seeds that surely could grow into a truly great future. It was "an enormous potential," promised Nicholson, although the shape of it was yet to emerge.

That potential now was being nurtured by a widening range of campus alumni and friends. Some of them had significant financial resources that could assist in the accomplishment of campus goals, and most of them represented various ideals for which the campus stood. A good example was the group of four persons celebrated by the campus in June, 1989, by the giving of honorary doctoral degrees (see Appendix P). Larry D. Contos had chosen to continue the legacy of his parents in the Anderson community by exhibiting initiative as a committed servant of the public good. Robert Culp (B. A., 1957) had provided courageous leadership, especially in Toledo, Ohio, both as a church and community leader, bringing hope and dignity to persons in need. Gloria Gaither (B. S., 1963) had become an articulate advocate for Christian values related to working mothers, rearing children, making responsible decisions, and risking vulnerability in serving others for Christ's sake. Sidney "Mac" Johnson (B. Th., 1952; M. Div., 1955)

(Left) David L. Sebastian, board chair   (Right) Louis E. Gerig, board vice-chair

had assisted in planting and nurturing Christian churches in Thailand, Taiwan, Singapore, Indonesia, Hong Kong, Nepal, and Burma, becoming known as a servant leader committed totally to the worldwide mission of the church. As a group these persons represented much of what the campus viewed as worthy goals for graduates.

There was obvious institutional momentum and a strong sense of additional frontiers available for crossing. Nicholson often had said that the campus was called to be "the Church of God at its best." The full definition of "at its best" might never have become wholly clear to all campus members. However, one aspect of this pivotal phrase that was clear was the dynamic nature of a "movement," a body of believers free to innovate and gripped with a sense of destiny. These surely were characteristics to which the university aspired. Now came a new president who knew well both the life of that church movement and the life of the campus.

Dr. James L. Edwards had just completed a pastorate of fourteen years in Columbus, Ohio, and a time as chief executive officer of Warner Press.[3] Reared in a Church of God pastor's family, he often had visited the campus during the later Morrison

(Top) Presidents Edwards (left), Reardon, and Nicholson,
with campus first ladies Deanna, Geraldine (standing), and Dorothy

(Middle) President James Edwards and A. Patrick Allen,
college dean and vice-president for academic affairs

(Bottom, left) President Edwards delivering his inaugural address
(Bottom, right) President Edwards on his inauguration day,
with (left) Robert Reardon, Ronald Fowler, and Robert Nicholson

years. While Reardon was president, Edwards had completed on the campus his bachelor's degree in 1965, his seminary education in 1970, and tenures as director of student recruitment from 1966-1970 and director of church and alumni relations from 1972-1975. As he said in his "My Faith Journey" statement sent by the board of trustees to all members of the General Assembly of the Church of God on May 5, 1990, "I am a child of the church: her Sunday school, her college, her Bible classes, her seminary, her fellowship, her circles of leadership, her unfolding history." The church's "unfolding history" now needed fresh leadership. Times were changing. Many new faces had appeared recently in the executive offices of the national church agencies in Anderson. Technology, diversity of many kinds, and crumbling social values across the nation were pressing against, if not penetrating the church's life. The campus had grown to record institutional headcount enrollments of 2,115 in the fall of 1989-90, 2,124 in 1990-91, and 2,162 in 1991-92 (see Table 32). Increasingly classrooms were being populated with students and faculty members from many Christian backgrounds.

Some undergraduate students had no religious commitments, only academic goals. Some college faculty members, while sympathetic with campus ideals, focused primarily on their professional competencies and were unsure of the spiritual roots and aspirations of the school or what such distinctives had to do with their own responsibilities. In various interviews with senior and retired faculty members conducted for this volume (see Appendix T), concern was expressed by these persons about the possible erosion of a crucial campus heritage. Things don't necessarily have to be again "the way they used to be." But, said this common voice of concern, there now is danger that, in all its diverse programs, busy schedules, and multiple constituencies, this beloved and special campus might slowly lose sight of its larger and distinctive mission (particularly the Christian dimension).

Clearly there now were seeds of greatness well planted throughout the school's life. To grow to maturity, however, this community of teachers and learners needed to share a dream. They needed to have articulated freshly for them a compelling cause that would capture the imagination and harness the commitment and creativity of a new generation of faculty and staff. The real story of Anderson University always lay just beneath the surface of the maze of people and events, catalogs and diplomas. The core issue still centered in the *why* of it all. Education was being offered and pursued *from what vision* and *for what purpose?*[4] Major attempts at clarifying and communicating mission had been made both in the 1970s and 1980s, but this crucial task seemed neverending and so central to the viability of an appropriate future.

Professors Bruce MacMurray, Willard Reed, and Merle Strege took one important form of initiative by launching early in the decade of the 1990s a campus project on "private morality and the public good." Soon funding was received from Lilly

Endowment (see Appendix S) to assist them with activities designed to help integrate intellectual and public life and to nurture a strong and responsible corporate consciousness on campus. Then another initiative came when the local *Anderson Herald/Bulletin* newspaper ran a series of pieces on "2,000 And Beyond: Where Is Anderson Headed?" President Edwards naturally was approached. What did he see as the university's future and its relationship to the future of the city? His response was thoughtful and enthusiastic.

The new president informed the public that the Anderson campus would be a "premier Christian university." Student size would remain relatively unchanged. The goals, he said, were quality, not quantity ones since the smaller, more intimate learning environment was prized. There soon would be more offerings at the master's level and a solidified partnership with the city's public school system. "We see ourselves as persons who ought to be interested in the public sector because we do educate the public," said Edwards. "Just because we're independently controlled and managed doesn't mean we're not in public education. We are. I'd like to see us make a difference."[5] Here was a young leader with vision and a willingness to act.

Steps in the Right Direction

Student enrollment, despite gloomy demographics and vigorous competition, particularly from publicly supported institutions, continued moving in a positive direction. Fall 1991 enrollments in the university's college were up one percent over the previous year, including a 2.1 percent increase in full-time undergraduates and a 4.8 percent increase in the adult division (now totaling 325 of the 2,050 undergraduates). See Table 32 for details. After several years of enrollment decline, the seminary also experienced an increase in the fall of 1991, an encouraging 19.1 percent over the previous year (112 as opposed to 1990-91s 94 graduate students). Institutionally the one-year growth was 1.8 percent. Important as were the numbers, however, President Edwards had said that the key question was one of quality, not mere quantity. For student enrollment that meant attracting and retaining students compatible with and qualified to profit from an Anderson University education. It also was intended to mean serving the special educational needs of the church constituency and of residents of Madison County, as well as maintaining a general student body drawn nationally, containing significant numbers of minority persons, and continuing to include the presence of international students. In the fall of 1991-92, 6.2 percent of the undergraduate student body represented minority populations (111 of these 128 persons were black, with another ten Hispanic, six Asian, and one native American).

For all of these enrolled students and for other constituencies, present and

TABLE 32

Student Enrollment: Fall Semesters, 1988-91

The figures are headcount enrollments. Full-time equivalent enrollments (calculated on a twelve-hour base) are shown in parentheses.

	1988-89	1989-90	1990-91	1991-92
Institutional	2,050 (1,871)	2,115 (1,945)	2,124 (1,925)	2,162 (1,970)
College (traditional students)	1,729 (1,693)	1,773 (1,737)	1,720 (1,690)	1,725* (1,701)
Adult Education (undergraduate)	200 (90)	242 (135)	310 (168)	325 (188)
School of Theology	121 (88)	100 (73)	94 (67)	112 (81)

*At least forty percent of the 1991-92 undergraduate student body (college plus adult education) was affiliated with the Church of God and fifty-two percent were from Indiana. However, many students typically do not declare a church affiliation and the local adult education students weight geographic origin in favor of Indiana. Church of God students remained a major presence and the campus continued to be diverse in places of student origin (forty-one states and fifteen countries were represented).

potential, there was continuing program energy and creativity. Quality, diversity, and relevance tended to characterize the ongoing parade of innovations. One example was the nursing program. On June 15, 1991, commencement day, the nursing department sponsored a special breakfast event on the campus, one of remembering and celebrating. Nursing education had begun on the Anderson campus during the 1960s with a cooperative program enabling students to transfer after two years at Anderson to Ball State University in nearby Muncie for the professional nursing courses. But that had been only the beginning.

In 1973 the associate degree in nursing had been launched at Anderson College in response to community need. St. John's Hospital in Anderson was then ending its diploma program and had requested the local campus to fill the vacuum, helped by an annual grant of $75,000. In the following years the campus had become a major educator of health care professionals locally, with accreditation by the National League of Nursing first achieved in 1975. By the 1980s, with many changes in the nursing profession itself, the decision had been made to move to a baccalaureate program. This four-year program first was offered by a Plus-Two approach (the associate degree plus two years, with the first BSN graduates in 1985), and finally by a generic BSN, with its initial accreditation anticipated in 1992. This 1991 breakfast, hosted by the nursing department chair, Patricia Bennett, marked the last associate degree graduating class in nursing and anticipated the first generic BSN graduates to come the following year. Present that morning were current and past nursing faculty members, university presidents, and college and school deans who had supervised and supported this program over the years. Present also were representatives of almost all of the graduating classes since the first in 1975. This one program had demonstrated curricular creativity and had reflected well much that the university holds most dear.

Another example of aggressive innovation was the business program. Added in 1991 to the three undergraduate schools, which had been created in 1983, was a fourth, the School of Business, with Dr. Kenneth Armstrong as dean. Combined to form this new school were the business/economics and computer science departments. Immediately in view was the potential of a master's degree in business administration. Differing from many business programs, this one would highlight the liberal arts, emphasize ethics, and be motivated by the desire to serve as well as profit in the business arena. Approved by the college faculty in December 1991, for availability beginning in September 1992, was a new computer science minor in electrical engineering technology. The specialized courses would be taught by faculty from Purdue University, already resident on campus (see chapter twelve).

The MBA program, the first graduate program to be offered by the university outside the seminary, was approved to begin in September 1992. Having been explored as a possibility for several years, in May 1992 the Board of Trustees also approved the offering of the institution's first doctoral program beginning in the fall of 1993. It would be an in-service Doctor of Ministry degree offered through the School of Theology. A new Graduate Degree Council under the direction of Dr. F. Dale Bengtson now was in place to guide in the exploration of still other graduate programs that might be in the university's future.

Examples of innovation, however, were not limited to academic departments and a primarily traditional student population. The adult education program now was

School deans, (left) Kenneth D. Armstrong,
F. Dale Bengston, E. Darlene Miller, Blake Janutolo

serving an older population, as the Center for Pastoral Studies of the School of Theology had been for nearly two decades. Since 1979 the In-Service Training Institute, sponsored by the National Association of the Church of God, had been hosted each summer on the Anderson campus. It specialized in providing a range of educational opportunities primarily for black lay leaders, bi-vocational ministers, and others. The campus recognized Rudolph Smith with an honorary doctorate in 1991 (see Appendix P), in part because of his significant role as dean of this Institute for twenty years.

In the summer of 1991 an *elder campus* was conducted on campus for the first time. The purpose was to help persons over sixty years old to broaden their experiences, make new friends, find new ways to interpret their stage of life, and learn more about the Church of God movement. An extension of such specialized focus for a particular constituency was the plan for a first Summer Arts Academy. The young and creative are to be invited to campus to identify their talents and gain instruction and inspiration that will support commitment to Christian art ministries. Emphasis will be on music, music industry, and communications. Inspiration for these senior high youth will be provided by people like Sandi Patti, Bill and Gloria Gaither, and F. Dale Bengtson, dean of the School of Music and Art.

The central campus preoccupation, however, has not been with summer programs and specialized student constituencies, significant as they have become. The resident, traditional student was still the heart of the institution. A review of the annual *Student Life Handbook* reveals much about the campus philosophy of undergraduate student life and the extensive range of student personnel services. The 1991-92 issue, for instance, invited students to "enjoy the unusual combination of academic exchange and

TABLE 33

Samples of Alumni: Areas of Service by Category As of January, 1992

Graduates of the college, now serving
  in Madison County, Indiana (as of Jan. 1992)

Public School Teachers .... (approx)220
Nurses.. (approx)240
Social/Mental Health Professionals............. (approx) 20
Attorneys... (approx) 10
Accountants.. (approx) 30
Public School Administrators .... (approx) 5
Christian Ministers............................... (approx) 75

Ministerial graduates of the seminary,
  Initial Placement, 1979-1991

Senior Pastor.................................223 (40.3%)
Associate Pastor..............................125 (22.6%)
Further Graduate Study.....................52(9.4%)
Missionary....................................41(7.4%)
Chaplain
      Institutional................................13(2.4%)
      Military 12 (2.2%)
Teacher
      Church School.............................11(2.0%)
      Public School..............................5(.9%)
Urban Ministry....................................5(.9%)
National Church Agency.....................11(2.0%)
Other..55(9.9%)

      Total....................................553 (100%)

Current Church of God Foreign Mission Personnel
      Missionaries (active)....................... 54
      Regional Directors (from total of five) 4
James Albrecht (B. A., 1959; M. Div., 1962;M. A., 1978).
      Europe and Middle East.
Robert Edwards (B. A., 1967; M. Div., 1972).Africa
Willi Kant (B. A., 1975; M. Min., 1976).Latin America
Michael Kinner (B. A., 1976; M. Div., 1982).Asia

Christian fellowship that's possible only at places like Anderson University." The section on residence life was led by the announcement that "We Are Family." Welcoming words of President Edwards said: "You are now a part of a community of friends, faculty, and staff committed to be of help to you" (1, 6-7). Many of those friends were then pictured, skilled and supportive people like Jerry Grubbs, Vice President for Student Life, H. L. Baker, Dean of Student Services, Donald Collins, Campus Minister, Lisa Pay, Director of Counseling Services, Jean Morehead, Director of Multi-Cultural Affairs, and others. There also were resident directors, the Campus Activities Board (CAB), the Anderson University Student Association (AUSA), and about a dozen social clubs (see Appendices I and U for listings of student organizations and selected student leaders for 1989-1991).

One symbol of the quality in view for all programs was the guest appearance in March, 1991 of the Anderson University Chorale at the national convention of the American Choral Directors Association meeting in Phoenix, Arizona. Chorale director Richard Sowers was pleased that this premier campus group would be so honored in this most prestigious of settings. In fact, Anderson University was becoming known as a center for the education of Christian musical artists. On November 29, 1990, the university went on the air with its new FM radio station, WQME. Station manager Gary Brummitt (B. A., 1979) signed onto the airwaves with a contemporary Christian format, beginning with Sandi Patti singing "Hosanna." This three thousand-watt commercial station reached as far as the major population center of Indianapolis and began providing excellent Christian witness and educational opportunities for communication and other students. Judging from the enthusiastic public response, it soon appeared that the station's on-air slogan, "a shade above normal" (based on its 98.7 spot on the dial), was an understatement. It was considerably above normal, as the whole campus was intended to be.

Pace-setting models of outstanding professional excellence were visible to students. Mort Crim, former Anderson student and now senior news editor and anchor of WDIV in Detroit, Michigan, was a campus trustee, frequent guest, and popular chapel/convocation and commencement speaker. In April 1990 two Anderson University alumni received major recognitions at the Gospel Music Association's annual Dove Awards ceremony in Nashville, Tennessee. Sandi Patti won an unprecedented ninth straight Dove Award as female vocalist of the year and Steven Curtis Chapman was honored as artist of the year, top male vocalist, and songwriter.[6]

Such examples of achievement could be cited in a range of other fields and vocations. Appendix N presents a selected group of alumni to whom the institution has awarded honorary doctoral degrees over the years because of outstanding achievements. Table 33 reflects the substantial impact the campus has had through its many alumni, particularly in the communities adjacent to it and in the Church of God movement across the nation and world.

Intercollegiate athletics also was the scene of outstanding individual accomplishments and program developments significant for the future. September 29, 1990, for instance, was not a likely day for all-time records to be broken by the university's football team. It was a home game, the fourth game of the season, and already the Ravens had suffered three loses. The opponent was Hanover College, the previous year's Indiana Collegiate Athletic Conference football champion. But when this afternoon was over, the record book had to be opened and partially rewritten. Anderson won the game 30-12, piling up an amazing total of 629 yards of offense. The running game was so successful that Anderson's strong passing game, featuring All-American receiver Brad Lamb,[7] was relatively unused. The rushing Ravens accumulated twenty-nine first downs as they rushed sixty-nine times for 504 yards, burying a forty-two year old school record by 116 yards! Fullback Ryan Bates, tailback Larry Bryant,[8] and quarterback Todd Stone ran for 186, 184, and 128 yards respectively. It was a spectacular display of offensive strength by an inspired team coached by Michael Manley (B. A., 1973). See Appendix J for a listing of athletic coaches, most valuable players, and selected team records.

Peter Prichett glided to the National Association of Intercollegiate Athletics national steeplechase crown in Texas in the spring of 1991, becoming Anderson University's first NAIA outdoor track national champion. He was coached by Larry Maddox who had become well-known for building small-college track and cross country powerhouses. Joining Maddox as a successful and nationally recognized coach was Donald Brandon in baseball. Nearly every year since 1979 Brandon's teams had enjoyed high national rankings in the NAIA, often winning against teams from much larger schools. Three times the Anderson baseball team has played in the NAIA world series, first in 1965 under coach Carl Erskine (former Brooklyn Dodger great), and then in 1984 and 1987 under coach Brandon. In 1991 that year's team participated for the first time in the play-offs of the NCCAA (National Christian College Athletic Association) and came away as national champion.

As the 1990-91 school year opened, the university was a member of two athletic conferences, the Hoosier Conference for Women (Anderson, DePauw, Goshen, Hanover, Manchester, and Taylor) and the Indiana Collegiate Athletic Conference (Anderson, DePauw, Franklin, Hanover, Manchester, Rose-Hulman, Taylor, and Wabash). National affiliation was with the NAIA (National Association of Intercollegiate Athletics) for both men's and women's sports.

Traditionally on the Anderson campus, reporting lines for athletics and the academic department of physical education were the same, both responsible to one school dean since 1983. But by letter on November 7, 1990, President Edwards shared his view with campus leadership that "the task of providing for the necessary supportive attention to facilities, conference relations, recruiting, coaching, staffing, transportation, etc., seems to be quite different from those issues considered through a departmental structure." So, in order to strengthen athletic programs, Jerry Grubbs, then Vice President for Student Life and Human Resources, was given general supervision of athletics. The responsibility for human resources shifted to Denise Kriebel. Barrett Bates, Director of Intercollegiate Athletics, now would report to Grubbs, a member of the president's executive staff.

Immediately Grubbs was asked to guide in the development of a mission statement, statement of philosophy, and overall goals for athletics. They were to be appropriate for an athletic program functioning within the larger mission of this Christian university which valued excellence in all programs, but, as first priority, valued pursuit of a quality education for all students, including athletes.

By the board of trustee's meeting of October, 1991, and with a major study completed during an executive leave, Grubbs proposed and the board received approvingly the perspectives and directions now being called for. Intercollegiate athletics would "exist within the overall mission of the university" and provide competitive opportunities "consistent with a strong liberal arts tradition and within a Christian context." They affirmed that the president, not the board, alumni, or any other organization, has full and final authority and responsibility to administer the athletic program. There would be commitment to excellence, but not to "professionalism in athletics," since "students are students first and athletes only secondarily."

These administrative and educational perspectives were essential in informing a major decision made earlier in 1991. For men's sports, the Indiana Collegiate Athletic Conference decided to leave the NAIA national affiliation and join the National Collegiate Athletic Association (NCAA) at the division III level (a non-scholarship division). The ideal of the scholar-athlete would remain primary. After initial hesitation because of some related unknowns, Anderson chose to participate in this national affiliation shift. This way the campus could remain with the ICAC which, said President Edwards, provides "superb competition with schools in a reasonable distance, enhancing collegiality and competition without requiring students to miss a great number of classes." Taylor University chose otherwise, thus becoming the only member to leave the area conference to be an independent.

Looking Long Range

Many forward steps were being taken. Each was intended to further insure the ongoing integrity of a distinctive institutional mission, while continuing to strengthen the foundation that would enable an innovative and expanding future for quality higher education. One step in that direction, of course, was to remain conservative in fiscal policy without sacrificing the willingness to act creatively, even courageously when a cause and time were right. The institutional treasurer, Ronald W. Moore, for instance, reported some dramatic statistics for the fiscal year ending June 30, 1991. Total institutional assets (without depreciation) had risen from $10,156,662 in 1965-66 to $68,157,557 in 1990-91. While in 1965-66 total institutional liabilities had represented 44.0 percent of total assets, by 1990-91 they represented only 32.8 percent. Progress had been both substantial and sound.

The year 1990-91 was the twenty-sixth consecutive year that the annual budget had finished with an operating surplus. In that year, $6.73 million were received in gifts and grants from all external sources. Federal and state agencies had provided $2.75 million in grants for student aid, scholarships, internships, and work-study programs. Gifts from other sources had totaled $3.98 million, $1.44 million of which had come from Church of God World Service, churches, and individuals. To make possible such remarkable financial development in the midst of the volatile world of private higher education had required careful planning, creative measures—and certainly the courage of institutional self-discipline. Those descriptive words of earlier years still applied to this institution, "not wealthy, but healthy."

Such health had been maintained in years that had not been easy for most colleges affiliated with the Church of God movement. In the six institutions in North America predominantly governed by the Church of God, there had been a total of 522 first-time Church of God first-year students in the fall of 1979-80. That number declined nearly every year to a low of 307 by the fall of 1989-90. In 1979-80 Anderson's share of the Church of God freshman total was 51.9 percent. In 1989-90 its share had risen to 55 percent, an increasing share of a decreasing total. During the 1980s there was a significant decline in the percent of the college-going Church of God high school graduates who chose any Church of God institution (about ten percent compared to about twenty-five percent in 1969 and 1979).[9]

As a result in part of this weakening enrollment pattern, various financial crises were experienced within the Church of God higher education community, particularly at Mid-America Bible College in Oklahoma.[10] The tendency of the church was to concentrate its available funding where the crisis and related need seemed most urgent. Since, of course, Anderson University had avoided crisis and demonstrated success in a major fund-raising effort, there was a noticeable shift of support away from Anderson, and especially to Mid-America Bible College. Specifically, between 1978-79 and 1990-91 the proration percentages of Church of God World Service funding decreased to the university's undergraduate college by 7.9 percent and to the School of Theology by 3.3 percent. During the same period such percentages rose by a modest 0.2 percent to Warner

Pacific College and by a dramatic 37.7 percent to Mid-America Bible College.

The long range intent, however, remained unchanged. The university intentionally would maintain its close relationship with the Church of God movement. This relationship was judged to be an essential and ongoing aspect of the school's very essence. But in the short term there was work to be done. Effort had begun late in the Nicholson administration to develop a formal "covenant" statement that would seek to define with new clarity the mutual expectations and obligations of the campus-church relationship. President Edwards would work to complete this crucial project. His work would proceed at a time when accountability increasingly was being called for across the church, but without clarity on how, in a voluntaristic church tradition, such accountability could be structured and assured. The complete covenant statement was approved by the board of trustees in May 1992 (content in part found in Appendix W).

Two actions of the university's board of trustees in October 1991 illustrated the delicacy and difficulty of the task ahead. First, the board decided that, beginning with the graduation ceremony concluding the 1992-93 school year, the university's commencement would be separate from the church's International Convention held annually on the campus. This schedule change had been discussed for years because of the inconvenience of graduating students having to be in Anderson some six weeks after school's end to fulfill a mandated graduation requirement of participating in the commencement ceremony. Now, triggered by the church's decision to alter slightly the convention's scheduling, adding further to the awkwardness for the school, the decision was made to do what was best for the students. Care would be taken to minimize the possible, but incorrect perception that the university, by this action, was moving away from the church's life. Alternative programming would be developed to keep the university visible at and valuable to the International Convention.

The other trustee decision was to respond appreciatively but cautiously to a January 1990 action of the church's Commission on Christian Higher Education. That action, based on the belief that the church's General Assembly "expects supervision of the broad higher educational functions of the Church of God movement," had called for schools to covenant "to coordinate cooperatively our institutional functions, consistent with our obligations, through the Commission on Christian Higher Education." The Commission had affirmed this concept in principle and forwarded it to the several governing boards for consideration. Anderson's board considered this "covenant" proposal in October 1991 and also affirmed it in principle, but "within the boundaries of the integrity of our various corporations." The schools involved, judged Anderson's trustees, exhibited sharp differences in size, type, and financial health. Therefore, Anderson University, on the one hand, was concerned not to make itself liable for decisions and debts of other institutions. On the other hand, it was anxious that the church benefit from the distinctive missions and range of diverse potentials resident in these schools. There should be no leveling to some standard model. The university was most willing to "continue the dialogue on matters of church governance which enhance the effectiveness of our units of church life and mission."

The university's future relationship with the church, of course, often would focus on the evolving life of the School of Theology. In August, 1990, at a summer retreat meeting of the board of trustees organized around School of Theology issues,[11] a mission statement developed by the seminary faculty was approved for the School of Theology. The seminary's purpose was "to educate at the graduate professional level both men and women for Christian ministry. To this end, we are committed to be a community of scholars who are church-related and in whose character and servanthood the following are vitally linked: biblical faith; academic integrity; Christian spirituality; love for persons; and a responsible relation with the created order and all humankind." I then identified for the trustees seven issue areas around which the seminary's future appeared to hinge. They are found in Appendix V because of the breadth of perspective they offer on both the history and future of the School of Theology.

Beyond the crucial issues of church relations in general and those of the School of Theology in particular, there were university-wide strategic issues as the institution took the long-range view ahead. There were, of course, the several issue areas identified and elaborated helpfully by the university's Strategic Planning Committee in 1988 (see chapter 12). Building on these, President Edwards listed six of his own in October 1991. After having experienced more than a year in the presidency, Edwards identified for the board of trustees the following as crucial and long range issues:

1. *Affordability.* Our students must be able to afford the quality education we offer. New attitudes of how one pays for an education will have to be developed while we continue to expand access to limited resources in the face of unlimited need.
2. *Positioning the Institution.* We are a far better and stronger institution than our price tag[12] or our general position in the academy of higher education would indicate. We do not seek an elite standing, but we do wish to be considered for the quality that is here and that is being developed. Moving to the next level will challenge our creativity and perceptions, within and without.
3. *Governance.* The Church of God is in a most important dialogue about governance issues. Whatever is decided, we will be involved. The impact will be significant. Our hope is that we can clarify the needs which are unique to a quality Christian university while strengthening our ties with the church. There is little clarity in this area, and we must find allies on this board and in the church to reach for our true potential in the life of the church and within our wider mission.

Candles and Carols, in Reardon Auditorium

4. *Program Development.* Within the great traditions of the liberal arts, we continue to search for an entrepreneurial spirit which responds to the changes necessary to serve our mission. Expansion alone is not the answer. Refinement will be required. Centers of excellence will encourage improvement across the campus. Faculty development will take on new demands. Staff effectiveness and efficiencies will be demanded as resources are pressed in light of new wants and needs.

5. *Productivity.* We will have to find new ways to be productive in the delivery of our educational services. This issue will require the attention of both faculty and staff as we find the technologies of efficiency and meet the higher standards of effectiveness.

6. *Competition.* Increased competition can be felt in the higher education marketplace at virtually every level. Competition is experienced for students, for dollars, for faculty, for minority involvement, for ideas and even values.

(Top, left) Fredrick H. Shively, Bible and Religion
(Top, right) James Earl Massey, School of Theology
(Bottom, left) Richard L. Sowers, Music
(Bottom, right) Susan P. Speece, Biology

Of very practical significance to an effective addressing of these strategic issues was an extensive study of constituency perceptions and expectations of the campus. Conducted in 1989 by the Marcon Corporation of Anderson, Indiana, samplings of present and prospective students, their parents, alumni, and pastors clarified some important matters—particularly in relation to future college student recruitment and retention. These campus constituencies placed high value on Christian life-style and the spiritual environment of the campus. But the highest value was placed on the quality of professors and the related academic reputation of the university. There also was obvious concern about the availability of adequate financial aid for needy students.

Very evident and gratifying in these survey results was the general sense of loyalty to and pride in the Anderson campus. A key conclusion drawn from the data was that alumni needed more assistance in becoming involved in the life and needs of the campus. They obviously believed in the school and often were in a position to be helpful. So, guided in part by findings of this study, a new set of college recruitment materials was prepared that projected a somewhat new institutional image. Highlighted now was the slogan "where quality learning and Christian service come alive." This was part of the needed "positioning" of the institution and an effective meeting of the competition in the demanding marketplace of student recruiting.

Light for the Darkness

From the beginning of this school in 1917, the central questions always were these: "Education from what vision?" and "Education to what end?" In those first years the institution was modest and the curriculum limited. But the fundamental vision and purpose were neither modest nor limited. Seventy-five years of courage, growth, experimentation, and faithfulness now have brought fragile beginnings to the point that President Edwards, in October, 1991, could articulate the enduring and maturing vision and purpose this way for the board of trustees:

> We aspire to be a premier Christian university. This will require a dynamic leadership team and a partnership with trustees which is solid, futuristic in thought, and creatively resourceful. I believe we are up to the task. What is that task? Said the president:
> We are first of all and always persons on a Christian mission.... Our sense of belonging to Christ and to a mission which is of eternal significance is all the motivation we need to give our best and to pursue goals at the highest levels. I am delighted, humbled, and very grateful for the calling which has come to me to serve with you for Christ's sake, for the kingdom, for His children, and for the future of His making.

The task was identified in different terms when President Edwards reported earlier to the Executive Council of the Church of God in the spring of 1991. On that occasion he quoted futurist Joel Barker as having said wisely: "A vision without action is merely a dream. Action without a vision is just passing time. However, a vision with action can change the world." Edwards then turned to the mission of Anderson University, saying that it is "an action oriented part of the church, with a vision for turning young people toward a needy world with superb tools and with the passion for serving."

Deidre Smothers, from Casper, Wyoming (B. A., 1991), was one student among many who clearly had been "turned" in this wonderful way. She had joined a group of students led by Donald and Gloria Collins (campus pastor and wife) on their way to India to learn and serve. Writing of her experience in February 1990, she said that "India changed my life. The way I feel about death, life, salvation, plenty, poverty, happiness, joy, misery, grief and pain has changed." She observed firsthand that "because of the dedication and passion with which Mother Teresa and her Christian sisters have served, the poor of Calcutta are not in poverty, because love and compassion have been graciously made available to them." Smothers concluded, "I want to use up my life in reckless abandon so that, when it's time for me to die, I will have nothing left to give." Surely the servanthood mission of Anderson University never had been stated more eloquently.

As always, teaching remained the university's central function and quality professors in the classroom constituted the heart of the institution. The 1990-91 year, for instance, saw the coming from England of Arlon Bayliss to head the new art glass program. The retirement of Gertrude Wunsch, who had served for thirty-five years as professor of physical education, came that same year. At the end of the 1991-92 year LaVern Norris, professor of sociology, also retired after more than three decades of effective service (Appendix F identifies these and all others who served on the full-time faculty for at least twenty-five years). Sid Guillen, native of Cuba and chair of the department of modern foreign languages, was serving as consultant to the Federal Office of Education and recently had co-authored a best-selling Spanish textbook. Susan Speece, chair of the biology department, was writing and lecturing widely on the critical subject of AIDS. Kenneth Ryden, of the art department, had been commissioned to design and create a ten-foot tall bronze statue of John the Apostle in commemoration of the upcoming centennial celebration of St. John's Health Care Corporation in Anderson. Walter Froese, born in Germany and now holder of the chair in church history at the School of Theology, was specializing in making the past come alive for the sake of the future. So was historian George Rable whose 1989 book *Civil Wars: Women and the Crisis of Southern Nationalism* was published by the University of Illinois Press and

awarded the Julia Cherry Spruill prize by the Southern Association of Women Historians.

These highly skilled teachers sought to inspire the light of knowledge in the context of faith. Their work was symbolized well by the seasonal "Candles and Carols" Christmas celebration. Musical excellence at this annual campus event had joined for years with readings of the biblical hope for humanity in Christ's coming and with the light from hundreds of candles held high in affirmation and gratitude. By 1990 this memorable community experience, involving a standing-room-only crowd in Reardon Auditorium, also was available to more than six hundred thousand Indiana households through the videotaping of Anderson University's Covenant Productions and statewide distribution to Indiana's network of public broadcasting stations. The light of learning and hope was being spread widely.

The beautiful campus continued to evolve as a setting appropriate for supporting the goals of quality learning and rich residential life. By the time University Terrace, a ten-unit condominium development located on the site of the old Park Place Church, was dedicated in October 1990, construction already had begun on the twenty-nine-unit University Village located north of the athletic fields. These attractive housing projects, sold on a life estate basis, represented significant investments by campus friends in the university's future. Joining such projects was active planning for a major renovation and expansion of Hartung Hall, projected to be ready by the fall of 1993. Science facilities would be modernized and a new home would be available for the Bible and Religion and Nursing departments. To honor quality leadership of the past and highlight again the centrality of the academic program, the board of trustees in May, 1992, authorized the recently expanded and unified university library to carry the name of Robert A. Nicholson.

In the meantime, initiative was being taken to have updated a campus master plan now twenty years old. Growth and change would be managed with an eye to educational function and campus beauty and safety. The future would be anticipated as carefully as possible and infused with that same pride which had characterized the past. Such was symbolized by a tradition of lights. During the homecoming of 1991, as had been the case for many years, the luminaries were a highlight. As darkness fell on Friday evening and large numbers of alumni families wandered the familiar campus, thousands of lighted candles outlined the perimeters and walkways, releasing their light so that all could see and feel again the pride. Flames of memory and appreciation had been kindled with joy.

(Top) Campus luminaries, front of Decker Hall
(Bottom) Nicholson University Library from "the valley"

Kindle the Flame
Celebrating Seventy-Five Years

ANDERSON UNIVERSITY
1917-1992

(Left) Logo, 75th anniversary   (Right) Campus seal, featuring open Bible, blazing torch

The future, of course, was full of unknowns. What was known was that campus tradition was rich, commitment was strong, and the opportunities many. Leadership was stable and innovative, with roots in the past and eyes on the future. The university, still crucial in the life of the Church of God movement, now also had become the school of choice for large numbers of young people from the wider evangelical community.[13] While more and more adults from the local community were finding the campus a good place for meeting a wide range of their educational, cultural, and recreational needs, the administration was giving special attention to defining the campus orbit to include the dynamic circle of the greater Indianapolis area. Trustee Bill Gaither reflected on the "unique niche" for Anderson University in the world of Christian higher education. He tended to see it in a distinctive combination of strong Christian identity and a freedom and creativity seldom found in Christian colleges. Surely this is part of what was meant by the university reflecting "the Church of God at its best."

So the time had come. The 1992-93 school year marked the university's time of diamond jubilee, three quarters of a century of distinctive educational service. The decision was made to take full advantage of this milestone opportunity. A large planning

402

committee was named and was co-chaired by President Edwards and former presidents Reardon and Nicholson, both yet living in the immediate community, active, and anxious to join again in working together for the future of the school. Here was a remarkable trio of seasoned leaders, prepared to join with Thomas Bruce, director of university relations, and many others to help enable a celebration of memories and achievement in ways that would enlighten the path yet ahead. In fact, the theme chosen for the year-long celebration was "Kindle the Flame."

The flame image stimulated memories of the early gas boom in Anderson, and long before that the prophecies of Isaiah about God's people being a light to the nations. As gleams of light reflect off a diamond's several surfaces, so this campus intended to move into the twenty-first century with its light of innovation and inspiration burning brightly and spreading its influence in many directions. This was to be more than a big institutional birthday party. It was to be a capturing of the moment, an inciting of the imagination, the launching of a new era, a passing of the torch in the ongoing search for educational excellence.

Decades earlier, in the midst of a terrible, worldwide economic depression, President John Morrison had been comforted by his pastor and friend, E. A. Reardon. The president was reassured that together, enabled by faithful colleagues and the Spirit of God, they would never let the lights of this school go out. When 1992 arrived, not only were the lights on, but the mission was very much alive and the call was to further kindle the flame! Here is a living tradition continuing to seek effective ways to assist coming generations of students to ask their questions, discover enduring values, and determine, in the light of Jesus Christ, how best to make a real difference in the world. Here is one campus where quality learning and Christian service would indeed come alive.

The official seal of Anderson University features three Latin words that mean truth, faithfulness, and service. They surround an open Bible, above which rises a blazing torch that is showering light in all directions. That seal, in a graphic way, tends to say it all. Here is the flame that should be kindled for the sake of generations yet to come. Here is a source for that flame, biblical truth, and a motive for its burning, faithfulness and service. Here is a vision that makes a difference in this troubled world. The 1923 *Echoes* affirmed that "each student, as he or she leaves the school, takes a lighted torch, and we see this torch of truth shining bright as the morning star in our home land as well as in the foreign land" (33). Back in 1923 the number of students available on the Anderson campus to carry this inspiring and transforming torch was relatively few. Now, after seventy-five years, the body of alumni has become many thousands strong.

Robert Nicholson, in his inaugural address as president in 1983, recalled a story by Harry Lauder, the Scottish bard. Lauder once had recounted his Edinburgh boyhood experience of watching an old lamplighter. At dusk this man climbed a ladder to light an old-fashioned gas street lamp, then went on to do the same from one lamp to another. Finally, the lamplighter himself was lost from sight. But, emphasized Nicholson, "the course of his journey was evident by the lamps he had lit." The new president's point in recalling this story was that, over the years of the history of the Anderson campus, many lamps had been lit in the midst of many kinds of darknesses. The names of the lighters easily slip from memory, but the flames they lit are bright and enduring.

The tasks yet remaining for the Anderson campus are to locate today's oppressive areas of darkness, usually caused by ignorance, sin, bigotry, and despair, and then to keep kindling the flame! Truth sets free, free to believe, to learn, to grow, to serve. In the noble cause of enabling such liberation of the spirit and intellect, Anderson University remains committed to being a "guide of soul and mind."

Echoes of the *alma mater*, the school's beloved theme song, linger on both in memory and in meaning. Decades of institutional life now have been invested in finding the best ways to fulfill this song's call to academic excellence, spiritual commitment, and service to humankind. But the task is far from complete. Thousands of Anderson alumni, now scattered in many nations and active in all walks of life, still ponder these poetic lines and seek ways to make their noble vision real in a troubled world.

Such treasured words and musical notes of the past call for fresh commitment and creativity. What has been must now be translated into insights, attitudes, skills and methods appropriate for the needs of a demanding future. So we who have shared in the Anderson University story are dedicated to continue remembering, learning, believing, serving—and singing:

> Anderson, our Alma Mater,
> *Guide of soul and mind,*
> Thou hast taught within thy borders,
> To aid all mankind.
> So, for this, Thy noble purpose,
> May our best avail;
> Friend of all that's good and upright,
> Hail to thee, all hail!

1. Recipients of the Robert Nicholson Award from 1989-90 through 1991-92 have been faculty members Dale Bales (chemistry), Gregory Heberling (business), and George Rable (history), and staff members Vickie Barton (counseling services), Margaret Camm (president's secretary), and Connie Profitt (registrar's office). In July 1992 Margaret Camm retired after serving for thirty-two years as secretary to Robert Nicholson (when dean and president) and to President James Edwards.

2. Joseph T. Wilson, founding principal, was never the school's "president" since, in his time, the school was not yet a corporation independent of the publishing company.

3. While a pastor in Columbus, Ohio, Edwards earned his Ph. D. from Ohio State University in educational policy and leadership. His doctoral research centered on issues relating to effective faculty development on small college campuses. Earlier he had married 1965 Anderson graduate Deanna Monteith. Having served on the church's Publication Board, he had assumed the presidency of Warner Press in a transitional period in order to effect a major restructuring and initiate a business turn-around. From that transitional role he was called to the university.

4. See Barry L. Callen, "The 'Higher' in Higher Education," in *Faculty Dialogue* (Spring 1991).

5. As quoted in the *Anderson Herald/Bulletin*, October 22, 1991, A-3.

6. In April, 1992 Sandi Patti was honored for the eleventh consecutive year as "female vocalist of the year."

7. After leaving Anderson in 1991, Brad Lamb was drafted by the NFL's Buffalo Bills and made the team.

8. Bryant went on to become the all-time leading ground gainer in Anderson football history (see Appendix J).

9. These studies were conducted by the church's Commission on Christian Higher Education. In 1989 about seventy-five percent of college-going Church of God high school graduates chose to attend publicly supported institutions.

10. Detail may be found in Barry Callen, *Preparing For Service* (Warner Press, 1988).

11. This retreat meeting was part of the trustee development grant program funded by the Lilly Endowment and focused on enabling the trustees to govern more effectively the seminary portion of the university (see chapter twelve). Another aspect of this grant program was the naming of a "Seminary Advisory Committee" to enhance communication with the seminary's "field" constituencies.

12. For 1992-93, the annual tuition rate for a full-time, traditional undergraduate student was $8,780, with a room charge of $1,680 and food service of $1,440. This

annual total of $11,900 for a resident college student was low in relation to many comparable institutions and now was assisted by a strong program of student financial aid of many kinds.

13. In the board of trustees meeting in October 1981, Robert Nicholson, then college dean, noted the declining percent of Church of God students in the college, a fact resulting in part from the school's increased attractiveness to evangelical young people from many church bodies. The board chair, Ronald Fowler, concluded the extensive board discussion of this development by saying: "Yes, we are right in moving toward any audience God gives us. . . . The College has become a major evangelistic outreach of the Church of God." This affirmation of a broader constituency, however, was coupled with renewed effort to recruit effectively within the Church of God.

Appendix A

Trustees, Cumulative List (1925-1992)

Not included are members of the campus "managing committee," which functioned prior to the school's 1925 incorporation as a body independent of the Gospel Trumpet Company.

Chairs, Board of Trustees

Joseph T. Wilson	1925-1931	Donald C. Richey	1970-1973
Albert F. Gray	1931-1946	Ray W. Keith	1973-1976
W. H. Hunt	1946-1951	Marvin W. Baker	1976-1978
E. E. Perry	1951-1962	Jack R. Anderson	1978-1979
Harold Achor	1962-1966	Marvin W. Baker	1979-1981
Denzel R. Lovely	1966-1967	Ronald J. Fowler	1981-1991
Glen E. Marshall	1967-1968	David L. Sebastian	1991-present
George W. Blackwell	1968-1970		

Board of Trustees

Achor, Harold	1946-1966	Crim, Mort	1974-1989
Adcock, Elver F.	1933-1953	Crockett Isom R.	1962-1982
Allison, Joseph D.	1988-present	Cross, Myrle	1939-1949
Anderson, Jack R.	1971-1984	Culp, Robert A.	1987-1992
Baker, Marvin W.	1953-1988	Dawson, I. K.	1935-1950
Bargerstock, Randy F.	1980-1986	Dickinson, O. Wayne	1985-present
Bate, Charles T.	1982-1992	Dunn, S. P.	1925-1957
Bauer, Esther K.	1972-1985	Edwards, James L.	1990-present
Beach Verda	1990-present	Erskine, Carl D.	1978-present
Berry, Robert L.	1925-1932	Flynn, Jeannette R.	1985-present
Blackwell, George W.	1946-1971	Fowler, Ronald J.	1976-present
Blevins-Dicus, Dorothy	1985-1990	Froehlich, Paul	1946-1971
Bohannon, Donald R.	1970-1986, 1988-present	Gaither, William J.	1973-1988,
		Gatton Walter R.	1962-1972,
Bontems, James W.	1960-1961		1978-1987
Bowman, Edward F.	1983-1988	Gerig, Louis E.	1988-present
Bradley, James W.	1978-1984	Goode, Richard A.	1985-present
Brown, Flavy B., Jr.	1960-1965	Gritzmacher, Victor J.	1954-1969
Burgess, O. A.	1925-1929	Grubbs, J. David	1975-1984
Byrum, Russell R.	1925-1933	Guilford, L. W.	1925-1933
Caldwell, Maurice	1959-1974	Hall, Billy Joe	1981-present
Carroll, Dennis D.	1990-present	Hatch, Ralph W.	1987-present
Caudill, R. C.	1932-1957	Hayes, Sherrill	1979-1988
Clausen, Barbara T .	1981-1985	Hency, Dale E.	1985-1990
Cook, H. Revere	1965-1975	Hines, Dalineta E.	1986-present
Cotton, Raymond E.	1987-1992	Howell, R. D.	1934-1939

407

Hunt, W. H.	1938-1953	Reardon, Robert H.	1956-1983
Hutchison, Jack D.	1960-1982	Reed, William E.	1967-1971
Huttenlocker, Keith E.	1970-1984	Reid, Benjamin F.	1982-1987
Kane, John Sr.	1935-1960	Reitz, Robert	1966-1970
Kardatzke, Elmer	1944-1948	Reynolds, Lawrence	1961-1970
Kardatzke, Jon K.	1974-1989	Ritchey, Donald C.	1961-1973
Keith, Ray W.	1950-1981	Roache, Leonard	1981-1984
Kinion, Kenneth E.	1956-1971	Robold, Claude L.	1984-1985
Kissinger, H. H.	1948-1953	Rohr, Loren	1978-1983
Koglin, Anna	1925-1930	Rose, Richard	1978-1981
Lehman, Glen	1957-1962	Rowe, A. T.	1925-1935
Lockhart, J. Kenneth	1982-1992	Schield, Wilbur L.	1963-1988
Lovely, Denzel R.	1949-1967	Seaton, Donald D. Jr.	1976-1981
Luquire, James F.	1972-1977	Seaton, W. T.	1929-1934
Macholtz, Adam	1962-1972	Sebastian, David L.	1986-present
Marshall, Glen E.	1953-1973	Settlemeyer, Lois A.	1990-present
Martin, Earl	1925-1946	Settlemyre, Thomas F.	1984-1986
Massey, Gwendolyn	1978-1980	Sharpe, Hollie W.	1983-present
McBride, Gilmer J .	1977-1992	Sherwood, Herbert A.	1925-1933
McCall, Maxine	1988-present	Shively, Fredrick	1978-1983
McCaw, Larry	1988-present	Shoemaker, Helen Achor	1978-1985
Menchinger, Fred G.	1985-1990,	Shriner, Neil G.	1989-present
	1991-present	Simpson, Oscar T.	1961-1974
Monday, M. A.	1934-1939	Slaybaugh, Daniel	1954-1959
Monk, W. E.	1933-1944	Smith, Ann E.	1992-present
Morris, E. J., Jr.	1960-1970,	Smith, Birdie M.	1925-1941
	1971-1976	Smith, Ruth M.	1984-present
Morrison, John A.	1925-1954	Smith, Steele C.	1930-1935
Naille, Ronald A.	1981-1991	Sorrell, Lovell J.	1972-1977
Neece, William C.	1981-present	Sterner, R. Eugene	1977-1987
Nevitt, Gerald	1973-1978	Strickler, Paul	1971-1981
Nicholson, Robert A.	1983-1990	Strobel, Lawrence	1953-1963
Oldham, Dale	1941-1954	Tarr, Charles	1991-present
Olds, John	1957-1962	Telfer, David	1978-1979
Olt, G. Russell	1925-1946	Thompson, William E.	1978-1979,
Perry, Estel E.	1947-1962		1979-1989
Perry, Guy	1978-1982	Towers, Frank	1953-1958
Pinyoun, Frederic	1970-1975	Wilson, Joseph T.	1925-1947
Poe, Carl M.	1975-1980	Wood, Robin J.	1990-present
Quinn, C. Lowery	1939-1954	Woodsome, Richard C.	1969-1976
Reardon, Eugene A.	1932-1934	Wright, Walker	1925-1933
		Wyatt, Lawrence P .	1984-1985

Appendix B

Institutional Aims and Objectives: 1954

The following statement appeared in the A. C. Catalog for several years, including 1954.

Anderson College is a Christian college. It seeks to give the student a unified philosophy of education and an over-all view of human life and destiny. It holds that the central factor of unification is theological and that true education must proceed in harmony with the Christian revelation. Thus does Anderson College seek to graduate men and women who are convinced Christians and who are prepared to present rational justification for their beliefs and manner of life.

The general purpose of the College is to give its students an understanding and appreciation of the cultural and scientific achievements of man, both past and present; to inspire them with a love for truth and beauty; and to prepare them to live in society effectively for themselves and helpfully for others.

The college recognizes as basic in the realization of its objectives that each student is a distinct personality, and that the fullest development of his personality can come only through a process of educational guidance sufficiently individualized to meet the particular needs of each student. The College believes that personality develops best under democratic processes; therefore it delegates to both faculty and students the fullest powers possible to determine and to reach life's highest goals.

In a more particular sense the aim of Anderson College is fivefold:

1. It would give to the students in his four years here the techniques of learning, so that clear thinking may be stimulated; that wholesome attitudes may be created in such relationships as involve homemaking, money-making, forming of friendships, practicing of professions; and that the student may adjust himself to the religious, social, political, economic, and physical world in which he lives.

2. It would provide a general education, especially in its lower division courses, so that the student may know, adjust himself to, and appreciate the world of which he is a part.

3. It would give such bases in preprofessional courses as are sound and as are required in the professions of medicine, law, engineering, and the ministry, and also lay the foundation for graduate study in the humanities, the social studies, and religion.

4. It would prepare students to enter the ministry, the fields of religious education, music, teaching, social work, and business; but it does not profess to complete training in these fields.

5. It would welcome students of all faiths. In a specific way the Church which supports and controls the institution looks to it for the training of her youth. Through Anderson College the Church seeks to conserve and to train for leadership the youth of the Church of God."

Appendix C

Board of Trustees' Statement on Educational Philosophy, June 1981

As part of its major report to the General Assembly of the Church of God, June 16, 1981, the Board of Trustees made the following statements about the educational philosophy of the campus. They were in direct response to the many related concerns expressed by various church leaders in the 1979-80 period.

"Humanism"

There is today a widespread and influential approach to truth and value, an approach which can be called "secular humanism." It has been formalized in documents like "Humanist Manifestos I and II" (1933 and 1973) and is popularized in many forms. It tends to exalt inordinately both human reason and potential, while failing to acknowledge the existence and relevance of God in all such matters. This secular humanism is alien to the assumptions of the Christian faith and to the very foundations of a Christian liberal arts college. Therefore, the educational philosophy of Anderson College does not subscribe to secular humanism. It seeks instead to approach the human condition and the human hope in the light of God's revelation of Himself and His will in Jesus Christ (7).

The Heart of a Christian Liberal Arts College

As a Christian liberal arts institution, Anderson College offers a comprehensive curriculum representing the full range of historic academic disciplines, presented in the context of Christian traditions and understandings. It prizes truth and wisdom, and demands honest inquiry into all areas of available knowledge. The integrity of the academic process is valued highly and enables this College to fulfill its mission of preparing Christian young persons to become competent and productive Christian professionals. For more than 50 years Anderson College has been a strong, growing and vital Christian liberal arts college, with several programs which distinguish it. The Board of Trustees is determined to continue and extend this commitment to be a Christian liberal arts college at its best (8).

The Faculty and Creed-Signing

It is the position of the Board of Trustees that the historic opposition of the Church of God Reformation Movement to standardizing and legislating formal creedal statements has been wise and should be maintained. The intended unity among Christians is not based on the achievement of full agreement on all theological questions. Rather, it is based on a common membership in the Church through the grace of God and is anchored by a common commitment to the centrality of Christ and the authority of the Word of God. Anderson College does care deeply about the theological convictions of its faculty; however, it believes that the signing of a belief statement or creed is both inappropriate and ineffective as a condition of employment (8).

The Kind of Faculty and Staff Desired

There are several existing patterns for the building of the faculty in a Christian college; they range from the model of planned diversity (securing a great range of faculty and scholars, Christian and non-Christian) to a model allowing for only faculty of one point of view (for example, persons willing to sign a particular theological creed). Anderson College through the years has rejected both of these models. By contrast, our model is this: for our faculty of more than 100 persons, teaching in 22 major areas, we require a considerable breadth of credential, competence and experience. Our educational program is stronger when there is breadth, weaker when uniformity is imposed. It is the position of the Board of Trustees that we shall aspire to selecting vital, practicing Christian persons; we shall be in our practice as close to that ideal as the range of qualified applicants would allow; that some positions will go unfilled rather than be staffed by persons unqualified academically or spiritually; that the welfare of the student always should be a primary consideration; that our diversity must be framed within our educational philosophy and mission; and that persons will not knowingly be employed or tenured unless they actively support the mission and goals of the College (8-9).

Employment Standards

Anderson College seeks to employ persons who subscribe to its educational mission and whose personal and professional lives reflect:

1. A belief in and commitment to Jesus Christ and the Christian faith as these are interpreted through the historic witness of the Bible and the contemporary ministry of the Holy Spirit.
2. A vitality of Christian experience which is maturing in insight and application and which is appreciative of differing viewpoints.
3. Evident competence and a commitment to the continuing development of one's abilities.
4. A commitment to liberal arts education and preparation to serve in an environment of purposeful and rigorous inquiry.
5. Obvious skills in the art of teaching and recognized mastery of relevant subject matter.
6. A capability, by temperament, preparation and will, to support students as they confront the intellectual, social, physical, emotional and spiritual challenges of their lives.
7. A sensitivity and support for the ethos and traditions of the campus community (19).

Appendix D

Institutional Mission: Statement, Sources, Implications, Applications (1982-1991)

MISSION STATEMENT   **(Adopted, Board of Trustees, October 1982)**
> To be an institution of Christian higher education at its best. We understand this to mean building that quality program which will enable each member of the campus community to become stronger in body, mind and spirit; to experience what it means to love God and "neighbor"; to purposefully adopt a style of servanthood in all of life.

MISSION SOURCES   **(Adopted, Board of Trustees, April 1988)**
The mission of Anderson University is informed significantly by the liberal arts tradition and relationship with the Christian community in general and the Church of God movement in particular. The rigor of academic inquiry, the dignity of persons, the cruciality of relationships and the authority of Biblical revelation all are fundamental in the design and implementation of the undergraduate, graduate, continuing education and community service programs of the institution.

Anderson University is a voluntary community of persons committed to learning, growing and serving. The central basis of this community is agape, which is understood to mean a seeking after the highest good of all persons in the community and, concurrently, the highest good of the community itself.

It is foundational to the nature, history and mission of this educational community to define the "highest good" in the context of the Christian faith, particularly the conviction that Jesus Christ is Savior and Lord and that discipleship is to be interpreted by the historic witness of the Bible and the contemporary ministry of the Holy Spirit.

MISSION IMPLICATIONS   **(Adopted, Board of Trustees, April 1988)**
There are a series of implications for the life of this community which grow out of the institution's mission. They are informed by and begin to illustrate the meanings of a servanthood style of life and a commitment to agape as defined above. Some of them were seen in the earliest Christian church (Acts 2) as it sought to translate faith into community life. All of them are central aspirations for the life of Anderson University. They include:

     A. An expectation that witness to the implications of God in Christ will characterize community life;

     B. An atmosphere of openness, honesty and questing after truth, recognizing that even traditional formulations of faith and knowledge are never fixed or understood similarly by all;

     C. A conscious breaking down of the barriers of gender, race and social class in favor of genuine valuing of persons as persons;

     D. A commitment of time, abilities and resources to those in need;

     E. A sharing of power, balancing the best use of gifts and experience and the need for functional community life with the desire to nurture the integrity and sense of participation of all community members;

F. A freedom to live, think and grow, but not a selfish, uninhibited freedom which does not serve the well-being of oneself or others in the community.

G. A responsibility of all community members increasingly to embody the community ideals, to represent the community in the world and, as necessary, to refine the community through constructive confrontation.

MISSION: CURRENT APPLICATIONS
(Approved as accurate, Board of Trustees, November 1988)

In carrying out her mission as a servant institution, Anderson University seeks to offer quality academic programs, primarily on campus but potentially in other settings, as follows:

1. Undergraduate Education. Through its undergraduate college, the University offers Bachelor or Associate degree work in a wide range of academic disciplines, primarily to the traditional, residential, undergraduate degree-seeking student.

2. Seminary Education. Through the graduate School of Theology, the University offers Master degree work for the professional education of pastors and specialized ministries in the life of the Church of God and the broader Christian church. Through its Center for Pastoral Studies, the School of Theology also offers wide-ranging in-service educational opportunities.

3. Adult and Continuing Education. Through its Division of Adult and Continuing Education and through cooperative programs with other institutions, the University offers a broad range of course work to non-traditional students in the Anderson area. These courses may be taken for life or professional enrichment, or may be applied to existing or specially developed degree programs of the University.

4. Graduate Education. The University will offer additional graduate programs in selected areas where a demonstrated need exists, where quality can be assured and where institutional mission is supported.

MISSION: SCHOOL OF THEOLOGY
(Approved, Board of Trustees, May 3, 1991)

The Mission of the School of Theology of Anderson University is: To educate at the graduate professional level both men and women for Christian ministry. To this end, we are committed to be a community of scholars who are church-related, and in whose character and servanthood the following are vitally linked: biblical faith; academic integrity; Christian spirituality; love for persons; and a responsible relation with the created order and all humankind.

413

Appendix E

Academic Freedom and Responsibility

The following statement was adopted by the Board of Trustees in April 1984 and remains the current stance of the institution in regard to the crucial issue of "academic freedom" as it relates to professional standards and Christian faith.

Anderson University, including its undergraduate and graduate schools, seeks to be a marketplace of ideas, experiments and growth experiences. It is dedicated to cultivating in each individual an awareness of the physical world, a sense of history, an appreciation of culture, a spiritual maturity, a social conscience and an interest in the worth of ideas regardless of their immediate utility.

The University has a responsibility throughout its curriculum to raise questions of truth, value, meaning and morality, not escaping easily into a false objectivity or sterile neutrality. The University maintains a Christian perspective, but does not wish to be guilty of an unexamined religious conformity. It lives in an atmosphere of free inquiry, even while it affirms that all knowledge is understood most fully in the light of God's redemptive activity in Jesus Christ. Its goal is to approach wisdom through a comprehensive study of human knowledge, experience and potential in the light of Biblical revelation. It assumes that Christian belief, rather than being an imposed restraint on the academic process, can and should be an enrichment of it and the basis for an integrated worldview.

All faculty members, whether tenured or not, are entitled to the privileges and obligated by the responsibilities of academic freedom. The privileges are: (1) a faculty member is free in the classroom to discuss openly and fully all issues which are within the member's area of academic competence and are relevant to the subject of the class; and (2) a faculty member is free to conduct research and then publish the results, subject to the time constraints of assigned institutional duties. The responsibilities are: (1) a faculty member, when speaking or publishing inside or outside the classroom, should at all times seek accuracy of statement, exercise appropriate restraint, show respect for the opinions of others and make clear that he/she, particularly outside the classroom, is not acting as a spokesperson for the University; and (2) a faculty member is to exercise academic freedom with discipline, responsibility and in the context of the assumptions of this policy statement and the particular mission of Anderson University.

414

Appendix F

FACULTY ROLL OF HONOR

The following faculty persons served Anderson University and successive generations of its students on a full-time basis for at least twenty-five years each. The competence, dedication and sacrifice of persons such as these have enabled the University to reach toward its mission of being "an institution of Christian higher education at its best." These represent scores of others who also served long and well. We of the present and the future have the opportunity and challenge to stand on the sturdy foundations laid by the following group of faculty men and women and their many distinguished colleagues over the years.

BEARD, Norman E.	1958-	International Education, Dean of Students, Director, TRI-S, 1964 to present
BENGTSON, F. Dale	1960-	Music, Dean of the School of Arts, Culture and Religion, 1983 to present.
BREITWEISER, D. Paul	1943-1972	Music
CALLEN, Barry L.	1966-	Christian Theology, Dean of the School of Theology, 1974-1983; Dean of the College, 1983-1988.
CLAUSEN, Henry C	1917-1945	Music
CLEAR, Valorous B.	1947-1980	Sociology, Social Work, Criminal Justice
COOK, Kenneth E.	1957-1990	Chemistry
COTTINGHAM, Elsie E.	1964-	Librarian
DEUBACH, Vila	1935-1974	English, Coordinator of Student Personnel, Librarian
FALLS, R. Glenn	1952-1987	Business, Accounting
FARMEN, William J.	1964-	Psychology
GOODMAN, Delena	1952-1983	Librarian
HALDEMAN, Walter S.	1933-1958	Religious Education
HARBRON, Thomas R.	1961-	Physics, Computer Science
HARPER, Elaine J.	1950-1985	English
HARTSELLE, Cecil H.	1924-1963	Music
JEENINGA, Gustav	1960-1989	Old Testament, Archaeology
KARDATZKE, Carl	1933-1959	Education
KOGLIN, Anna	1923-1956	German, Greek
KUFELDT, George	1961-1990	Old Testament
LASH, Howard	1961-1986	Education
LINAMEN, Harold F.	1949-1987	Business, Economics

MACKENZIE, Elbridge	1949-1980	Education
MACHOLTZ, James D.	1953-1985	Physical Education; Dean of the School of Theoretical and Applied Sciences, 1983-1985
MARTIN, Earl L.	1930-1957	Applied Theology; Dean of the School of Theology, 1950-1953
MAYO, Marie Joiner	1950-1989	Biology
MILLER, Adam W.	1945-1962	Bible. Dean of the School of Theology, 1953-62
MILLER, E. Darlene	1965-	Education, Dean of the School of Social and Professional Studies, 1983 to present.
MORRISON, John A.	1919-1958	Pastoral Ministries, President, 1925-1958
NEWBERRY, Gene W.	1946-1980	Christian Theology, Dean of the School of Theology, 1962-1974
NICHOLSON, Robert A.	1945-1990	Music. Dean of the College, 1958-1983, President, 1983-1990
NORRIS, M. LaVern	1958-1992	Sociology
OLT, G. Russell	1925-1958	Psychology. Dean of the College, 1925-1958
OSBORNE, Nancy	1943-1973	French
PISTOLE, Hollis S.	1959-1984	Pastoral Ministries
REARDON, Robert H.	1947-1983	Pastoral Ministries. President, 1958-1983
RENZ, Russell R.	1959-1989	Education
SALTZMANN, Paul W.	1959-	Mathematics
SHOOT, Frederick	1953-1980	Religion, Dean of Instruction
SMITH, John W. V.	1952-1980	Church History
SNYDER, Richard E.	1964-	Librarian
STRONG, E. Marie	1952-1978	Religion
TURNER, Kenneth V.	1966-	Mathematics
WEBBER, Gibb E.	1962-	English
WUNSCH, Gertrude E.	1955-1991	Physical Education
YOUNG, Richard M.	1962-	Physical Education

Appendix G
School of Theology
CUMULATIVE DIRECTORY OF FULL-TIME FACULTY

NAME	DISCIPLINE	YEARS OF SERVICE
Aukerman, John H .	Christian Education	1984 to present
Blackwelder, Boyce W.	New Testament	1963-1976
Bradley, James W.	Pastoral Ministries	1984 to present
Caldwell, Irene S	Christian Education	1966-1973
Callen, Barry L.	Christian Theology, Ethics	1972-1983
Coody, Burt E.	Psychology of Religion	1954-1965
Courtney, Donald	Christian Education	1961-1966
Crose, Lester	Christian Missions	1975-1978
Dwyer, Timothy R.	Old Testament	1990 to present
Froese, Walter	Church History	1980 to present
Goodman, Delena	Library Science	1952-1983
Gough, Louis F.	New Testament	1957-1961
Grubbs, Dwight L.	Applied Theology	1978 to present
Grubbs, Jerry C.	Christian Education	1973-1988
Hall, Kenneth F.	Christian Education	1978-1992
Johnson, Donald D.	Pastoral Care & Missions	1965-1968
Joiner, Ronald E.	Pastoral Ministries	1958-1963
Kendall, Charles T .	Library Science	1983 to present
Kufeldt, George	Old Testament	1961-1990
Leonard, Juanita L.	Church and Society	1987 to present
Martin, Earl L.	Christian Theology and Ministry	1950-1953
Massey, James E.	New Testament and Preaching	1981-1984, 1989 to present
Miller, Adam W.	New Testament	1950-1962
Miller, Gene	New Testament	1985 to present
Miller, T. Franklin	Pastoral Ministries	1975-1981
Newberry, Gene W.	Christian Theology	1950-1980
Phillips, Harold L.	Homiletics, New Testament	1976-1979
Pistole, Hollis S.	Pastoral Ministries	1959-1984
Shively, Fredrick H.	Pastoral Ministries	1974-1978
Smith, John W. V.	Church History	1952-1980
Stafford, Gilbert W.	Christian Theology	1976 to present
Stoneberg, Theodore A.	Pastoral Care	1981 to present
Strege, Merle D.	Historical Theology	1980 to present
Vayhinger, John M .	Psychology and Pastoral Care	1968-1981
Welch, Douglas E.	Christian Missions	1978 to present

*Other persons have provided crucial service to the seminary as part-time faculty members, and some of the above have taught part time in years other than those of their full-time service.

Appendix H

Undergraduate Departmental Organization and Chairs: 1992-93

School of Music and Art   F. Dale Bengtson, Dean
   Art   (acting)
   Music   F. Dale Bengtson

School of Science and
  Humanities   Blake Janutolo, Dean
    Bible/Religion/Philosophy   Merle D. Strege
    Biology   Susan Speece
    Chemistry   Dale Bales
    English   Kevin Radaker
    Mathematics   Stanley Stephens
    Modern Foreign Languages (acting)
    Nursing   Patricia Bennett
    Physical Education   Rebecca Hull
    Physics   Lawrence Shaffer
    Psychology   Curtis Leech

School of Business   Kenneth Armstrong, Dean
   Business/Economics   Kenneth Armstrong
   Computer Science   James Lewis

School of Social and
Professional Studies   Darlene Miller, Dean
   Communication   Donald Boggs
   Education   Barbara Jones
   History/ Political Science Douglas Nelson
   Sociology/Social Work
    Criminal Justice   Bruce Mac Murray

Note: Comparable information for 1960-61 found in Table 16.

Appendix I

Student Organizations: 1977-78 and 1990-91

	Approx. No. of Participants 1977-78	Approx. No. of Participants 1990-91
1. Academic		
Honor Societies		
Alpha Chi (Upper Class Academic)	70	63
Alpha Lambda Delta (Freshmen Women/Men)	46	NA
Alpha Lambda Delta (Freshmen Women)	NA	20
Alpha Mu Gamma (Foreign Language)	NA	20
Alpha Psi Omega (Drama)	30	13
Delta Mu Delta (Business)	30	13
Delta Sigma Rho/Tau Kappa Alpha (Forensics)	NA	1
Kappa Delta Pi (Education)	69	25
Kappa Mu Epsilon (Mathematics)	14	14
Phi Eta Sigma (Freshmen Men/Women)	20	NA
Phi Eta Sigma (Freshmen Men)	NA	51
Pi Kappa Lambda (Music)	12	4
Sigma Tau Delta (English)	12	19
Sigma Zeta (Science)	40	30
Recognition Groups		
Society for Collegiate Journalists	8	NA
Music		
AU Chorale (Choir)	56	56
Brass Emsemble	NA	19
Concert Band	NA	65
Jazz Combo	NA	10
Jazz Ensemble	NA	25
Male Chorus	52	58
Percussion Ensemble	NA	10
Symphonic Choir	NA	80
Wind Ensemble	47	50
Women's Chorus	NA	68
Brass Quintet	5	NA
Campus Chorale	76	NA
2. Religious Life		
Fellows in Ministry (ACUME)	243	386
Anderson University Center for Ministry Education		
Religious Life Council	8	NA
Campus Ministries Committee	NA	2

Campus Ministries Student Association	NA	2
Workcamps	NA	25
Prison Ministry	NA	15
Adopt-a-Grandparent	NA	32
Students Offering Unconditional Love (SOUL)	NA	50
Study Buddies	NA	60
Search Groups	NA	50

3. Residential

Men and Women's Representative Councils	52	NA

4. Student Government

Student Government Association	12	NA
Anderson University Student Association	NA	33

5. Social Life

Adelpha Philos	30	20
Adelphos	25	8
Agathos	45	40
Amici	28	50
Arcita	24	NA
Arete Pep	48	39
Booster	64	13
Business Club	40	NA
Camarada	50	113
Campus Activities Board	NA	10
Dativus	18	54
Eniteo	NA	60
God Squad	45	NA
International Club	70	NA
International Student Association	NA	30
L'Amifidel	NA	30
Multi-cultural Student Union	NA	40
Novus Dux	NA	4
Sachem	35	25
Sourettes	30	NA
Student Activities Department	49	NA
Taeda	15	14
Xenos	NA	26

6. Athletics (Men's)

Baseball	23	24
Basketball	36	19
Cross-Country	15	14
Football	60	74
Golf	20	12

Softball	18	NA
Tennis	25	7
Track	30	NA
Volleyball	15	NA
Wrestling	10	NA

7. Athletics (Women's)

Basketball	NA	13
Cross-Country	NA	10
Softball	NA	13
Tennis	NA	17
Track	NA	25
Volleyball	NA	13
Intramurals	624	910
Bowling Leagues	60	NA

8. Special Events Committee

Homecoming	15	NA
May Festival	20	NA
October Fest	20	NA

9. Interest Groups

Accounting Club	NA	30
American Marketing Association	NA	50
Business Club	40	NA
Debate Team	15	7
French Interest Circle	20	NA
Student Nurse Association	30	20
Students in Free Enterprise	NA	20
Model United Nations Team	15	17

10. Special Services

Center for Public Service	50	40
VITA (Tax assistance program)	NA	20

11. Publications

The *Andersonian* — Student Newspaper	15	12
The *Echoes*—School Yearbook	20	12

Appendix J

Intercollegiate Athletics
Head Coaches, Most Valuable Players, and School Records

Three men's sports are highlighted here because of their longevity of play, visibility to the public, and availability of records. See Table 27 which lists the beginning years of all intercollegiate sports, women's and men's.

FOOTBALL

	COACHES	MOST VALUABLE PLAYERS
1947-48	Frank Hedden	James Macholtz
1948-49	Frank Hedden	Carter Byfield
1949-50	Robert Kerr	Robert Absher
1950-51	Robert Kerr	James Macholtz
1951-52	Robert Kerr	(Not Available)
1952-53	James Bronson	Ronald Patty
1953-54	James Macholtz	Ronald Patty
1954-55	James Macholtz	James Wehsollek
1955-56	James Macholtz	James Wehsollek
1956-57	James Macholtz	James Wehsollek
1957-58	James Macholtz	William Norris
1958-59	James Macholtz	Gordon Taylor
1959-60	James Macholtz	Paul Lambert
1960-61	James Macholtz	Gus Carlson
1961-62	James Macholtz	Nat Johnson
1962-63	James Macholtz	Ronald Parr
1963-64	James Macholtz	Larry Davy
1964-65	Richard Young	Richard Sharp
1965-66	Richard Young	Richard Sharp
1966-67	Richard Young	James Dunnhoft
1967-68	Richard Young	Ted Williams
1968-69	Richard Young	Mike Wood
1969-70	Richard Young	Terry Murawski
1970-71	Richard Young	Ray Monroe
1971-72	Richard Young	Neal Rector
1972-73	Richard Young	Lee Mack
1973-74	Richard Young	Buckie Bookhart
1974-75	Richard Young	David Courtney
1975-76	Richard Young	Donald Courtney
1976-77	Donald Brandon	David Courtney
1977-78	Donald Brandon	John Bargfeldt

1978-79	Kevin Donley	Phil Kalbaugh
1979-80	Kevin Donley	Phil Kalbaugh
1980-81	Kevin Donley	Mike Shelburne and Brian Stoneking
1981-82	Kevin Donley	Mark Gittins and Charles Rhudy
1982-83	Michael Manley	Kevin Vogt
1983-84	Michael Manley	Kevin Vogt
1984-85	Michael Manley	Ronald Norton
1985-86	Michael Manley	Kenneth Dodson
1986-87	Michael Manley	Dennie Mitchell
1987-88	Michael Manley	Ryan Moe
1988-89	Michael Manley	Trent Garrett
1989-90	Michael Manley	W. Brad Lamb
1990-91	Michael Manley	W. Brad Lamb
1991-92	Michael Manley	Larry Bryant

SCHOOL RECORDS

Most Team Victories in a Season.....9 in 1970
Most Total Offense in a Season......4,136 yards in 1990
Career Rushing Leader....................Larry Bryant, 1988-91, 3,287 yards
Career Passing Leader....................Terry Murawski, 1966-1969, 5,778 yards
Career Pass Receiving Leader.........Brad Lamb, 1988-1990, 3,205 yards
Career Touchdowns Scored.............Brad Lamb, 1988-1990, 36

BASKETBALL

	COACHES	MOST VALUABLE PLAYERS
1947-48	Frank Hedden	John Wilson
1948-49	Frank Hedden	John Wilson
1949-50	Robert Kerr	James Woodward
1950-51	Robert Kerr	Charles Harris
1951-52	Robert Kerr	Richie Brown
1952-53	Ernest Rangazas	Jack Howell
1953-54	Ernest Rangazas	Richie Brown
1954-55	Robert Macholtz	Robert Culp
1955-56	Robert Macholtz	Jack Wilson
1956-57	Robert Macholtz	Jack Wilson
1957-58	Robert Macholtz	Gary Ausbun
1958-59	Robert Macholtz	Pete Culp
1959-60	Robert Macholtz	Kenneth Strawn
1960-61	Robert Macholtz	Kenneth Strawn
1961-62	Robert Macholtz	KennethStrawn
1962-63	Robert Macholtz	Kenneth Strawn

1963-64	Robert Macholtz	James Fisher
1964-65	Robert Macholtz	Gary Pate
1965-66	Robert Macholtz	Gary Pate
1966-67	Robert Macholtz	Charles Hise
1967-68	Ronald Parr	Ronald Long
1968-69	Robert Macholtz	Ronald Long
1969-70	Robert Macholtz	Doug Jennings
1970-71	Robert Blume	Tim Miller
1971-72	Robert Blume	Steve Lewis
1972-73	Robert Blume	Entire Team
1973-74	Robert Blume	Arte Lawson
1974-75	Robert Blume	John Carswell
1975-76	Barrett Bates	Jeff Jenness
1976-77	Barrett Bates	James Scoby
1977-78	Barrett Bates	DeNorris Boyd
1978-79	Barrett Bates	Curt Moreillon
1979-80	Barrett Bates	Larry Griffin
1980-81	Barrett Bates	Larry Griffin and Mike Burton
1981-82	Barrett Bates	Norm Bass and Doug Reams
1982-83	Barrett Bates	Rick Lantz
1983-84	Barrett Bates	Brian Stevens
1984-85	Barrett Bates	Jeff Howard
1985-86	Barrett Bates	Jeff Howard
1986-87	Barrett Bates	Jim O'Bold
1987-88	Barrett Bates	Tom Slyder
1988-89	Barrett Bates	Kenlin Kropf
1989-90	Barrett Bates	Brennan Lein
1990-91	Barrett Bates	Chris Lewis
1991-92	Barrett Bates	Pat Roberts

SCHOOL RECORDS

Most Team Victories in a Season.....26 in 1960-61
Most Total Offense in a Season........2,609 points in 1960-1961
Most Points Scored in a Season........681 points, Jack Wilson, 1957-1958
Most Career Points Scored...............2,142, Kenneth Strawn, 1959-63

BASEBALL

COACHES		MOST VALUABLE PLAYERS
1947-48	Frank Hedden	(None named until 1960-61)
1948-49	James Sibert	
1949-50	Donald Barnett	
1950-51	Donald Barnett	
1951-52	Ernest Rangazas	
1952-53	Ernest Rangazas	
1953-54	Robert Macholtz	
1954-55	Robert Macholtz	
1955-56	Ernest Rangazas	
1956-57	Ernest Rangazas	
1957-58	Ernest Rangazas	
1958-59	Ernest Rangazas	
1959-60	Paul Stravakos	
1960-61	Carl Erskine	Robert Adcock
1961-62	Carl Erskine	Robert Adcock
1962-63	Carl Erskine	Robert Adcock
1963-64	Carl Erskine	Robert Weigle
1964-65	Carl Erskine	Robert Weigle
1965-66	Carl Erskine	N/A
1966-67	Carl Erskine	N/A
1967-68	Carl Erskine	Terrell Tierney
1968-69	Carl Erskine	Joseph Snowden
1969-70	Carl Erskine	N/A
1970-71	Carl Erskine	Scott Kirksey
1971-72	Donald Brandon	Hollis Sharpe
1972-73	Donald Brandon	David Coolidge
1973-74	Donald Brandon	Randy Wilson
1974-75	Donald Brandon	Randy Wilson
1975-76	Donald Brandon	John Bargfeldt
1976-77	Donald Brandon	Maury Hoover
1977-78	Donald Brandon	Michale Getkin
1978-79	Donald Brandon	Rod Nealeigh
1979-80	Donald Brandon	Rod Nealeigh
1980-81	Donald Brandon	Donald Morris
1981-82	Donald Brandon	Donald Morris
1982-83	Donald Brandon	Robert Fields
1983-84	Donald Brandon	Tom Price
1984-85	Donald Brandon	Jeff Wild
1985-86	Donald Brandon	Craig Wilson

1986-87	Donald Brandon	Rick Hurni
1987-88	Donald Brandon	Andrew MacLachlan
1988-89	Donald Brandon	Brian Heigle
1989-90	Donald Brandon	Brian Heigle
1990-91	Donald Brandon	Bryan Spetter
1991-92	Donald Brandon	Brian Cruz and Chris Hoeppner

SCHOOL RECORDS

Most Team Victories in a Season.....47 in 1990
Most Career Pitching Victories........37, Brian Heigle, 1987-1990
Highest Career Batting Average......397, Rod Nealeigh, 1979-1980
Most Career Hits............................264, Andrew MacLachlan, 1984-1988
Most Career Home Runs.................39, Jeff Griffith, 1985-1987

Appendix K

Senior Class Presidents: 1922-1968   Homecoming Queens: 1949-1991
May Queens: 1939-1980

Year	Class Presidents	Homecoming Queens	May Queens
1921-22	Edgar Busch	(First in 1949-50)	(First in 1939-40)
1922-23	Emil Hollander		
1923-24	Daniel Ratzlaff		
1924-25	E. Earnest Branch		
1925-26	Amy Lopez		
1926-27	Benjamin Fansler		
1927-28	Alfred Pontius		
1928-29	Walter Haldeman		
1929-30	Gilbert Swart		
1930-31	Ralph Coolidge		
1931-32	John Lackey		
1932-33	Frank Towers		
1933-34	David Gaulke		
1934-35	Cecil Brown		
1935-36	Ida Byrd Rowea		
1936-37	Ralph Halverson		
1937-38	Kenneth Crose		
1938-39	Louis Gough		
1939-40	Fletcher Edmondson		Mona Morrison
1940-41	Frances Merrill		Deedie Leonard
1941-42	Guy Perry		Doris Martin
1942-43	Robert McDonald		Juanita Hunnex
1943-44	Maurice Berquist		June Cima
1944-45	Louis Meyer		Naomi Hunter
1945-46	Russell Whalen		Wilma Hurst
1946-47	Ralph Hatch		Thelma Whalen
1947-48	I. Joe Crane		Lois Miller
1948-49	John Kinney		Velma Snyder
1949-50	Donald Rice	Joyce Hensley	Maxine Grunwald
1950-51	Daniel Harman	Betty Harp	Yvonne Fortner
1951-52	Philip Kinley	Marilyn Riedlinger	Barbara Switzer
1952-53	Neil Shriner	Rowenna Dodge	Velma VanHoose
1953-54	Arthur Williams	Pat Beach	Cathy Bailey
1954-55	Richard Lau	Marian Panton	Janet Phillips
1955-56	David Day	Lois Stephenson	Donna Preston
1956-57	Robert Routt	Judy Wells	Judy Ballard
1957-58	A Thomas Cappas	Hester Click	Barbara Jo Rhoda

1958-59	O. Earnest Niehaus	Donna Roush	Carol Stevenson
1959-60	J. Gordon Palmer	Neoma Benson	Judy Ballard
1960-61	Nathan D. Williams	Judy Weeden	Juanita Evans
1961-62	Ruben Schwieger	Berniece Still	Kaye Hughes
1962-63	Ronald Parr	Sandra Haynes	Carolyn Lauteret
1963-64	Harold Smith	Mary Starkey	Karen McCurdy
1964-65	Charles Fox	Twila Tucker	Becky Davidson
1965-66	Carl Caldwell	Karen Seibert	Jeannine Thompson
1966-67	David Lewis	Zola Troutman	Sandy Adams
1967-68	Kenneth Hatch	Cozette Beach	Mona Hoffman
1968-69	(Last elected)	Jeanne Cook	Sheila Smart
1969-70		Carol Richardson	Linda Watkins
1970-71		Vicki Richards	Rose Marlowe
1971-72		Eunice Hollaway	Mary Mulford
1972-73		Debbie Conrad	Denise Reese
1973-74		Patsy Stofko	Sherry Hill
1974-75		Pam Miller	Cheryl Eckert
1975-76		Barb Bryant	Carol DeLong
1976-77		Lana La Viere	Rhonda Fair
1977-78		Pam Neidert	Cindy Carey
1978-79		Jody Shropshire	Kathy Newman
1979-80		Pam Snapp	Helen Van Straten
1980-81		Audrey M. Liechty	(*)
1981-82		Melanie Green	
1982-83		Rebecca Hart	
1983-84		Ellen Turner	
1984-85		Cindy Wiggins	
1985-86		Lori Fair	
1986-87		Lisa Dickerson	
1987-88		Georgana Pentz	
1988-89		Glendora Evans	
1989-90		Kelly Spaulding	
1990-91		Dana Ausbun	
1991-92		Martha Cameron	

*Ended program because of introduction of the January Term calendar.

Appendix L

Students, College, by Degree, Division and Major: 1956-57

I. Bachelor of Arts Degree.. *294*
  A.The Division of the Humanities
    1.   Art   2
    2.   English   15
    3.   Speech   4
    4.   French   1
    5.   German   0
    6.   Spanish   2
    7.   Philosophy   2
    8   Psychology   30
  B. The Division of the Sciences
    1.   Biology   18
    2.   Chemistry   17
    3.   Mathematics   0
  C.The Division of the Social Sciences
    1.   Accounting   1
    2.   Business Administration   2
    3.   Secretarial Science   0
    4.   Education   1
    5.   Home Economics   8
    6.   Physical Education   0
    7.   History   21
    8.   Sociology   26
  D. The Division of Bible and Religion
    1.   Applied Theology   1
    2.   Bible   82
    3.   Religious Education   3
  E. The Division of Music
    1.   Music   2
  F. Pre-Professional Courses
    1.   Pre-Nursing   4
    2.   Pre-Medicine or Dentistry   9
    3.   Pre-Medical Technologist   0
    4.   Pre-Engineering   11
    5.   Pre-Law   4
    6.   Not specified   28

II. Bachelor of Science Degree.. ***495***

    A. Business

1.	Accounting	18	
2.	Business Administration	28	
3.	Secretarial Science	1	
4.	Not specified	19	

    B. Teacher Training

       1. Secondary Education   191

              a. Language Arts   31

              b. Languages

                     French   1

                     German   0

                     Spanish   2

                     Not specified   1

              c. Social Studies   36

              d. Biological Sciences   16

              e. Physical Science with Math   32

              f. Business   3

              g. Health & Physical Education   42

              h. Not Specified   23

       2. Elementary Education   100

    C. Music   72

1.	Sacred	13	
2.	Piano	4	
3.	Voice	4	
4.	Violin	0	
5.	Organ	0	
6.	Public School Music	32	
7.	Not specified	19	

    D. Religious Education   42

    E. Not specified   14

III. Bachelor of Theology Degree *42*

    A.Bible and Religion   42

IV. Two-Year Certificate *3*

V. Three-Year Diploma *0*

VI. Not specified for any degree (*includes four graduates*)............................ *47*

      Total (not including evening school, special art
          or music, or graduate school)...**881**

Source of the above information was the final report of the President's Study and Planning Commission, 1955-1957.

Appendix M

Graduates by Majors: 1981-1991

In cases where a student completed multiple majors, only the first is listed.

	1981	1983	1985	1987	1989	1991
Accounting	25	28	23	23	21	24
Administration of Criminal Justice	7	9	9	6	13	6
American Studies	3	2	2	1	1	2
Applied Music	0	7	4	6	4	3
Art	5	2	5	2	1	0
Arts & Crafts	1	0	0	0	0	0
Athletic Training	0	1	1	5	3	6
Bible	2	6	6	6	4	1
Bio-Chemistry	12	13	9	11	10	11
Business Administration	20	1	3	3	0	0
Business Education	1	0	0	0	0	0
Chemistry	4	4	4	6	6	2
Christian Education	7	6	7	6	2	4
Church Music	2	1	0	1	1	4
Computer Science	2	10	18	5	9	2
Computer Science-Business	5	1	6	9	6	3
Computer Science-Math	3	2	0	2	0	0
Drama	0	0	0	1	0	1
Economics	4	3	9	3	2	1
Education	16	32	24	5	1	1
Elementary Education	19	29	27	32	26	39
English	11	9	4	4	11	6
English-Secondary Education	0	0	0	0	0	5
Family Science	0	0	0	0	0	5
Fine Arts/Studio	0	0	0	0	0	1
French	2	2	2	2	0	0
General Business	0	0	0	1	7	6
Government	12	6	8	5	0	0
German	1	0	3	0	1	1
Graphic Design	3	3	4	10	4	0
History	6	7	5	4	3	1
International Business	0	0	1	1	0	0
International Education	0	0	1	0	0	0
Journalism	0	1	0	1	0	0
Management	53	59	58	63	36	28

	1981	1983	1985	1987	1989	1991
Marketing	17	27	22	24	30	25
Marriage & Family	6	9	11	7	6	0
Mass Communication	4	10	20	13	16	10
Mathematics	9	5	7	5	6	4
Muesology-Museography	1	0	0	0	0	0
Music Education	8	6	4	3	6	11
Music Industry	2	7	1	2	1	0
Music-Business	0	0	0	1	7	8
Nursing	0	0	4	3	12	0
Philosophy	0	1	1	2	0	0
Physical Education	4	5	9	6	8	5
Physical Education-Secondary Ed	0	0	0	0	0	2
Physical Education & Health	7	0	0	0	0	0
Physics	2	2	2	1	3	1
Political Science	0	0	0	1	8	3
Psychology	22	22	15	17	13	18
Public Affairs	1	1	0	0	0	0
Public Relations	1	0	0	0	0	0
Recreation Leadership	1	2	0	0	0	0
Religion	32	28	26	14	9	9
Sacred Music	1	0	0	0	0	0
Science	1	1	0	4	1	0
Science-Secondary Education0	0	0	0	2	28	0
Social Studies	3	5	5	3	8	4
Social Work	10	7	7	11	15	19
Sociology	22	14	22	10	8	3
Spanish	4	4	5	1	1	2
Spanish-Secondary Education	0	0	0	0	0	1
Speech (General)	2	1	0	0	0	1
Speech Communication-Theatre	2	3	1	1	1	1
Speech-Broadcasting	3	3	1	0	1	0
Speech-Drama	2	2	2	0	0	0
Visual Arts	1	2	2	1	3	1

Appendix N

Record of Alumni Awards: 1977-1992

Year Honored	Seminary; Distinguished Senior	Seminary: Distinguished Service/Ministry
1977	Timothy Foreman	Harold Phillips
1978	Larry Logue	Ronald Fowler
1979	David East	Rodney Bargerstock
1980	Milan Dekich	Naftali Tsumah
1981	David Markle	Hillery C. Rice
1982	Bernard Barton	Sidney Johnson
1983	Donna Merrell	Barry Callen
		Robert Reardon
1984	Peggy Young	Leroy Fulton
		Ralph Anderson
1985	Robert Christensen	Gene Newberry
		Thomas Settlemyre
1986	Gordon Steinke	Donald Courtney
		Oral Withrow
1987	Dale Fontenot	Robert Edwards
		Wilfred Jordan
1988	Gregory Giles	Amelia Valdez Vasquez
		George Kufeldt
1989	Donald Taylor	Jerry Grubbs
		Gary Ausbun
1990	Sandra Hildebrand	James and Dorothy Sharp
		Mary Morgan
1991	Micheal Thompson	C. Richard Craghead
		Gilbert Stafford
1992	David Kardatzke	James Earl Massey

Year Honored	College: Alumni Service	College: Distinguished Alumni
1977	Marie Strong	Gertrude Collins Evans
		Nathan Smith
1978	Adam W. Miller	Larry Brown
		Lillian Meier*
1979	Ronald Fowler	
	Lottie Franklin	Grace Donahew
1980	Cleda Anderson	Carlton Cumberbatch
		Al Bennett
1981	Glenn Falls	Louis Gerig
1982	Geraldine Reardon	Ronald and Carolyn Patty
		Sandi and John Helvering
1983	Dale Bengtson	Hans Fictenberg
1984	Maxine Linamen*	Julian Ridlen
	Larry Maddox	
1985	LaVern Norris	Shirley King Coolidge
1986	(None)	Bessie Brown Willowby
		Melvyn Hester
1987	Walter Kufeldt	Robert Hugh Moss
1988	Frederick Shoot	Dorothy Nelis Nicholson
	Gustav Jeeninga	Sherrill Hayes
1989	Margaret Camm	Paul Ward
1990	Gertrude Wunsch	Robert Nicholson
	Kenneth Cook	Opal Bengtson
1991	Richard Snyder	Charles and Charlotte Wood
	Gladys Roark	
1992	Franklin Kenneth Hall	Rodney Bargerstock

* Awarded posthumously

Appendix O

Gallery of Distinguished Alumni

A select group of graduates in whom the Anderson campus takes pride, each also having been chosen to be the recipient of an honorary doctoral degree from his or her alma mater in recognition of distinguished lives of Christian service. These few represent thousands of others who have gone from this campus to make a significant difference in many walks of life. For a listing of all honorary degrees granted by the institution, see Table 8 and Appendix P.

Elver F. Adcock
B. Th. 1938
Dr. Divinity 1940

Esther (Boyer) Bauer
B. Th. 1930
Dr. Divinity 1980

Cauthion T. Boyd
B. Th. 1944
Dr. Divinity 1977

Milo L. Chapman
B. Th. 1939
Dr. Letters 1981

G. David Cox
B. A. 1955; M. Div.
Dr. Divinity 1978

John D. Crose
M. Div. 1983
Dr. Divinity 1939

Lester A. Crose
B. A. 1945
Dr. Divinity 1959

Robert Culp
B. A. 1957; B. D. 1961
Dr. Divinity 1989

Walter M. Doty
B. A. 1939
Dr. Letters 1981

Chester Edwards
B. S. 1955
Dr. of Laws 1970

Arthur R. Eikamp
B. A. 1943
Dr. Letters 1985

Ronald J. Fowler
M. Div. 1966
Dr. Divinity 1986

W. Shirell Fox
B. A. 1950
Dr. of Laws 1985

Leroy M. Fulton
B. A. 1953; M. Div. 1960
Dr. Divinity 1977

Gloria Gaither
B. S. 1963
Dr. Letters 1989

William (Bill) Gaither
B. S. 1959
Dr. of Music 1973

Max R. Gaulke
B. A. 1933
Dr. Divinity 1970

J. Horace Germany
B. Th. 1944
Dr. Letters 1981

J. David Grubbs
B. A. 1960
Dr. Divinity 1974

C. Wilbur Hatch
B. Th. 1925
Dr. Divinity 1957

Sandi Patty B. A. 1979
Dr. Music 1991

Betty Jo Hutchinson
B. S. 1944
Dr. Divinity 1984

Sidney M. Johnson
B. Th. 1952
Dr. Divinity 1989

Elmer E. Kardatzke
B. A.; 1935; B. D. 1937
Dr. Divinity 1966

Louis P. Meyer
B. S. 1945
Dr. Divinity 1987

Adam W. Miller
B. A. 1939
Dr. Divinity 1940

Arlo F. Newell
B. A. 1950
Dr. Letters 1992

Robert A. Nicholson
B. A. 1944
Dr. Laws 1990

Harold L. Phillips
B. Th. 1938
Dr. Divinity 1954

Leslie W. Ratzlaff
B. A. 1940; B. Th. 1941
Dr. Letters 1981

Robert H. Reardon
B. A. 1940
Dr. Laws 1983

Hillery C. Rice
B. Th. 1940; 1942
Dr. Divinity 1953

Ida Byrd Rowe
B. A. 1938; B. Th. 1938
Dr. Letters 1941

Helen A. Shoemaker
B. A. 1960
Dr. of Laws 1978

Ann (Espey) Smith
B. S. 1958
Dr. Divinity 1977

Steele C. Smith
B. Th. 1924; B. A. 1934
Dr. of Laws 1949

E. Marie Strong
B. S. 1945
Dr. Divinity 1978

Paul A. Tanner
B. Th. 1946
Dr. Divinity 1969

Oral Withrow
B. A. 1955; M. Div. 1961
Dr. Divinity 1988

E. E. Wolfram
B. A. 1947
Dr. Divinity 1962

Appendix P

Honorary Degrees Awarded 1937-1992
(Degrees awarded prior to 1937 are listed in Table 8.)

1937	Earl L. Martin, D. Div.		1961	Harry B. Mitchell, D. Div.
1937	M. Clifford Townsend, D. Laws		1961	Frank K. Zoll, D. Laws
1938	Arthur Campbell, D. Laws		1962	Herman B. Wells, D. Laws
1938	Rodney C. Caudill, D. Div.		1962	Oscar T. Simpson, D. Science
1939	John D. Crose, D. Div.		1962	E. E. Wolfram, D. Div.
1940	Elver F. Adcock, D. Div.		1962	Ivy Kahn, L. H. D.
1940	Adam W. Miller, D. Div.		1963	Harold W. Boyer, D. Div.
1941	Elsie E. Egermeier, D. Lit.		1963	Charles M. Shultz, L. H. D.
1941	Ida Byrd Rowe, D. Letters		1963	Izler Soloman, D. Music
1942	Floyd I. McMurray, D. Laws		1964	Archie A. Kinion D. Div.
1942	Estel E. Perry, D. Div.		1964	Everett A. Hartung, D. Laws
1943	(none)		1965	(none)
1944	(none)		1966	Birch E. Bayh, D. Laws
1945	W. Dale Oldham, D. Div.		1966	Donald L. Boyes, D. Laws
1946	(none)		1966	Elmo A. Funk, D. Laws
1947	(none)		1966	Elmer E. Kardatzke, D. Div.
1948	(none)		1966	Charles V. Weber, D. Div.
1949	William H. Hunt, D. Div.		1967	Bessie Hittle Byrum, L. H. D.
1949	Steele C. Smith, D. Laws		1967	John R. Emens, L. H. D.
1950	Harold E. Achor, D. Laws		1967	R. Eugene Sterner, D. Div.
1951	Ernest P. Kersten, D. Div.		1968	(none)
1951	Warren C. Roark, D. Div.		1969	Paul A. Tanner, D. Div.
1951	Henry F. Schricker, D. Laws		1969	Robert L. Kessler, D. Div.
1952	(none)		1969	Wilbur L. Schield, D. Laws
1953	John H. Kane, D. Div.		1969	William B. Harper, L. H. D.
1953	Theodore R. McKeldin, D. Laws		1969	Charles H. Malik, L. H. D.
1953	Hillery C. Rice, D. Div.		1970	Raymond S. Jackson, D. Div.
1954	Harold L. Phillips, D. Div		1970	Max R. Gaulke, D. Div.
1954	Harriet W. Toner, D. Lit.		1970	Richard G. Lugar, D. Laws
1955	Theodore A. Distler, D. Laws		1970	Chester L. Edwards, D. Laws
1956	T. Franklin Miller, D. Div		1970	Chester L. Edwards, D. Laws
1957	C. Wilbur Hatch, D. Div.		1970	Theodore M. Hesburgh, L. H. D.
1958	(none)		1971	Ross H. Minkler, D. Div.
1959	Frank H. Allis, D. Laws		1971	Ezekiel J. Morris, Jr., D. Div.
1959	David W. Gaulke, D. Science		1971	James Farmer, D. Laws
1959	Lester A. Crose, D. Div.		1971	Thomas E. Wilson, D. Laws
1959	William E. Reed, D. Div.		1971	E. Joe Gilliam, L. H. D.
1960	Denzel R. Lovely, D. Div.		1972	Bernard Gale Hetrick, D. Div.
1961	Landrum R. Bolling, L. H. D.		1972	Edith Green, D. Laws
1961	Gerhard Klabunde, D. Div.		1973	Nellie Snowden, D. Div.

1973	Marvin J. Hartman, D. Div.		1983	Robert H. Reardon, D. Laws
1973	William J. Gaither, D. Music		1984	Charles W. Colson, L. H. D
1973	Otis R. Bowen, D. Laws		1984	Carl D. Erskine, D. Laws
1974	Pansy Melvina Brown, D. Div.		1984	Edward L. Foggs, D. Div.
1974	J. David Grubbs, D. Div.		1984	Betty Jo Hutchison, D. Div.
1974	A. Morton Crim, D. Letters		1985	Arthur R. Eikamp, D. Letters
1974	Percy K. Jenkins, D. Science		1985	W. Shirell Fox, D. Laws
1974	Mark O. Hatfield, D. Laws		1985	Samuel G. Hines, and
1975	(none)			Louis H. Evans, Jr. L. H. D.
1976	David E. Martin, D. Laws			(granted jointly)
1976	Addie Wyatt, D. Laws		1986	Ronald J. Fowler, D. Div.
1976	Thomas R. McMahan, D. Laws		1986	Wilber Hardacre, D. Laws
1976	Sam J. Ervin, Jr. D. Laws		1986	Coretta Scott King, L. H. D.
1977	Wilbur S. Roby, D. Laws		1986	Fidel Zamorano, D. Div.
1977	Cauthion T. Boyd, D. Div.		1987	Steven C. Beering, D. Science
1977	Leroy M. Fulton, D. Div.		1987	Philip S. Cooper, D. Law
1977	Ann Espey Smith, D. Div.		1987	Hattie Downer, D. Div.
1978	Helen A. Shoemaker, D. Laws		1987	Richard C. Halverson, L. H. D
1978	G. David Cox, D. Div.		1987	Louis P. Meyer, D. Div.
1978	E. Marie Strong, D. Div		1988	Myron S. Augsberger, D. Laws
1978	John Nelson, D. Music		1988	Doris J, Dale, L. H. D.
1979	(none)		1988	Oral Withrow, D. Div.
1980	Fouad B. Melki, D. Div.		1989	Larrry Contos, D. Laws
1980	Ester Boyer Bauer, D. Div.		1989	Robert Culp, D. Div.
1980	Donald A. Noffsinger, D. Laws		1989	Gloria Gaither, D. Letters
1981	Milo L. Chapman, D. Letters		1989	Sidney M. Johnson, D. Div.
1981	Walter M. Doty, D. Letters		1990	Robert A. Nicholson, D. Laws
1981	James H. Germany, D. Letters		1991	Raymond Cotton, D. Div.
1981	Leslie W. Ratzlaff, D. Letters		1991	Sandi Patty, D. Music
1982	Helen E. Canaday, D. Laws		1991	Rudolph Smith, L. H. D.
1982	Edward P. Czapor, D. Laws		1992	Arlo F. Newell, D. Letters
1982	Benjamin F. Reid, D. Div.		1992	Cleve Grant, D. Div.
1982	William H. Hudnut,III, D. Laws			

Names and Numbers of Honorary Degrees
Awarded, 1957-1992:

	Number	Percent
A. Doctor of Divinity	43	39.1
B. Doctor of Laws	34	30.9
C. Doctor of Humane Letters	16	14.6
D. Doctor of Letters	8	7.3
E. Doctor of Music	5	4.5
F. Doctor of Science	4	3.6
TOTALS	110	100.0

Appendix Q

Commencement Speakers

1923	Four Students
1924	Joseph T. Wilson, Pastor, Evangelist, Louisville, Kentucky
1925	Robert L. Berry, Evangelist, Writer
1926	Charles E. Brown, Pastor, Detroit, Michigan
1927	A. T. Rowe, Pastor, Atlanta, Georgia
1928	Herbert M. Riggle, evangelist, author
1929	Eugene A. Reardon, Pastor, Denver, Colorado
1930	J. Raymond Schutz, Pastor, Professor of Sociology (Manchester College)
1931	Mack M. Caldwell, Alumnus, Church of God Pastor (Iowa)
1932	Fred B. Fisher, Methodist Pastor, Missionary to India
1933	Charles E. Brown, Editor,, Gospel Trumpet Company
1934	John A. Morrison, President, Anderson College
1935	Otto F. Linn, Professor of New Testament, Anderson College
1936	W. G. Spencer, President, Franklin College
1937	M. Clifford Townsend, Governor of Indiana
1938	C. Oscar Johnson, Pastor, Third Baptist Church, St. Louis
1939	W. H. Hunt, Pastor, First Church of God, Hamilton, Ohio
1940	Merton S. Rice, Pastor, Metropolitan Methodist Church, Detroit, Michigan
1941	Roy L. Smith, Editor of The Christian Advocate
1942	Floyd I. McMurray, Extension Dept., Indiana University
1943	Clyde E. Wildman, President, DePauw University
1944	Albert W. Palmer, President, Chicago Theological Seminary
1945	Clement T. Malan, Supt. of Public Instruction, Indiana
1946	James W. Clarke, Presbyterian Pastor, St. Louis
1947	D. Elton Trueblood, Professor, Earlham College
1948	Roy L. Smith, Editor of The Christian Advocate
1949	John A. Morrison, President, Anderson College
1950	Harold A. Bosley, Dean, Duke University Divinity School
1951	Henry Schricker, Governor, State of Indiana
1952	Denzel R. Lovely, Church of God Pastor, Los Angeles
1953	Theodore R. McKeldin, Governor, State of Maryland
1954	Russell J. Humbert, President, DePauw University
1955	Theodore A. Distler, Exec., Association of American Colleges
1956	Robert H. Reardon, Exec. Vice President, Anderson College
1957	Richard C. Raines, Bishop, Methodist Church, Indiana
1958	John A. Morrison, President, Anderson College
1959	David W. Gaulke, Physician, Houston, Texas
1960	W. Dale Oldham, Church of God Pastor, Anderson, Indiana
1961	Landrum R. Bolling, President, Earlham College
1962	Harold L. Phillips, Editor, Warner Press
1963	Carl F. H. Henry, Editor, Christianity Today
1964	Robert H. Reardon, President, Anderson College

1965   A. Blair Helman, President, Manchester College
1966   Birch E. Bayh, United States Senator, Indiana
1967   Robert H. Reardon, President, Anderson College
1968   O. P. Kretzman, President, Valparaiso University
1969   Charles H. Malik, Past President, U. N. General Assembly
1970   Theodore M. Hesburgh, President, University of Notre Dame
1971   James Farmer, U. S. Asst. Secretary, Health, Education, and Welfare
1972   Edith Green, Member, U. S. House of Representatives
1973   Robert H. Reardon, President, Anderson College
1974   Mark O. Hatfield, United States Senator, Oregon
1975   A. Morton Crim, News Anchor, Philadelphia
1976   Sam J. Ervin, Jr., Former U. S. Senator, North Carolina
1977   Otis R. Bowen, Governor, State of Indiana
1978   Robert H. Reardon, President, Anderson College
1979   Richard G. Lugar, United States Senator, Indiana
1980   Robert H. Reardon, President, Anderson College
1981   James Earl Massey, Speaker, Christian Brotherhood Hour
1982   William H. Hudnut III, Mayor, City of Indianapolis
1983   Robert H. Reardon, President, Anderson College
1984   Charles W. Colson, President, Prison Fellowship
1985   Louis H. Evans, Jr., Presbyterian Pastor, Washington, D. C.
1986   Coretta Scott King, President, Center for Nonviolent Change
1987   Richard C. Halverson, Chaplain, United States Senate
1988   Myron S. Augsburger, President, Christian College Coalition
1989   A. Morton Crim, News Editor, T V Anchor, Detroit
1990   Robert A. Nicholson, President, Anderson University
1991   Ronald J. Fowler, Pastor, Akron, Ohio (Retiring Board Chair)
1992   Robert H. Reardon, President Emeritus, Anderson University

Appendix R

Campus Buildings

BUILDING	**DEDICATION**	**PERSON(S) HONORED**

Morrison Hall October 1949 Dr. John A. Morrison

The first new building constructed on the Anderson University campus. It houses women and is named in honor of the late Dr. John A. Morrison, who came to the faculty in 1919 and served as Anderson College's first president and chief executive officer for 39 years (1925-1958).

Dunn Hall October 1954 Dr. S. P. Dunn

Memorializes the late Dr. S. P. Dunn, veteran Afro-American pastor who was a charter member of the Anderson College board of trustees and whose motion changed the institution's name from Anderson Bible Training School to Anderson College and Theological Seminary. (1925). He was the pastor of Metropolitan Church of God in Chicago for many years. Originally dedicated in 1954 as the "New Men's Residence Hall," it was officially named Dunn Hall in June 1960.

Wilson Library October 1957 Charles E. Wilson

(Prior to library expansion and joining with Byrd Library in 1989) Honors the late Charles E. Wilson, one-time general manager of Delco-Remy Division in Anderson, who was president of General Motors Corporation when invited by President Dwight Eisenhower to serve as U. S. Secretary of Defense.

Martin Hall June 1958 Dr. Earl Martin

Named for the late Dr. Earl Martin, who served Anderson College as trustee, vice president, acting president and was first dean of the graduate School of Theology. Houses women.

School of Theology June 1961

Serves ministerial students pursuing graduate degrees. The building houses classrooms and offices, the Jeeninga Museum of Bible and Near Eastern Studies, and Adam Miller Chapel, added in May 1974 and named in honor of Dr. Adam W. Miller, second dean of the School of Theology. From 1964 until the unification with Wilson Library in 1989, the building also housed Byrd Memorial Library.

O. C. Lewis Gymnasium October 1962 O. C. Lewis

Named for the late O. C. Lewis, widely known Church of God layperson and businessman in Sikeston, Missouri, Lewis Gymnasium houses classrooms and offices along with the basketball courts and other athletic facilities.

Olt Student Center October 1963 Dr. Russell Olt

Named for the late Dr. Russell Olt, first dean of Anderson College who served from 1925 until his death in 1958. Olt Student Center serves Anderson University students in numerous ways—food service, recreation, lounge facilities, student activities office, and bookstore.

Smith Hall   1964   Lillian Odell Smith
Residence hall for men memorializes Lillian Odell Smith, active laywoman in the Church of God.

Hartung Hall   October 1964   Everett & Ersele Hartung
Contains Anderson University's science complex as well as many classrooms that serve other areas of study. Hartung Hall is named in honor of the late Everett and Ersele Hartung, Anderson College benefactors and active leaders in the Church of God. A major expansion project was begun in 1992 to house the Bible and Religion and Nursing departments and to add general class-rooms and modernize science laboratories.

Mansfield Apartments   1967   C. C. & Ina Mansfield
The first housing units constructed to serve married students. They were named in appreciation for the generosity of the late C. C. and Ina Mansfield, veteran Church of God leaders in Oklahoma.

Boyes House   1968   Don & Beverly Boyes
Is the official home of the President of Anderson College, made possible through a generous gift of Don and Beverly Boyes, former general manager of Delco Remy Division in Anderson and vice president of General Motors Corporation on his retirement.

Myers Hall   October 1970   Linfield Myers
A women's residence hall named for Linfield Myers, Anderson banker and civic leader who had been a benefactor of Anderson College since its founding in 1917. Mr. Myers was chairperson-emeritus of the board of directors of the Anderson Banking Company.

Decker Hall   June 1971   Philip & Katherine Decker
The most imposing building on the Anderson University campus, housing classrooms, administra-tive offices, Center for Public Service, Instructional Materials Center, Computer Center, and other central campus functions. It is named for the late Philip and Katherine Decker, pioneer residents of the community of Anderson and parents of the late Mrs. Herman Krannert. A major gift from Mr. and Mrs. Krannert made the construction of Decker Hall possible.

Bennett Natatorium   October 1972   Dr. & Mrs. Rollie Bennett
Provides excellent swimming facilities for academic programming, intramural activities and inter-collegiate competition. It was a gift of Dr. and Mrs. Rollie Bennett, long-time Anderson area resi-dents.

Byrum Hall   June 1975   The Byrum Family
The first permanent tabernacle erected in Anderson by the Church of God after it had brought its publishing work to Anderson in 1906. The structure, dating from 1908, has been renovated as a home for Anderson University drama, musical, and other programs. Byrum Hall honors one of the foremost families in the history of the Church of God. Enoch E. Byrum became editor of the "Gospel Trumpet" upon the death of D. S. Warner. Noah Byrum, his brother, was business man-ager of the operation, serving as the company's first secretary-treasurer. Robert Byrum was archi-tect and builder of this structure as well as the campus Old Main (razed to build Decker Hall). Russell R. Byrum, son of Robert, was a member of the first faculty of Anderson Bible Training School. Bessie Byrum was the wife of Russell Byrum, missionary and a member of the first facul-

ty of the Anderson Bible Training School. Ruthven Holmes Byrum was founder and chair of the Anderson College art department.

Byers Hall   1977   A. L. Byers

Was purchased and remodeled to house the university's nursing department. The building original-ly was the home of Andrew. L. Byers, an early pioneer in the Church of God and managing editor of the Gospel Trumpet Company for many years.

Athletic Field Complex   October 1977

Consists of football and baseball fields, an all-weather running track, stadium seating, tennis courts, weight room, and practice fields. In 1985 the football field was named Macholtz Stadium to honor Dr. James Macholtz.

Krannert Fine Arts Center   April 1979   Ellnora Decker Krannert

Provides the first permanent campus facilities designed for art and music. The center consists of five structural units--two for music, one for art, one for classrooms, and one for art galleries. The facility honors the late Ellnora Decker Krannert, whose philosophy was influential nationwide in many educational disciplines, including the arts. The Krannert Fine Arts Center consists of several wings honoring Bill and Gloria Gaither, Wilbur and Eileen Schield, and Rev. Marvin L. Forbes, whose ministry had made a strong influence on the personal and professional life of Charles Schulz (artist of "Peanuts" fame).

Reardon Auditorium   April 1984   Robert H. Reardon

Honors Robert H. Reardon, second president of Anderson University. This 2,200 seat auditorium hosts numerous campus and community events, as well as the undergraduate chapel programming.

Robert A. Nicholson University Library   October 1989   Rober tA.Nicholson

Honors Robert A. Nicholson, third president of Anderson University. This university library has housed since 1989 the collections of the former Wilson and Byrd Libraries. It was named in Dr. Nicholson's honor in 1992.

Appendix S

Selected Campus Grants, Lilly Endowment, Inc.

Lilly Endowment, Inc., Indianapolis, Indiana, has been a major partner in assisting the campus to accomplish vital research, professional development, and building construction, program initiation, evaluation, and endowment.

YEAR	AMOUNT	PROJECT
1956	$ 50,000	Library Construction-matching grant
1957	$ 15,000	Improvement of Instruction
1960	$ 25,000	Four-year grant to buy books for Wilson Library
1961	$ 30,000	Three-year matching grant to add faculty to School of Theology
1963	$ 75,000	Hartung Hall
1964	$ 50,000	Hartung Hall
1965	$ 1,000	Support for TRI-S Initiation
1966	$ 13,500	School of Theology Jerusalem Seminar
	$ 25,000	School of Theology Library Development
1967	$ 5,000	Purchase of books for School of Theology Library
	$ 50,000	Annual Grant/ Science classrooms, land acquisitions, musical instruments
1968	$ 50,000	Annual Grant/Land acquisition, construction of bookstore
1969	$ 50,000	Annual Grant/Mobile offices, TRI-S, equipment purchase
1970	$ 50,000	Annual Grant/TRI-S, purchasing site for Myers Hall, equipment
1971	$ 50,000	Annual Grant/Remodel Hartung Hall for psychology department
1972	$ 50,000	Annual Grant/Relocate art department to Olt Student Center and remodel Wilson Library
1973	$ 50,000	Annual Grant/Unrestricted reserve
	$300,000	Center for Public Service (payable over three years)
	$500,000	Challenge grant, endowment campaign
	$ 25,000	Volunteer Teachers for Kenya
1974	$ 50,000	Annual Grant/Unrestricted Reserve
	$ 50,000	Volunteer Teachers for Kenya
	$250,000	Byrum Hall remodeling
1975	$ 50,000	Annual Grant/Unrestricted reserve
	$100,000	School of Theology Chapel Project

1976	$ 12,700	Flying Carpet Seminar
	$210,000	The AC Plan (three-year grant)
1977	$ 70,670	Two year grant for faculty development
1980	$ 21,368	Partial replacement funds for Indiana Educational Grant Awards Program
1983	$150,000	Curriculum Revision
	$ 23,360	Linkage with Public Schools
1986	$ 75,000	Institutional development & strategic planning
	$ 24,325	Faculty development
1987	$500,000	Dream of Distinction/Library Computerization and Expansion of Micro-Computer Lab
1988	$ 44,795	Nursing curriculum revision
1989	$ 47,000	Curriculum development
	$ 28,525	Trustee development for School of Theology Governance
1990	$ 75,000	Faculty Development Program
1991	$ 10,000	Institutional Ethics Program

(Left) Dr. Robert Glenn Falls   (Right) Dr. Marie Joiner Mayo

445

Appendix T

Record, Audio Taped Interviews
Oral History of Anderson University

Anderson, J. & C	8/15/89	Lambert, Lloyd	6/30/89
Baker, H. L.	1/31/90	Lash, Howard	8/30/89
Baker, Marvin	7/31/90	Lawson, David	1/4/90
Baker, Theodore	2/7/90	Linamen, Harold	5/18/89
Batdorf, J. & D.	6/30/89	McMahan, Thomas	11/9/8
Bauer, Esther	7/20/89	MacKenzie, Elbridge	6/6/89
Beard, Norman	8/2/89	Massey, James E.	2/14/90
Bengtson, D. & O.	8/23/89	Meyer, Louis	1/5/90
Blevins-Dicus, D.	8/11/89	Miller, Darlene	9/9/91
Boyer, Harold	9/26/89	Miller, F. & G.	8/15/89
Brown, Alfred	8/30/89	Miller, F. & G.	8/15/89
Byrd, C. & E.	11/15/89	Miller, Howard	9/28/89
Byrum, Russell	2/25/75	Moore, Ronald	3/12/90
Byrum, Russell	1/6/76	Newberry, Gene	7/20/89
Clear, Val	7/21/89	Nicholson, Robert	3/5/80
Crose, Kenneth	5/17/89	Nicholson, Robert	7/5/89
Edwards, James	2/22/90	Nicholson, Robert	11/30/89
Erskine, Carl	9/5/89	Nicholson, Robert	2/14/90
Falls, Glenn	5/31/89	Nicholson, Robert	3/22/90
Fox, Sherill (I)	9/26/89	Nicholson, Robert	6/4/90
Fox, Sherill (II)	1/10/90	Norris, Lavern	1/19/90
Franklin, Lottie	11/7/89	Olive, Gloria	10/11/89
Gaither, B. & G.	7/27/90	Patty, R. & C. & S.	6/29/90
Goodman, Delena	7/7/89	Phillips, Elwood	5/22/91
Grubbs, Jerry	1/30/90	Phillips, Harold	1/17/80
Hall, Kenneth	6/4/91	Pistole, Hollis	8/11/89
Hannah, James	6/27/89	Prunty, K. & F.	11/7/89
Harman, Daniel	1/18/90	Ragsdale, Elva	7/6/89
Harper, Elaine	5/31/89	Reardon, Robert	10/5/89
Hester, Melvin	7/29/89	Reardon, Robert	1/17/90
Hoffman, Mona	9/24/89	Reardon, Geri	10/5/89
Jeeninga, Gustav	5/12/89	Rees, James	6/6/89
Johnson, Donald	3/2/90	Reithmiller, Bill	11/16/89
Johnson, Sidney	12/5/89	Renz, Russell	6/30/89
Jones, Kenneth	6/23/89	Reynolds, Lawrence	6/14/90
Kane, J. & E.	3/16/90	Rice, Hillery	1/12/90
Kardatzke, Eva-Clair "Tip"	7/21/89	Rock, Robert	11/10/89
Kilmer, J. & R.	1/19/90	Schemmer, Betty	10/25/89
Koglin, Anna	3/11/75	Schieve, Jessie	12/14/89
Kufeldt, George	9/19/89		

Shoemaker, Helen	8/14/89	Tiesel, W. & M.	6/28/89
Shoot, Fred	7/6/89	Tjart, Peter	5/17/89
Schultz, Clair	8/31/89	VanDyke, Jack	6/12/89
Snowden, Roscoe	1/3/90	Weir, F. & E.	11/21/89
Sibert, James	2/2/89	Williams, Emery	1/11/90
Sowers, Austin	8/11/75	Wilson, John	6/5/89
Strawn, Lucille	7/20/89	Wood, Ray	5/22/91
Strege, Merle	3/16/90	Wunsch, Gertrude	6/8/90
Strong, Marie	12/18/89	Young, Richard	8/14/89
Tanner, Paul	1/3/90		

Appendix U

Selected Student Leaders: 1989-1992

	1989-90	1990-91	1991-92
Officers, Anderson University Student Association (AUSA)*			
President of the Student Body	Brad Colwell	Rudy Pyle, III	Rudy Pyle, III
Vice Presidents:			
Student Dev.	Beth Olson	Jeff Stutzman	Chris Mefford
Student Services	Rudy Pyle, III	Christi Kidwell	Debbie Williams
CAB	Marla Jenkins	M. Whittington	Christi Kidwell
Public Relations	Bart Caylor	Bart Caylor	Todd Hillwig
Chair of Senate	Tim Johnson	Mark Yoder	Dave Adams
Chief Justice	Steve Smith	Nichole Pugh	Nichole Pugh
Treasurer	Nichole Pugh	Angel Bates	Mark Yoder

Social Club Presidents*

Women

Aldepha Philos	Amy Moore	Melody Fletcher	Michelle Merckx
Arete Pep	Amy Schlieve	Julie Dinius	Donna Boner
Camarada	Judi Jo Boewe	Beth Apple	Cara Santeusanio
L'amifidel	Kate Kramer	Beth Holmes	Amy Overdorf
Taeda	Bridget Young	Robin Woodard	Susan Graves

Men

Agathos	Scott Martin	Scott Martin	Jason Esposito
Amici	Mark Savidge	Scott Edwards	Goose Gainey
Booster	Larry Wooley	Kevin Mitschelen	Dan Metzger
Dativus	Dwayne Goldman	Chris Mefford	Jeff Bell
Novus Dux	Dan Starr	Dan Combs	Chris Buyer
Sachem	(none listed)	Jeff Sherrill	Adam Brown

*(Source: As listed in the respective Student Life Handbooks)

448

Community Council, School of Theology

1989-90	1990-91	1991-92
Gerald Cullison	Bruce Applegate	Bruce Applegate
Jerry Davisson	Melanie Owens Cole	Steve Delisle
Dan Dudley	Steve Delisle	Cali Depue
Mike Hamm	Cali Depue	Owen Facey
Mark Lawson	Kelly Fair	Kelly Fair
Melanie Owens	Jon Grubbs	Jon Grubbs
Ann Sandlin	Judith Jennings	David Kardatzke
Ben Seutter	David Kardatzke	Mark Lawson
	Mark Lawson	Mitch Ripley
	Tim States	Tina True
	Carl Willans	Carl Willans

(Left) Brad Colwell, president, A. U. Student Association, 1988-90
(Right) Rudy Pyle, III, president, A. U. Student Association, 1990-92

449

APPENDIX V

Strategic Issues for the School of Theology

The following were listed by Dr. Barry L. Callen for the
board of trustees in August, 1990.

1. Through its Task Force on Governance and Polity, the Church of God is asking major questions of itself. The independence of the School of Theology from the university is not at issue now as it has been at times in the past—although the School of Theology could virtually disintegrate through uncoordinated, independent, and competitive programs in the church. *The issue*: The School of Theology, very much at the core of the university's structures and mission, must also be seen and function as the seminary of the whole church. The university has a stewardship of the seminary which it has carried well in the past for the whole church, in fact founded for the church primarily out of the vision of a few campus leaders thinking for the whole church.

2. The School of Theology is seeking a fresh path within the life of the changing structures of the university itself. Early ATS accreditation standards encouraged heavy and inefficient independence of the School of Theology within the university. The name change to "university" in 1987 was motivated in part to accommodate the results of that separateness within a larger whole. The undergraduate college greatly deemphasized the professional dimension of ministerial education after 1950, giving many people the impression that the college now was largely out of the business of ministerial education. Recently, however, these internal separations have undergone major change: "Christian Ministries" major in the college; college and seminary alumni organizations merged; libraries merged; admissions and other service areas under review; trustees structures, such as the separate SOT committee, under review as part of the Lilly grant program on trustee development. *The issue*: How best to program, staff, and support a seminary inside the larger university.

3. The original question posed in 1947-49 is being asked again in several ways. The question then was: "Do we in the Church of God need *our own* seminary?" Fifty years ago some of our best young leaders were going to "denominational" seminaries. It, therefore, was said that we needed graduate theological education "in a wholesome theological atmosphere . . . especially designed to fit them for the pastoral, evangelistic, religious education, and other fields of activity in the Church of God." Thus the School of Theology came into being. *The issue*: Is that distinctive Church of God focus still a driving motive for the SOT's continued existence? Is it what we now have? Is that distinctiveness what the church currently expects of the School of Theology? How ecumenical should the SOT's faculty and student body be in order to provide quality education and maintain a viable enrollment, without losing a particular reason for being? Are ecumenical alliances appropriate? Are there new alternatives in sight? Should we be looking for them?

4. How localized on the Anderson campus should the School of Theology of the future be? Many questions of educational philosophy surround this question. Community, e.g., is

assumed to be crucial to quality ministerial education and faith development, but it is hard to foster with a commuting adult population.[1] Theological education by extension is a contemporary phenomenon often called for, but it raises questions of quality control and loss of the community of learning. The desires to be relevant to the needs of minority ministerial students and to prepare students for ministry in an urban world sometimes are seen in tension with programs largely localized in Anderson, Indiana. *The issue*: How should new media technologies and extension opportunities be related to future School of Theology staffing and programming?

5. The Center for Pastoral Studies now is nearing twenty years of service and has been well accepted in the church as a crucial, practical arm of the School of Theology. The need for ministerial education in the Church of God is great and diverse because of widely ranging levels of preparation for it and time availability to pursue it. *The issue*: How central in the future of the School of Theology should be the continuing education of ministers, some with seminary degrees and some without even college degrees? What about the offering of the Doctor of Ministry degree as a specialized continuing education opportunity for some? How far can available resources be stretched? Where is the priority?

6. A perennial continuum in theological education is the one between a seminary being, on the one hand, a practical, professional school operating at the graduate level and, on the other hand, a graduate school of religious studies that includes some professional opportunities in the midst of its academic orientation. The School of Theology began with very practical, professional outcomes in mind, but also with programs like Oberlin in view and full accreditation as a goal. Academic standards were to be high, but not at the expense of the preparation of students for professional functioning in the real life of the church. *The issue*: Where is the School of Theology now on this continuum? Where ideally should it be? Accreditation has been achieved and a well-credentialed faculty assembled. Seminary graduates typically complain that they were not well prepared for practical things (maybe ones such as college students always complain about food service, no matter what is done!). Is the seminary to prepare both scholars and pastors for the life of the church?

7. It appears that the Church of God today, more than ever, needs visionary leaders and disciplined insight into the nature and demands of the faith in a fast-changing world. Surely, more than ever, the School of Theology can and must be central to the church's future. The Church of God movement agreed in principle in 1976 that "seminary training is the normal, the ideal level of initial preparation for the future young minister." That was quite a step forward from where the church was in 1950 at the seminary's founding. But it has been a step largely in principle only. Today, for a range of reasons, fewer students are seeking seminary education in the Church of God than were a decade ago, particularly in the church's seminary in Anderson. *The issue*: How can the importance of seminary education for ministerial candidates in the Church of God movement be transformed from a mere statement of ideal to functioning reality?

1. By 1990 the average age of a student in the School of Theology was about thirty-four.

APPENDIX W

THE COVENANT RELATIONSHIP
Anderson University and the Church of God Movement

A process was begun in the Robert A. Nicholson administration to develop a formalized "covenant" statement describing the relationship and commitments between Anderson University and the Church of God movement. Under the leadership of President James Edwards, this process was completed in 1992 with the statement's approval by the campus board of trustees. The statement sought to go beyond the existing legalities of such things as articles of incorporation and bylaws to a fresh articulation of how the campus and church are "bound together in mutual support and accountability through a voluntary, purposeful commitment."

As stated in May, 1992 by the University after a series of clarifying consultations with groups of representative church leaders, the specific covenant elements were worded as follows.

The University covenants with the Church of God:

• to maintain in an excellent manner its undergraduate, graduate and seminary programs of Christian higher education;
• to respect and treasure the authority of the Bible and the distinctive heritage of the Church of God;
• to provide preparation for Christian ministry both in the undergraduate schools and the graduate School of Theology; to offer meaningful in-service training opportunities to current ministers;
• to work diligently to attract and provide assistance to Church of God students who enroll in its programs; to be open and hospitable to other students to whom it can minister effectively;
• to reflect in its community life a commitment to diversity as found in the life and mission of the Church of God;
• to represent the Church of God well in the world of higher education;
• to exercise good stewardship of its human, physical and financial resources;
• to be accountable, through its board of trustees, to the Church of God which founded it and helps sustain it;
• to work with other ministries of the Church of God — international, national, state, regional and local — in a supportive and interdependent manner.

The University understands that the Church of God covenants:

• to seek to understand the functional distinction of a college or university and to support the particular ministry of Christian higher education with prayer, dialogue and caring;
• to share Anderson University's vision for the future and to assist in achieving that vision;

• to support Anderson University and its programs with appropriate financial resources through World Service;

• to exult constantly the calling to Christian ministry and to elevate the worthiness and importance of careful preparation through undergraduate and seminary education;

• to minister to and with Anderson University graduates and to provide a vital community of faith into which these gifted persons can be welcomed;

• to open and enable paths of communication between Anderson University (and other Church of God colleges) and young people who are thinking about attending a Christian college or university;

• to offer the friendship and fellowship which sustains this covenant in renewed experiences of the grace of Christ and the common life we hold together in the church, the body of Christ.

Such a covenant relationship was said to be founded on several premises that had been stated in the 1981 campus document "Anderson College: In Partnership with the Church." Those premises, repeated and reaffirmed in this 1992 covenant, were:

• Anderson University seeks to provide a superior quality of education;

• Anderson University has a faith perspective and is prepared to raise questions of truth, value, meaning and morality;

• Anderson University values the church relationship in which the thought and practices of the church and the methods and perspectives of the academic disciplines are enabled to probe and inform each other;

• Anderson University shares in the mission of Christ and therefore strives to have all aspects of campus life reflect His redemptive spirit and reverence His way of life;

• Anderson University exists as a vital link between the church and the literary, political, religious and scientific worlds of the day.

Bibliography

Alumni News. 1956. April:2.

Anderson College Report to the National Council for Accreditation of Teacher Education. 1963. Anderson, Indiana. August.

Andersonian. 1948. February 24:

"Anderson Rotary Club." 1964. A brief history released by the club. Typescript.

Broadcaster. 1929. April:1, 3, 4.

_____. 1929. May: 3, 5.

_____. 1934. March/April:10.

Echoes: Annual of the Senior Class. Anderson, Indiana: Anderson University.

*Gospel Trumpe*t. 1918. July 25:16.

_____. 1927. February 17:8.

_____. 1938. May 14:14.

National Council for the Accreditation of Teacher Education (NCATE) Self-Study. 1963. August.

New England's First Fruits. n. d. Old South Leaflets. Vol. III. No. 51. Boston: Directors of the Old South Work.

Report to North Central Association of Colleges and Secondary Schools. 1970. Anderson, Indiana: Anderson College.

Signatures: Anderson University Names and News. 1989-90. Anderson, Indiana: Anderson University Office of Publications. Winter.

_____ 1990. Anderson, Indiana: Anderson University Office of Publications Summer.

*Student's Handboo*k. 1945-46. Published by the Anderson College Student Council for 1946-47 school year.

Adams, Robert. 1980. "The Hymnody of the Church of God (1885-1980) as a Reflection of That Church's Theological and Cultural Changes." Doctoral dissertation, Southwestern Baptist Theological Seminary.

Beard, Norman E. 1958 "Anderson College: Its Contribution to the Training of the Ministry of the Church of God. Master's thesis, Anderson School of Theology.

Bengtson, Opal. 1988. "Like It Wuz—Then and Now: Memories of Opal Bengtson." October. Typescript.

Berry, Robert L. 1931. *Golden Jubilee Book.* Anderson, Indiana: Gospel Trumpet Company.

Blanchard, John. 1892. *Congregational News.* January.

Bock, Gene. 1971. "History of the Anderson Kiwanis." Typescript.

Brooks, H. A. 1912. "Advantages and Value of Education." *Gospel Trumpet.* June 20:4-5.

Butts, R. F. and L. A. Cremin. 1953. *History of Education in American Culture.* New York: Holt.

Byrum, E. E. 1895. *Gospel Trumpet.* December 26.

Byrum, Russell R. 1917. "The Preacher Among His Books." *Our Ministerial Letter.* April.

_____. 1917. "A Course of Study for Ministers." *Our Ministerial Letter.* August.

Callen, Barry L. 1983. "Faculty Academic Freedom in Member Institutions of the Christian College Coalition." Ed. D. dissertation, Indiana University.

_____. 1988. *Preparing for Service.* Anderson, Indiana: Warner Press, Inc.

_____. 1990. *Listening to the Word of God.* Anderson, Indiana: Warner Press.

_____. 1991. *Faith, Learning and Life.* Anderson, Indiana: Warner Press.

_____. 1992. *Thinking and Acting Together.* Anderson, Indiana: Warner Press.

Clear, Valorous. 1953. "The Church of God: A Study in Social Adaptation." Ph. D. dissertation, University of Chicago.

_____ 1977. *Where the Saints Have Trod.* Chesterfield, Indiana: Midwest Publications.

Dieter, Melvin. 1990. "If It Preaches, It Will Sing!" *Holiness Digest.* Fall:15, 17.

Farlow, Clarence Robert. 1960. "A Study of the Life of Ruthven Byrum, Indiana Artist, as it is connected with his contribution to Indiana art." Master's thesis. Ball State University.

Forney, C. H. 1914. *History of the Churches of God.* Harrisburg, Pennsylvania: Publishing House of the Churches of God.

Gray, A. F. 1966. *Time and Tides on the Western Shore.* Autobiography published privately.

Harper, William Rainey. 1905. *The Trend in Higher Education.* Chicago: University of Chicago Press.

Hofstadter, Richard and C. DeWitt Hardy. 1952. *The Development and Scope of Higher Education in the United States.* New York: Columbia University Press.

Hofstadter, Richard. 1962. *Anti-Intellectualism in American Life.* New York: Alfred A. Knopf.

Jay, John Edwin. 1951. *Narratives of My Years at Wilmington College: 1915-1927.* Wilmington, Ohio: Willmington College.

Jones, Timothy K. 1989. *A Century of Faith, Learning and Service: Manchester College, 1889-1989.* Manchester, Indiana: Manchester College.

Koller, Charles. 1949. "As Goes the Seminary So Goes the Denomination." *Alumni News.* February.

Lowery, Howard. 1950. *The Mind's Adventure.* Philadelphia: The Westminster Press.

Martin, Warren Bryan. 1982. *College of Character.* San Francisco: Jossey-Bass, Inc.

Massey, James E., editor. 1984. *Educating for Service.* Anderson, Indiana: Warner Press.

Mayhew, Lewis B. 1979. *Surviving the Eighties.* San Francisco: Jossey-Bass, Inc..

Mikesell, William H. 1961. *The Power of High Purpose.* Anderson, Indiana: Warner Press.

Morison, Samuel Eliot and Henry Steele Commager. 1950. *The Growth of the American Republic.* New York: Oxford University Press.

Morrison, John A. 1917. *Gospel Trumpet.* December 27:8.

_____. 1918. *Gospel Trumpet.* October 17:2.

_____. 1918. *Gospel Trumpet.* December 12:19.

_____. 1919. *Gospel Trumpet.* January 23:22.

_____. 1929. *The Broadcaster.* April:3.

_____. 1930. "The Church College." *The Broadcaster.* February:1.

_____. 1931. *The Broadcaster.* July:1.

_____. 1931. "Why the Church College?" *The Broadcaster.* September:1-2.

_____. 1934. *The Broadcaster.* January:3.

_____. 1938. *Gospel Trumpet.* May 14:9, 14.

_____. 1953. *Alumni News.* November:2.

_____. 1955. *Alumni News.* January:2.

_____. 1956. *Alumni News.* April:2.

_____. 1962. *As the River Flows.* Anderson, Indiana: Anderson College Press.

Myers, Linfield. 1973. *As I Recall: The Wilson-Morrison Years*, edited by Larry G. Osnes. Anderson, Indiana: Anderson College Press.

Oldham. Dale W. 1973. *Giants Along My Path.* Anderson, Indiana: Warner Press.

Olt, George Russell. n.d. "Little Journeys at Home and Abroad" (a collection of personal papers). typescript.

_____. 1936. "Anderson College Commencement." *Young People's Friend.* June 21.

_____. 1956. *An Approach to the Psychology of Religion.* Boston: The Christopher Publishing House.

Pace, C. Robert. 1972. *Education and Evangelism.* The Carnegie Commission on Higher Education.

Pelikan, Jaroslav. 1984. *The Vindication of Tradition.* New Haven: Yale University Press.

Prather, Paul. 1991. "Asbury's Sweet, Sweet Spirit" *The Asbury Herald.* Summer: 3-6.

Phelps, J. W. 1917. Foreword. *Our Ministerial Letter.* April.

Phillips, Harold L. 1950. "The New Graduate School." *Alumni News.* June:3.

_____. 1979. *The Miracle of Survival.* Anderson, Indiana: Warner Press.

Reardon, Robert H. 1943. "The Doctrine of the Church and the Christian Life in the Church of God Reformation Movement," S. T. M. Thesis, Oberlin School of Theology.

_____. 1967. *Anderson College News.* Jubilee Issue. September:4.

_____. 1979. *The Early Morning Light.* Anderson, Indiana: Warner Press.

_____. 1991. *This Is the Way It Was.* Anderson, Indiana: Warner Press.

Ringenberg, William C. 1973. *Taylor University.* Grand Rapids: Eerdmans.

Smith. F. G. 1908. *The Revelation Explained.* Anderson, Indiana: Gospel Trumpet Company.

_____. 1914. *What the Bible Teaches.* Anderson, Indiana: Gospel Trumpet Company.

_____. 1919. *The Last Reformation.* Anderson, Indiana: Gospel Trumpet Company.

Smith, John W. V. 1980. *The Quest for Holiness and Unity.* Anderson Indiana: Warner Press.

Smith, Robert N. 1987. "Drama at Anderson College: 1917-1986." Typescript.

Smith, Timothy L. 1957. *Revivalism and Social Reform.* Nashville: Abingdon Press.

Solberg, Winton. 1990. "The Sabbath on the Overland Trail to California." *Church History.* September:341.

Strege, Merle. 1991. *Tell Me the Tale.* Anderson, Indiana: Warner Press.

Tarr, Charles. 1972. *A New Wind Blowing!* Anderson, Indiana: Warner Press.

Thacker, Joseph, Jr. 1990. *Asbury College: Vision and Miracle.* Evangel Press.

Thornburg, Opal. 1963. *Earlham: The Story of the College, 1847-1962.* Richmond, Ind: Earlham College Press.

Warner, D. S. 1883. *Gospel Trumpet.* December 1.

_____. 1884. *Gospel Trumpet.* October 15: 2.

Warner, D. S. and H. M. Riggle. 1903. *The Cleansing of the Sanctuary.* Gospel Trumpet Company.

Willard, W. Wyeth. 1950. *Fire on the Prairie.* Wheaton, Ill: Van Kampen Press.

Wilson, J. T. 1917. *Gospel Trumpet.* October 18:10.

_____. 1918. *Gospel Trumpet.* July 4:7

INDEX

Selected Subjects and Persons

In addition to the many names and subjects below, many others appear in the footnotes, tables and appendixes. Note especially the listings of trustees, faculty members, student leaders, outstanding athletes, and honor graduates. "Ta." indicates Table, "Ap." Appendix, and "Ph." photograph.

Blevins-Dicus, Dorothy (see: Morrison, Dorothy)
Bloom, Robert, 336; Ap. J
Board of Church Extension, 39, 117, 120, 145, 179, 301
Board of Trustees: 62; charter members, Ta. 5; church membership, 331; committee struc ture, 293, 353, 378; cumulative list, Ap. A; development grant, seminary, 293, 366; role, 352
Boggs, Donald, Ap. H
Boosters Club (see: social clubs)
Boren, LaRita and Leland, 358
Bowser, Elsie, 49
Boyer, Esther (see: Bauer, Esther)
Boyer, Harold, 112, 119, 128; Ap. P
Boyes, Donald (Boyes House), Ta.18; Ap. P, R
Brandon, Donald, 2, 106, 391; Ap. J
Brandon, Janet, 106
Breitweiser, D. Paul, 87, 123; Ta. 12, 13; Ap. F; Ph., 244
Broadcaster (see: alunmi)
Brooks, H. A., 20, 33
Brooks, Lawrence, 19, 108; Ta. 10
Brown, Alfred, 118, 124
Brown, Charles E., 98, 215; Ta. 6, 8, 12; Ap. Q; Ph., 321
Brown, Cecil, 122; Ap. K
Brown, Delwin, 200, 238
Brown, Larry, 249, 252; Ap. N
Bruce, Thomas, 403
Brumfield, Donald, 233
Brummitt, Gary, 390
Bryan, William Jennings, 80
Bryant, Larry, 391, 405; Ap. J
Buehler, John, 232; Ta. 13,16
Buettner, Milton, 140, 200, 228, 249
Buildings (see individual names; Ap. R)
Burnett, Fredrick, 252, 276
Business/Economics Department, Ap. H
Business/Professional Men's Foundation, 222
Byers, Andrew L., 18, 324
Byers, C. E., 101, 104
Byers Hall, Ta. 24; Ap. R
Byrd, Esther (Sample), 115
Byrd, Cecil K., 115, 126, 128-29, 272, 361

Byrd, G. M., 115, 272
Byrd, Wendell, 115, 126, 272
Byrum, Bessie L., 30, 36-39, 93, 121, 123, 212, 324; Ap. P; Ph., 38, 141
Byrum, Enoch E., 18, 22, 29, 132, 145, 169; Ph.,128, 324
Byrum Hall, 30, 119, 266, 324; Ta. 24, 25; Ap. R
Byrum, Noah, 29, 324
Byrum, Robert, 29, 31, 39, 324
Byrum, Russell R., 29, 33, 35-36, 38-39, 45, 49, 62, 78, 92, 95-98, 213, 324, 338, 351; Ta. 5, 8; Ap. A; Ph. 212, 321
Byrum, Ruthven H., 235, 322, 324; Ta. 12, 13; Ph., 185

C

Caldwell, Irene (Smith), 105, 158, 237, 295; Ap. G
Caldwell, Mack M., 73, 76, 79, 109, 193; Ta. 10; Ap. Q
Callen, Barry L., xiii, 250, 257, 289, 304, 343, 353, 361, 364, 369, 374, 378; Ap. F, G, N; Ph., 346, 357, 362
Camarada (see: social clubs)
Camm, Margaret, 405; Ap. N
Campaign for Anderson University, 356-62; Ta. 28, (see: finances)
Campbell, Arthur, 142-43; Ap. P
Campbell, J. E., 36
Campbell, Maggie, 378
Candles and Carols, 401; Ph., 397
Cantley, Shelby, 339
Carrington, John, 202, 249, 352
Carroll, Dennis D., 379; Ap. A
Center for Pastoral Studies, 287-292, 295, 301, 316
Center for Public Service, 199, 315-16; Ap. I, S
Chapel, 45, 66, 72, 164, 213, 250, 285, 369
Chapman, Milo, 128, 305; Ap. O, P
Chapman, Steven Curtis, 390
Cheap Thrills, 336, 377
Cheeks, Charlie, 208, 221
Chemistry Department, Ap. H
Chicago, University of, 145, 160

Warren, Leonard and Zella, 301
"We Believe" Statement (SOT), 304
Webb, Charles H., 324
Webber, Gibb, E., Ap. F
Weigel, Stella, 51, 65, 108, 110; Ta. 3
Weir, Esther (Elsaser), 65-66, 87, 98, 122 ; Ph.,
   66
Weir, Forrest, 66, 87, 98, 122-23, 125, 158;
   Ph., 66
Welch, Douglas E., 258; Ap. G
Wells, Earl, 123; Ph., 128
Wesley Center for Biblical Studies, 298
Whalen, Paul, 162
Wheaton College, 13
Wiley, Joseph W., 142; Ta. 12
Wilkins, Ernest Hatch, 157
Williams, Edgar, 108
Williams, Emery C., 193
Williamson, Lowell J., 222
Wilmington College, 67, 106
Wilson, Charles E., 47, 188, 226, 228, 324;
   Ph., 187
Wilson Galleries (see: Galleries)
Wilson, Jack, Ap. J
Wilson, John ("Jumpin' Johnny"), 2, 172-73,
   193; Ap. J; Ph., 166
Wilson, Joseph T., 30, 32-36, 38, 40, 54-56, 62,
   84-85, 134, 208-09, 351, 380; Ta. 5, 8; Ap.
   A, Q; Ph., 28, 34
Wilson Library (see: library)
Withrow, Quentin, 172
Womack, Joe, 199
WQME, 360, 390
Wright, Walker, Ta. 5
Wunsch, Gertrude E., 399; Ap. F, N

Y

Yale University, 10, 98
Young, Richard M., 336; Ap. F, J

Z

Zazanis, Nick, 109
Zoll, Frank, 171; Ap. P